GUIDING
YOUNG CHILDREN'S
LEARNING

GUIDING YOUNG CHILDREN'S LEARNING

A Comprehensive Approach to
Early Childhood Education

Sara Wynn Lundsteen

Professor
North Texas State University

Norma Bernstein Tarrow

Professor
California State University, Long Beach

Primary Illustrator:
Sara Wynn Lundsteen

McGRAW-HILL BOOK COMPANY

New York   St. Louis   San Francisco   Auckland   Bogotá   Hamburg
Johannesburg   London   Madrid   Mexico   Montreal   New Delhi
Panama   Paris   São Paulo   Singapore   Sydney   Tokyo   Toronto

To my parents and Alex
S. W. L.

To my mother and the memory of my father
N. B. T.

This book was set in Century Expanded by Monotype Composition Company, Inc.
The editors were Phillip A. Butcher and Susan Gamer;
the designer was Joan E. O'Connor;
the production supervisor was John Mancia.
The illustrations signed "SWL" were drawn by Sara Wynn Lundsteen;
all other drawings were done by J & R Services, Inc.
R. R. Donnelley & Sons Company was printer and binder.

Cover photograph by Erica Stone.
© Peter Arnold, Inc.
© Erica Stone, 1978.

GUIDING YOUNG CHILDREN'S LEARNING

1234567890 DODO 8987654321

See Credits on pages 491–495.
Copyrights included on this page by reference.

Library of Congress Cataloging in Publication Data

Lundsteen, Sara W
Guiding young children's learning.

Includes bibliographical references and index.
1. Education, Preschool. 2. Education, Primary.
3. Child development. I. Bernstein Tarrow,
Norma, joint author. II. Title.
LB1140.2.L883   372'.21   80-20777
ISBN 0-07-039105-X

CONTENTS

CONTRIBUTORS

JILL BARDWELL
Director of Early Childhood
    Education
East Texas State University, Dallas

JAN FISH
California State University,
    Northridge

PAULETTE FULLER
Principal, Willow Elementary School,
ABC Unified School District,
    Cerritos, California

JAMES L. HOOT
North Texas State University

NORMA C. McGEOCH
California State University,
Long Beach

KATHERYN SAMPECK
East Texas State University

VELMA SCHMIDT
Program Director of Early Childhood
    Education
North Texas State University

ROSE SPICOLA
Texas Women's University

ELLEN STEADMAN
M. C. Lively Elementary School
Irving, Texas

GLORIA TANSITS
Doctoral Candidate
University of New Mexico

PATRICIA KIMBERLY WEBB
Director of Early Childhood
    Education
Southern Methodist University

PREFACE

We begin the first chapter of *Guiding Young Children's Learning* with a scene in the office of a faculty member at a school of education. Three students—Pat, Chris, and Lee—are charting their careers and seeking an understanding of the field of early childhood education. This setting provides the starting place for our exploration of that dynamic and rapidly changing field. We have written this textbook for students who, like Pat, Chris, and Lee, are beginning their study of early childhood and hoping to become early childhood educators—but we have also tried to meet the demands of this endlessly fascinating area in such a way that our text will be useful as a continuing reference for practicing teachers and caretakers of young children.

Our text covers early childhood from infancy through the primary grades—a span of ages which is, as far as we know, unique in this field. It is true that the largest number of our readers will work with children aged four, five, and six, but we have included material about the entire range in each chapter. We have also included not only "typical" children but also the gifted, the handicapped, the disadvantaged, and the culturally different; and we go beyond the school and its staff to discuss the involvement of parents and the community. We believe that we have covered many topics which are given little or no treatment in other current texts.

Naturally, each of our readers has different needs and perceptions. We have tried to meet common needs; but we have also preserved the integrity of our own point of view. Our orientation is developmental-interactionist, and we emphasize creative problem solving by young children and respect by teachers for each child as a developing, autonomous learner—a "whole child," moving, feeling, and thinking creatively.

This text consists of four parts. Part One provides background: it examines the history of early childhood education, the current "state of the art," and possible future careers for our readers. The scenes enacted in Chapter 1 give a sampling of several different types of early childhood programs and also foreshadow many ideas to be developed later in the book. Chapter 2 is a brief presentation of the roots of our profession and some present international influences and perspectives. Chapter 3 brings the readers up to date, discussing trends since the renaissance of early childhood education in the United States in the mid-1960s. A continuum of programs is presented.

Part Two covers the development of the child. We believe that an understanding of child development is essential to anyone concerned with planning educational experiences for children. The chapters in Part Two suggest directions for educators, help establish a theoretical base for education, and present a point of view based largely on developmental research. As developmental-interactionists, we believe that curriculum planning must grow from and interact with knowledge of developmental principles. Although, as we noted above, our interest is in the "whole child," we have found it necessary in Part Two to discuss each developmental domain—cognitive, affective, and motor—independently. Chapter 4 describes development in terms of physical growth and motor and perceptual development. Chapter 5 describes development in cognition and language; we have treated these two areas together in order to stress their interrelationship, a point that is rarely emphasized in the literature of this field. Chapter 6 deals with the affective domain—social and emotional development. Finally, Chapter 7 discusses the developmental assessment of children and programs, and also a related topic—the assessment and accountability of teachers.

Part Three deals with curriculum designed to promote cognitive, affective, and psycho-physical-motor abilities. The chapters on development in Part Two have counterparts in Part Three: Chapter 4 corresponds to Chapter 8; Chapter 5 to Chapters 9 and 10; and Chapter 6 to Chapter 11. Examples have been drawn from important content areas. We should point out that by "curriculum" we mean far more than separate subject areas (mathematics, reading, social studies) for children in the primary grades or block play, story time, and dramatic play for toddlers and preschoolers. Our *examples* are simply that: we do not intend to let subject areas be overemphasized. Part Three, then, presents goals and *illustrative* curriculum areas related to the discussions of development in Part Two. Chapter 8 takes up curriculum for the psycho-physical-motor area, stressing the informal aspects of developing perceptual and motor skills and movement education but mentioning specific school programs in these fields. This chapter also examines nutrition, health, and safety. As we mentioned above, both Chapter 9 and Chapter 10 relate to Chapter 5, on development of thought and language. Chapter 9 is concerned with goals and curriculum for cognitive development beginning in the earliest years; here we use examples from mathematics and science. New "process approaches" to science and experiences with numbers are emphasized; this is in tune with Piaget's ideas and with recent research. Chapter 10 presents goals, curriculum, and sample activities in the area of language development. The first part of Chapter 10 covers the informal aspects of developing oral language; the second part takes up reading and writing readiness and approaches to beginning reading. We discuss literature for young children and how Piaget's ideas are applicable to reading readiness. Chapter 11 deals with curriculum in the affective area. Informal curriculum in this area is concerned with developing a healthy self-concept and personality, sound value systems, and good social relationships. The affective curriculum can extend to almost all fields; we have taken our examples from social studies, music, and art.

Part Four takes up the special strategies teachers will need. Chapter 12 deals with teaching and learning strategies; here we discuss the importance of children's symbolic play and problem solving. Our emphasis on problem solving is another aspect of this text which we believe to be unique; and we have carried it through much of the book. Chapter 13 is concerned with the needs of special children—those who are environmentally, educationally, or physically different from the norm. Chapter 14 discusses how environment, or structure, and materials can be designed and used to create a special world for children. Here we view planning, management, and discipline as going hand in hand with artistry. Chapter 15 discusses the relationship of the school setting to parents and the community.

Following Part Four is the Epilogue, in which our students Chris, Pat, and Lee reappear. Here we recapitulate some important themes and issues and look briefly to the future.

It is our hope that each of our readers will find a place in this field, as Chris, Pat, and Lee do. Teachers, like children, learn and discover from the inside out. But in learning, everyone needs a point of view, a theoretical base, and exposure to the thoughts of others. It is these things which we have attempted to provide.

Many of our readers will, we hope, be interested in our accompanying activities book, *Activities and Resources for Guiding Young Children's Learning* (McGraw-Hill, 1981), which relates developmental knowledge specifically to the curriculum. Here we present objectives, activities, and resources for various developmental and curriculum areas; in essence, this accompanying book serves as an extension of the theories and implications presented in the text.

ACKNOWLEDGMENTS
In writing this book, we have received very important contributions from several early childhood educators: from Jill Bardwell and James L. Hoot for Chapter 1; from Velma Schmidt for Chapter 2; from Patricia Kimberly Webb for Chapter 6; from Jan Fish for Chapter 7; from Katheryn Sampeck for Chapter 11; from Norma C. McGeoch and Ellen Steadman for Chapter 13; from Rose Spicola for Chapter 14; and from Paulette Fuller and Gloria Transits for Chapter 15. We are very grateful to them for their work on these chapters; but we must point out to our readers that the responsibility for any mistakes or shortcomings is ours alone.

In addition, we are indebted to hundreds of students, teachers, colleagues, consultants, administrators, and young children who have stimulated us. Special thanks are due to Carol Mason Wolfe, who, as Sara Lundsteen's research assistant, read and weighed every word again and again, providing a fresh interdisciplinary view and an incisive yet humanistic approach; to Linda Varvas, Norma Bernstein Tarrow's assistant, who performed many clerical tasks and did much reading and criticism of the manuscript; to Alex Lundsteen, who provided the continuing support and encouragement essential to long-term projects; and to Irv Howard and Arthur, Marc, and Jonathan Bernstein, for their patience, their understanding, and their tolerance of the time and efforts devoted to this project. Another expression of gratitude goes to our production editor Susan Gamer for her remarkable patience, care, and persistence in helping to shape the emergence of this book in its final form. Our focus on creative problem solving as a central theme owes much to cross-cultural research and testing in Swedish kindergartens. This project was directed by Göran Stromqvist and included the following teachers in Gothenberg, Sweden: Anna-Lena Lundstrom, Kerstin Swensson, Katarina Wahl, and Lisbeth Watson. We also express our thanks to the American kindergarten project: to Ann Kieschnick, principal; Benna Jones, teacher; and the children and parents at Gooch Early Childhood Center in Dallas Independent School District. Finally, we must include Burr and Meese, who supervised our creation of large portions of this book.

Sara Wynn Lundsteen
Norma Bernstein Tarrow

GUIDING
YOUNG CHILDREN'S
LEARNING

PART ONE

EARLY CHILDHOOD—
PAST, PRESENT, AND
YOUR FUTURE

The first part of this book contains three chapters exploring present settings in early childhood education, kinds of jobs you might find, and perspectives from distant history up to the present.

Chapter 1 gives you as vivid an image as we could conjure of present exemplary settings for early childhood education. You will get to know our students—Pat, Chris, and Lee—and experience principles of early childhood education pulled from their whirlwind tour of some settings, principles you will meet again in subsequent chapters and in your own teaching. Their experiences move you easily into an analysis of job opportunities in your future.

Chapter 2 helps you to understand the present and predict the future by looking at past history. You can trace significant practices "back to their roots."

Chapter 3 completes the time line by bringing you up to date since the reawakening to the importance of early childhood that has taken place in this country (and abroad) since the mid-1960s.

Some of the other parts to this book have longer introductions because we felt the group of chapters needed some extended explanation. In Part One, the chapters can speak for themselves. They are designed to appeal to your senses, to your pragmatic need for satisfying employment, and to your intellectual needs for understanding your place in time (historically speaking) and in space (internationally speaking). With background such as this, you increase your professional knowledge and develop more appropriate attitudes.

CHAPTER 1

*"Early childhood experiences
leave long-lasting impressions."*

WHAT'S IT LIKE AND WHERE DO I FIT?

Jill Bardwell and James L. Hoot

Largely out of curiosity, Pat, Chris, and Lee approached the office of a well-known professor of early childhood education on a college campus.

Pat spoke, "I like this motto on the door, 'Early childhood experiences leave long-lasting impressions.' "

"How about this one?" said Lee. " 'Children are our greatest resource.' "

"Let's go on in," suggested Chris, "and ask some questions about early childhood education. I hear there are some good jobs, and I'd like to know more about the field."

The professor opened the door. "Couldn't help overhearing your conversation. I'd like to talk with you about the field. But I'm leaving to go by some early childhood settings. Have to drop off some brochures."

"Could we have some of the addresses so we could visit?" asked Linda.

"It's a bit more complicated than that—phone calls, appointments. . . . I'll tell you what; if you'd like, you can come along with me. In an hour's time you can see three settings, and we can talk along the way."

What's It Like?—Scenes to Remember

SCENE 1:
A DAY CARE CENTER

"The Shirley Smith Child Development Center. . . ." Pat read the big letters adorning the far-left corner of the Maddox Corporation office building and assembly plant.

"This is an example," said the professor, closing the car door, "of an important and growing trend in child care. Facilities like this, associated with private industry, make it possible for working parents to be close to their children, to have them located in the same spot. Also, the father or mother is saved from taking one child to infant care, one to preschool, and one to yet another location for kindergarten."

"During work breaks the parents can come to see the children?"

"Right. The children feel they are not all that far away from the parents. They can even go, on occasion, to see where the parent works and what he or she does."

"What is the age range cared for here?"

"Infancy to age 5½."

Leaving the smell of freshly mixed tar, boiling and ready for new construction across the street, the group entered the imposing brick and glass building. Inside, the first thing Pat, Chris, and Lee saw was a two-story atrium with palms and other trees reaching for the skylight, a quiet pool with goldfish, and tropical plants embracing each other in the filtered sunlight.

"Children are allowed to come here on escorted walks, especially when the weather is too bad for them to use even the covered part of their playground. Interestingly, the administration of this company planned for this center from the beginning."

"Why?"

"Partly from a humanitarian commitment, partly from ideas gained from visits to foreign countries where such facilities are a common accompaniment to industry, and partly with the following thought in mind: when customers have two equal prospects, they are more likely to do business with a company engaging in humanitarian enterprises, such as offering child care facilities for the employees."

"Do the parents pay?" asked Chris.

"Yes, about $25 a week for the first child, and $20 a week for each additional child. But since the company is committed to the best in equipment, maintenance, and qualified personnel with degrees (paid well—in order to retain them), the operation does not make a profit. Some children whose parents are employed in neighboring businesses are admitted for a slightly higher charge."

By now the group had approached the office of the child care director, which was glassed in and displayed various kinds of first aid equipment, medicines prescribed for certain children, some of the children's paintings, and a license for child care issued by the state.

The director greeted them warmly and agreed to give them a quick tour.

"How many people work here? What kinds of backgrounds do they have?" asked Chris.

"I have three teachers with professional degrees in child development or early childhood education. These teachers have four assistants who have two-year junior college degrees. In addition to a full-time cook, we have an assistant cook who also works with the children. Just this year she began working toward a degree in early childhood education. From a high school work-study program, I have a student who will spend two years with us. We still have our first high school student who went on to college for her degree. We also have a number of college students who are observers or student teachers. We are not using parent volunteers on a regular basis at present. We have to be a bit careful that parents don't leave their regular work hours to come down to help us. The management, however, is considerate about emergencies."

"What do you mean? What kind of emergencies?"

"I don't mean just times when several staff members are ill and we can't find help to cover or when a child suddenly becomes ill. I mean more subtle problems. For example, the other day one of our four-year-olds accidentally tore a hole in his picture when the big felt-tip marker he was using ran out of ink. This seemed to be the last straw. First he was mad, and then he cried unconsolably. Finally, I took him into a quiet place (the room we use for staff meetings and conferences with parents) so I could listen to him. When that didn't work, I asked if he would like me to call his mother. When he said, 'Yes,' it didn't take long for his mother to appear."

"Then what happened?" asked Pat.

"She talked to him, saying that her work consisted mainly of typing and that she made mistakes, too. She didn't usually tear a hole in her paper, but she had torn it taking it out of the machine. And sometimes she discovered she'd run out of ribbon when she'd been typing along. When this happened, she simply had to stop, take the paper out, get up and stretch, and start over. After his mother left, he was perfectly happy for the rest of the day. This incident gave us some direction in establishing program goals for this child. We set goals here for each individual child. But I tell you this incident mainly to show how well it works out to have the parents working close by."

After making her point, the director moved down the hall displaying (at child's eye level) huge drawings of some of the fours and fives. When the trio commented, she explained that the children had lain on the floor and had had the outlines of their bodies traced. Then each painted in the details, revealing a great deal of their concepts of themselves and their abilities. There was four-year-old Jennifer's tracing with every finger and almost every tooth. There was immature Sandra's depiction of a belly button and very little else.

Then the director slowly opened the door leading into the brightly painted infant room. Two walls contained low, full-length windows looking out on a landscaped courtyard. A third wall was covered with glass cupboard doors, and behind the doors were pillars of paper diapers, multicolored utensils, infant paraphernalia, and a variety of baby food. Toward the back of the room, flanked by an oak rocking chair and two swing sets, were the carefully placed cribs, each with its colorful dangling mobile. On a well-padded rug in the front of the room sat an energetic teacher conversing with four attentive infants tucked about her.

Awed, Lee whispered to the director, "The babies look at the teacher as though they understand what she is saying."

"Although they certainly cannot understand the meanings of the words our teacher, Jan, is using, we believe that speaking to infants definitely encourages them to want to speak and communicate," replied the director.

"What are the age ranges of these infants?" questioned Pat.

"Roosevelt is 7 months, Rafael 8½ months, Steven 11 months, Medalian 12 months, and Nietta, back there in the crib, is 3 months," replied the director. The professor gave the students a significant look when the director displayed this much knowledge about each infant.

Intrigued, Lee moved to the back of the room to get a peek at the quiet infant, Nietta. Expecting to find Nietta sleeping, Lee was surprised to see the baby intently examining an erupting mass of foliage protruding from a planter hanging beside her bed. The infant's bright eyes appeared to search each leaf with the interest of a microbiologist viewing a strange organism through a microscope. Nietta's enchantment was soon interrupted by the tired cry from Roosevelt. When an avalanche of cries followed, the director suggested the group move on.

In this part of the hallway, there was a paper collage of freight trains made by the children. They had pasted on all manner of brightly colored shapes representing cargo—inspired by a field trip.

As the group moved into the spacious room for two- and three-year-olds, Pat spotted an attractive aquarium. "One of the fathers," said the director, "who was previously in the pet business provided one aquarium for each of our rooms. On his breaks he sometimes comes in and gives the children instructions on care and maintenance of aquariums."

Chris noted the large expanse of draped picture windows overlooking the roadway. Several children were squatting on the broad ledge peering out.

"The children sit there and watch workers coming and going," the director explained. "They can watch the construction across the street progress. Those children whose parents are from neighboring businesses can wave good-byes and watch for arrivals. It gives them a sense of control and security."

"Everything is child-sized!" exclaimed Pat. "They can get their own drinks, wash their hands, and reach the toys and blocks in the cubicles without help."

The twos and threes were carrying large, colorful pillows (almost as big as they) in the shapes of toys and animals from storage places to their cots in preparation for their afternoon naps.

"They dearly love those toy pillows we made," said the director, "and even talk to them sometimes. Each child has his or her own for sleeping with or just for cuddling. They help to make nap time very attractive. When it's obviously time to give the children new pillows, they part with the old ones very reluctantly."

Three-year-old Viva, with fourteen neat, tiny braids on her black head, confidently approached the three students.

"What's your name?" queried Viva.

"Pat."

"Lee."

"Chris."

"Look behind you. Fishes!" Viva flashed a smile.

Viva was soon joined by her age-mate Supra, dressed in a paisley-print sari. On Supra's ears, tiny gold earrings twinkled through dark hair.

"When we get on our cot, we go to sleep. I'm going to sleep like a four-year-old," confided Supra.

The professor and the director exchanged glances.

"We stress social and communicative development," said the director. Normally, you'll find our children eager to talk to you, and some use many complex language patterns. We read to them a lot and encourage their parents to, also."

"I notice that your children represent a variety of ethnic origins," said Lee.

"Yes," replied the director. "Perhaps that's where my own culturally different background comes in handy. Several of our parents have said to me, 'I'm putting my child here not only because it's handy, attractive, and run well, but because you're here and I feel my child's cultural heritage will be respected.' We are also fortunate in having a bilingual aide who is very good with the children."

"I hate to rush us," said the director, "but we have two more stops. We'll catch the fours and fives at the next site just down the street. Thank you for the visit."

Talking about scene 1

In the car Lee spoke first.

"I can't believe how well the teacher in the infant room worked with all those babies. Her arms were going like the tentacles of an octopus, winding up musical mobiles, shaking rattles, pinning diapers, and tickling tummies."

"I was impressed that the director knew each baby as an individual," Pat added. "When I asked about the range of ages in the room, she knew each child's exact age."

"The director leads by example much of the time," inserted the professor. "She can substitute for any member of her staff if need be."

"I noticed that she didn't miss much that was going on," added Pat.

"She and the other teachers are all skilled in observing small, significant details of behavior—for example, the kinds of things their children like and do. Careful observation of significant detail is important in *any* career in early childhood education. I like to think I can put my observations of details of children's behavior together to identify patterns of development, relate these to abstract concepts, and build systems to be tested. You gain this ability early in your career (say, as an aide), and you can go on refining it, upgrading your training, and moving up a career ladder.

"I liked the facility itself," commented Chris. "With all the greenery and windows, it reminded me more of a home than a school."

"First of all," responded the professor, "educators are becoming increasingly aware that the physical environment speaks to us all. For example, consider eating in an atmosphere that is sterile, like a fast-food mart. Then consider eating much the same dish but with soft light, soft chairs, soft music, and a fresh carnation at your table. Although you're not likely to die from eating the food at either place, the *qualitative* aspects of the experience are greatly enhanced in a more comfortable milieu. If you want to have quality education for young children, it seems reasonable to hope that an esthetically enriched physical environment might have similar effects upon the children's learning.

"Second, the center's resemblance to a home reflects the view that schools are an 'extension' of, rather than a replacement for, the home. Nurturing effective home-school relationships is especially important in early childhood education."

"I've been wondering," said Chris. "What are some of the other things the twos and threes do besides get ready for their nap?"

"A typical day might include health inspection on arrival, free-play period, snack, lunch, nap time, more free-time selection, and perhaps a story time. All activity here is relatively unstructured, with emphasis placed upon children making selections from available materials such as water, sand, clay, paint, and blocks. But beyond all these outer things, this director sees her school as an environment having stability, consistency, challenge, and patterning, as time spent making a *quality* base for the rest of a child's years."

"I would like to work in a place like this. Are there lots of business-sponsored programs?" asked Pat.

"I should emphasize that, at present, few industries provide programs for employees' children. Where these work-associated centers are not available, some parents—maybe I need to say 'guardians' in this day of changing family structures—anyway, some parents send their children to full-day centers. These centers are either private or agency-sponsored. Those who can't pay the costs of private centers may use agency centers. These generally charge in terms of ability to pay."

"What else can guardians do for their children?"

"If they don't want to place their children at the kinds of centers I've mentioned, they have still another option—family day care homes. At these sites, adults care for a number of children at their residence, for a given fee.

"You mean nearly any adult can open up a home center?" asked Pat.

"Well, just about anyone. Licensed homes do have to meet a number of minimum qualifications. Many home centers, however, fail to apply for a license. This failure is a concern for professionals interested in the quality of education for young children."

"Looks as if there are lots of places for young children of working guardians. But suppose a child reaches school age? Is anything going on for the older ones? I can see a problem when children are dismissed from school around 2 or 3 P.M. and guardians don't get home till much later."

"Yes, early childhood professionals are becoming more and more aware of the need for programs focusing upon school-age children. Some centers have initiated extended-day programs. These programs provide older children with a place to go before or after school, a place where they may play under supervision, complete homework, even receive help with special school difficulties. Some extended-day programs are in public schools. Here we are at the next site."

SCENE 2:
A PRESCHOOL
PARENT
COOPERATIVE
Alighting from the car in front of the Creative Preschool of Hillsborough, the group approached a white frame building flanked by a small church.

"Last time we smelled tar; this time it's petunias," remarked Lee as a riot of pink color greeted their eyes.

"This is an example of a cooperative preschool, owned and run by the parents living in this little suburb."

Their path of approach took them by the playground. To the west was a large multilevel wooden construction built by some of the fathers. Wooden beams, fashioned abstractly, could easily represent a ship, a truck, a play house, or whatever the children's imaginations could conjure up. Much decision making by the children was involved in where to climb, how high, and in what manner. To the south was a water-play area, a shallow, winding, concrete trough. To the east was the digging area with sand and small gravel, and beside this portion of the playground, a small vegetable garden was staked off. Cucumbers and carrot tops were in evidence. To the north were tire swings dangling from overhanging beams. These swings were hung horizontally (or flat) so that several children could share them (encouraging cooperative play). Circling the play area was a concrete track for wheeled toys, and surrounding that was a wooden fence with some of the children's paintings fastened to it.

"Freddie, Freddie!" Some of the four-year-olds approached a teacher. "They've had that swing all day. We want a turn!"

The teacher, accustomed to being called by her first name, stooped down to listen.

"What are you going to do about it?"

"We're going to . . . No, we won't do that. . . . We're going to tell them that we've waited a long time—to let us swing a little."

"This school," remarked the professor to Chris, Pat, and Lee, "takes special care to allow the children opportunities to solve their own problems as much as possible."

Entering the narrow hallway, the group saw a bulletin board displaying lunch menus, requests for specific items needed by the center (e.g., old shirts, spools, corks), special instructions for a perceptually impaired child, a list of mothers and fathers assigned each day as the "floating parent" for the school, and class schedules showing the theme of the week. Since the current theme was Mexican culture, the children were painting designs on paper ponchos; this activity had overflowed into the hallway.

"You'll find this facility small and cramped in comparison with the spacious rooms of the Maddox Corporation. But every inch is cleverly used," said the professor, "and it is indeed a *creative* preschool."

As the trio entered a room for fours and fives, they saw the small space artfully housing a painting center with pull-up-to-the-ceiling hanging lines for drying pictures and a tiny housekeeping area where the children bathed and cuddled dolls. The partition partially enclosing this area displayed fine new picture books. Small group tables accommodated a collection of classification materials, matching activities, bingo games of various sorts, and letter-number form boards for tracing. Shelves within easy reach housed the puzzles. Beans, which were being recorded in various stages of growth, sprouted in paper cups on the window ledge. A pile of cushions in a corner created a cozy environment for looking at books or using earphones to listen to tapes and records. Finally, a set of small plastic, interlocking blocks furnished equipment for the creation of marvelous machines. The "floating parent" (the mother or father whose day it was to serve as an aide) skillfully mixed paints and provided brushes for the poncho makers while the remaining children peopled the rest of the centers of activity. The teacher sat at the table encouraging a group of children involved in classification activities.

"Oh, I'm so glad to see you." said the teacher, rushing up and hugging the professor. "We've had so many good problems this week!" she said, smiling enthusiastically and hugging a nearby child. Then she and the professor both laughed.

Explained the professor to the trio, "That's not how people usually act when they have a lot of problems. But, as I told you earlier, this school welcomes problems as challenges, differentiates them carefully, matches them with appropriate strategies, and tolerates a variety of resolutions."

"For example," said the teacher, "yesterday I was trying something new with music, and it wasn't going well. I wasn't sure whether it was (1) an environmental problem (too cramped in here), (2) a personal problem between me and one or two children, (3) an interpersonal problem between several children, (4) a special problem for one child who was triggering the rest, or (5) a combination of *all* these. So I decided to stop and let the children talk about the situation. I was about to resolve the problem by either getting another teacher to take them for music or simply forgetting it until I had a chance to bring it up in the staff meeting. While I was pausing, Josephine came up with the idea of having music outside. The children got busy and planned who would carry what and what we'd do. I was so proud of them."

"Let me introduce Chris, Pat, and Lee," said the professor. "They're considering careers in early childhood education, and for their benefit, I'd like to ask you a few questions. First, why do you feel that early childhood is an important period of life?"

The teacher looked thoughtful. "It's a time when growth is so great and learning is so rapid. Much that happens now, in my room, affects the quality of their later lives and learning. What happens to young children shouldn't be left to chance."

"Thanks. Now my next question: What do you like about young children?"

"I love their joy, their innocence, the sense of beginnings. I like their strong emotions, their wonder, their curiosity, even their anger that flares up as they learn control of themselves and their world. Yet each one is so different. I need so many different approaches. Each child teaches me! I love the messes, the hugs, the questions. I like this direct way of contributing, myself, to the development of children."

Just then a child flew into the room, planted a kiss on the teacher's cheek, and flew off.

"Stay for puppet time, if you can." said the teacher.

"Afraid we must be off," replied the professor.

"Thanks for bringing the brochures for the ECE meeting," said the teacher.

Talking about scene 2

Sliding into the car, Chris said, "What struck me most was the affectionate atmosphere. Children kissed teachers and teachers hugged colleagues. No one's afraid to touch someone else. That, and the teacher's commitment—why she loved her job—those things impressed me."

"It takes more than love," commented the professor. "And it is well for you to consider what degree of involvement with children and parents is best for you. It's not all sweetness and light. Some of the parents in the cooperative are penny-watchers, some are always agitating for more prereading skills and take-home work, and some of the children are rejected by the others. The director, who was busy teaching today, and whom we saw only briefly on the playground, handles these pressures well.

"As you noticed, feelings are important to the staff here. They even have a very small space in the center called the 'feelings room,' where distressed children can go with the director or a trained parent. There, they can look at pictures showing different feelings, verbalize the ones they are experiencing, act them out using a furnished dollhouse, and even fight with the director using *batakas*—soft padded bats. This school also encourages the children to express their feelings in stories which they dictate to parents. These stories, with carefully noted authorship, are later read to the children."

"Are the parents always willing to work their turn in the school?" asked Chris.

"While not all parents are always able to work in the classroom during school hours, they do compensate by participating in other needed functions, such as assisting in hiring staff for the center, serving as board members, handling repairs, or making arrangements for field trips. So, although they contribute in varying ways, all parents *do* contribute to the program. The parents have chosen this type of school with much thought. They are financially involved in it. And generally, the teachers are highly skilled at working with parents. Needless to say, the parents—who run the school—visit at any time they please."

"What do we get to see next?" asked Pat.

"A kindergarten–first grade."

"That's for me," said Chris, "I can remember what my first grade was like."

"It probably wasn't very much like this one. Some of the changes may seem small. But many small changes merge to form a big change.

"I wish you could see some other settings, for example, a Montessori school, a program for developmentally delayed infants, a bilingual early childhood program, or a center for American Indians. And there are many other settings also. What I'm trying to say is that the variety is nearly infinite. It takes a long time to learn about the major types of early childhood programs and the common core of assumptions and practices that unite most of them."

"How do we learn all that?"

"That, in part, is what our program of college courses is all about. We begin by studying the roots of early childhood education, its history, and its current status. In addition, we try to nurture an understanding of child development and curricular areas that are appropriate in terms of our developmental insights. We then explore various roles played by the teacher, including the expansion of education beyond the school. These concepts are taught in our program by a variety of professors with many different styles of communicating and a variety of perspectives.

SCENE 3: A COMBINED KINDERGARTEN –FIRST GRADE

"Here we are now, the third and last stop on our early childhood 'tour'—an elementary school. This facility is divided into two major wings—the primary or early childhood section, which includes grades K through 3; and the intermediate wing, which includes grades 4 through 6. Each wing has its own administrator. I'll introduce you to the early childhood principal, who is working with me on a presentation for a meeting next month."

The professor introduced the administrator as a person who takes children very seriously, who knows and respects the community she serves and who knows, respects, and supports her teachers. The curious group of students, accompanied by the principal and professor, moved down a long, carpeted corridor until arriving at an opened door labeled "Mr. Robinson, K–l."

"Go on in and take a look around while we make some plans for our upcoming presentation. We'll be back in a few minutes," said the professor.

Slowly, the visitors moved inside the human beehive and encountered a classroom very dissimilar to the ones they recollected from their elementary school experiences.

"So we can see as much as possible," suggested Lee (demonstrating some administrative skill), "why don't we each pick a different section of the room to observe and then discuss our observations later?"

Pat, drawn by a series of competing odors, moved down a narrow aisle, past the smell of fresh sawdust in the guinea pigs' cage, toward the sound of sizzling food coming from a large island hut in the back of the room. Behind the grass-covered shelter, four children, dressed in native garb, were preparing a meal. Between glances at a recipe (given in pictures), the children (supervised by a Hawaiian child's mother) cut crisp vegetables, measured them in appropriate containers, and slowly poured the ingredients into two large woks.

"What are you making?" asked Pat.

A girl with unusually fair skin and pale blue eyes looked up from her stirring and announced, "We're making Teriyaki vegetables. Us Hawaiians like food cooked like this. You can taste some after it's finished."

"OK. Do you mind if I see what's happening inside your hut while things are cooking?" asked Pat.

Following an affirmative gesture, Pat pulled back the dangling strands of mongo grass from the narrow doorway and peered inside. The chalky smell of drying tempera came from a mural of an island which covered an entire interior wall. Across from the mural, an automatic projector clicked, displaying brilliant slides of island scenes.

In the far corner, three children swayed to the rhythm of taped Hawaiian music. Between selections, a resonant voice was heard on the tape, encouraging the dancers to move other parts of their bodies to the rhythms which followed.

"That's Mr. Robinson's voice!" volunteered one of the performers. "He's a real good dancer!"

A tug on the pants and an invitation—"It's ready to eat!" beckoned Pat from the hut. While savoring the carefully prepared meal, Pat noticed Lee picking her way through a morass of block structures across the room.

Through a maze of tracks, buildings, and bridges Lee carefully moved to the center of the activity where an older-looking girl was kneeling beside a pile of blocks, building a towering edifice. Blocks were added to this structure by slow, deliberate movements of the girl's slender fingers. Each gesture was accompanied by the meticulous wag of a slightly protruding tongue.

"Can you tell me about your building and these other constructions?" asked Lee.

"We're building a city for Hi-There. This is going to be his skyscraper. Todd and Bill over there" (she meant the woodworking area) "are making an elevator so Hi-There can get to the top floor."

"Who's Hi-There?" asked Chris.

"He's the guinea pig in the cage by the door. We couldn't agree on what to call him. Just kept saying, 'Hi there!' Then we decided we'd found him a name."

Glancing toward the door, Lee observed a hefty boy playing at the other end of the block city. Holding a block car at eye level, the boy cautiously inched across a narrow plank bridge raised on each end by one small block. Totally disregarding what was happening in the room, the boy almost appeared to *be* the small car crossing a mile-high bridge.

After observing the block center, Chris began looking around the classroom for a noticeably absent feature—the teacher. Unlike teachers of a decade ago, who usually stayed in the front of the classroom stage while the pupils sat still and listened, Mr. Robinson was inconspicuously sitting on a couch in the far corner of the room. A girl, standing on the couch with her arm affectionately draped around the teacher's neck, appeared to be telling Mr. Robinson a story. He promptly printed it on a large wide-lined pad hanging from a metal frame in front of them. Another child watched the process, engrossed. Some others were writing their own stories. Others were curled up in beanbag seats, devouring books.

At that point the professor entered the room, signaling that it was time to leave. After thanking the principal for allowing them to observe, the professor and students left to return to the university.

Talking about scene 3

Once inside the car, a barrage of comments began.

"The children seemed to do so much by themselves without the teacher's help!"

"Not entirely without the teacher's help," responded the professor. "Although Mr. Robinson is sometimes hard to find in the classroom, he does play a critical role in structuring learning experiences so the children can discover much on their own."

Pat quickly added, "I like the way he spoke on a tape between music selections the children were dancing to inside the hut. The kids were very pleased with his suggestions and felt his presence even though he wasn't there."

"Yes," the professor inserted, "this teacher makes excellent use of media, allowing groups of children to engage in worthwhile activities while he works with individuals."

"What about the 'K–1' situation?" asked Lee. "I know, for example, that blocks are fine for kindergarten children, but what happens when first-graders play with them rather than working on first-grade things? Won't they be behind in second grade?"

"As you probably noticed," the professor explained, "it is difficult to distinguish the kindergartners from the first-graders. This combination of students reflects this philosophy: We need to pay more attention to each child's unique developmental level rather than trying to fit a child into things he or she should be doing at a prescribed age or grade level.

"As for the blocks, observation of children involved in block play at almost any level provides much insight into themes that interest the children and into their ability to solve problems. In addition, older children effectively develop concepts of many other curricular areas such as math and science through block play."

"But is it really like that? I mean, all those great places we saw— are there lots more like them?" asked Pat.

"I should point out that the quality of early childhood centers varies widely. These programs you have seen today are the types most consistent with the theory and practice emphasized in our college course work. It is in centers like these that we prefer to place our teacher candidates for their professional field experiences. We hope that work in our program will prepare students to have an impact on—that is, to improve—the quality of education for young children wherever they go. It's important—you noticed the motto on my door, 'Early childhood experiences leave long-lasting impressions.' If we give *you* a 'quality' experience, you are more likely to give children a quality educational experience. A career with young children entails a long-term commitment, directed toward acquiring and continuing training.

"Well, we're back. I know we had to rush through those few centers, but maybe you have at least enough of a taste of early childhood programs to help you to make a tentative decision."

Pat responded, "We really appreciate your taking us with you. But how can we find out more information about where we might fit?"

SOME IDEAS TO REMEMBER   If you, the reader, are wondering where you "might fit"—as Pat, Chris, and Lee were—then you will wish to go on to the following sections of this chapter. (We meet Chris, Pat, and Lee twice more: when they have gone through the early childhood program and are ready to think seriously about setting the tone of their own classrooms—Chapter 14— and when they come back—in the Epilogue—after a year of teaching to think about the issues in their newly chosen career.) Now let's summarize some of the ideas that were illustrated in the whirlwind tour designed to give them a taste of "what it's like." These ideas are key concepts which reappear throughout this book. They are grouped in three categories: the learner, the environment, and teaching.

It helps to summarize the experiences we've described and to try to determine ideas worth remembering. We hope you have abstracted your own responses and notions from the experiences of Pat, Chris, and Lee. The list below is a reminder of some of the key ideas woven into this episode. Chapter numbers following certain items indicate where these subjects are to be found discussed more fully.

The Learner
1 Early childhood experiences leave long-lasting impressions.
2 Children are our greatest resource.
3 Children's art reveals their development (Chapter 11).
4 Early childhood education extends downward to infancy and upward to age eight.
5 Attending to a child's unique developmental level is more important than age or grade level.

The Environment
1 Some industries are beginning to act upon a humanitarian responsibility to provide child care facilities. This trend is part of society's growing sense of responsibility for optimal child care and development facilities (Chapter 3). Many small changes can merge to form a big change.
2 An esthetic environment is a right of children, and children's art can contribute to it (Chapter 11). Schools are an extension of the home rather than a replacement for it.
3 Optimally, children's outdoor play areas are constructed to promote creative imagination; decision making, social cooperation; and physical, cognitive, and affective development (Chapter 8).
4 Feelings are important. Children's feelings are respected. Genuine affection adds a caring, loving, cheerful tone to a setting (Chapters 6, 11).
5 Settings contribute to multicultural activities and interests (Chapter 13).
6 Special children are mainstreamed into schools (Chapter 13).
7 One aspect of modern early childhood settings is multiple interest centers (Chapter 14). Other more general aspects are stability, consistency, challenge, and patterning.
8 Early childhood education is found in a wide variety of settings and on all economic levels (Chapter 3).

Teaching

1 High school students in work-study programs are beginning early to start on careers in early childhood education.

2 Early childhood educators set individual goals for children in light of each child's unique developmental level (Chapters 4 to 6).

3 Fathers are involved in early childhood education as family patterns change (Chapter 15).

4 "Children as problem solvers" can be an important goal for a setting (Chapters 5, 10, 12).

5 Discipline (or self-management) includes careful delineation of a problem, active listening, respect for feelings, involvement of the children in problem finding and solution finding, and appropriate matching strategies. Solutions to problems are multiple (Chapter 14).

6 Movement education may be an important part of the curriculum (Chapter 8).

7 Reading and writing can be a natural process involving children in many types of activities, selected by individual children themselves (Chapter 10).

8 Grouping can be small or large, depending on children's purposes and discoveries (Chapter 14.)

9 Teaching roles change as developmental knowledge leads the way (Chapter 12). A career in early childhood education allows upward mobility, a career ladder.

10 Early childhood educators need to be able to explain their ideas and actions to other adults.

11 Early childhood education takes more than love.

Where Do I Fit?—Examining Job Alternatives

Part of finding out where you might fit among the many kinds of openings in early childhood education is asking yourself some questions. In general these questions deal with: (1) why you want to work with young children, (2) what degree of involvement with learners, parents, and others is best for you, and (3) what skills and abilities you already have. Then you are ready to consider types of settings in which you might work, in more detail (than was possible in the whirlwind tour Pat, Chris and Lee took). And last, we offer some ideas on just how you might go about getting a job.

SOME QUESTIONS FOR FUTURE TEACHERS Answering the following questions may help you achieve clarity and insight regarding your career choice. Considering the questions may also help you determine the most compatible teaching level or work situation for you. Although we frequently use the words "teacher" and "teaching," these labels no longer adequately encompass the range of career patterns now possible for those who wish to work with or on behalf of young children. The following questions have been adapted from Kohl (1976):

1   What do I want to teach?
2   Why do I want to work with or for young children? Why do I want to spend so much time with young children? Am I afraid of adults? Have I spent much time with children recently, or am I mostly fantasizing about how young children behave?
3   What do I want from the children? Do I want them to like me? To do well on tests? To learn particular subject matter? Like each other? Be self-directing? Be creative?
4   With what age child do I feel most comfortable?
5   What attitudes do I have regarding racial and class differences?
6   What kind of young children do I want to work with? Do I want to work with children who have special needs?
7   What degree of involvement with children is best for me? How will I react to spending a lot to time with, for example, twenty people in one room?
8   What kind of school do I really want to teach in?
9   What skills and abilities do I have? (Education, experience, and attitudes, and qualities, such as initiative.)

Let's assume you have read and reflected on the foregoing list and think you want to work with young children. What next? Try to find as many opportunities as possible to observe and interact with young children in a variety of settings. You can gain experience from summer camps, baby-sitting, volunteer work, and working as an aide (with or without pay). Visit and observe professionals as they perform their daily tasks. Take courses. Read about jobs (e.g., Seaver, Cartwright, Ward, & Heasley, 1979) and interview people who have a job you might like.

One of the advantages of a job in the field of early childhood education is the aspect called "career ladders." The next section explains this aspect.

CAREER LADDERS   The concept of career ladders (Figure 1-1) allows an individual to enter a profession at the lowest level and then, with additional training and experience, to fill increasingly complex roles. For example, someone who begins in the position of a classroom aide can, with additional training in child development and curriculum (and credit for work experience), move into the position of teacher and later become the director of a children's center. Individuals are not frozen out for life because of the lack of a traditional sequence of professional preparation. Nor do they

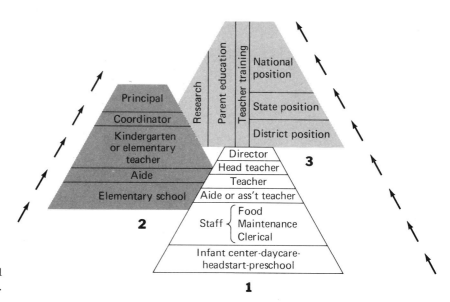

Figure 1-1
Career ladders.

have to wait through years of professional preparation before they can practice.

Part of the concept of career ladders is that there are job openings for you before you finish your preparation. These opportunities in early childhood education at the beginning of the ladder can provide income so that you can continue school. They give you flexibility of hours, since some day care centers are open all day (and well into the night). And this ladder offers you experience that is of value to you in your own field. There are not too many professions that offer such opportunities. You may not start on the level that you ultimately want to reach, but you can be doing meaningful work in your area.

There is also entry to adjacent systems, such as the elementary school with its structure of aide, teacher, coordinator or consultant, and principal. From either of these ladderlike systems, the individual can move into positions of educational leadership at the district, state, or national level, or into the fields of parent education, teacher training, and research. A table showing some early childhood settings, typical ages served, description, and examples follows later in this chapter (see Table 1-2 on pages 25–26). For sample job descriptions and relevant qualifications, see Table 1-1.

Movement into other related fields

Other career options include the possibility of movement into related fields. Some of these are research in child development, child psychology, nutritional science, community work (e.g., child-abuse intervention).

Table 1-1 JOB DESCRIPTIONS

TITLE	Teacher*	REPORTS TO:	Principal
	(Public school)	(Relevant to kindergarten and primary)	

QUALIFICATIONS: As set by state certification authorities

SUPERVISES: Teacher aide and volunteers assigned

JOB GOAL: To help students learn subject matter or skills or both that will contribute to their development as mature, able, and responsible men and women

PERFORMANCE RESPONSIBILITIES

1 Plans a program of study that, as much as possible, meets the individual needs, interests, and abilities of students
2 Creates a classroom environment that is conducive to learning and appropriate to the maturity and interests of students
3 Guides the learning process toward the achievement of curriculum goals and—in harmony with the goals—establishes clear objectives for all lessons, units, projects, and the like to communicate these objectives to students
4 Employs instructional methods and materials that are most appropriate for meeting stated objectives
5 Assesses the accomplishments of students on a regular basis and provides progress reports as required
6 Diagnoses the learning disabilities of students on a regular basis, seeking the assistance of district specialists as required
7 Counsels with colleagues, students, and parents on a regular basis
8 Assists the administration in implementing all policies and rules governing student life and conduct, and, for the classroom, develops reasonable rules of classroom behavior and procedure, and maintains order in the classroom in a fair and just manner
9 Plans and supervises purposeful assignments for teacher aide(s) and volunteer(s) and, cooperatively with department heads, evaluates their job performance
10 Strives to maintain and improve professional competence
11 Attends staff meetings and serves on staff committees as required

JOB DESCRIPTION FOR INFANT CENTERS, HEAD START, DAY CARE, AND PRESCHOOLS†

RESPONSIBILITIES OF DIRECTOR, OR HEAD TEACHER	QUALIFICATIONS
This person has the responsibility for operating a day care center for children in a manner that contributes to their growth and development through:	Ability to supervise staff of varying backgrounds
	Administrative ability
	Sensitivity to needs of children
Developing and implementing programs	Emotional maturity and stability
Supervising and evaluating all personnel	Bachelor's degree or equivalent and three years experience in a preschool program
Maintaining the physical environment	
Operating in conformity to government and agency standards	
Enrolling children	
Keeping financial records	
Scheduling assignments of personnel	

(Continued)

Table 1-1 (CONTINUED)

JOB DESCRIPTION FOR INFANT CENTERS, HEAD START, DAY CARE, AND
PRESCHOOLS†

RESPONSIBILITIES OF DIRECTOR, OR HEAD TEACHER	QUALIFICATIONS
Teaching groups of children, as required Planning and conducting staff meetings Requisitioning and inventorying supplies Supervising record keeping as required by agency and government policy, including personnel evaluations, children's attendance, and progress, health and safety inspection, and requisitions and inventories	(See preceding page.)

TEACHER'S RESPONSIBILITIES	QUALIFICATIONS
Responsible for planning and conducting daily program for group of children through: Planning and conducting daily activities for children Supervising assisting personnel Preparing educational materials Maintaining orderly physical environment Participating in staff and parent meetings Sharing information with other staff members Relating to parents to plan activities Observing and recording children's behavior and performance	Bachelor's degree or equivalent in early childhood education, or related field Emotional stability and maturity Ability to relate to children Stamina and energy Ability to recognize and record significant behavior

ASSISTANT TEACHERS	QUALIFICATIONS
Assist teachers as directed Supervise activities including participating in games with children, enforcing safety rules, providing adult supervision Maintain orderly environment Observe and record behavior Aid individual children Assist with meal and snack service	High school diploma or equivalent Preferably, previous experiences with children Dependability Emotional stability and maturity Ability to keep simple records Sensitivity to children's needs

* This model job description is a working paper to be edited as necessary to meet local school requirements. It is distributed for information purposes to subscribers of "Job Descriptions in Education," a service of the National School Boards Association, and does not necessarily reflect official NSBA policy.

† These requirements are established (ideally) by the Child Development Associate Consortium. In practice, there is great variation and flexibility in meeting the formal educational requirements.

Source: Adapted from National School Boards Association, 1973.

Flexible schedules—Family day care

This field also can adapt to a life-style that involves a prolonged period of working at home—while remaining in the "field." Family day care is a program that licenses individuals meeting certain criteria, to use their own homes as a milieu for providing care and educational experiences for young children. The field of early childhood education offers the possibility of a schedule that meets individual or family needs (e.g., children's school hours or vacation periods).

Opportunities to create your own job

In this field, you can be your own boss, eventually opening your own school; or you can at least be your own manager, running one of the mushrooming franchise businesses in early childhood education.

If you can find a need, and if you are persistent and creative, the field of early childhood education provides almost unlimited new opportunities to create your own job. For example, one ECE student combined service in the navy with opening a day care center on the base; another convinced a large business corporation that it needed an early childhood center—and a director. Another ECE graduate was the motivating force behind the creation of a preschool designed to serve the needs of American Indians in an urban community. Some have created careers out of parent education.

Reciprocity

In the field of early childhood education, although there are differences from state to state in our country, you will find there is a degree of cooperation that allows an individual to take his or her professional expertise across state borders. Thus, if you have earned credentials in one state you may find that reciprocal agreements between states will grant you entry into similar positions elsewhere. In some instances, additional course work may be required. You can determine the requirement by contacting your state department of education or state department of teacher accreditation, or your nearest local teacher training institution. If you change institutions before you complete professional requirements, you will be able to transfer much of what you have done. In some instances, there are matriculation agreements between two-year and four-year colleges assuring transfer credit.

There are fifty different states with fifty different, frequently changing, requirements for certification or accreditation. Because of this diversity (which contrasts with the uniformity in many foreign countries), it is impossible to give details of specific requirements in each state.

Some ideas to consider

Although working in the field of early childhood education has many advantages (as implied in the scenes visited by Chris, Pat, and Lee earlier), it also has, for some, disadvantages you may want to consider.

Disadvantages (or sources of frustrations) might include these:

- Tremendous physical energy and stamina are required.
- Long hours are required. Despite the popular idea that teachers have "great hours," responsible teachers of young children spend much time in planning and preparation in addition to the actual teaching hours.
- Salaries are not always commensurate with the work load or comparable to those in other fields. However, teachers' salaries have been steadily improving in most states.
- Stress may occur when one is not really able to help children—that is, when children have problems that are beyond the control of the teacher (e.g., family problems).
- Bookkeeping-type chores often get in the way of real teaching.
- There is little contact or interaction with other adults during the typical workday.
- Constantly having to be "in charge" and responsible may create mental and emotional stress.

WHAT IS THE JOB OUTLOOK?

It is likely that job opportunities for working with young children will increase as more mothers, out of necessity or desire, join the work force. The burgeoning fields of infant care, day care, and parent education also offer job possibilities. You can also consider several nontraditional teaching situations: businesses, social agencies, hospitals, parks, after-school tutoring programs, and delinquency-prevention programs (Kohl, 1976). Professionals who are concerned about young children and families can be found in legislatures, agricultural extension services, high schools, public relations firms, courts, churches, government offices, television and radio, newspapers, large factories, and department stores. Along with this increasing diversity of settings, there is a growing interest in adequate preparation of professionals, since more and more specialized education and skills are being required. Special education and bilingual capabilities also up one's employable skills. In sum, the outlook is highly encouraging.

WHERE WILL I WORK? —CHARTING MANY POSSIBILITIES

You might work in a place like one visited by Chris, Pat, and Lee earlier in this chapter or in one of the less typical places just mentioned. Table 1-2 will acquaint you with many options. (For ideas about basic philosophies of programs see Chapter 3 and 12.)

Table 1-2 SOME EARLY CHILDHOOD SETTINGS

SETTING	TYPICAL AGES SERVED	DESCRIPTION	EXAMPLES
Day care center	Birth–16	Custodial care and educational programs generally serving infants through five-year-olds. Extended-day programs sometimes provided to care for older children after school. Trained staff and aides. (In this chapter, the Shirley Smith Child Development Center.) (Times: e.g., 6 A.M. to 6 P.M.)	Public agencies, industrial enterprises (e.g., Maddox Corporation in this chapter), franchise centers, campus child development centers, hospital, prison and "drop in" ("Mother's day out") programs.
Home day care	Birth–6	Program operated by people in their own homes, providing care for from one to five children of preschool age or after-school care for older children. Licensed, must meet health and safety standards, financed by public and by private funds. Sometimes supervised by district-wide coordinator trained in early education.	Private residence.
Compensatory programs	4–8	Summer and year-round educational programs supported by federal, state, or local funds (or a combination) for economically disadvantaged and culturally different children. Supplemented by health and social services. Trained staff and aides, volunteers, and parent assistants (usually from local area).	Head Start, Follow Through (see Chapter 3).
Home visitor programs	Birth–5	Trained workers come to the home to instruct children or parents (in working with children). May demonstrate use of educational toys.	See Chapters 3 and 15.
Infant programs	Birth–2	May be part of day care program, home visitor program, or parent-child center program. Includes "infant stimulation" programs. Trained staff of varying qualifications.	See Chapters 3, 8, 15.
Kindergarten	5–6	Program geared to the needs of five-year-olds and intended to serve as transition between home or preschool programs and elementary school. Includes public and private facilities. Generally taught by accredited teacher with assistants. (Recall the sample scenes.)	Public school kindergarten (see Chapter 14 for bilingual kindergarten) or kindergarten–first-grade combination derived from British infant school model (as in this chapter).

(Continued)

Table 1-2 (CONTINUED)

SETTING	TYPICAL AGES SERVED	DESCRIPTION	EXAMPLES
Primary grades	6–8	Public, private, or parochial school. Accredited teacher, sometimes with advanced degree or preparation. (Recall the last sample school scene in this chapter.)	Infant school including flexible grouping, scheduling, and learning centers as well as traditional programs (see Chapter 10).
Laboratory or demonstration school	Birth–5	Primarily intended to train teachers or for research. Commonly located on college or university campus. Student teachers from sponsoring institution work under supervision of teachers from school faculty.	University laboratory schools (serve as model programs).
Nursery school	2–5	Half- or full-day sessions. Most often privately owned. Some financed as cooperative; some church-run or under adult-education program for local school district. Head teacher usually is accredited and has assistants, aides, and volunteers to help.	An array of private nursery schools is listed in the Yellow Pages of the telephone book. Montessori schools are a special type of nursery school—and often serve the elementary grades also (see Chapter 2).
Parent-child centers	Birth–5	Offers educational programs for parents and children—separately and together. Trained staff at varying levels.	See Chapter 15.
Parent cooperative	2–5	Formed by parents to provide program for children. Costs lowered by parents participating regularly along with trained teachers. Some night meetings with fathers and mothers.	In this chapter, the Creative Preschool of Hillsborough.
Play school or group	2–6	Private facilities in homes, churches, and other locations where owners are licensed (in some states) to take children for supervised play in small groups, or parents rotate responsibility for supervision of children's play.	See Chapter 15. See Chapter 2 for British equivalent (play groups).
Special programs	Birth–16	Services for children with special needs, including private and publicly funded programs. Teachers trained in child development, special education, or related disciplines.	Programs for physically, mentally, emotionally handicapped and gifted, also developmentally delayed infants (see Chapter 13). Programs for linguistically different children (see Chapter 13).

There are a few things that need to be said about these settings that cannot be squeezed onto a chart. The chart covers well what we'd like to say here about three kinds of infant and toddler programs (home visitor, center, and combination).

Further information

Campus child care centers On many college and university campuses, students now have the attraction of on-campus child care (not to be confused with laboratory schools). These programs, resembling day care centers, may be custodial or educational in nature. Typically the director and all leading teachers are fully certified early childhood teachers. Part-time and full-time assistants are usually undergraduate students majoring in child development or early childhood education.

Montessori schools Montessori schools vary in program content and design. Montessori teachers consider the environment and materials an integral part of the design for learning. A central theme is the interest of the child in *real work*. Even the youngest children are involved in caring for the environment and in learning to care for their own needs. Ideally, the teacher—often referred to as the "director—serves as a consultant and guide. The children work at tasks they themselves select. Learning occurs through experience and activity, especially with materials that teach in and of themselves, reaching children through their senses. (See Chapter 2, page 40.) Curriculum, even for the prekindergarten, includes subject matter such as reading, writing, geography, geometry, and mathematics. Children are placed in multiage groupings rather than in chronological-age groups.

Becoming a Montessori teacher requires selecting from among various approaches to the specialized training, because Montessori educators differ from one another philosophically. The several "brands" of Montessori education each conduct their own teacher training.

Kindergartens The kindergarten is the central program in early childhood education serving the five-year-old child. Often kindergartens operate full-day, nine-month programs. The number of private half-day programs has dwindled during the past decade, largely because of the dramatic increase in the number of public school kindergartens. This growth in publically supported programs has enabled large numbers of children to attend kindergarten who could not otherwise afford to do so. Typically, kindergartens include learning centers for language, art, music, building with blocks, mathematics and manipulatives, science, housekeeping, and woodworking.

In most states a kindergarten teacher needs to hold a teaching certificate, with an early childhood or kindergarten endorsement. Other positions available in the kindergarten program include curriculum specialist, supervisor, parent volunteer, and aide. If you become a kindergarten teacher, the chances are that you will work six to seven hours a day and spend time in extensive preparations. Being a kindergarten teacher requires involvement with parents, often after regular school hours (e.g., parent-teacher conferences, home visits, or both). You will keep up with current developments in the field and often take part in in-service training. You will need to have knowledge of appropriate activities and materials to foster learning, interpersonal skills, appropriate expectations for individuals, plus an attitude which favors letting children have opportunities to act responsibly without too much adult interference. You'll also need skills in helping children to reflect on and evaluate their activities and experiences, in informing parents about their children, and in evaluating daily activities and each child's progress, and these are only a few of the abilities and attitudes you'll need.

Optimally, the primary classroom, providing a continuation of first-hand experiences, is highly similar to the kindergarten room in arrangement, appearance, and materials. Primary-grade teachers, supervisors, curriculum specialists, and consultants hold degrees in early childhood education, elementary education, or both.

HOW DO I GET A JOB?   It isn't always easy to find a job, and this can be disheartening. If you have studied hard and worked hard, and have much to give, it is frustrating not to be able to put all this enthusiasm and energy immediately to work. But there are jobs out there. You may have to work for a while as a substitute, or in some area of early childhood other than your first choice. Sometimes you need to check again and again with the employer's school or center. Last-minutes needs in hiring frequently occur. Be persistent! Some of the things you can do are these:

- Build a placement file at your college or university.
- Draw a circle on a map around the areas you are willing to travel to from your home and start a card file on every school district or early childhood center within that circle. Make notations on the card of each call or visit you make.
- Canvass all personal contacts (even somebody-who-might-know-somebody-who-would-know-somebody in the field).
- Visit schools and centers; meet the staff and administrators.
- Do some volunteer work in the kind of centers you are interested in. This builds experience and contacts.
- Act out an interview situation.
- Prepare a complete résumé.

- Find out what the needs are in the places you are considering. Then, if you can indicate how *you* can fill those needs; you might be able to let *them* talk *you* into the job.
- Be well-groomed, enthusiastic, articulate, and well-prepared whenever you meet staff and administrators.
- Be willing to be a good listener. Listen to what they have to say. Let them feel that you are interested and want to learn more about them.
- Ask questions. Even if you are desperate for the job, it is important to convey the idea that you have a philosophy and ideas about teaching methods and that you want to be sure this center matches *your* needs and ideas. Convey a sense of self-assurance and sincerity, and sincere interest in children. These are the kinds of qualities a prospective employer looks for; the kinds of qualities that will assure an employer that you will be an asset to the field of early childhood education.

Summary

The decision to teach young children needs to be made in as well-informed and deliberate a way as possible. Asking oneself specific questions, engaging in many firsthand experiences with children, and observing others at work will help one reach a sound decision. This chapter has described settings and careers in early childhood education and suggested how you might fit in. First, we took you on a tour with three students guided by a professor of early childhood education. These dramatic episodes illustrated many significant ideas to be developed further in later chapters. Next, we took a closer look at quite a few careers that you might fit into. We included the possibility of using the concept of career ladders to gain experience while in training.

The second half of this chapter also considered the advantages of possible movement into other related fields and of finding employment with a schedule adaptable to changes in your life-style or preferences at different periods in your life. These adaptations include opportunities for family day care, for self-employment, and for creating your own job. We also noted some responsibilities of, and qualifications for, various positions in the field. (If you can do many things at once; possess an abundance of patience, humor, and stamina; work well with your hands; feel comfortable touching and being touched; are enthusiastic about life; and are intelligent—then working directly with young children may be for you. Being creative to the point of knowing forty uses for egg cartons might be helpful, too.) But variation in job qualifications and constant changes in regulations from state to state make it impossible to give a complete list of responsibilities and qualifications.

As for the job outlook, we noted that teachers of young children are still in demand—especially in infant and day care centers. Many jobs are available for those with interest and ability in the fields of bilingual and special education. Finally, you found in this chapter some specific suggestions for techniques to use in getting a job.

A Look Ahead

Now that you have had a taste of what it's like and how you might fit in, Chapter 2 searches out the historical roots of our early childhood profession that affect us today. We find that the history of the early childhood education movement, like any other movement, began in the hearts of men and women.

References

Child Development Associate Consortium. *CDA in the states*. Washington, D.C.: Office of Human Development, Department of Health, Education, and Welfare, 1976.

Kohl, H. R. *On teaching*. New York: Bantam, 1976.

National School Boards Association. *Job descriptions in education*. Washington, D.C.: National School Boards Association, 1973.

Seaver, J. W., Cartwright, C. A., Ward, C. B., & Heasley, C. A. *Careers with young children: Making your decision*. Washington, D.C.: National Association for the Education of Young Children, 1979.

CHAPTER 2

CHAPTER 2

*"Come, let us live with our children
and learn from them."*

—*Friedrich Froebel*

BACK TO THE ROOTS AND BEYOND: HISTORICAL AND INTERNATIONAL PERSPECTIVES

Velma Schmidt

Early childhood education didn't begin yesterday—or the day before. Its roots turn, twist, and intertwine—reaching into the depths of our past and around the world. Many individuals have dedicated themselves to the improvement of this form of assistance to very young children. Many of these individuals seem quaint and peculiar to us now. The thoughts of others are amazingly relevant to today's child—partly because basic human nature changes relatively little. We can learn from early beginnings and from current efforts around the world. Thus, we gain a sense of pride, heritage, and increased professionalism.

With this broadening perspective in mind, consider the following questions that this chapter will explore.

- Why is it important for you today to understand the history of the study of the child?
- How were the beliefs and practices of the early leaders the same? How did they differ?
- What are some ways in which nations of the world differ in the care and education of young children?

What Can We Learn from The Past?*

Through the centuries, the people who were concerned about young children advocated homes and education which nurtured children. In Europe, John Amos Comenius (1592–1670) envisioned a school system which respected the spontaneity and human dignity of the child. He believed that the home was the first school. He described his preschool program in his *School of Infancy*, and he wrote the first picture book, *Orbis Pictus*. A revolutionary thinker, Jean Jacques Rousseau (1712–1778), was the first to champion the rights of children as children rather than recommend their treatment as miniature adults. Rousseau believed that the child was inherently good. In his book *Emile*, he described a process of education which relied on the use of spontaneous interests and activities related to the natural development of children. Johann Heinrich Pestalozzi (1746–1827) started a school for orphans in order to experiment with his ideas about education. His homelike school looked like a workshop, and he used the outdoors as well. The children in Pestalozzi's school were disciplined in a mild and loving way, very different from the strict and harsh discipline inflicted on most children in Pestalozzi's day.

---

* At the conclusion of this chapter, you will find a list of selected historical milestones in early childhood education (see page 49).

In eighteenth- and nineteenth-century America, many parents used the Bible to train their children; and as children grew older, they learned to read so that they could read the Bible as well as the laws of the land. To make a democracy work, America needed educated citizens. As the industrial revolution caused a rapid growth of cities, many undesirable conditions prevailed, including poverty, vice, and child labor (children worked in factories as young as age seven). A reform movement set out to improve life through education. Horace Mann led the fight during the 1800s for publicly supported education for all children. However, early childhood education developed mainly outside of the public sector.

In this chapter, we start with the first kindergarten, then move to milestones at nursery school age, and then to significant events in early day care. Our progress parallels a historical evolution toward increasingly younger age groups served by early childhood education. We also use a series of imagined interviews to introduce you to some important historical figures and to their influence on early childhood education.

THE FIRST KINDERGARTEN (FRIEDRICH FROEBEL)

Friedrich Froebel (1782–1852), when a young man in Germany, searched for a vocation which would be satisfying to him personally. His experience of tutoring led to his interest in education. Let's "interview" Froebel.

"Mr. Froebel, what led to your interest in education?"

"I taught in an orphanage and then started a school for older boys. I liked teaching, but I didn't know much about it. I had heard about Pestalozzi's school in Switzerland, where children were treated with love and understanding and where recreation and construction activities were combined with the usual school subjects. I was interested in this school because the schools in Germany were very strict and authoritarian and I felt that there had to be a better way to teach children. I enjoyed teaching in Pestalozzi's school, and I liked the way the children were treated."

"Tell me, how did you start your famous Kindergarten?"

"After watching the mothers in the German villages, I decided to start a school for young children in order to extend the training in the home. I gathered a group of children, ages one through seven, in the village of Blankenburg, and we met in an old powder mill in 1837. I used many of the games and activities with the children which I had seen them play in the villages. I developed my program by watching their reactions to the activities I introduced. I named my school 'Kindergarten' ('children's garden') because I believed that the young children would develop with nurture just as plants grow with good care. I wanted a school which would provide activities corresponding to the child's present stage of development. I used the materials to stimulate the child's senses and natural play activity. As my program developed, I arranged the activities of the children in more systematic ways."

"Would you describe the materials you used in your Kindergarten?"

"I called my main materials 'gifts.' The six gifts I developed were a sequence of small wooden boxes, each one containing different geometric shapes in different sizes and combinations. For example, the third gift contained eight 1-inch cubes; the fourth gift contained eight 2-inch brick-shaped blocks. Each child was given the same gift and followed the instructions of the teacher in handling and learning about each piece in the box. I also developed a series of 'occupations' (learning activities), inside and outside my class. These activities—such as laying small sticks in patterns, weaving paper strips, folding paper, and drawing in sand or on checkered paper—helped the children express the impressions they received from the gifts. The children also participated in circle games and movement plays. They tended a garden and took nature walks every week. I compiled a book of songs, poems, pictures, and hand plays for mother and teachers to help children learn about their community and about the value of work."

"Were you surprised at the spread of your 'kindergarten' ideas?"

"Yes! Many of my friends were surprised, too, at how the idea of kindergartens spread all over Germany. Some of my best teachers, trained in my school, even planned to start kindergartens in other countries."

"I understand that some of your 'Froebel teachers' came to America."

"Yes. Mrs. Carl Schurz started a German kindergarten in Wisconsin in 1855. Elizabeth Peabody, liking the idea, began an English kindergarten in Boston in 1860. To interest others in starting kindergartens, she traveled all over the United States. Because of her lectures on the West Coast, kindergartens were established there very early."

"Thank you, Mr. Froebel."

Early kindergarten teachers in America used the same program Froebel and his teachers had used in Germany, but they used it very rigidly. This was not the "children's garden" Froebel had envisioned. The kindergarten was also used in America in an attempt to solve the new social problems which developed with the great influx of immigrants. Churches, settlement houses, and philanthropic organizations established kindergartens in the slums in order to fight disease, crime, and vice. The kindergarten teachers taught the children in the morning and worked with the parents in the afternoon. Gradually, some kindergartens were housed in empty schoolrooms in public schools. After Susan Blow was successful in having kindergartens adopted in the St. Louis public schools in 1873, many school districts added kindergartens to the elementary schools. Because of the large classes in the public schools, each teacher had two kindergarten classes each day; thus, the work with parents fell by the wayside. A conflict developed between the kindergarten and first-grade teachers as to what children should be learning in kindergarten

ISSUE

and what children of kindergarten age really needed. This conflict became more intense with the beginning of the child study movement.

THE AMERICAN KINDERGARTEN (PATTY SMITH HILL)

Most of the kindergartens in America followed the Froebel program. But after the study of the child started, some of the kindergarten teachers began to question some of the Froebel principles and materials. Patty Smith Hill (1868–1946) emerged as a leader in reforming the program for young children. Let's "interview" her in New York City.

"Tell me, Ms. Hill, how did your career begin?"

"I taught underprivileged children in a kindergarten in Louisville, Kentucky, under Anna Bryan, who believed that each teacher should have freedom to develop a program. We spent our summers studying and attending meetings to learn more about young children. In 1895 we were invited to join thirty-five kindergarten teachers in Chicago to study with G. Stanley Hall, who advocated learning about children by using questionnaires and anecdotal records. After the first meeting, all the teachers left except Anna and me. We stayed for the summer. Hall felt that the Froebel program neglected health problems and erred in not developing larger muscles before the smaller ones. Hall called for larger equipment, more activity, and greater freedom for children. Hall's program also stressed the child's emotional life, holding it to be more fundamental than the child's intellectual life. The next year I experimented with these ideas in our kindergartens in Kentucky."

"What happened?"

"Somehow the word got out that we were trying different methods, and we were flooded with visitors for some years. Parker, who had a progressive school, and John Dewey, from the University of Chicago, were among the visitors. I studied with both of them. Dewey had a subprimary school which had a family atmosphere and where the children planned their activity, carried out their plans, and judged the results. I experimented with applying Dewey's principles of social interaction, the relationship of interest to effort, and optimal conditions for thinking. I was interested in the creativity and imagination the children developed with a program that gave them large blocks of time. Also, I was observing the *process* children used in their activities rather than the *product*."

"When did you make up your mind about an appropriate and effective program for young children?"

"I really never stopped experimenting. In 1905 I was fortunate enough to join the faculty at Teachers College, Columbia University. It was an exciting time to be there. W. H. Kilpatrick was applying Dewey's principles in his project method and in his process of social reconstruction. Many educators from all over the world came to visit our experimental schools.

"My staff and I continued at the Speyer School for children of poverty, and at the Horace Mann School. We used different methods and materials and then observed and recorded the children's reactions and activities. Gradually, I developed the large blocks, added large climbing equipment, included outdoor play, provided materials to encourage dramatic play, and gave children time for free play. With the help of Edward L. Thorndike, we organized our experiments into a program for young children including a series of *'habits.'* Typical 'habits' or activities were listed with the desirable changes in thought, feelings, and conduct that should take place. This program is described in the book *A Conduct Curriculum for the Kindergarten and First Grade*" (Burke, 1923).

"How did the Froebel kindergarten teachers react to the changes that were taking place as a result of child study?"

"The Froebel disciples were incensed and defensive over attention to health, large-muscle activity, and emotional development. We had intense arguments for twenty years. During my first summer at Teachers College, Susan Blow, chief spokeswoman for Froebel philosophy, and I taught a class together. The students must have been utterly confused. The International Kindergarten Union (today the Association for Childhood Education International, or ACEI) formed a committee to try to settle this controversy. We met for years. Each side reported its views and gave evidence to support them. Also, books and articles by Dewey, Kilpatrick, and others criticized the 'sit still and small-muscle activities' of the Froebel program.

"Finally, enough research was available; the results of programs for young children illustrated and supported our point of view. The main changes were increased size and variety of materials, opportunities for creativity, freedom for activity and construction, and a social organization which was informal and flexible, and which provided for the physical and mental health of children (Forest, 1935).

"Thank you, Patty Smith Hill."

MONTESSORI SCHOOLS (MARIA MONTESSORI)

During the same time that early childhood programs were changing in America, another system of education was gaining publicity.

The educational achievement in teaching writing and reading to young children in the Montessori school brought recognition to **Maria Montessori** (1870–1952) in Italy early in her career. She was an intelligent, persistent, and hard-working woman whose son has headed the European Montessori headquarters in the Netherlands. Let's "interview" Maria Montessori.

"Dr. Montessori, we have heard much about your system of education. How did it start?"

"I was the first woman in Italy to become a medical doctor (much against my parents' wishes). When I was an intern, I worked in the psychiatric clinic in Rome. I became very interested in the 'idiot' children who were placed in the asylum there. They were kept in a blank room, and it occurred to me that they were starved for experiences. They saw no one but each other, doing nothing but staring, sleeping, and eating. For seven years, I studied psychology, anthropology, and education, and Seguin's work with retarded children. I decided that deficiency was an educational problem rather than a medical one. So I started working with these deficient children. I was surprised at what they could learn! When these children were able to pass the same examinations as the normal children, I felt that the education for normal children needed improvement."

"What did you do next?"

"In 1907, I took a job in a tenement in a poor section of Rome to keep the children occupied while their parents worked. The tenement had been remodeled, and the owner wanted his property protected. (The children had been quite destructive!) I had a big budget for carpentry for my building and used some of the funds and available skills for construction of many of my educational materials. It was here that I developed my program, observing the children, making equipment, trying it out on them, and then changing it until it worked. I lived within the community so that I could understand the parents and meet with them often. The parents had to see me once a week, and they had to promise that they would follow through at home on my suggestions. These children and parents needed to learn to take care of themselves, to keep clean, and to have a neat appearance. The children learned so much that many visitors came to the Casa dei Bambini ('Children's House')."

"Would you describe your program?"

"I can best describe it by having you visit a Montessori school. If you'll take a few steps with me, we'll be at one. Notice how busy the children are. Each child has a different piece of equipment. Notice the child-sized tables and chairs and the low shelves. (This child-sized furniture is a unique contribution of mine. Another is my Montessori equipment, which allows the children to direct and correct themselves.) The children get all of their own materials and put them away. They don't need the director often. She watches the children and is ready to introduce the next piece of equipment when a child has mastered the one he or she has been working on."

"How long does it take a child to master a piece of equipment?"

"That depends on the child. Individual children repeat the process until they can do it very well. They select what they will do and for how long they want to do it. We have been amazed at how long a child works with one piece of apparatus when he or she has chosen it. Look at the practical life area. The children do real work—wash the tables, sweep the floor, and clean the mirrors. The carrots Sara is cutting will be shared with all the children."

"I don't see the children playing with blocks or toys."

"In this program, the children's activity is directed into cognitive learning. Young children can learn many things. They do real work—keep the room clean and orderly, take care of themselves, and take care of the garden. They learn by using special apparatus designed to help them discover specific concepts. Notice the children using the beads to learn the arithmetical concepts of units and tens. Observe the children using the bells to learn the musical concept of the scale. My apparatus has been copied all over the world. I hope this visit has given you some idea about my program."

"Thank you, Dr. Maria Montessori."

Montessori came to America in 1913 and again in 1915 to lecture and to acquaint Americans with her system of education. The rise and fall of her popularity is illustrated by the fifty-eight magazine articles which were written about her between 1910 and 1914 and by the eight articles published from 1915 to 1918. Kilpatrick, a popular educator at that time, criticized her method as having limited scope and limited opportunities for children to express themselves (Kilpatrick, 1914). Others criticized Montessori for lack of opportunity for imaginative play and language development. She harnessed children's play to the service of social adaptation.

Since 1958, there has been a vigorous rebirth of Montessori in America. Nancy Rambusch began this movement with her school in Connecticut and by beginning the American Montessori Society (AMS). The AMS schools, responding to criticism, added opportunities for self-expression (more art, music, and social interaction) to the basic Montessori curriculum. The majority of the Montessori schools are private. However, during the past few years there has been an increase in Montessori-type classrooms in the public schools as an alternative program. (See Figures 2-1 to 2-8 for examples of equipment.)

Figure 2-1
Cylinder blocks. These are wooden blocks containing ten inset cylinders, increasing in height and diameter. The knobless cylinders shown in Figures 2-2 through 2-5 have the same dimensions but add the attribute of color. (Source for Figures 2-1 through 2-8: Nienhuis Montessori catalogue.)

Figure 2-2
Yellow knobless cylinders. As these cylinders get wider, they also get taller.

Figure 2-3
Red knobless cylinders. These cylinders vary only on the dimension of diameter, or width.

Figure 2-4
Green knobless cylinders. These cylinders vary on both dimensions—height and diameter. As they get taller, they get thinner.

Figure 2-5
Blue knobless cylinders. These cylinders vary on only the dimension of height.

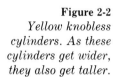

Figure 2-6
Pink tower. This consists of ten wooden cubes varying in size from 1 cubic centimeter to 10 cubic centimeters.

Figure 2-7
Broad stair. This consists of ten rectangular prisms which have a constant length (20 centimeters) but vary in width and height (from 1 to 10 square centimeters).

Figure 2-8
Red rods: ten wooden rods increasing in length from 10 to 100 centimeters.

NURSERY SCHOOLS   Margaret McMillan's open-air nursery school for deprived children in London (1909) caught the interest of leaders like Abigail A. Eliot and Patty Hill. As a result of the publicity, many nursery schools were established in America. With the help of money from a foundation, nursery schools were established at leading universities during the 1920s as centers for research in child development and early childhood programs and as training centers for teachers. Other nursery schools were opened by organizations concerned with improving the life of the deprived child. The nursery school teachers checked the children's health and cleanliness daily and provided nutrition and rest time. Private nursery schools opened to serve the middle class as an extension of the home, adding parent education. Free expression and play were valued. Children had the freedom to play with others because social adjustment was a major goal.

CHILD DEVELOPMENT MOVEMENT

Between the 1930s and late 1950s, an effort was made to put theory into practice. The research in child development continued and was better designed. Gesell was recording the growth of infants over a period of years at Yale. He emphasized the process of maturation and concluded that all children develop through the same stages. Many children were raised by his monthly "stages and ages"—his normative scales. Freud's stress on the danger of repression gradually caused a greater awareness of a need for a sense of security and of giving children a chance to express their feelings (Weber, 1969). Watson's training through conditioning had some effect on rearing in early childhood. Hymes expressed the prevailing view in his book *A Child Development Point of View* (1955), as did Frank (1938) in his speech on the "fundamental needs of the child"—sympathetic understanding, patient support, and tenderness so that the child can accept the process of socialization without becoming resentful, hostile, or overly aggressive (Weber, 1969, p. 180). Even though the terms "whole child" and "total personality" were commonly used, the emphasis was on social-emotional development. Early childhood programs were very similar, and children were viewed as a homogenous group.

PROGRAMS FOR INVOLVING PARENTS

Through the years, parent involvement and education has been a part of many programs. Merrill-Palmer was founded in 1922 under the name "Merrill-Palmer Motherhood and Home Training School." In California in 1927, twenty mothers formed a group, located a building, and hired a teacher (Taylor, 1967). Children three and four years old attended several mornings a week. Each mother worked in the school one morning a week. The business of the school and child study sessions were conducted at monthly meetings (Hymes, 1978). A working relationship between parents and teacher, the atmosphere for learning how children develop, and the lower cost have made the *parent cooperative* a valuable sort of program. Such programs have increased steadily through the years in the United States and in foreign countries. (See Chapter 15, the example in Chapter 1, and the section on the play group movement later in this chapter in the discussion of developments in Great Britain.)

CONCERNS ABOUT CHILD CARE

Beginning in the 1880s, poor immigrants came to American cities by the millions to take jobs in the new industries. Because mothers had to work and many children were without care, charities and religious organizations began day nurseries to provide what was later named "day care." Children from two weeks to six years old had all-day care, and older children had after-school care. Gradually, standards were set to alleviate crowding and improve inadequate facilities. Mothers' clubs met at night to discuss child care and training of mothers for employment. From about

1920 on, the day nurseries began to change from a useful, broadly defined, simple child-helping service to a marginal and limited agent of family and child welfare (Steinfels, 1973). Stress on the importance of the mother, the effect of the separation of the young child from the mother, and the advantages of breast feeding over bottle feeding resulted in a common attitude that the working mother was abnormal. Therefore, adequate finances, facilities, and staff were not made available.

Only during emergencies—the depression and World War II—has the federal government provided funds for child care. The increase of funds for nursery schools during the depression of the early 1930s later set a precedent to free women to take the many war-related jobs that needed to be filled. The increase of working mothers necessitated child care during World War II. A notable program was the Child Service Centers in the Kaiser shipyards, directed by James L. Hymes, Jr. The buildings were located where the parents worked and were designed for young children. Hymes gathered a competent staff including a nurse, a nutritionist, and a family consultant. He adjusted the program to respond to the needs of the children and families at Kaiser. Services included 24-hour care year round for children from eighteen months through six years of age. Recreation for school-age groups, emergency care, sleeping shifts for older children, and care in the infirmary were also available. Also, mothers could order precooked food for family suppers.

Predictions that after the war the mothers would give up their jobs proved inaccurate. The number of working mothers has increased steadily since World War II. In recent years, the number of single parents who need child care services has increased sharply. Some change in attitude toward working mothers—but not a commitment to comprehensive child care—is evident today. Research gives evidence that separation of a young child or an infant from the mother need not be harmful. Recognition of the importance of the early years in an enriched environment means developmental rather than custodial child care. Chapter 3 deals with the local, state, and federally funded programs that developed in response to this recognition and to the awakening to the problems of culturally different and economically disadvantaged children.

What Can We Learn beyond Our Borders?

Many countries have developed programs for young children which are based on sound principles of child development and meet specific needs. The sections which follow describe some of these programs.

FRANCE   Pauline Kergomard (1838–1925) in France had views which were advanced for her time. She had faith in the power of education to further progress and equality of educational opportunity. She promoted education in the context of child care, but she warned that the program should avoid forcing knowledge. In fact, she did not allow the teaching of readiness skills until after the age of six. She viewed child care as an enlarged family with a climate of joy and affection. She was appointed inspector general of preschool education in 1879 and held this post until 1917. Her influence is evident in the *école maternelle* today. Kergomard consolidated the principles of protection, health, and nutrition, provided a wider variety of social and physical activities—and added educational elements (Austin, 1976).

GREAT BRITAIN   The British have made two major contributions to ECE: the *play group movement* and the *informal British infant schools.*

In England, about 1960, mothers who could not afford private nursery education gathered a small group of children to play together. As they outgrew the facilities in the backyard and interest increased, the government provided play group leaders to help organize these playgrounds. Today, a group of mothers organize, and with help they find a place, hire a teacher or leader, secure equipment, and finance the operation. A maximum of twenty children under five years of age play together five or fewer times a week for about 2½ hours each time. Mothers assist the leader. Priority for government support is given to "socially deprived" children (Jarecki, 1975). As more mothers work outside the home, a need for all-day child care has developed which has not as yet been filled.

The Plowden Report of 1967 on infant (early childhood) schools recommended child-centered education. These recommendations were based on cumulative research [Central Advisory Council for Education (England), 1967]. The official position had been in favor of child-centered education since the 1920s. Suggestions had been made that education and the school must fit the child and that much more flexibility was needed in the programs because of differences in growth. Teachers of young children had been studying the research for thirty years, gradually changing from a subject-oriented to a child-oriented approach. About one-third of the British infant schools have changed to a more informal approach, making slow, cautious, and sensible changes.

Children ages five through seven are placed in one classroom in a "family grouping" in an informal activity-based program. Children are trusted to "initiate their learning and the work of the teacher is to help them develop interest into knowledge, using all the tools and resources of civilization along the way" (Smith, 1976, p. 10). Rather than being presented in separation from each other, subjects are integrated into meaningful relationships. For example, children learn about their community through firsthand experiences (science, social studies). They talk and write about their experiences and extend them through reading (language arts). The informal British infant school incorporates the best of what we know about how children develop and learn.

SWEDEN
The Swedish view is that everyone who needs help from the community has a right to it. Child care is part of a comprehensive social policy beginning at birth. The major concern is providing optimal care for children in a country where many families have two working parents. Thus, legislation has provided subsidies for either parent who takes leave from employment to care for a child and for the building and staffing of a network of centers to provide care outside the home. For the most part, these centers are concerned with social and emotional development rather than cognitive or academic skills. Also related to the belief that everyone has a right to help from the community is the practice of providing allowances for children and free health services for children to age sixteen (Roby, 1973).

ISRAEL
Israel is faced with educating a diverse population. Separate systems have evolved for educating Arab children and Jewish children; those children whose parents seek a religious approach to education and those whose parents seek a secular approach; and those whose parents subscribe to the collectivist philosophy of the kibbutz. Each of these sectors manages an independent system supported by the state. Among the major contributions to the field of early childhood education has been the significance accorded to the early years by the adoption of universal education from age five since 1948 and by the extension of universal education to most disadvantaged three- and four-year-olds in recent years.

The education of diverse disadvantaged cultures represented in Israel has led to the establishment of institutes concerned with research and programs for this population. The research of Sarah Smilansky (1968) has focused on fostering sociodramatic play in disadvantaged children of ages three to six—a type of play quite rare with these children, yet typical of children from advantaged homes. She believes that disadvantaged children should be stimulated to learn how to play and that play skills will contribute to cognitive development. (See the section on play in Chapter 12.) Other researchers have been working in the field of parent education and parent involvement.

Israel also provides comprehensive, government-subsidized prenatal and postnatal health care for over 90 percent of its infants and mothers. An extensive network of child care facilities is available to working mothers. These are provided largely by voluntary organizations.

On the kibbutzim, full-time care for infants and young children is focused on the spontaneous creative activity and play of children and on social and emotional growth. On most kibbutzim, children live in "children's houses" and spend afternoons and Saturdays with their parents. Strong ties develop within the children's peer groups and so do self-direction, problem-solving skills, and social responsibilities.

SOVIET UNION   The Soviet Union began an extensive day care system in 1917, and it does not have an urgent need for additional child care. In the cities, where there is a high percentage of working mothers, care is available for children from two months to seven years old. The larger number of children receiving child care usually enter at the age of two or three. The child care situation is far less developed in the rural areas.

A mother has fifty-six days paid maternity leave before and after the birth of a child with the option of a year's leave of absence without penalty. Free health services are available. The facilities are well-equipped, spacious, cheerful, and occupied by cheerful children and caring adults.

The philosophy of the program is dictated by the Central Committee and is identical all over the country. Specific programs and manuals are provided to child care workers, who generally have a nursing background. The objectives of child care are physical health, socialization, and character education for the benefit of the group and the country. Emphasis on the importance of working for the collective good rather than for individual benefit begins in infancy. In order to emphasize a "collective spirit," the caretaker will put as many as nine infants in a playpen with one toy. After one child has played with it for a while, the caretaker tells the child to share it with another child; this goes on until each has had a turn. The idea is to make the child give up the toy for the sake of a comrade, not just when finished, but when the child still wants to retain it (Chauncey, 1969).

CHINA   After 1949, Mao Tse-Tung used the nurseries (two months to three years) and kindergartens (three to seven years) to help build a new society to produce the desired attitudes, values, and emotions in children (Kessen, 1975). Mothers are given an eight-week maternity leave. The purposes behind Chinese nurseries and kindergartens are said to be to help liberate mothers for the working forces, to ease the burdens of working parents, to promote the all-around moral, intellectual, and physical development of the children, and to educate children so that they may become skillful and disciplined, and able later to assume adult responsibilities as "successful revolutionary workers" (Kessen, 1975, p. 37). Children are taught to be quiet and shy, orderly, and conforming.

Visitors see very little negative behavior. American visitors are also amazed to see the physical prowess of children, their skills in song and dance and recitation of long passages. Every child engages in productive labor, like folding cartons, testing flashlight bulbs, and assembling parts.

Moral development is taught from stories based on pictures with a strong moral tone and through language development (Kessen, 1975).

INTERNATIONAL RESEARCH   In addition to its involvement in international activities through different governmental agencies, the United States is also cooperating in cross-cultural research through the Center for Educational Research and Innovation of the Organization for Economic Cooperation and Development (OECD), based in Paris (Austin, 1976). The OECD was established in 1961, and twenty-three nations are members of it. One of the four areas of focus is "educational growth and educational opportunity"—the identification of successful programs for the socially disadvantaged and on alternative strategies to achieve equality of educational opportunity in the world. Because a considerable number of the member countries expressed interest in early childhood education, ECE is one project in this area (Austin, 1976). Two evaluations of programs for the disadvantaged indicate that attempts at intervention have been somewhat disappointing. Children in most programs make initial gains, but as time goes on, the measured effectiveness of preschool experiences decreases. Perhaps, through continued international cooperation, ways can be found to improve the education of the socially disadvantaged children and to improve methods of research.

Summary

Many leaders have contributed to our understanding of the development and learning of young children. The research and philosophies of these leaders have not always been interpreted accurately. At times they also changed their views during their careers. Some remnants of most of the ideas and programs of the past remain, even some undesirable ones. We have considered, in this chapter, the ideas of leaders who have had a major or lasting impact on early childhood education.

Whether the beliefs of a leader or a philosophy came from observing children or from research, a continuous thread runs through the history of early childhood education. Those leaders who were committed to the education of young children, who were sensitive to children, and who started all planning for children with the question, "What are the characteristics of these children and what are their needs?" all had very similar programs. These programs valued, e.g., play, children's interests, spontaneity, activities initiated by children, and creativity.

We also need to be aware of those programs which started from the needs of society. Such programs arose from the need to deal with such problems as working parents, collective philosophies, or the assimilation of diverse cultures, and they attempt to be optimal programs for young children while meeting these needs.

What is needed in the future is a belief that our future will be determined by how we care for our children, and a commitment to act accordingly. What is needed is a comprehensive social policy for *all* children. Do all children have a right to health, education, protection—a right to a quality of living which enhances their well-being? You will have the chance, as an early childhood educator, to affect the quality of life of the children you touch and to stand on the shoulders of the historical figures that came before you. History—while we are reading it, we are making it.

Historical Milestones

Another way to summarize is by creating a selected list of historical milestones in early childhood education. For your reference now and later, such a list follows.

Early Educators
1658 *Orbis Pictus*, first picture book, by Comenius

Kindergarten
1854 Kindergartens established in England

Montessori (1870–1952)
1913 and 1915 Dr. Montessori visited America
1929 Association Montessori Internationale established

Child Study
1880s and 1890s Kindergartens established in the United States; poor, immigrant children came to the United States from southern and eastern Europe
1883 Hall's survey on *The Content of Children's Minds* published
1896 University Laboratory School at the University of Chicago established by Dewey (included the subprimary age groups)
1904 Department of Kindergarten established at Teachers College, Columbia University, and at the University of Chicago

Federal Government Support
1916 First child labor law (later ruled unconstitutional)
1938 Fair Labor Standards Act set guidelines for employment of young people
1962 National conference on child abuse held
1965 Head Start program established
1967 Follow Through program established

Nursery School and Child Care
1916 Cooperative nursery established at the University of Chicago
1917 Iowa Welfare Research Station established (first of a number of university-related nursery schools)
1921 Laboratory nursery school established at Teachers College, Columbia University, by Patty Hill
1929 Susan Isaacs' *The Nursery Years* published in England; other books followed

1943 Comprehensive day care centers established in New York City, Cornelia Goldsmith, director
1960 Play groups organized in England

Professional Organizations Established
1892 International Kindergarten Union, later the Association for Childhood Education International, publishes *Childhood Education*
1920 Child Welfare League of America
1926 National Committee on Nursery School, today the National Association for the Education of Young Children, publishes *Young Children*
1948 Organisation pour L'Education Préscolaire (World Organization for Early Childhood Education)

Other Significant Events
1897–1911 Binet's individual intelligence test developed and revised
1932 Kilpatrick's project method popular in kindergartens
1946 Beginning of impact of television on young children
1961 Publication of *Intelligence and Experience* by J. McVicker Hunt
1964 Publication of *Stability and Change in Human Characteristics* by Benjamin Bloom

References

Austin, G. R. *Early childhood education: An international perspective.* New York: Academic Press, 1976.

Burke, Agnes, et al. *A conduct curriculum for the kindergarten and first grade.* New York: Charles Scribner's Sons, 1923.

Central Advisory Council for Education (England). *Children and their primary schools: A report of the Central Advisory Council for Education (England)* (Vol. 1: The report). Department of Education and Science, report. London: H. M. Stationery Office, 1967.

Chauncey, H. (Ed.). *Soviet preschool education* (Vol. I: *Program of instruction*) (Educational Testing Service). New York: Holt, Rinehart, and Winston, 1969.

Forest, I. *Preschool education.* Boston: Ginn, 1935.

Frank, L. L. The fundamental needs of the child. *Mental Hygiene,* 1938, *22* (July), 353–379.

Hymes, J. L. *A child development point of view.* Englewood Cliffs, N.J.: Prentice-Hall, 1955.

Hymes, J. L. *Living history interviews: Early childhood education. Book 1: Beginnings.* Carmel, Calif.: Hacienda Press, 1978.

Jarecki, H. *Playgroups: A practical approach.* London: Faber and Faber, 1975.

Kessen, W. (Ed.). *Childhood in China,* New Haven, Conn.: Yale University Press, 1975.

Kilpatrick, W. H. *The Montessori system examined.* New York: Houghton Mifflin, 1914.

Roby, P. E. (Ed.). *Child care, who cares? Foreign and domestic infant and early childhood development policies.* New York: Basic Books, 1973.

Smilansky, S. *The effects of sociodramatic play on disadvantaged preschool children*. New York: Wiley, 1968.

Smith, L. A. H. *Activity and experience: Sources of English informal education*. New York: Agathon Press, 1976.

Steinfels, M. O. *Who's minding the children? The history and politics of day care in America*. New York: Simon and Schuster, 1973.

Taylor, K. W. *Parents and children learn together: Parent cooperative nursery schools*. New York: Teachers College Press, 1967.

Weber, E. *The kindergarten: Its encounter with educational thought in America*. New York: Teachers College Press, 1969.

CHAPTER 3

*"The philosophic aims of education
must be to get each one
out of his isolated class and
into the one humanity."*

—*Paul Goodman*

WHAT'S GOING ON?

During the 1960s, the federal government became a sort of fairy godmother waving a wand over a newly resplendent Cinderella—early childhood education. A resurgence of interest in programs for young children (especially disadvantaged young children) was based on (1) the belief that early childhood education (ECE) could meet severe social needs in this country and (2) the backing of a federal government willing to put its money to work to see that things happened.

After reading this chapter, you should be able to answer the following questions:

- What are some of the major sociological factors and research findings leading to the growth of early childhood programs?
- What are Head Start and Follow Through and what were the conclusions and reactions derived from evaluation of these programs?
- What are the features of some of the types of specific programs or "models" for disadvantaged young children?
- What are some of the conclusions that we can draw from an analysis of research findings about various infant and preschool programs?

This chapter traces some reasons for the resurgence of interest in early childhood education. After discussing *intervention* strategy and the rationale behind it, we describe compensatory programs and research conducted under Follow Through, Head Start, Home Start, various infant-toddler programs, and other programs conducted in various states and local communities. An analysis of the research findings tells us to be more realistic about the relationship between various social problems in this country and "what's going on" in early childhood education.

Renaissance of Early Childhood Education

What are some of the factors leading to the rediscovery of childhood as a previously underestimated and overlooked national resource and to the renaissance of early childhood education? Naturally, the reasons are complex, and these are only four of them:

1 Research conducted by social scientists on the development and education of young children indicated that the early years are of crucial importance to cognitive and intellectual growth. Bloom's analysis of a vast number of research studies led to interpretations that the major portion of human intellectual development takes place before the age of five and that 50 percent of measured intelligence at age seventeen is developed by the age of four (Bloom, 1964).

2 The belief that development could be enhanced by improving the environment was a logical outgrowth of the work of Hunt (1961), who stressed the role of environment in relation to intelligence. It was felt that if one could improve conditions of the less fortunate in our society, one would also be providing an environment more favorable to cognitive growth. Thus intellectual functioning would improve substantially.

3 With the confidence that something *could* be done by intervening at an early age, there came the idealistic commitment that something *should* be done. Since "all men are created equal" according to our democratic principles, it was felt that those who are less fortunate should not have to suffer simply because they were born into less advantageous surroundings.

4 Changes in our society have led to the need for finding adequate custodial care for more young children. As increasing numbers of women entered the work force, for example, they started looking for places where they could leave their children during the day.

The civil rights movement tended to increase recognition of the fact that children of the poor and culturally different frequently arrived at school seriously deficient in skills that assure success in the educational system, and were overrepresented among school dropouts. A growing concern over the inequality of educational opportunity for minority children nurtured the hope that programs for young children could serve to defuse the social dynamite in the urban ghettos and rural slums. Early childhood education was seen as a potential cure-all for social problems; vast amounts of federal and state money were made available to help ECE realize this purpose.

The Intervention Issue

In and out of such upheavals, a historical pendulum of educational practice appears to swing back and forth between: belief in (and practice of) basic education and an emphasis on allowing children to develop freely; between direct instruction in a predetermined curriculum and confidence in the value of play as a learning vehicle for young children. (See Chapter 12.)

The activity-oriented primary programs and the child development programs of the 1930s and 1940s were challenged (along with a great many other American educational practices) when the first Russian sputnik was launched in the late 1950s. Critics of American education gave reasons why they thought the Russians had attained technological superiority over the United States. These critics focused attention on the reading disabilities shared by many American children. Pressure was brought to teach more and to teach it earlier. The effects were felt all the way down to the preschool level, where great stress was placed on children's cognitive skills and on language learning—"back to the basics."

The research and the somewhat frenzied fundings of the 1960s and early 1970s were based on the assumption that intervention in the form of a rich, intellectually stimulating environment for children who do not otherwise have access to such environments would foster the greatest increase in their intellectual abilities. Thus, these programs also favored intervention and structure over the "free play" philosophy of those who believed in the child's inalienable right to play without intervention. Even within the interventionist camp, however, there was and is an issue about the character of intervention (Feshbach, Goodlad, & Lombard, 1973). Is intervention to be with formal academic format and content or with nondirective activities stressing cognitive and language development?

Thus, the many programs that grew up because of federal funding reflected different attitudes toward the amount and type of intervention thought to provide for optimal growth. Head Start, one of the pioneer federal programs (still going strong today), is described in the next section.

HEAD START In the early 1960s—even before the days of Head Start—a number of researchers (such as Kamii, Gray, and Karnes; and the program known as DARCEE) in different parts of the country were responding to the challenge of developing programs of intervention or compensation to meet the needs of disadvantaged and culturally different children. Some of these researchers were committed to definite rationales, specific techniques and materials, or both. Others were committed to more "free" time and to the encouraging of children to construct their own knowledge. Some of the elements of these compensatory programs included:

- Helping children acquire the sorts of skills that most middle-class children acquire before going to school, particularly in the areas of language, sensory skills (e.g., visual discrimination), mathematics (e.g., basic number concepts), and classificatory skills
- Helping children acquire the sorts of attitudes most middle-class children appear to have when they enter school (e.g., independence, persistence, and ability to delay gratification)
- Improving relationships with peers and adults
- Providing materials and opportunities for children to manipulate and and find things out for themselves, constructing their own knowledge
- Parent training

Following on the heels of early compensatory models just mentioned was the massive effort known as Head Start, created as one of the major efforts in President Lyndon Johnson's "war on poverty." The original Head Start program was rather hastily put together in the spring of 1965 and planned to begin that summer. Just 89 days after the initial White House announcement, 2,500 centers were opened in every state and territory, serving 689,000 children in the first summer. It was one of the largest peacetime mobilizations ever (Osborn, 1979).

Objectives of Head Start

Major objectives of Head Start included:

- Improving the child's physical health and abilities
- Fostering positive emotional and social development
- Improving mental processes and skills (especially in the verbal and conceptual areas)
- Establishing patterns of success leading to self-confidence
- Strengthening relationships between child and family
- Developing a responsible attitude toward society on the part of child and family

Components of Head Start

While early childhood education was at the forefront of Head Start, it was seen as only one part of a multicomponent enterprise. By intent, there was no single design for individual Head Start programs. There was no attempt to impose control from the top. No specific philosophy or techniques were required. Community decision making was one of the goals of the program. Every Head Start program was required, however, to include the following components: health services, mental health services, social services, nutrition, parent involvement, career development, and education. When appropriate, services included these functions: prevention and early detection, correction, continuing service, and parent education. Parents were encouraged to participate in decision making, in classroom activities, in activities for parents, and in working with their own children. The educational component included the objectives of providing an environment that would foster intellectual, physical, and emotional development, appropriate to the age level; identifying and reinforcing home experiences; and assisting parents to improve knowledge and skills crucial to effective child development.

Head Start guidelines required an adult-to-child ratio of 1 to 5—that is, one adult for every five children. Usually, there was a limit of fifteen children per class, with one teacher, one aide, and one volunteer. Although there were some full-day programs, for the most part programs were morning-only programs that met the requirements of a minimum of fifteen hours per week.

The guidelines encouraged experimentation and variety and created an assortment of programs stemming from many different bases—school systems, churches, community centers, and others. From the outset, there was a strong commitment to supportive, unstructured, socialization programs. A typical program included between 1 and 1½ hours of work-play activity period, during which the children engaged in block play, dramatic play, creative experiences, and play with manipulative materials, such as games, puzzles, and building sets. There was usually provision for discussion, music, and story time, some group sharing, and outdoor play when the weather was favorable. Some programs offered breakfast, others a morning snack. Most offered the children a hot lunch. Those programs that ran a full day included a long rest period and then some quiet games, stories, or art activities, and possibly outdoor play between the time the children awakened and dismissal time (U.S. Department of HEW, 1973a).

The broadness of the educational objectives obviously provided a great deal of freedom in deciding what specific activities would be undertaken or emphasized in each program. This freedom was important for several reasons. First: much of the research and many of the experimental compensatory programs upon which Head Start was based stressed specific training in language and cognitive processes; in practice, however, the emphasis in Head Start was on development of the "whole child" (and programs of a traditional type). Second: educational objectives for Head Start were (and are) sufficiently broad to permit personnel in local programs to conduct just about any kind of educational program they felt appropriate. Thus, if a center director had adequate training, then working within the rather loose guidelines of the Head Start objectives could be an advantage. If, on the other hand, teachers and directors were poorly prepared, then individual programs could be full of directionless activity (Morrison, 1976).

Assessment of Head Start

From the very beginning of Head Start, a portion of effort and cost was directed toward research and evaluation. The majority of the studies, which used primarily cognitive measures, showed positive results immediately after the program followed by a leveling-off effect. Thus, either the original gains were lost or the initial advantage to Head Start children faded as the control children caught up with them.

Hundreds of studies have been conducted in an attempt to assess the effectiveness of Head Start programs. It has been as difficult to measure the effectiveness of this project, which has almost as many constantly changing variables as there are programs, as it is to measure the shoe size of a squirming child who will not sit still long enough to be measured! Head Start has been a squirming, growing, changing entity. Many variables have not been subject to control.

The high hopes of Head Start supporters were somewhat dashed by early studies indicating that Head Start was not accomplishing the hoped-for miracles. Attempts to measure gains from the expenditure of great amounts of money were discouraging. Dauntlessly, researchers offered many alternative explanations and hypotheses to be tested: e.g., (1) Head Start began too late; (2) when the Head Start children entered the traditional public school, they lost the gains from the innovative programs; (3) the home environment had not been sufficiently influenced; (4) the time for Head Start was too short (the time during the day needed to be longer); (5) programs denied the children's own cultures, trying to assimilate them overnight.

Table 3-1 summarizes Head Start as of the end of the 1960s.

Table 3-1 HEAD START AT THE END OF THE 1960s

IMPLICATIONS DRAWN FROM RESEARCH	MEASURES UNDERTAKEN	EXAMPLES
1 Head Start efforts were begun too late.	Programs for infants and toddlers	Harlem Research Center Infant Research Center Verbal Interaction Project
2 Head Start was unable to counter negative influences in home environment and expectations	Programs sending educators and other support workers to homes to work with parents	Home Start Health Start Florida Model (Gordon)
3 Effects of Head Start were nullified by traditional approach of public schools	Continuation of approach and support systems of Head Start in elementary schools	Follow-Through California ECE
4 The enrichment approach adopted by many Head Start programs was not specific enough to meet needs of disadvantaged	Emphasis on programs with specific intervention strategies; broad range of programs encouraged	Planned Variations and individual model programs and evaluation
5 Two-hour daily or summer-only programs were insufficient.	Extension of programs to full academic year and half or full day	Year-long Head Start
6 Conflicts were caused by aiming at quick assimilation of minority children into the majority culture.	Development of culturally relevant programs	Programs stressing black and American Indian culture; bilingual programs.
7 Head Start was based on what may be two erroneous assumptions: (a) the impact of environment is crucial and (b) early childhood is the critical period.	Long-term research, including modifications and supplementation as indicated above	Planned Variations and other longitudinal studies

Experimentation and Research in the 1970s

In light of Head Start's uncertainties, public and legislative reaction demanded more than a "buckshot approach"—that is, an approach analogous to aiming a gun loaded with buckshot at the side of a barn, so that one is assured of hitting *some* spot on the building. If one wants to hit a specific point, it was felt, the approach needs to be more concentrated and more directed, and bullets are more effective than buckshot. Huge appropriations of federal funds were in danger of being cut off unless research could show significant and lasting benefits from compensatory programs—direct hits.

Teaching techniques and materials directed at the specific needs of disadvantaged children rather than the original "hit or miss" concept and controlled research to assess the effectiveness of these techniques on a long-term basis seemed to be the logical next step. These were some of the ideas that brought about the birth of planned variation. What did this new thrust in research hope to do?

The concept of *planned variation* represented an attempt to implement and evaluate programs more specifically directed at the special needs of disadvantaged children, programs based on models with a carefully thought-out rationale and evidence of success in pilot studies. This concept formed the basis of a new program generated out of Head Start, the program known as "Follow Through."

FOLLOW THROUGH Project Follow Through, one of the earliest major efforts to deal with the disappointing research results of the 1960s, was designed to maintain and supplement, in the kindergarten and primary grades, the gains made in the Head Start program. No mere enrichment program this time—instead, this project was committed to specific program approaches (known as "models"), developed by university or privately based research organizations (known as "sponsors"). Each of these models used specific learning strategies and materials to meet the needs of the disadvantaged child, but each model was unique. Built into the Follow Through design was the principle of *planned variation* rather than selection of a single model for all programs.

Planned variation meant that each community involved selected the model preferred. Representatives of the sponsor helped implement and oversee the program in that community, and mutually agreed that they would preserve this arrangement for the period of the study. Thus, among the most significant features of Follow Through were:

- Participation by parents
- Planned variation involving a variety of educational approaches from kindergarten through grade 3

- Implementation in a variety of ethnic, cultural, and geographic settings
- Longitudinal research and development

The success of the sponsorship idea as a strategy for change was confirmed by the Follow Through program. Two sources of power—the community and the sponsor—were harnessed to work in harmony, with each strengthening the other. The strength of planned variation rests in the acknowledgment that there is no one best way to approach a problem as complex and value-laden as the education of children. Beers (1976) notes that this is an idea very close to the anthropological concept of cultural relativism, implying respect for different ways of dealing with the human experience.

Since the concept of cultural relativism should not permit applying the standards of one culture to judge the work of another, the evaluation of a program based on numerous and different approaches required evaluation from a variety of perspectives. There was, however, concern that undue emphasis was placed on the results of standardized achievement tests (e.g., reading and mathematics). Moreover, there was concern that such standards were considered the most significant criteria—even the only criteria—for judging the worth of all the programs. Assessment was not sophisticated enough to command public respect for measures of traits such as initiative, self-direction, motivation, curiosity, creative problem solving, autonomy, and love of learning.

Summarizing the results of several studies, Frost and Kissinger (1976, p. 86) noted, "Attitudes of teachers are more positive, children are responding to school in a more favorable manner, there are fewer attendance problems, and children are exhibiting greater curiosity, self-direction, and creativity than before. In addition, achievement in academic skills has increased in many classrooms."

A critique by House, Glass, McLean, and Walker (1978) agrees that the effectiveness of a teaching approach varies greatly from one school to the next but rejects the finding that models which emphasize basic skills succeed better. House et al. believe that this conclusion is the result of a vague and ill-defined classification scheme, poor choices of measurement instruments, and flawed statistical analysis.

HEAD START PLANNED VARIATION

The Head Start Planned Variation study, launched in the fall of 1969, had the express purpose of assessing the relative impacts of different, specific preschool models.

These models had four major similarities and one major difference. First, all models were considered to be promising methods for working with disadvantaged or culturally different children and families. Second, all sought to develop children's learning abilities, were convinced of the importance of individual and small-group instruction and frequent interchange between children and concerned adults. Third, all believed that children's successes in learning are inseparable from their self-esteem, and all attempted to promote successful development in the affective domain while fostering cognitive goals. Fourth, all had a Follow Through model in existence in the community, so that continuity was provided for a longitudinal study. The sponsors differed among themselves in the *priorities* they assigned to these objectives and in the degree to which they felt that the end justifies the means. We won't go into detail as to each of the models; but we will illustrate a continuum and compare three types of models placed along this continuum. First, we consider criteria for comparison.

Three types of programs compared: Discovery-oriented, cognitive-oriented, and academic-oriented

Several attempts have been made to identify significant criteria to serve as the basis for analyzing and comparing any programs for young children (Lay & Dopyera, 1972). One such list is shown in Figure 3-1. Such a list may be useful as you try to compare various early childhood settings that you visit. (Recall Chapter 1.)

We have selected and combined some of the criteria from Figure 3-1 to form seven points that seemed most illustrative of differences among three general types of programs. (See Table 3-2.) These three general types fall on a continuum from less structured to more structured. Reading through the differing approaches on the chart gives some of the flavor of the range of programs going on then (and now) and the views of the intervention issues described earlier.

In brief overview: the *discovery-oriented* approach is more committed to free play and less to structure; the *cognitively-oriented* approach is

Figure 3-1
Criteria for the comparison of early childhood programs.
(Source: Bernstein, 1972.)

☐ 1. Goals and rationale
☐ 2. Classroom environment
☐ 3. Materials
☐ 4. Curricular and extracurricular experiences
☐ 5. Language development
☐ 6. Ethnically relevant experiences
☐ 7. Cognitive experiences
☐ 8. Affective development
☐ 9. Psycho-motor development
☐ 10. Creative experiences
☐ 11. Individual needs

☐ 12. Scheduling
☐ 13. Classroom management and techniques
☐ 14. Staff
☐ 15. Role of teacher
☐ 16. Role of student
☐ 17. Role of aides, parents, and community workers
☐ 18. Provision for testing and evaluation
☐ 19. Provision for continuity of the model
☐ 20. Support to ensure effective implementation

Table 3-2 A COMPARISON OF THREE PLANNED VARIATIONS MODELS REPRESENTING A CONTINUUM FROM LESS STRUCTURE TO MORE STRUCTURE

CRITERION	BANK STREET MODEL (DISCOVERY-ORIENTED)	RESPONSIVE MODEL (COGNITIVELY ORIENTED)	ACADEMIC PRESCHOOL MODEL (ACADEMICALLY ORIENTED)
Role of teacher and of student	Teacher interacts freely with children. Child takes responsibility for own learning (freely choosing and planning activities) and behavior (according to understandable rules).	Teacher stimulates the child to develop concepts through manipulating objects and verbal interaction with the environment. Child constructs concepts through activities and verbally interacts with the teacher.	Teacher asks or directs, following exact sequence of the program. Child responds with correct answer, loudly, often in chorus.
Curricular experiences	No prescribed curriculum or methodology; a wide variety of experiences are available. Many informal opportunities for language development. Process orientation.	Provides a responsive environment which includes experiences with real objects, their pictures, and abstract symbols for them. At every possible occasion the teacher uses and encourages use of words conveying relational concepts. Process orientation.	Stress on learning basic skills. Formal lessons directly teach language constructions; e.g., articles, prepositions, negative statements. Content orientation.
Classroom management, techniques, rewards	Encouragement of self-discipline and self-direction. Intrinsic rewards; i.e., learning provides its own satisfaction.	Child encouraged to finish activities selected by himself or herself. Intrinsic reward.	Attention demanded, held by rapid pace of group work and extrinsic rewards, e.g., tokens and praise.
Scheduling	Sequence of activities that is smooth-flowing, flexible but generally consistent, alternating quiet and active activities.	Major portion of morning, child selects own learning activities from environment structured by teacher.	Three academic periods 20–30 minutes each. Short periods of music, art, refreshment, physical activity are used to break the academic routine and to reinforce language.

(Continued)

Table 3-2 (CONTINUED)

CRITERION	BANK STREET MODEL (DISCOVERY-ORIENTED)	RESPONSIVE MODEL (COGNITIVELY ORIENTED)	ACADEMIC PRESCHOOL MODEL (ACADEMICALLY ORIENTED)
Materials, environment	No special materials, but a great variety. Environment loosely structured with many interest areas.	Many manipulative and self-correcting materials. Environment structured so child can freely explore but will make discoveries leading to learning.	Printed work sheets for math, reading, and language. Most other materials considered a distraction. Separate, distinct areas with partitions for study of math, reading, and language.
Testing and evaluation	Direct observation and continuous informal assessment.	Standardized testing to determine cognitive developmental level. Continuous informal assessment.	Standardized testing. Formal (criterion-referenced) testing in reading, language, and math.
Goals and rationale	Stimulate positive attitudes and children's involvement in directing their own learning. Develop positive self-concept as this is a prerequisite to development in learning.	Enhance a child's cognitive processes and build autonomy. Develop positive self-concept because the welfare of the whole child is considered important.	Provide academic skills necessary for children to compete successfully in public schools. Bring about positive self-concept as a result of success in academic areas.

committed to a view in which children have time to develop on their own but are provided with some structure as well as a stimulating environment; the *academic* approach stresses a high degree of structure designed to provide children with the necessary skills for a successful academic career as it tries to overcome their deficits. Examples follow:

Preacademic
Academic Pre-School (Engelmann & Becker)
Behavior Analysis (Bushell)
Learning Research and Development Center (Resnick)

Cognitive Discovery
Responsive Environment Corporation (Caudle)
Institute for Developmental Studies (Deutsch-Wolfe)
Responsive (Nimnicht)
Cognitively Oriented (Weikart)
Florida Parent Education (Gordon)
Tucson Early Education (Henderson)

Discovery
Bank Street (Gilkeson)
Open Education (EDC-Hein)

In order to further fix the idea of the general differences of programs in your mind, we'd like to use an analogy, a horse race: see Figures 3-2, 3-3, and 3-4 on pages 66–67. The horses were drawn by a five-year-old named Tara, whose father made the connection (Rayder, 1976). If you forget everything else we've said, you may remember these horses. Consider them one at a time.

Evaluation

What about the evaluation of Follow Through and Head Start Planned Variations? Here again Rayder's analogy is helpful.

The sponsors were encouraged to develop programs consistent with their individual and varied orientations. Each of them did this, and there were tremendous differences in both short- and long-range goals, in methods, and in materials. Some stressed academic content, even if this led to conformity and passivity. Others stressed self-direction, positive self-concept, and initiative, even if, as a result, academic content was to be delayed. Although the "measures" of success paid lip service to all these goals, it was clear that what really counted was immediate gain in cognitive skills. This was like inviting horse breeders to breed a variety of horses for different purposes and then judging the "best" horse by performance in a specific race.

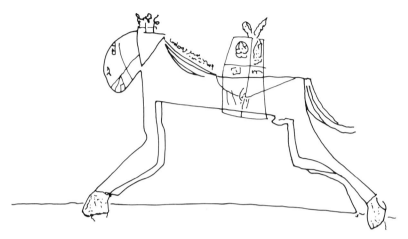

Figure 3-2   *"This horse likes to graze in the field, to romp around, and to deliver gifts to others. This horse likes to be touched and feels good with others around. This horse certainly doesn't look competitive and, if it had its choice, would not race against others. This horse seems independent, but in touch with itself. It is a self-starter, simply takes great joy in running, and would never be found in a mechanical starting gate."*

To the reader: What program indicated on Table 3-2 (and elsewhere in your experience) stresses building positive self-concept, self-direction and self-discipline as a prerequisite to any formal learning? In our Table 3-2, the program labeled "Discovery-oriented" reminds us of this horse.

(Source for Figures 3-2, 3-3, and 3-4: Rayder, 1976.)

In fact, Rayder has raised a crucial question, related to the ethics of considering educational programs for children in the same manner as we treat horse races. Can we evaluate social and educational projects of the comprehensiveness and diversity of Follow Through and Head Start Planned Variations according to a design and methodology appropriate for horse races?

Obviously, the state of the art of evaluation is not yet advanced enough that we can devise trustworthy measures of important areas outside the cognitive domain. Rather than ignore or downgrade such areas as self-concept, values, motivation, aspiration, social adjustment, and creativity, we must make concerted efforts to develop means for assessing progress in these areas as well.

Figure 3-3 *"Here is another horse. It has long legs and looks strong and intelligent. From the feather on its legs you can tell it's probably a Clydesdale. It could pull heavy loads, solve problems, and overcome obstacles that would be insurmountable for a speedy race horse. Speed is not one of this horse's characteristics, but where long-term strength is required, this horse would probably do very well.*

To the reader: What program in Table 3-2 (and elsewhere in your experience) apparently takes a slow but sure approach to children's learning? The program in our Table 3-2 labeled "Cognitively oriented" reminds us of this horse.

Tara

Figure 3-4 *"Here's a horse that might do exceptionally well in a horse race. It's slim and peppy and could get a good jump on the pack. It probably runs short races best and may have trouble with a race over 6 furlongs."*

To the reader: What program indicated on Table 3-2 (and elsewhere in your experience) "teaches" hard and fast and apparently shows "amazing results" in recognizing numbers or words after a few months? In our Table 3-2 the program labeled "Academic" fits the description.

Status of Head Start and Follow Through Today

What is the status of Head Start and Follow Through models today? There appears to be widespread agreement that the models, in their pure form, are not being implemented in the field except under the controls of an experimental design. Most programs not under such controls combine features of a number of different models. It might be said that the models served their purpose in providing demonstrations of a variety of materials and strategies, in bringing these to public and professional awareness, and in having many of their features adopted or adapted in programs all over the country.

There also appears to be widespread agreement that the successful implementation of any specific programs or strategies is dependent more on the background, personality, and motivation of the individual teacher than on any features of the program itself. The teacher's commitment to a program is more of a guarantee of its success than anything inherent in the program itself (Klein, 1973). That is, you, the teacher, are the key to success.

We turn next to other programs of the 1970s that attempted to meet the criticisms of the early Head Start efforts. These programs included Home Start and a variety of infant-toddler programs.

HOME START In response to the hypothesis that programs such as Head Start could not counter negative effects of home environment and expectations, Home Start was conceived as a home-based program for low-income preschool children and their families. Building upon existing family strengths, it was meant to assist parents in their role as the first and most important educators of their own children. It was implemented for the first time in 1972. Since the program was designed to take Head Start expertise to the parent *in the home*, home visitors came regularly and assisted the parents in learning how to work with their children.

The principal way of providing services to families was the home visit, which took place an average of twice a month and lasted about 1½ hours with each family. Most home visitors followed a curriculum for the visit to ensure that all four components (education, health, nutrition, and social-psychological services) were covered during the visit. Each home visit was specifically geared to the needs of the individual parent and child being visited. Home visitors frequently left materials in the home and encouraged the parents to follow up with related activities. Monthly group activities for parents were added to the program in the course of the demonstration phase. Comprehensive social-emotional, health, and nutritional objectives were adopted as part of the core program.

Objectives of the three-year demonstration project were:

- To involve parents directly in the educational development of their children
- To help strengthen the parents' abilities in facilitating the general development of their own children
- To demonstrate methods of bringing comprehensive Head Start–type services to children and parents (or substitute parents) for whom a center-based program was not feasible
- To determine the relative costs and benefits of center and home-based comprehensive early childhood development programs, especially in areas where both types of programs might be feasible (U.S. Department of HEW, 1973b)

The evaluation design provided information about the overall effectiveness of the program by measuring changes in both parents and children using eleven measures with experimental and control groups. At the end of one year, significant differences were found between experimental and control children on the school-readiness measures, in task orientation, and in health care. There were no differences in areas of social-emotional development, physical development, or nutrition. As for parents, after one year mothers in the experimental group showed significant gains in the quantity and quality of their interactions with their children, their teaching skills, the amount of educational materials in the home, and their involvement in the community. More than one year in the program did not result in any appreciable additional gains for either mothers or children (Kresh, 1976).

INFANT-TODDLER PROGRAMS

In response to the hypothesis that the somewhat disappointing results of Head Start evaluation studies might be a result of starting programs too late in the child's life, a number of researchers moved into the areas of infancy and "toddlerhood." Some of these programs provided tutoring which included one-on-one interaction, play, and instruction. This was done at the child's home or at a nearby center. However, on looking back on his program, Schaefer, one of the program developers, felt that his efforts had not been successful. Effects on level of intellectual functioning of even an intensive training program appeared to "wash out" within two years of the termination of these efforts. He believed that his program should have started earlier (at birth), continued through the school years, and concentrated on working with the parents directly. In this way, parents would have been encouraged to take an interest in and assume responsibility for a more active role in the children's intellectual development (Schaefer, 1973). These thoughts are apparently echoed successfully in the "verbal interaction" project, guided by Levenstein.

VERBAL INTERACTION PROJECT

A study by Phyllis Levenstein of her home-based parent-child interaction program lends support to Schaefer's analysis. Working with children two to three years of age, 90 percent of whom were black, she created five different experimental groups. The groups differed in age of entry, length, and intensity of the experience. All were exposed to Levenstein's unique kind of intervention—semiweekly half-hour visits in the home by a trained worker who stimulated *interaction between mother and child* with the aid of a kit of toys and books. The intervention was focused in purpose, with guided involvement in activities aimed at the development of language and thought.

The methodology differed from the group instruction of Head Start or the tutoring approaches just mentioned. First, Levenstein's target was not the child but the mother-child pair as an *interactive system.* Second, the principal agent of change was not a teacher or tutor but the child's own mother (or primary caretaker). Intervention may thus endure as long as the mother-child interaction endures. In fact, those children who entered the program as two-year-olds maintained significant gains in IQ even three and four years after termination of the program.

To further fix the idea of this important program in your mind we have another one of Tara's horses, which we again use as an analogy: see Figure 3-5.

CONCLUSIONS

What conclusions can be drawn about the effectiveness of the programs we have just discussed?

Bronfenbrenner (1974) has made an excellent analysis of preschool and infant-toddler programs. He waded through the morass of studies published in recent years and discussed those that tended to meet three important criteria he established. The three criteria were:

1   Systematic follow-up data were available for at least two years after termination of intervention efforts.
2   Similar information was provided for a control group matched on relevant personal characteristics and background variables.
3   The data were comparable from one project to another.

He then analyzed evaluations of three different types of programs—preschool programs in group settings, home-based infant tutoring programs, and home-based infant parent-child interaction programs.

First, let's take a look at what he had to say about all the research on *preschool programs* (i.e., programs for three- to five-year-olds). What trends were clearly discernible?

• Preschool intervention is effective in producing substantial gains in IQ that are generally maintained as long as the program lasts.

TARA

Figure 3-5 *"This horse appears with her foal. The mother-child interaction is more important for both of these horses than horseracing. This little foal learns a lot about running from its mother. Since the foal is off to such a good start, it will probably still be a good runner when it is older."*

To the reader: Does this scene remind you of Levenstein's program, which placed stress on improving interaction in the home environment as a prerequisite to any formal learning? (Source: Rayder, 1976.)

- Experimental groups do not continue to make gains when intervention is continued beyond one year.
- Neither earlier entry into a program (from age one) nor a longer period of enrollment (up to five years) results in greater or more enduring cognitive gains.
- After termination of the program, children begin to show a progressive decline, and by the third or fourth year of follow-up they have fallen back into the problem range of IQ scores—in the low 90s and below.
- The period of sharpest decline occurs after the child's entry into regular school. (Follow Through appears to indicate, however, that continuation of intervention *with strong involvement of parents* may counteract this factor).
- The children who profit least are those from the most disadvantaged backgrounds.
- For the most disadvantaged students, the greatest loss takes place during the summer months; the less disadvantaged tend to maintain their status or even make some gains.

- The most significant gains are associated with the cognitively oriented programs.

Now let's examine Bronfenbrenner's conclusions about programs for infants and taddlers. In *home-based tutoring programs* (e.g., Schaefer's Infant Education Project), Bronfenbrenner notes results similar to those arising from center-based preschool programs, with dramatic gains that are lost when the program is terminated. He notes that in both the center-based and the home-tutoring programs, although the parents are involved, the role of the parents is secondary. The most striking aspect of his analysis is the sharp change that can be seen in the picture when one examines *home-based parent-child interaction programs*, in which the parents have the primary role and the focus is on the interaction between child and parent rather than between teacher or tutor and child (e.g., Levenstein's Verbal Interaction Project). In these programs, *where parents work directly with their children*, Bronfenbrenner finds reliable reports of the following dramatic results:

- Initial gains are maintained even three to four years after intervention has been terminated.
- Effects are cumulative from year to year and even after intervention.
- Greatest gains in IQ scores are made by children who enter programs at the earliest ages.
- Benefits to younger siblings of the target child are noted.
- Positive changes in the attitude of the mother toward her child and toward herself, and in her opinions, are noted.

Bronfenbrenner's analysis provides valuable insights for planning programs for disadvantaged or culturally different children. It seems that many program developers, even today, continue to naively "invent" and implement programs as if we had no indication of the most promising and feasible approaches. We do *not* have to keep rediscovering the wheel; we *do* have a clear direction indicated to us.

STATE AND COMMUNITY PROGRAMS Early childhood education programs got their initial push from the federal government, but with President Richard Nixon's clampdown on federal spending for social and educational programs, it became clear that the individual states would have to assume a larger share of the responsibility in the years to come. Thus, individual schools and communities have taken up the banner of early childhood education. Recognizing the importance of the early years in improving children's chances of success in school and the opportunity to move out of the cycle of poverty, individual schools and communities have responded with programs of the "homegrown" variety, designed to meet specific needs of specific communities.

AN INVITATION TO THE READER

We would like to invite you to check on the programs for your own state and community—to find out what's going on. For example, does your state have funded kindergartens for *all* fives whose parents want them to attend? Do your local primary grades have open-space programs, open education, team teaching, and individual programs? What kinds of children's educational television programs are available to serve your community? How many franchised day care programs do you have locally? What provisions are being made for young children with respect to Public Law 94-142 in your community (a free, appropriate public education available for all handicapped children beginning at age three)? (See Chapter 13, on the special child.) The twentieth century has become known as the "century of the child" (the first White House Conference on Children was held as early as 1909). We've come a long way *and* we still have a long way to go. Keeping informed on what's going on is important. Modern history: while we're reading it, we're making it.

Summary

This chapter deals with a resurgence of interest in early childhood education, with special attention to the milestone of intervention for the economically disadvantaged and the formulation of programs with far-reaching impacts that can roughly be classifed on a continuum. This continuum moved from more discovery-oriented (developmental inter-action) to more narrowly academic-oriented.

The 1960s brought a resurgence of interest in early childhood education, sparked by two major factors: research and sociology. (1) Research revealed the influence of the environment in modifying IQ and early childhood as a critical period in the development of intelligence. (2) Sociological factors included responses to the civil rights movement and the recognition that a large number of economically disadvantaged and culturally different children started school irrevocably behind their peers.

Many individuals and institutions designed intervention strategies to augment the child's natural developmental processes. Opinion still differs as to how, when, and where to intervene. Experimentation was conducted in a variety of settings with program models based on specific intervention strategegies.

Early studies of Head Start results indicated a high degree of support for the programs among parents, initial gains on the part of children, and a leveling-off in longer-term comparisons with control groups. Different reasons were given for the disappointing results, and redesigned compensatory efforts were developed. Thus Follow Through attempted to carry on the multifaceted approach of Head Start in kindergarten and primary grades; some programs strengthened parent education; Head Start's Planned Variations Study was launched to compare the different effects of specific models; infant-toddler programs and Home Start were implemented. Federal efforts and programs were matched by state and local programs—some small-scale and some as massive as California's ECE program.

What have we learned from this huge movement? What kinds of compensatory education programs are most effective? From infancy until the child is about three years old, the direct interaction between child and parent (aided by a trained person) seems to be more effective than direct training of the child by a trained person (tutoring). Economically disadvantaged children and their families benefit greatly from programs that give parents training and support they need to engage in verbal interaction (with a strong cognitive base) in a one-to-one relationship with their children. From about age three through the elementary years, it appears that preschool programs providing cognitive stimulation are effective. Moreover, strong involvement by parents and the use of other support systems (such as health and social services) can help programs to be more effective.

We need to realize, however, that educational programs such as those exemplified by Head Start, Follow Through, and the infant programs, do not take place in a vacuum. For the most part, they represent only a fraction of the child's life and interactions. We need to look toward interventions that will effect radical changes in the immediate environment of the economically disadvantaged family and child, if we are truly to make a difference in their lives.

Such programs represent a fraction of other forces currently seething in our nation to make the twentieth century the century of the child. You will find many more forces discussed in this book and as you become a careful and insightful observer.

What's going on? Much! And as professionals in the field of early childhood education, we all need to keep informed and involved.

References

Bloom, B. *Stability and change in human characteristics.* New York: Wiley, 1964.

Beers, C. D. Principles of implementation: The lesson of Follow Through. Paper presented at meeting of the American Education Research Association, San Francisco, April 1976.

Bernstein, N. An analysis of early childhood models along selected criteria. Long Beach, California: California State University at Long Beach Foundation, 1972 (unpublished).

Bronfenbrenner, U. *A report on longitudinal evaluations of pre-school programs: Is early intervention effective?* Washington, D.C.: U.S. Department of Health, Education and Welfare, Pub. No. (OHD) 75-25, 1974.

Feshbach, N., Goodlad, J., & Lombard, A. *Early schooling in England and Israel.* New York: McGraw-Hill, 1973.

Frost, J. L., & Kissinger, J. B. *The young child and the educative process.* New York: Holt, Rinehart, and Winston, 1976.

House, E., Glass, G., McLean, L., & Walker, D. *No simple answer: Critique of the Follow Through evaluation.* Urbana, Ill.: Center for Instructional Research and Curriculum, University of Illinois at Urbana, 1978.

Hunt, J. M. *Intelligence and experience.* New York: Ronald Press, 1961.

Klein, J. Making or breaking it: The teacher's role in model (curriculum) implementation. *Young Children,* 1973, *28* (6), 359–366.

Kresh, E. *Findings from the Home Start evaluation.* Paper presented at the National Association for the Education of Young Children, annual conference, Anaheim, Calif.: November 1976.

Lay, M., & Dopyera, J. *Analysis of early childhood programs: A search for comparative dimensions.* Urbana: College of Education Curriculum Laboratory, University of Illinois, 1972.

Morrison, G. S. *Early childhood education today.* Columbus, Ohio: Merrill, 1976.

Osborn, K. Speech before the Sixth Annual Conference of the National Head Start Association. Denver, Colorado, May 1979.

Rayder, N. *Methodological and ethical problems of research in early childhood education.* San Francisco: Far West Regional Laboratories, 1976.

Schaefer, E. S. Learning from each other. In J. Frost (Ed.), *Revisiting early childhood education.* New York: Holt, Rinehart, & Winston, 1973.

U.S. Department of Health, Education, and Welfare, Office of Child Development. *Head Start program performance standards.* Washington, D.C.: U.S. Government Printing Office, 1973a.

U.S. Department of Health, Education, and Welfare, Office of Human Development. *The Home Start demonstration program: An overview.* Washington, D.C.: U.S. Government Printing Office, 1973b.

PART TWO

THE WHOLE CHILD: AREAS OF CHILD DEVELOPMENT

This second part of the book contains four chapters examining areas of child development and their evaluation. What is included in each developmental area?

We think . . . and we feel . . . and we move. Sometimes we do one without the others. But most of the time we do these things together. Although the chapters in Part Two deal separately with each area of development, they do so only because restrictions of language and thought do not allow us to treat them all together. We obviously do not believe that cognitive and language development (Chapter 5) is perfected before the child begins to "work on" affective development (Chapter 6). Each developmental area not only develops simultaneously but also is affected by the others. This interrelationship is part of the reality of the whole child.

In Part Two, we deal with development of movement (Chapter 4, Psycho-Physical-Motor Development); of thinking (Chapter 5, Growth of Thought and Language); and of feeling (Chapter 6, Becoming: Affective Development in Early Childhood, which includes social, emotional, moral, and creative areas). Chapter 7 (Assessment) deals with evaluation of development in each of these areas (by means of both tests and observational techniques), with accountability, and with program evaluation.

How can you use developmental knowledge in planning programs for young children? This part is designed to give you a foundation for laying the building blocks of curriculum, materials, and teaching-learning strategies (the substance of Part Three). Each chapter treating a developmental area in Part Two has a matching curriculum chapter in Part Three.

What is the most important base of early childhood education? If we had to choose, we'd say, "Developmental knowledge." Of course, curriculum is important. But planning and choosing materials and programs for young children without prior attention to developmental bases is like having an audience show up for a performance before the actors have even learned their lines.

What can Part Two do for you? The descriptive science of child development can provide you with useful information—sometimes about what you need to avoid doing at a particular point in children's development—if you want them to learn appropriately, productively, and joyously. And this science can provide you with information about readiness stages for learning. That, and much more (detailed at the beginning of each chapter), is what this part of the book can do for you. (Part Three tells you how to apply this scientific information as a teacher-artist.)

CHAPTER 4

"You've got to walk before you can run."

PSYCHO-PHYSICAL-MOTOR DEVELOPMENT

W hat does the statement on the opening page of this chapter—
"You've got to walk before you can run"—mean? It refers to the idea that some skills generally have to come before others. You need a basic vocabulary before you can speak in sentences. You need basic arithmetic skills before you can do algebra. Although we use this expression figuratively in many areas, it is most appropriate in the area of motor development, where, yes, you must *literally* be able to walk before you can run.

This chapter will trace the sequences of psycho-physical-motor development from conception through the primary grades and give implications for those who work with young children. It will help you to answer the following questions:

- What are the principles, sequences, and environmental influences bearing on development of perception, physical growth, and motor skills from infancy through childhood?
- What are the implications for working with young children?
- What attitudes are advocated in dealing with toilet training and masturbation?
- What do educators need to know about child abuse?

Why have we chosen such a complicated title for this chapter—
"Psycho-Physical-Motor Development"? "Psycho" has to do with perception (the biologically based prerequisite to cognition); "physical" has to do with growth and maturation; and "motor" has to do with physical skills and movement. We consider each of the three elements—perceptual, physical, and motor—separately and break each down into separate age-related periods (infancy and toddlerhood, preschool, and school age). How do the three processes operate and interrelate?

Picture little Sandy in her crib, a brightly colored exercise bar stretched across the rails. Sandy's eyes focus on the exercise bar. We are aware that she has begun to perceive this new addition to her environment. Her little hands twitch and move in the direction of the toy. Within days or weeks she has grown and matured physically sufficiently to reach for the bar. As her motor skills develop, she can grasp the bar and even progress toward a further achievement as she begins to stretch and strain to pull herself erect. Note how all three developmental processes, perceptual, physical, and motor, are involved and interacting.

Introduction

PRINCIPLES OF PHYSICAL, MOTOR, AND PERCEPTUAL DEVELOPMENT

Principles underlying the growth and development of all body systems appear to be related to four areas: (1) rate of growth, (2) direction of growth, (3) differentiation and integration, and (4) sequence of development.

1 Rate of growth

Physical, motor, and perceptual development each follow growth rates that are typical for each age or stage and for all cultures. These rates rarely differ or change. However, development can be delayed under conditions of extreme hardship. If this abuse is prolonged over a long period, it tends to do permanent damage. If, however, deprivation is for a relatively short time, it appears that the body can overcome the negative effect and compensate for it. The child, in effect, catches up. For example, in the Netherlands during World War II, children who were subjected to very restricted diets lacking in many of the required nutritional components were able to overcome the negative effect in a relatively short time once they were returned to the normal conditions they had known in prior years. The implication for educators is that if damage is prolonged in a particular area during critical periods of growth (that is, when growth is greatest in that area), then it may be irreversible, and even our best educational efforts may not allow the child to catch up. But if we can intervene during a critical period of growth—if we can make special efforts at that time to counteract the effects of deprivation—then we may be able to reverse the negative pattern. Also, it should be pointed out that the effect of a period of acute deprivation may be reversible if it represents a relatively short period in an otherwise normal history.

While on the one hand we have knowledge of the possibility of overcoming delayed development, on the other hand we have interest in the possibility of acceleration of development. Training or extra stimulation does appear to give children to whom it is offered an immediate (but short-lived) advantage over their peers. This advantage is not sustained, except in the case of highly individualistic skills dependent more on specific training than on maturation. For example, consider fifteen-month-old twin boys. Training one of them to walk up stairs will allow him to accomplish this act sooner than his brother; but within a matter of months, the untrained child will catch up. A young child trained in skiing, swimming, or skating (skills which do not develop just on the basis of maturation) can be expected to maintain an advantage in these skills over an untrained child. Thus training appears to be effective in areas where highly specific skills are involved—that is, skills which are not universally developed.

2 Direction of growth

Physical, motor, and perceptual development are governed by the principles of *cephalocaudal* (head-to-foot) and *proximodistal* (central-parts-to-outer-parts) development. (Think of a dot that stretches and expands to a cross.) The cephalocaudal principle is evidenced by the fact that the brain develops more rapidly than any other part of the body, that it occupies more space and weight than any other part in the infant. Movement and motor control also become more specific and complex from head to toe. Babies can lift their heads before they can control their legs. The direction of growth from the center to the outer parts (proximodistal) is also clear. Children can perfect gross movements of their arms and legs before they can cut or tie shoelaces or perform other skills which require the use of the more-distant fingers.

Consider some examples. Four-year-old Amy enviously watches her brother win all his opponent's marbles. For the time being, Amy is better able to catch a large playground ball by hugging it to her chest than to shoot marbles between her thumb and forefinger. A teacher striving for perfect manuscript writing skills may be making these efforts prematurely if a youngster has not yet developed the fine motor skills needed. Children's choices or avoidance of activities often give us clues as to their needs. The child who prefers climbing, building with blocks, or riding a tricycle may not yet be ready to succeed at activities that require the use of the more-distant fingers, according to the principle of proximodistal development.

3 Differentiation and integration

Differentiation means that the baby's skills become increasingly more distinct and specific. From early thrashing toward an object, infants can focus on, reach for, and grasp what they want. Integration allows them to coordinate various segments of behavior patterns with each other. Babies who have learned to differentiate their mother's face from other faces can learn to integrate their visual impression with their differentiation of her voice from other voices. Complex responses require the baby to combine and integrate many distinct skills. Older children (for example), when crossing a street, must be able to differentiate the red, yellow, and green lights and what each represents, to look in both directions to check traffic, and differentiate the speeds of approaching vehicles, to walk between the painted "walk" lines, *and* to *integrate* all these skills.

4 Sequence of development

The sequence of development is universal and does not change. Although not all babies demonstrate the same behaviors at the same time, babies all over the world first learn to sit without support, then to crawl, then to pull themselves upright, to walk with support, to stand alone, and then to walk alone. (See Figure 4-2, page 90.) Norms give those of us who work with young children a general idea of when most children will develop each of these skills.

NORMS Norms are based on simple mathematical calculations that reflect the average growth tendencies for a large number of children. Norms do not tell us what is abnormal or unacceptable. They do not explain growth or development; they merely describe it. Norms do not tell us what is ideal; they merely indicate what is most likely to appear in the development of children at particular chronological ages. (CRM, 1975, p. 112)

If used properly, norms can be helpful in giving us a picture of how children develop. They are useful in studying the effect of some variable on development (e.g., the effect of dietary deficiency on physical growth). Norms are not useful, however, in prediction or diagnosis for an individual child. In contrast to the *normative* approach (based on norms for each age or stage), an *ordinal* approach takes into account the fact that, although the sequence of development will be the same for all children, each child's rate of growth is individual, and comparisons are made between where the child was and where he or she is now. (See Chapter 7.)

Expectations of children based on age norms are not always realistic. One of the authors recalls sitting in a neighborhood park watching her two-year-old—an unusually big child for his age—play in the sandbox. As he inverted his pail, some sand came out of the box and a park maintenance man warned him to "Keep the sand in the box." He looked at the maintenance man and smiled, not understanding the brusque command. A few minutes later he again spilled some sand out of the box, and the maintenance man repeated the command a little more vigorously.

Then the man turned to the mother, asking, "What's the matter? He retarded, or something?" No, the child was not retarded—but the *norm*, or behavior expected, for most children of his size was beyond this child's understanding.

A general implication is that we must be careful to base our expectations on a knowledge of each individual child and his or her abilities. We need to avoid basing our expectations on descriptions of what is typical for children of different ages, sizes, or grades.

The Neonate Period

Those of us involved with young children need to be aware of the variety of different experiences and influences on babies—even at the ripe old age of one day. Some children have conditions that are the result of a genetic abnormality (e.g., some kinds of mental retardation) or the result of events or conditions that occurred during their sojourn in the womb (e.g., deformation because of drugs the mother took) or the result of events or conditions that took place during birth (e.g., cutting off of oxygen that may cause brain damage). Even from that first day, mothers differ in their approaches to their babies. Some are more loving and cuddling; others more cool and aloof. Babies, too, seem to differ in their responses to caretakers, thus prompting different treatments. These experiences establish the foundation for how their needs are met, how they interact with significant adults, and how they see themselves and perceive their world.

The first month of a baby's life is referred to as the "neonate period." After some initial loss of birth weight, neonates begin to grow physically in both weight and length. The foundations of *perception* are established as they begin to use their senses to learn about the world. The sensory capabilities of the neonate have been verified by many researchers.

> The sensory capabilities of the newborn keep him in touch with his environment. Visually, he becomes capable of accommodation, or focus; of convergence, or seeing one image with both eyes; and of acuity, or seeing detail. The newborn's auditory sense allows him to discriminate loudness and pitch, and his senses of taste and smell are functioning. (CRM, 1975, p. 101)

The foundations of *motor* development (see Table 4-1) are evident in the presence of certain reflexes such as the grasping reflex and the Moro reflex (thrusting out the arms when support of neck or head is withdrawn). Babies tend to respond to discomfort with mass, or general, movements and crying. Specific reactions come later.

Table 4-1 MOTOR BEHAVIOR OF NEONATES

Eyes
1 Opens and closes lids both spontaneously and in response to stimuli.
2 Pupils widen and narrow in response to light. Narrow upon going to sleep. Widen upon waking. Widen with stimulation.
3 Following moving stimulus. Also jerky movements.
4 Oscillatory movement.
5 Coordinate, compensatory movements when head is moved quickly.
6 Coordinated movements.
7 Convergence.
8 Eye position in sleep frequently upward and divergent, as in adults.
9 Tear secretion (unusual).

Face and mouth
1 Opens and closes mouth.
2 Lips licks, compresses, purses in response to touch.
3 Sucks.
4 Smiles.
5 Pushes material from mouth.
6 Yawns.
7 Grimaces, twisting mouth, wrinkling forehead.
8 Retracts lips, opens mouth to touch. Turns lower lip.

Throat
1 Cries. Sometimes sobs.
2 Swallows, gags to noxious stimuli or touch at back of throat.
3 Vomits.
4 Hiccoughs.
5 Coughs, sneezes.
6 Coos. Holds breath.

Head
1 Moves upward and backward when prone, especially to stimuli.
2 Turns face to side in response to touch. Turns from side to side when prone or when hungry or crying.
3 Head shudders to bitter stimuli.
4 Moves arms at random. Arms slash when crying.

Trunk
1 Arches back.

2 Twists, squirms. When head rotates, shoulders and pelvis turn in same direction.
3 Abdominal reflex in response to needle prick as stimulus.

Reproductive organs
1 Cremasteric reflex (testes raised when inner thigh stroked).
2 Penis erects.

Foot and leg
1 Knee jerk reflex.
2 Achilles tendon reflex.
3 Leg flexes. Plantar flexion accompanies leg flexion (reverse of adult response).
4 Leg extends in response to gentle push. May support some of weight on first day.
5 Protective reflex (if one foot or leg is stimulated, the other pushes against source of stimulation).
6 Kicking, usually during crying.
7 Stepping movements, when held upright with feet against a surface.
8 Toe usually extends when sole of foot is stroked.

Coordinate responses
1 Resting and sleeping position: legs flexed, fists closed, upper arms extended.
2 Back arches from head to heels often during crying or when held upside down.
3 Backbone reflex (the side that is stroked or tickled bends in concave direction).
4 Tonic neck reflex or "fencing position" (head turned to the side, facing an extended arm, the other arm bent up near the head).
5 Springing position (when held upright and forward, arms extend forward and legs are brought up).
6 Stretches, shivers, trembles.
7 Startle response (Moro reflex).
8 Crying and mass or general movements.
9 Creeping movements when prone.
10 When held upright and rotated around vertical axis, arms and legs are extended in the direction of the rotation.
11 Body jerks to loud noises.

Source: Dennis, 1934.

At the end of the neonate period, we find an infant who has adapted to temperature changes, developed a fairly regular pattern of waking and sleeping, as well as one of eating and elimination. Little Julie yawns, grimaces, smiles and sucks, follows an object with her eyes, turns her head in response to stimuli, makes kicking and "stepping" movements, and even makes the beginning of "creeping" movements when placed on her belly.

The neonate can and does learn. In some cases, learning is related to survival—as is the case with learning to suck. Julie learns to establish a relationship with other human beings, to respond to her caretakers and to create responses in the caretaker related to her level of motor activity, her general nature, and her responsiveness. Attention is currently being focused not only on how parents set the tone for the infant's developing personality but on the interaction between parents' and infant's styles. See Segal and Yahraer (1978) for interesting insights into "how babies train their parents."

Infancy and Toddlerhood: The First Two Years of Life

Parents and teachers in the throes of dealing with the "terrible twos" are convinced that *if* they can make it through that trying period, life has to run smoothly from then on. But some of them insist they are not sure they *can* make it! What occurs in the psycho-physical-motor development of children in these first two years? What are children like in this period? What are reasonable goals and expectations on the part of adults? Physical, motor, and perceptual development proceed according to the four universal developmental principles discussed above.

PHYSICAL DEVELOPMENT DURING INFANCY AND TODDLERHOOD Although the newborn child has all the necessary body organs, it is essential to remember that many of these organs and parts require further development before they can function fully. Although the newborn's body structure is almost complete at birth, the bones still have a lot of developing to do. Bones are softer than the bones of older children, and some of them are shaped differently. Some bones are not fully joined together—e.g., the soft spot (or fontanelle) on top of the head. Bones are still soft and delicate; hardening (ossification) takes place at different rates in different parts of the body. Muscles are present at birth, but they will change in size, shape, and composition. The muscles of the young child are more delicate and less firmly attached to the bones than those of the adult. The child's tendency to develop fat (adipose tissue) is related to hereditary factors, body build, eating habits, and age. From birth to nine months, fat increases; thereafter, fat decreases rapidly until age 2½.

Growth is rapid: babies usually triple their birth weight and grow one-third taller during the first year. By the end of the second year, the child usually reaches about one-quarter of adult weight and about one-half of adult height. Different parts of the body have their periods of slow and rapid growth. Growth appears to come in four distinct periods—two slow and two rapid. The period of birth to two years of age is characterized by rapid growth, followed by a period of slow growth until the onset of puberty (between ages eight and eleven). It speeds up again in adolescence and then slows down until maturity.

The nervous system develops rapidly before birth and in the first three or four months of life. Coordination of movement appears to follow the development of the nervous system. Different areas of the brain develop at different rates. As a certain area develops, corresponding sensory and motor abilities appear and assist in the development of perceptual skills.

Educators must consider the fact that changes in strength, coordination, size, and body build have a strong impact on the child's personal and social development as well as on cognitive skills. Physical development influences behavior both directly and indirectly. Directly, it determines what children can do; indirectly, it influences their attitudes toward themselves and others and others' attitudes toward them. Thus, a roly-poly two-year-old boy may not be able to make any headway on a climbing frame, although his leaner friends get half-way up. He begins to see himself as less than successful and also may become the butt of jeers and other more subtle criticism. Later, he may be the last one chosen for teams—or the recipient of a teacher's (or his parents') overprotectiveness.

PERCEPTUAL DEVELOPMENT IN INFANCY AND TODDLERHOOD

In general, perception pertains to the processes by which we read messages that are conveyed by our senses. The growth of perceptual ability includes both a gradually increasing sensitivity of a child's receptors (eyes, ears, and so forth) to the information provided by his or her environment and an increasing ability to register and interpret this information. Among the mental processes, perception probably makes the greatest progress during the first couple of years of life. (Elkind & Weiner, 1978, p. 80)

Perceptual development, however, must be inferred from other behaviors. We cannot tell what the infant is feeling or experiencing, although newer research has devised ingenious methods to determine the sequence of perceptual development. Piaget's research pinpoints this age range as the sensory-motor period—a time when children operate on their environment (largely through the senses) to acquire new information. (See Chapter 5.)

The sense of sight develops rapidly. Visual acuity is limited during the first month, when the baby can focus only on objects that are close at hand. Yet before the end of the first year, a baby's visual system functions in many respects like that of an adult, although the baby may not derive the same meanings as at a later age. There is evidence that even during the first month of life babies are selective as regards what they look at and for how long. By age six to eight weeks, babies can begin to judge distances. At first, infants are attracted largely to the familiar; but by the third month they begin to be attracted by the different. (This transfer of interest, which indicates an ability to differentiate among patters, is called "dishabituation.") By six or seven months, babies develop depth perception.

Hearing is present at birth, and neonates can discriminate sounds. They are sensitive to the frequency, duration, and intensity of sound. By the end of the first year, they have learned through experience to coordinate hearing and vision. They are sensitive to the differences in sound combinations and recognize many words. This *auditory perception* allows them to derive meaning from what they hear.

Other senses that are present at birth in simple form and that develop through infancy are the senses of smell, taste, and touch. There appears to be a connection between the skin and the sympathetic nervous system which is aided by skin-to-skin contact and the stimulation of patting, cuddling, and carrying. (Caretakers need to keep that idea in mind.) Eye-hand coordination also develops and evolves (e.g., holding, mouthing objects, pulling, pushing, and letting go).

Attention is crucial to learning. The child gives selective attention to certain stimuli through the senses. Thus sensation (or attention to sensation) underlies perception. For example, Julie learns to recognize a certain tone when her caretaker calls her name. And this tone means she had better *stop* what she is doing. Perception, considered the foundation of cognition and learning (Figure 4-1), has roots that lie in infancy. (See Chapter 5, on development of cognitive abilities.)

What are the implications for those of us who work with young children? Clearly, we must provide many opportunities for the child to use his or her senses to explore the environment, take in and transform

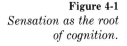

Figure 4-1
Sensation as the root of cognition.

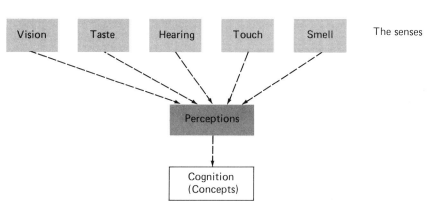

new information, and synthesize learning. Freedom within safe limits can allow the child to touch, taste, see, hear, and smell—to operate directly on his or her environment and gather the information upon which to build accurate concepts.

MOTOR DEVELOPMENT DURING INFANCY AND TODDLERHOOD

Motor development appears to follow a universal sequence that is unrelated to sex, birth order, geographic location, or parental ability. Although the sequence may be universal, some children develop some motor skills more fully than others. The greater development of some motor skills may be encouraged by the child's family or culture. Sex differences in motor development do not begin to appear until around kindergarten age, leading to speculation that perhaps parents' and teachers' expectations contribute to boys' having more "advanced" motor skills.

Several researchers have concerned themselves with the sequence of motor development. (See Figure 4-2 for one researcher's work—Bayley's summary.) Thumb sucking, smiling, and voluntary motor action appear between the second and fourth months. The baby learns to sit up, to crawl, to chew, to shake. By nine months, the infant usually attempts to increase mobility and locomotion by standing up, creeping, and crawling. By the end of the first year, children are well on the way to motor independence. By the end of the second year, they are climbing and walking unaided. Toddlerhood is said to begin when the infant starts to walk. During this period children establish hand and eye preferences and learn to walk smoothly, to jump with both feet leaving the ground, and to drag or push a toy.

As toddlers move into the preschool period, they are gaining speed, accuracy, economy of movement, and strength and steadiness in all the motor skills. It appears that a child needs two elements for growth—simple maturation (which accomplishes much) and a sufficiently stimulating environment which provides security and encouragement.

Toilet training

Toilet training (on many a day care teacher's mind) is one of the major motor accomplishments of the toddler (and his or her parents). Training depends on several factors—the child's sex (girls tend to achieve control earlier than boys), the maturity of the muscles controlling the sphincter and anus, and parents' attitudes. Bowel control is generally achieved before bladder control, and most children tend to be toilet-trained by the age of three. Maturation makes learning easier and allows you to accomplish their training in less time. The optimal time for beginning a regular toilet routine appears to be between fifteen and eighteen months, when children can recognize elimination signals, can restrain the impulse

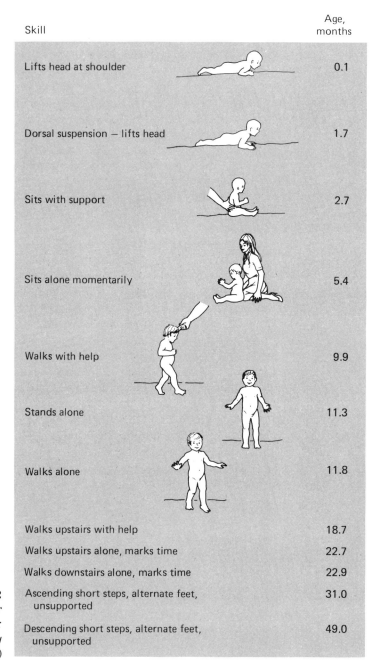

Skill	Age, months
Lifts head at shoulder	0.1
Dorsal suspension — lifts head	1.7
Sits with support	2.7
Sits alone momentarily	5.4
Walks with help	9.9
Stands alone	11.3
Walks alone	11.8
Walks upstairs with help	18.7
Walks upstairs alone, marks time	22.7
Walks downstairs alone, marks time	22.9
Ascending short steps, alternate feet, unsupported	31.0
Descending short steps, alternate feet, unsupported	49.0

Figure 4-2
Sequence of motor development. (Source: Ages reported by Bayley, 1965.)

long enough to get to the toilet, and can exercise control over the muscles involved.

Unfortunately, toilet training in western societies does not remain a matter of simple motor development. A great deal of ego on the part of parents seems to be involved in early toilet training. Adults' attitudes and concerns affect the manner and age in which toilet training is approached, the success of the training, children's long-lasting attitudes about themselves and their bodies, and the relationships between children and adults, especially parents. Caretakers must, for example, realize that children are sensitive to even the most subtle reactions to messiness or fascination with feces.

ENVIRONMENTAL INFLUENCES: IMPLICATIONS FOR EDUCATORS

We can and should provide environments that encourage infants to explore and to improve their skills safely and securely. We should also give them our own encouragement: we can provide motivation and reinforcement and offer guidance and supervision. We should also act as models—that is, we ourselves should be enthusiastic about our own exploration and development of skills. As has been noted earlier, instruction is of value primarily in specialized areas, such as swimming.

The Preschool Child

During the transition from dependent toddlerhood to independent childhood, preschool children's expanding skills and interests influence their personal development and affect their behavior. This is the period where autonomy and initiative develop, giving unique color to each child's individual personality. This is the period in which sex differences begin to manifest themselves, specialized skills responsive to training begin to develop, and children come to terms with their increased strength, speed, and coordination.

PHYSICAL DEVELOPMENT IN THE PRESCHOOL YEARS

Fortunately, growth rate slows down, or we would be a species of giants. The average child grows 2½ inches in height and gains between 5 and 7 pounds a year. There appears to be strong indication that the growth rate is dependent more on adequate nutrition than on racial or genetic factors. Bodily proportions change, because different parts of the body grow at different rates. The trunk, lower face, and legs grow more rapidly than the head, and children lose their babyish features.

Some bodily systems show signs of maturing; for example, the child's heart rate slows down and becomes more stable. The brain is more nearly complete than the rest of the child's body, reaching about 75 percent of its adult weight by the age of three. By about four, the child is capable of fine control of voluntary movement. However, many instances of immaturity in bodily systems may be found. The digestive tract becomes easily irritated by roughage and seasonings. (Be careful what you feed a child!) Bones, joints, and muscles of young children are still much more susceptible to injury than those of older children.

MOTOR DEVELOPMENT IN THE PRESCHOOL YEARS

Preschool children are busily developing new skills and abilities that allow them to expand their world and refine their skills. Many of these skills and abilities develop through maturational processes—given the opportunity, the place, and the encouragement to practice them. The preschooler, however, is responsive to training in specialized skills, and early training in such fields as dancing, skiing, swimming, and skating appears to give children advantages in these fields. Strength doubles between the ages of three and eleven, with boys gaining strength more rapidly than girls. Increased speed in various activities and shortened reaction time allow the child to participate in more complex games and activities. The preschooler develops natural rhythm, smoothness, and accuracy, which lead to increased coordination. Although boys appear more advanced than girls in large-muscle coordination, girls excel in manual dexterity. Some of these differences may be related to sex-typing experiences which dictate how and with what children play.

Smart and Smart (1972) have compiled information from several sources indicating the sequence of motor development in the preschool years: see Table 4-2.

PERCEPTUAL DEVELOPMENT IN THE PRESCHOOL YEARS

Preschool children function in the realm of preoperational thought and base their thinking on momentary perceptual experience; as a result, they pay little attention to transformations, or changes. What preschool children perceive at any moment, therefore, is only a fraction of what more mature children would perceive. The senses which determine perceptions are still developing at this age. The young child is farsighted and, even at age six, generally has not yet achieved 20/20 visual acuity. The ear is not fully developed. The young child is highly susceptible to ear infection, a fact that a preschool teacher needs to keep in mind.

Application of sensory judgment

Much of human behavior depends upon accurate interpretation of inputs received from the senses—accurate judgments of size, shape, and location of objects, direction and speed of motion, the relation of the body to objects in space. Each sensory experience gradually takes on meaning as the child learns to *interpret* the things he or she sees, hears, touches, and tastes.

Perception of size becomes more accurate as the child experiments

Table 4-2 SOME LANDMARKS IN MOTOR DEVELOPMENT DURING THE YEARS FROM 2 TO 6, FROM BASIC NORMATIVE STUDIES. THE ITEM IS PLACED AT THE AGE WHERE 50 PERCENT OR MORE OF CHILDREN PERFORM THE ACT. (Initials in parentheses refer to sources. See footnotes.)*

AGE TWO	AGE THREE	AGE FOUR	AGE FIVE
Builds tower of 6 or 7 blocks (GA)	Builds tower of 9 blocks (GA)	Cuts on line with scissors (GI)	Folds paper into double triangle (TM)
Turns book pages singly (GA)	Makes bridge of 3 blocks (TM)	Makes designs and crude letters (GI)	Copies square (TM)
Spoon into mouth without turning (GA)	Catches ball, arms straight (MW)	Catches small ball, elbows in front of body (MW)	Catches small ball, elbows at sides (MW)
Holds glass in one hand (GA)	Spills little from spoon (GA)	Dresses self (GI)	Throws well (G)
Imitates circular stroke(GA)	Pours from pitcher (GA)		Fastens buttons he can see (GI)
Puts on simple garment (GA)	Unbuttons, puts shoes on (GA)		Copies designs, letters, numbers (GI)
	Copies circle (TM)		
	Draws straight line (TM)		

LOCOMOTION

AGE TWO	AGE THREE	AGE FOUR	AGE FIVE
Wide stance, runs well (GA)	Walks tiptoe (GA, B)	Gallops (G)	Narrow stance (GI)
Walks up and down stairs alone (GA)	Jumps from bottom stair (GA, B)	Descends small ladder, alternating feet easily (MW)	Skips (G, MW)
Kicks large ball (GA)	Stands on one foot (GA, B)	Stunts on tricycle (G)	Hops on one foot, ten or more steps (MW)
Descends large ladder, marking time (MW)	Hops on both feet (MW)	Descends short steps, alternating feet, unsupported (G)	Descends large ladder, alternating feet easily (MW)
Jumps 12″ (MW)	Propels wagon, one foot (J)		Walks straight line (GI)
	Rides tricycle (GA)		
	Descends long steps; marking time, unsupported (MW)		
	Jumps 18″ (MW)		

* Key to sources:
B—Bayley, N. Development of motor abilities during the first three years. *Monographs of the Society for Research in Child Development,* 1935, *1*.
GA—Gesell, A., & Amatruda, C. A. *Developmental diagnosis.* New York: Hoeber, 1951.
GI—Gesell, A., & Ig, F. L. *Child development.* New York: Harper, 1949.
G—Gutteridge, M. V. A Study of motor achievements of young children. *Archives de Psychologie,* 1939, No. 244.
J—Jones, T. D. *Development of certain motor skills and play activities in young children.* New York: Teachers College, *Child Development Monographs,* 1939 (No. 26).
MW—McCaskill, C. L., & Wellman, B. L. A study of common motor achievements at the preschool ages. *Child Development,* 1939, *9,* 141–150.
TM—Terman, L. M., & Merrill, M. A. *Stanford-Binet intelligence scale.* Boston: Houghton Mifflin, 1960.
Source: Smart & Smart, 1972, p. 218.

with such toys as nesting blocks, stacking rings, and Cuisenaire rods.*
Perceptions of shape are aided by sorting blocks as well as by sorting a
variety of objects from the kitchen cupboard. Judgments of weight,
distance, space, and time intervals are all part of the child's expanding
world. Although specialized toys and equipment aid in this development,
we must not lose sight of the fact that children all over the world develop
these perceptions as they mature (and have done so all through the ages).
In fact, with our increased recognition of the significance of accurate
perception as a basis for the development of cognitive and language
skills, we must be careful not to overteach.

We need to allow children the freedom to manipulate materials and
to experiment with them with a minimum of instruction. They will add
the meanings which make their perceptions more complete. They learn
through play as they mix colors, complete puzzles, or fill measuring cups
with sand. These sensory experiences and perceptions provide the facts
to be used in reasoning, the ideas to be expressed in language, and the
basis for much that is later learned (Rand, Sweeney, & Vincent, 1953).

Awareness of the body

From infancy on, babies have been exploring their own bodies, learning
the parts of the body, its capabilities, its contours. They learn where
they end and the rest of the world begins. They learn about the space
they occupy. In addition, they learn many images of, and attitudes
toward, their bodies which summarize their interactions with themselves
and their world.

One aspect of awareness of the body is exploration of all the external
organs—toes, fingers, ears, noses, and genitals. Children learn that
different parts of the body produce different sensations. Often, a toddler
or preschooler learns that rubbing the genital organs produces a particularly pleasing sensation and returns to this type of body exploration
more frequently than to playing with toes. The attitude of parents and
teachers toward such masturbation has far-reaching effects on children's
attitudes toward themselves and their sexuality. It is important to
remember that masturbatory activity is part of the general exploratory
behavior of the young child.

ENVIRONMENTAL INFLUENCES: IMPLICATIONS FOR EDUCATORS   A number of environmental factors can affect the child's physical, motor,
and perceptual development. What are the implications for parents and
educators?

*Cuisenaire rods are a set of proportional, rectangular, color-coded blocks used in
mathematics education.

Socioeconomic status

Research indicates that children of more affluent families tend to be taller and healthier than those of lower socioeconomic status. The inadequate nutrition of poor children over an extended period of time (especially in the critical period of infancy and early childhood) can have a more lasting effect than short-term starvation.

Nutrition

The child needs a diet that supplies high-quality protein for growth, carbohydrates for energy, and the proper amounts of minerals, fats and vitamins to allow other nutritional elements to be properly used. The majority of children in the world do not have an adequate diet or do not get the fullest benefit from the foods that are available. In many countries, the men are served the meat and beans (protein foods) while the mother and children subsist on a largely carbohydrate diet. *The four-year-old needs 50 percent more protein per pound of body weight than his or her father.* In affluent western societies, there is a tendency toward overfeeding; and obesity, with its concomitant social and emotional effects, often results. The preschooler tends to have a somewhat diminished appetite and has begun to develop preferences. The preparation of food, the way it is presented, the timing of the meals, the attitudes of stress or calm at mealtimes—all affect getting the most out of what is eaten (Schneour, 1974).

In recent years, there has been much concern over the effect of sugar, artificial substances, and food additives. Some success has been claimed in the treatment of hyperactive children through dietary controls—usually eliminating sugar and food additives. We are just beginning to understand the connection between diet and learning ability, motivation, and energy level (Feingold, 1975). Parents and educators must ensure that young children receive balanced and adequate diets, that children's preferences are considered, that snacks are wholesome dietary supplements rather than junk food, that research into the effect of sugar and additives is taken into account, and that stress at eating times is regular routine at bedtime.

Sleep and rest

Children vary in their need for sleep, in sleeping patterns, and in the effect of other factors on sleep. Generally, preschoolers take no more than one nap a day in the afternoon. Caretakers should take their cues from the child's sleep needs on the basis of factors such as relaxation, cheerfulness, and reduction of activity before bedtime, and following a regular routine at bedtime.

Illness and accidents

Preschoolers should undergo regular physical and dental check ups and immunization against diseases. Parents need guidance in the areas of nutrition, health habits, first aid, attention to special needs, and safety. Meeting the social and emotional needs of children appears to reduce their predisposition to accidents.

Child abuse

The subject of child abuse has only recently come into prominence. The "battered child syndrome" is a clinical condition in young children who have received serious physical abuse—often with permanent physical and psychological effects. Although the majority of such cases are not reported, there is evidence that child beating ranks second only to motor vehicle accidents in causing injuries to children from direct attack and that child neglect creates extensive problems of malnutrition. Although this problem exists worldwide, it is more prevalent in countries where the nuclear family is totally responsible for the rearing of children and often isolated from the extended family and its supportive role.

Those of us who work with young children need to be aware of the extent of this problem and of clues to its existence. We need to be sensitive to the facts that personality disturbances are not a sufficient explanation of child abuse, that usually only one child in a family is a target, that it occurs most frequently in homes with a destructive kind of emotional climate or where the parent has a history of having been abused as a child, and that it is found in families at *all* socioeconomic levels. Often adults who were themselves abused as children view their behavior as in the best interests of the child and a rightful exercise of their parental authority. Appeals to a sense of responsibility tend to aggravate the problem for immature adults who are disappointed because their children are not able to satisfy the parents' emotional needs for nurturance and protection.

One method of dealing with the problem is to recognize that both these adults and their children need intervention by some authority. Social workers can often intervene to help the family develop new patterns of interaction. The approach of appointing surrogate parents for the *adults* has met with some success (Hielfer & Kempe, 1974). Both parent and child must be viewed as victims in these cases—both need help. It is the law in some states that one must report suspected child abuse. Check your local situation to determine your *legal* responsibility. It is the *moral* responsibility of those who work with young children to help eliminate child abuse.

The School-Age Child: Ages Five to Eight

This is the period of relatively slow growth—the calm before the storm of pubescence. Freed from the energy-consuming concerns with development of skills and of the illnesses of early childhood, the child in kindergarten and the primary grades can focus on developing and perfecting many motor coordinations, enjoying the sense of accomplishment that accompanies successful mastery of motor skills.

PHYSICAL DEVELOPMENT OF THE SCHOOL-AGE CHILD

Boys and girls continue their growth in this period, with boys being generally taller and heavier until they enter the pubescent period. Their legs have gotten longer and their trunks slimmer, and they are steadier on their feet. Fat diminishes and is redistributed. Muscles continue to grow in size and strength but are still not fully mature and are easily subject to strain. The skin appears less delicate; hair often darkens.

By school age, the digestive system matures considerably and can tolerate more unusual foods and less regular eating patterns. The heart grows slowly and respiration becomes slower, deeper, and more regular. The bones continue to ossify, and the deciduous teeth are replaced by permanent teeth.

MOTOR DEVELOPMENT OF THE SCHOOL-AGE CHILD

Children of ages five through eight are able to run and climb well. They can throw and catch a ball easily. During this period, they learn to skip and to jump rope. Other specialized skills that develop include swimming, bicycle riding, skating, and skiing. Comfortable with the elemental skills, the child undertakes the coordination of many skills into games. Many of these games involving running, chasing, and jumping are almost universal.

By the end of this period, the child's motor activities reveal increasing strength, speed, flexibility, precision (including steadiness, balance, and aiming), as well as reduction in reaction time.

PERCEPTUAL DEVELOPMENT OF THE SCHOOL-AGE CHILD

The sensory mechanisms involved in perceiving continue to mature. The eye changes shape and overcomes early farsightedness. Binocular vision is usually well developed around the age of six. Hearing acuity increases with age, and there is less likelihood of ear infections once the eustachian tubes assume their mature character. This is the period when the brain organizes into laterally specialized functions: that is, into right- and left-hemisphere functions. In general, the right hemisphere—which is involved in perception of nonverbal sounds and spatial relationships—appears to be dominant in boys; the left hemisphere—which is involved in language—appears to be dominant in girls.

ENVIRONMENTAL INFLUENCES: IMPLICATIONS FOR EDUCATORS

Although child-mortality rates are down in the United States, we must be aware of the fact that mortality rates for children between ages five and nine are five to nine times greater in poor countries than they are in affluent countries. Disease, injury, pollution, and malnutrition are all threats to the young child.

Children in this age range have fewer illnesses in general than younger children, and particularly fewer respiratory and gastrointestinal problems. Widespread use of immunization in the United States has considerably reduced the incidences of the communicable "childhood diseases" such as measles, mumps, chicken pox, whooping cough, and scarlet fever. (Not all children, however, are fortunate enough to be immunized against these threats.) Many illnesses can be prevented by practice of habits of good health, safety, and nutrition, and by provision of adequate rest and exercise.

Poor nutrition becomes a problem even in families which are concerned about nutrition when children have more access to snacks and sweets without adult supervision. Dental problems also result from this tendency. Obesity, with its concomitant psychological problems, is another problem stemming from poor nutrition. All these dangers must be the concern of adults responsible for the welfare of children. The preschool child is physically able to tolerate more unusual foods, and parents (and teachers having the opportunity) can encourage these children to expand their dietary repertoires constructively.

Chronic illnesses, such as diabetes and long-term disabilities, have an adverse effect on growth and motor development. Accidents are responsible for death or injury to boys more than to girls during this period, when children become increasingly independent and involved in peer-group activities. This is the age of involvement in competitive sports. Adults, at times, meet their own ego needs by pushing children beyond reasonable limits in the pursuit of achievement or victory. The effect of such approaches must be carefully weighed in relation to the child's still-developing and vulnerable bones and muscles as well as to significant social and emotional ramifications.

Summary

As we conclude this discussion on physical, motor, and perceptual development (each considered separately and each broken down into separate age-related periods), we must be aware of the intertwining of all aspects of human development. This development appears to proceed in predictable sequence. We must realize, however, that although the sequence is universal, children progress at varying rates. Norms describe the general sequence of development, but in assessing the development of an individual child, we must also consider his or her own pattern of growth. Those of us who work with young children may use normative scales to derive a general picture of where the child is in relation to others. But we also need to compare children with themselves in order to arrive at realistic expectations for them.

The relative roles of genetics, heredity, and environment are still not fully understood. It is clear, however, that all three are also interacting as the child grows in physical, motor, and perceptual skills.

During the period of *infancy and toddlerhood*, growth is rapid, bones and muscles develop, and the nervous system matures. The child is well on the way to motor independence, and the sensory systems needed for accurate perception become increasingly refined. The effect of deprivation during the prenatal and infancy period is related to the extent and duration of the deprivation.

Preschool youngsters change in bodily proportions and in body processes. As they approach their mature state, many new skills and abilities develop. Those skills most responsive to training are such individualistic and specific ones as swimming, skating, and bicycling. More general skills appear to develop through the process of maturation. Children grow in their abilities to apply sensory judgment. Their feelings about their bodies stem from their own awareness of their bodies and from their experiences, such as exploration of the body and attitudes toward toilet-training. Environmental influences that affect development include nutrition, socioeconomic status, patterns of sleep and rest, illness, and child abuse.

The *school-age-child* continues to develop physically, with sex differences becoming more evident. Motor development reveals increasing strength, speed, flexibility, and precision. Use of sensory mechanisms and effective perceptual skills lead the child into more mature cognitive skills. (See Chapter 5, on cognitive development.)

This chapter has attempted to increase your understanding of psycho-physical-motor development and to sketch its implications for those working with young children. Clearly, children change not only in size and in ability, but also in how they organize and respond to experiences. Their responses change both in character and in degree of complexity. Thus children's interaction with the environment and the interrelationship among the cognitive, affective, and psycho-physical-motor areas are major concerns of parents and teachers. We have tried to indicate *what* children can do and *why* they can do it, and thus provide a background for teaching-learning strategies in the psycho-physical-motor area. Chapter 8 gives specific ideas about curriculum; with your understanding of development, you will be able to expand on them and confidently help children develop.

Implications

What are the implications for those who work with young children? We need to be aware of the different rates at which both different children and different parts of the body develop in order to provide challenging opportunities without stress. The direction of growth (head to toe and center to outer parts) needs to be taken into account in planning learning activities. As different parts of the body grow at different times and rates, awkwardness is natural. While bones are still soft and muscles underdeveloped, it is unwise to push children beyond their capabilities. Even when the child's growth in autonomy and initiative indicates a readiness for further development of physical skills, we need to remember that highly competitive activities at too young an age tend to push the child—at times beyond safe limits.

The gradual growth of sensory skills places limits on what the child can reasonably be expected to do at any given time. Near-point vision and eye-hand coordination, for example, develop over a period of time. (Be cautious about early reading and writing; know the individual child well.)

Parents and educators need to be conscious of the sex-typing that has, in the past, begun to be felt most strongly in the preschool period. If we indicate that certain activities are more appropriate for boys or for girls, we, in effect, are guaranteeing that there will be *less* involvement and *less* success for the other sex.

Finally, we can and should provide environments that encourage children to explore and improve their skills. While we provide motivation and reinforcement, we can offer guidance and supervision and serve as models. Most of the time, maturation will do the rest.

References

Bayley, N. Comparisons of mental and motor test scores for ages 1–15 months by sex, birth order, race, geographical location and education of parents. *Child Development*, 1965, *36*, 379–411.

CRM. *Developmental Psychology Today* (2d ed.). New York: Random House, 1975.

Dennis, W. A description and classification of the responses of the newborn infant. *Psychological Bulletin*, 1934, *31*, 5–22.

Elkind, D. & Weiner, I. B. *Development of the child.* New York: Wiley, 1978.

Feingold, F. Hyperkinesis and learning disabilities linked to artificial food flavors and colors. *American Journal of Nursing.* 1975, *75*, 797–803.

Hielfer, R. E., & Kempe, C. H. *The battered child* (2d ed.). Chicago: University of Chicago Press, 1974.

Rand, W., Sweeny, M., & Vincent, E. *Growth and development of the young child*. Philadelphia: Saunders, 1953.

Schneour, E. *The malnourished mind*. New York: Doubleday, 1974.

Segal, J., & Yahraer, H. Bringing up mother. *Psychology Today*, 1978, *12* (November), 90–96.

Smart, M., & Smart, R. *Children: Development and relationships* (2d ed.). New York: Macmillan, 1972.

CHAPTER 5

*From the beginning, children think
and use language creatively:*

*"I saw it start to rain. The dirt got holes in
it."*

*"Look at the fingerpaint water. The blue
water. The blue-green water. It's dreamable."*

*(Child tries to thread a needle.) "Open your
mouth and say 'ah.'"*

GROWTH OF THOUGHT
AND LANGUAGE

The quotations on the opening page of this chapter are samples of basic creative thinking in the young child's development of thought and language. You will find this idea extended in this chapter. Such knowledge of development helps us to know better when to get out of a child's way and when to step in and assist.

More specifically, this chapter answers the following questions:

- How does a child come to think and to talk? By what private logic do children reach their conclusions—reasonable to them but illogical to us?
- What frameworks are useful to us in terms of organizing information and guiding instructional decisions? For example, what does the work of leaders such as Piaget and the work of linguists tell us? What milestones are common?
- How can we adults help to promote—instead of trampling on—children's creative thought and language?

Why bother to read this chapter? First, consider that the individual differences found in adult thought and sensitive, fluent language may have originated in early childhood. Knowing patterns of development found in this chapter gives the teacher background and perspectives needed for teaching. Teaching includes skilled selection of learning activities appropriate to the child. To help children develop their powers of thinking, you need to understand how they think and express their thought in language. You need to understand why children make so-called errors. With such a background, we won't absolutely guarantee that you'll be a better teacher, better able to select activities for children, but you probably will be!

Introduction

HOW DOES A CHILD LEARN TO THINK?

How do children come to *think* at all, and how do they move their thought patterns toward a supposedly adult stage? In overview, some major ideas are the following.

Piaget (a famous theoretician from Switzerland) has given us a useful description of children's stages of thought (Figure 5-1). A child's intelligence apparently develops in sequential stages. Each stage is marked by typical ways of thinking, interestingly different from adult thought. Through a series of classic experiments, he derived this explanation. His theory, which focused on four main mental stages, gives us a compressed picture of children's behavior at certain points in time. Starting from the very first experiences of the world, children themselves build up concepts such as distance, size, quantity, and space. A progression of ways of knowing emerges.

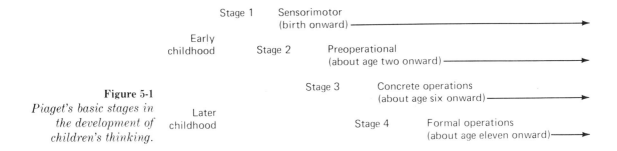

Figure 5-1
Piaget's basic stages in the development of children's thinking.

For example, ask young children of various ages: "What makes clouds move?" A child between three and five years old might say:

"You do" or, "It's magic."

A child between five and seven years old (who tends to attribute life to nonliving things) might say:

"Clouds follow us" or, "Clouds move so they can get to different places."

An eight-year-old might say:

"The wind pushes them." (Charles, 1974)

Try these questions yourself with children of several different ages and note the results.

The next part of this overview explains Figure 5-1, Piaget's four stages. Note that the first three stages encompass children's behavior during *early childhood* (birth to age eight). Piaget tends to characterize each period by the highest forms of thinking observed in children at that stage. The age levels given are *rough* approximations referring to group behavior—not to individual children. We should note that Piaget sees these stages as universal and independent of environment or training; and that, although their sequence does not change, children do pass through them at different rates.

One dimension of Figure 5-1 is continuity. The extended arrows suggest this extension. Even though the sequence emerges in stages, each continues to expand after others have come into existence. Each stage of development overlaps phases that follow. That is, much learned in earlier stages continues as a way of thought in later stages. (For example, sometimes even adults go back to earlier ways of knowing. Maybe we don't say that clouds move because they want to follow us; but most of us are occasionally guilty of animism in some form—for example, berating the hammer that hits your thumb.)

How do ways of knowing and thinking change? Consider the example of a small child in Piaget's stage 2 who wanted to hide her father. She suggested, "You stand behind me." She couldn't grasp the idea that he would show, that he would not be hidden by her little body. She could not see him from *her* point of view; so, he must be out of sight (Sharp, 1969). This *egocentric* attitude is a typical way of thinking at her stage. But a typical person in Piaget's fourth stage (formal operations) has changed. Such a person realizes that people have different perspectives, depending on their view of a scene. And yet, we have all seen supposedly mature persons regress to perception-bound, egocentric conclusions, to thinking that everyone should see a situation in exactly the same way that they do.

The arrows in Figure 5-1, then, remind us that at certain times certain individuals will engage in earlier ways of thinking. In some areas, however, they will have truly constructed higher ways. Advanced stages of thought do not automatically cut across all content areas and all contexts. That is, a profile of an individual's abilities in, say, science, mathematics, and social behavior might show a very jagged line.

A BRIEF OVERVIEW OF PIAGET'S STAGES

Briefly, the first—*sensorimotor*—stage shows the child to have constructed knowledge of objects, knowledge tied to specific sensory awareness or to actions of the body (e.g., nipples give food and are for sucking). Babies don't perceive objects the way we do; out of sight means out of mind. (A hidden rattle is simply and completely gone, forever, as though it never existed.) Typically, intellectual development at this earliest stage goes from simple reflex activity to simple adaptation to environment. Then development progresses to separation and recognition of "self" as differing from environment (e.g., from mother). The "knowing" leads to some attempts to act upon the physical world (e.g., to get a rattle by pulling the edge of the blanket it sits on toward oneself). All this development is tied mainly to body activity and to the senses.

The next stage—*preoperational*—indicates more symbolic knowledge (e.g., "chair" refers to lots of things you can sit on.) But this symbolic knowledge is still tied to self and to concrete objects.

The third stage—*concrete operations*—shows knowledge defined by groupings and rules, representing relationships within the physical world. Some sample operations are: classification, serial ordering, and addition and subtraction. But the child applies such mental operations only to objects considered to be real (or concrete). (For example, you pick up the real sticks and put them in an order, or take some away, in order to represent subtraction.)

The fourth stage—*formal operations*—shows knowledge to be manipulated systematically by means of abstract hypothetical propositions. The way of knowing in this last stage shows mastery of "thinking about thinking," a second-order removal from concrete reality to abstract relationships. Having given a brief overview, we next go into more detail.

Section 1: INFANCY TO AGE SIX

Beginnings are important. This half of the chapter covers Piaget's first two stages. We move back and forth between his ideas and discussions of language development, as the two go hand in hand, complement each other, and together give us a more complete picture.

Piaget's Stage 1:
Sensorimotor—Birth through about Two Years

If we have to choose, perhaps the most outstanding characteristics of this stage are adaptation, intention, and object constancy.

As might be suspected from the term "sensorimotor," in this stage infants and young children construct much learning through sensory contact and body movement. Infants do not appear to distinguish between the world and themselves. Intelligence begins with knowledge of the interaction of the self with things outside the self as infants go about creating their world of objects. Infants look at, reach for, handle, manipulate; they watch faces, rattles, flies—anything they can. Gradually they learn to look at what they hear, to touch what they see; adaptation to the physical world has begun.

It is an exciting milestone—and a distinguishing mark of intelligence—when infants begin to show intention and the deliberate use of an instrument to reach a goal. For example, in order to get an object that is too far away, infants learn to pull on whatever movable substance an object rests upon. When such actions become more general than one instance, then they become an example of a mental connection ready for use and reuse. The sum total of these connections represents what these children know.

We can see these young children's actions gradually becoming more and more precise and deliberate, showing the beginning of understanding about relationships in space and time and about cause and effect. The young child repeats and applies such understanding. For example, at eight months we might see a child push a caretaker's hand in order to set a complex toy in motion—an act that the hand has already performed before. In short, lacking internal symbols, the infant "knows" through motor interaction with objects in the surrounding physical world. The infant knows, adapts, and shows intention.

Object constancy is another milestone of this period. Children are not born knowing, but rather gradually learn about, the stability or constancy of objects. The young child (eight to twelve months) learns that objects exist even when they cannot be seen—that is, learns concepts of *permanence*. The child realizes that an object does not vanish into thin air when hidden. For example, Piaget's little son, Laurent, would follow his father with his eyes as Piaget hid behind the buggy. Then the young son would swing around with the expectation of seeing his father emerge on the far side of the buggy. Understanding the concept of *object constancy* adds to our picture of the early developments in infants' intelligence.

But what is happening to a child's language development about this time? We next see in a child's beginning language learning one of the most marvelous events of human existence. This miracle is a testimony to the creative genius of early childhood.

How Does a Child Learn Language?—A Brief Overview

How does a child come to talk at all? Coming to think and coming to talk are two *related* processes. Teaching in early childhood necessarily puts the two processes together. Another question this section addresses is, "How does a child *use* language?"

A PIAGETIAN PERSPECTIVE The child first uses language to gain egocentric, self-expressive ends ("Me want . . ."); next, to gain social ends ("Will you play with me?"); and finally, to represent symbolically relationships in the physical world ("If you put the rollers under it, it'll move easier"). As for motivation, children soon learn that it is useful to be able to say a few words to express oneself more precisely. This motivation from within is part of coming to talk. (The list on pages 110–111 and the descriptions following it give language milestones.) But first, consider the extreme importance of feeling as an accompaniment to language learning.

AN AFFECTIVE PERSPECTIVE: VERBAL AND NONVERBAL SUPPORTS

Although it is important for language development that babies hear speech sounds, positive affective tone is also crucial. All the nonverbal, physical accompaniments and subtle intonations critical in the beginning—the hugs, the pats, the tender touches—give an immediate sense of human communication. As the caretaker is feeding, bathing, or changing the infant, the caretaker coos, sings, and in general expresses joy and wonder. An infant does not understand the words but is nevertheless learning that language makes one feel happy—so happy that the infant tries to "talk," too. As the saying goes, "We learn what we love and what we love shapes us."

Thus, probably *the major linguistic assistance that an adult can give the young child is to keep the large part of language thrust at the child pleasant, playful, and joyous.* When the language directed to children has positive, supportive associations (as in "word play" and later in storytelling), children find language rewarding and attractive. If, however, much of the language directed to the child implies punishment ("No, no!" "Shut up!"), the sender lays a foundation for problems in listening, speaking, and reading. Fortunately, most children grow up hearing a great proportion of pleasant words, and motivation for language mastery is high. But when this positive tone has been lacking, a helpful program is needed to compensate.

A LINGUISTIC PERSPECTIVE: STAGES OF LANGUAGE DEVELOPMENT

One way of describing and organizing the child's process of learning the language of others is by three stages—"before language," "not quite" language, and "true" language: prelinguistic, protolinguistic, and linguistic. These stages (as was the case with Piaget's stages) correspond to certain ages, but with *great individual variation.* For example, Jean at two years of age can, rather precociously, name all of the objects in her environment; Jim at age five cannot. The point is that while the order of language stages is relatively stable, ages are merely approximate.*

Language Development

Prelinguistic
• Birth to three months (gurgle—coo)
• Three to twelve months (babble)

Protolinguistic
• Twelve months to two years (walk-talk)

* For sample references, see: Lenneberg (1967); Landreth (1967); Britton (1970); Cazden (1976); Dale (1972); MacGinitie (1969).

Linguistic
- Two to six years and beyond (progressive lengthening of sentences and progressive refinement of social uses of language)

Prelinguistic stage

From birth to three months, the child is busy making reflexive sounds (associated with physiological states) and squealing or gurgling sounds called "cooing." From about three months to twelve months, the child engages in "babbling," that is, a profusion of almost unlimited sound types. Examples are repetitions of /ma/, /da/, /di/. This practice ends at about eighteen months. At about eight months, the child produces intonation patterns resembling, e.g., a question or an exclamation. This level of language production corresponds roughly to the early part of Piaget's first major stage of intellectual development, the sensorimotor stage.

Protolinguistic stage

From about twelve months to twenty months, children react to words and sounds produced by people in the immediate environment as they move ahead interactively. The child moves from vocalizing in unison with adults, to imitation of adult sounds already in the child's repertory, to echoing (after a pause) what the adult has said. The child imitates sounds using an average stock of around thirty words (more than three and less than fifty) for naming and for one-word sentences. During this stage, sometimes referred to as the "walk-talk" stage, children show evidence of listening to simple commands (for example, "Show me your eyes").

The child eighteen to twenty months old uses one-word sentences to cover many meanings. For example, "Drink," might mean anything, from "Bring me one," or "Look at it," to "I didn't like it, so I knocked it off the tray." In other words, the human infant is already communicating complex underlying thoughts with single-word utterances—a highly respectable accomplishment!

At the end of this protolinguistic period, children give up this single-word approach upon making a dramatic discovery. They can combine words into two- or three-word sentences that reduce uncertainty. This protolinguistic stage, incidentally, corresponds roughly to the latter part of Piaget's *sensorimotor* stage.

Linguistic stage

From about two to six years of age, the child progressively and rapidly increases vocabulary. For example, at age two, a child typically has a vocabulary of about 200 to 300 words. Some children are able to name all items in their environments. The joining of words into original sentences continues. The child develops what appears to be a rudimentary grammar. According to linguists this grammar is genuinely constructed *by the child*. It does not occur in adult language and is not a mere random throwing together of words. Again, the child accomplishes wondrous feats.

By age six, the child has use of most of the simple grammatical structures and sounds that are characteristic of the dialect closest to the child. On into the elementary school years, however, some complex sentence structures (with less easily determined referents) are still being mastered (e.g., "John promised Mary to go" and "John asked Bill what to do"; Chomsky, 1969, 1972). Spoken communication units are about six to seven words long.

With respect to connected discourse, at about four years of age children can generally share a connected account of some recent experience. A sequence of instructions consisting of two simple directions is usually successfully carried out. By age five, children hold conversations with others when the experiences and language are familiar. Their language is usually easily understood. As their thoughts forge ahead of their performance, children may repeat words and phrases. This repetition is sometimes mistakenly judged to be stuttering.

Vocabulary development is incomplete, of course, at age six. Children typically reach that age with approximately 3,000 words and add about 1,000 words a year thereafter. Some children are still struggling with verb tenses, pronoun use, and plural forms ("two feets").

Thus, in these stages we see a natural, regular, and typical order of language development that is part of how a child learns language. Another part is the breakthrough in understanding that names stand for things and experiences in the world. Piaget has called this development to our attention, and we next examine it in detail.

Beginnings of symbolic representation and vocabulary

During the end of the protolinguistic stage (the last part of Piaget's sensorimotor stage and the first part of his preoperational stages) some children first discover the idea that *names stand for things*. However, there is no way for children who are just beginning to use language to be sure about the meaning of certain terms they hear. They are likely to believe that a term refers to whatever they had in mind when they first heard it. For example, if the mother or caretaker says "plant," a child might think that a plant is anything that looks green or anything that sits on a particular window ledge. What children think in association with a word or phrase depends on what they are noticing at that instant.

Moreover, they also believe that what is foremost in their thoughts at any instant is also what others must be attending to—another example of children's egocentricity. As children gain intellectual maturity, they realize that other people are not necessarily paying attention to the same things they are—but this is a hard lesson that many of us never learn entirely (Duckworth, 1973).

An example of beginnings of symbolism in language is seen when a young child holds two potato chips together and says, "Butterfly!" (Figure 5-2). You can observe these beginnings in children's dreams and fantasies. Today they may be a bear, tomorrow they may be playing "mommy" and "daddy." The use of such symbolism, such transformation, is an important marker of developing intelligence. See the extended section on play in Chapter 12.

Figure 5-2

Although Piaget has identified age two as typical of the beginning of language with symbolic representation, an illustration of much later development helps to clarify this crucial concept. The case is that of Helen Keller, who was blind, deaf, and mute. She discovered this concept of symbolic representation by means of association: her teacher spelled the word "water" in her hand (using finger signs) while water was actually flowing over her fingers. In this way, Helen Keller achieved the idea that *things have arbitrarily assigned names*. Within a few hours, Helen added thirty new words to her vocabulary.

In the same way that Helen Keller's language learning was suddenly accelerated, the language and thought development of typical children speeds up once they have grasped this basic idea, "Words are labels for things!" They begin to ask the names of objects continually, turning into "label demanders." In the beginning, one label may fulfill their needs for a great many things. For example, all men may be called "daddy"; and if, say, the household has a pet duck, all members of the bird family may be called "duck."

We will leave Piaget and his thoughts on language used for symbolic representation. Outside of this idea, he has had little to say to us about language development. The next section draws more information from the field of developmental linguistics.

Language Development of the Child—Ages One to Two

The description just given of stages of language development touched on: (1) sound production, (2) vocabulary, and (3) sentences. Further description follows. For the sake of analysis, we treat these features one at a time. But keep in mind that a child learns these aspects of speech—sounds, words, sentences—*at the same time, not in fragments*. This developmental fact implies that we should avoid fragmented teaching.

DEVELOPMENTAL FEATURES OF SOUND PRODUCTION

The contrast between vowels and consonants (e.g., "am"—"pam" is probably the first one to be learned. The mastery of the initial consonant in a word precedes its use in other places (e.g., "*t*oy" before "nu*t*" (Ervin & Miller, 1963). In other words, children in this early stage of life may have difficulty with final consonants when they learn to say words (no matter what their language or culture). Such information needs to be considered (more appropriately than in the past) when designers attempt to create language programs for young children, or when speech therapists prescribe premature remediation at the insistence of anxious parents.

DEVELOPMENTAL FEATURES OF CHILDREN'S GRAMMAR, SEMANTICS, AND ONE-WORD SENTENCES

Figure 5-3

"Doggie!" shrieks the thirteen-month-old, careening after the neighbor's spaniel; "See doggie!" shouts the twenty-month-old child, who in a short time has made extraordinary progress in generating two-word sentences instead of one-word ones (Figure 5-3). A child appears to move through several grammars in speaking, successively approaching adult norms and variety. Children in the sensorimotor stage are not just naming (not for long), as they use words. As was suggested earlier, usually children use a word with a variety of meanings. "Car" may mean, "That's mommy's car"; "Mommy is in the car"; "I want the toy car"; "Where did the car go?" "Do you want the car?" or, "The car is over there."

We suspect that the ambiguity of their one-word sentences (peaking at nineteen to twenty months) motivates children toward a more complex sentence system. *Any early childhood teacher can use this basic motivating force—the urge of human beings to make sense out of their mental world.*

TWO-WORD SENTENCES: THOUGHT CONTENT AND GENERATION

After one-word sentences, children create two-word sentences. On the surface, this performance seems like a very simple development. It is highly complex, as careful study has shown. When we know more, we feel like giving a lot of credit to children.

One point of view—the behaviorists'—is that language learning is a simple matter of imitating and copying what adults say, leaving out endings and minor words. Examination of language learning, however, shows that this idea is far too simple an explanation. It is fascinating to study children's progressively developing grammars and rule-governed behaviors. Of course, the children cannot tell you the rules abstractly;

the rules are not at their level of conscious verbalization. We cannot resist touching on a few examples.

First, one can see meaning groupings in children's two-word sentences. Their meanings refer, for example, to recurrence ("More ball"), disappearance ("All-gone ball"), possession ("Daddy chair"), and attributes ("Big dog"). Next, one can see children reversing the order of language; this is again suggestive of more than mere copying. For example, an adult would say, "The lunch is all gone," but a child may say, "All-gone lunch." Other groupings show relations of agent to action ("Daddy hit"), and action to object ("Hit Daddy") (Brown, 1973).

We can note more rule-governed behavior. Examine children's two-word sentences such as "See truck," "See lettuce"; "My milk," "My vitamins"; "Blanket on"; "Coat on"; "All-gone vitamins"; "All-gone doggie." The first class of words is small and serves as a pivot ("see," "my," "on," "all-gone"). The second, large class is open and can be added to continually ("milk," "vitamins," "blanket," "doggie"). Finally, when a child says, "Hi sock" (a greeting to an inanimate object) or "All-gone outside" (for the closing of a door) it is highly unlikely that the utterances were merely copied. Thus, in their use of language, children show rule-governed abilities and a creative imagination that is fresh, naive, and delightful. (See, e.g., Braine, 1963; Brown & Bellugi, 1964; Smith, 1971.)

Gradually young children expand and further distinguish their two-word sentences (e.g., "All-gone big, big doggie"). Showing even more complex use of sentence-generating principles, they transform sentences to questions ("Does doggie drink milk?") and to negative phrasing ("Doggie doesn't drink milk"). They learn how to invert the subject of a sentence and the auxiliary verb (e.g., "You are going"; "Are you going?") That is, the child's rule-governed language behavior includes knowing what *function* a word has, not just what it is. Children often appear to be testing their ideas about the "rightness" of new words and combinations (within the context of their primitive grammars). Although they mainly begin their speaking careers by referring to (and probably living much in) the present, we infer a sense of the future from such sentences as "In a minute" or "I'm gonna" (Clark, 1971; Cromer, 1968). About half, however, of what children of this age say is a sort of monologue, egocentric, without regard for molding the speech for a listener. Most important, from the beginning of children's speaking careers (as they master sound and sentence) they are *creative problem solvers*.

Now we leave the contributions to our understanding from linguists and return to Piaget, continuing with what he has identified as the second major stage of intellectual development. You will find children's ways of knowing in this stage still fascinatingly different.

Piaget's Stage 2:
Preoperational—About Ages Two through Six

DISTINGUISHING FEATURES

What distinguishes children in Piaget's preoperational stage? Because of creative (though not-too-accurate) interpretations of events in the world, we can usually note some conceptual confusions on the part of children in this stage. These confused concepts show important growth toward more mature concepts. We can also see not only rapid acquisition of language on the part of these incessant thinkers, talkers, and idea testers, but we can also see beginnings of differences related to culture.

By "operations" (as in the term "preoperational") Piaget means complex mental acts that are beyond the capacity of children in this stage—thus the prefix "pre" in "preoperational." Distinguishing features of this stage include children's (1) preconcepts, (2) egocentricism, and (3) beginnings of the ability to *conserve*. (But by and large, children at this stage are "preconservers.") We consider each in turn.

1 Preconcepts

The child in this period may shout, "See the car!"—whether it is a car, wagon, bicycle, cart, truck, or train. Or the child may use the word "daddy" or "uncle" no matter who the strange male may be. Generally found during the preoperational period, these overgeneralizations are examples of *preconcepts*, rather than true concepts. But this behavior represents an important step in a complex process—concept development. Simple, even erroneous, conceptions are prerequisites for more complex ones. For example, children in this stage might believe that the sun comes up because we pull up the shade or that walking makes the clouds move. (Note the cartoon shown in Figure 5-4.)

Figure 5-4
An illustration of cause-effect thinking and the preconceptions of a child. (Source: United Features Syndicate, © 1973; reprinted by permission.)

2 Egocentrism

Earlier we mentioned children's tendencies to view the world only from their own perspective. (Recall the not-very-much hidden father.) That is, children find it extremely difficult to imagine, for example, that the view from a new physical position would change. In this stage, children consider their one view the only one possible.

To gather data, Piaget devised a square board with mountains arranged in a pattern (as shown in Figure 5-5). Piaget's interviewers would ask a child to sit at the table so that he or she saw a certain view.

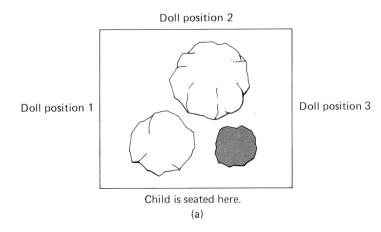

Doll position 2

Doll position 1   Doll position 3

Child is seated here.

(a)

Figure 5-5

(a) The model of the mountains is arranged on a square board or table as shown here from a bird's-eye view. (b, c, d, e) These are samples of the test pictures: (b) From the place where the child to be interviewed is seated, the mountains are viewed in this relationship. (c) This is the view from doll position 1. (d) The view from doll position 2. (e) The view from doll position 3. (Source: Adapted from Wilson, Robeck, & Michael, 1974.)

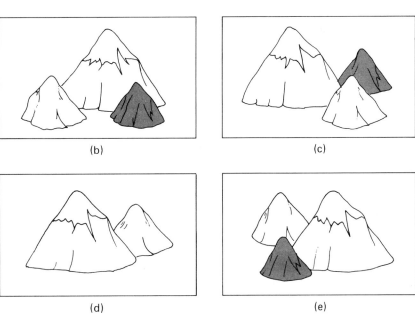

(b)

(c)

(d)

(e)

Then the interviewer showed the child drawings of the mountains and asked the child to select the one seen. Next the interviewer presented a doll who "walked" along the outer edges of the table, looking at the model of mountains from three other perspectives. The child, who remained seated, was then to select the pictures as the doll saw them. Children in the preoperational stage make only random guesses or select their own view. Not until about age ten can the child make the selections with confidence, though some transformations are selected earlier (Inhelder & Piaget, 1958). Early childhood teachers learn to work with, not against, a young child's natural egocentricism.

We should mention that some recent work (e.g., Donaldson, 1978) suggests that the nature of some of Piaget's tasks may occasionally lead us to underestimate children's cognitive abilities. When a doll is, say, hiding from a policeman doll, children can more successfully imagine different perspectives—probably because this situation is more easily understood and more meaningful than the setup with the mountains.

3 Preconservation

Children up to and during this stage are generally unable to counterbalance effects of how things look in the present by how they looked in the past. For example they think that a piece of clay pushed into a ball and then rolled into a snake *can't* weigh the same at the end as it did at the beginning.

The logical process of counterbalancing is called "conservation." The basic idea is that aspects such as quality, length, or number are constant in the face of certain transformations. Children at the preoperational stage don't reason (as we would) that because nothing was added or taken away, the amount is the same.

Detailed illustrations of conserving and not conserving will be given in our discussion of Piaget's next stage—concrete operations. When they reach this stage, children have succeeded in constructing such understanding from their experience. It helps, however, to understand children's difficulties by actually trying conservation tasks with young nonconservers. Examine the following task.

A TASK TO TRY WITH CHILDREN— CONSERVATION OF NUMBER

The task described in this section will give you an insight into the preoperational stage. Try it with nonconserving children of about five years of age. You might even try repeating it several times.

> Take some pretzels (or pennies, or other objects) and make a row of, say, six items. Next invite a child to take more of the items and make a row to match yours.

Thus:

O O O O O O

O O O O O O

Next spread your row out, so that it extends farther than the child's:

O   O   O   O   O   O

O O O O O O

Ask the child, "Do we still have the same?" The chances are that the young child will say, "No, you have more." Then you suggest, "Can you count them?"

The child counts:

O   O   O   O   O   O
1   2   3   4   5   6

O O O O O O
1 2 3 4 5 6

You then ask, "Do we have the same?" Child: "No, you have more."

Language (in this case ability to say numbers in order, to count) *is not necessarily an index of intellectual development.* The child's apparent ability (e.g., to count) can be misleading to adults. In the case just demonstrated language performance was not an index of the child's ability to understand the "true" concept of number and to conserve it.

Children must be able to handle two concepts at once to do this task. They must have constructed the idea for themselves that *number is both a class and a relationship.* Any number is a class concept because it is like every other number. But it is different from every other number in order of enumeration. The child in the example just given still needs maturation and many natural classificatory experiences in grouping, sorting, and one-to-one counting before the connections will be grasped. Then the child can attain the concepts and rules necessary in this conservation task.

Educationally speaking, this concept, conservation, is of great importance. It is useless for example, to expect children to understand measurement as long as they think the length of an object changes each time it is moved to a different position (e.g., that two sticks of equal length change length when the end points aren't aligned). This preconcept would affect not only objects being measured but the measuring rod itself. It's like trying to use a melting marshmallow as a ruler. Children's lack of conservation also has many implications for reading readiness. (See Lundsteen, 1980; and Chapter 10.)

Rather than merely say, however, that children at this stage cannot do this and that, it is more productive to look also at *positive* developments. As children in this preoperational stage collect names for objects, they begin to form ideas of sameness and to make some general categories (e.g., "These are all round."). They also form some relational concepts such as "bigger," "older," "taller," and "too much," and they begin to use these labels.

There are, of course, individual differences. But by being aware of *typical* development in this preoperational period (or any other) teachers have a starting point for understanding the *differences* among children. Piaget's work has been aimed at the "typical" child, not at individual variation. We do need to take variation into account.

Next we move to a parallel description of language. We first give some consideration to cultural variation.

Language Growth during the Ages Two to Six

We turn again to developmental linguists for illuminating ideas on language development. After a word on cultural differences (or similarities), we examine sound production, vocabulary, and sentences typical of ages two to six and older.

CULTURAL VARIATION AND OVER-GENERALIZATIONS Are there any class or cultural differences in language at this early stage? Consider apparent errors in standard English. Generally all children about this age make overgeneralizations of language rules they have attained. For example children may say, "I cutted my finger," "I goed to the store" or "He doed it." They are overgeneralizing the use of "ed" to form the past tense, making irregular verbs regular, and generally making the rules fit an easier pattern. Such errors are not a crime at all; they show high creative, cognitive levels. Children from cultures with different dialects appear to have highly similar grammars up to a point—even when their parents do not.

MASTERY OF SOME SOUNDS; ERRORS IN OTHERS Talkative three- and four-year-olds in this stage have mastered a number of sounds. Templin (1957) reported ages at which 75 percent of pupils she studied produced certain consonant sounds "correctly." By age three, these were—/m/, /n/, /ng/, /p/, /f/, /h/, /w/, and /y/; by age four—/k/, /b/, /d/, /g/, /s/, /sh/, and /ch/. It is not surprising that three-year-olds have developed this accuracy of sound production. Normally talkative, they get a lot of practice. In fact, they may be silent about only twenty minutes out of their waking days. Typically, about 80 percent of these utterances are intelligible, even to strangers (Lenneberg, 1967).

Looking beyond the achievements, we find some typical articulation errors made by children in this stage. Some children fail to enunciate certain difficult sounds properly until they are seven or eight (e.g., /j/,

/r/, /s/, /z/). Children in this stage may use "ting" for "thing," illustrating that they can articulate a single consonant before a cluster of them. They may tend to say "wabbit" for "rabbit," illustrating that they confuse sounds having the same manner of articulation but not the same placement.

Development of sound production is a matter of making increasingly finer contrasts. When contrasts occur frequently in adult speech (e.g., "fit" and "hit"), they are learned earlier than when they occur infrequently (e.g., /s/ and /sh/ in "occasion" and "nation") (Landreth, 1967).

DISTINCTION BEFORE PRODUCTION

In other words, children learn by sharpening their language concepts through the use of *contrasts* (a fact important to any language instruction). Another fact is that children have the internal *competency* to make these distinctions before they can actually produce and use them. An example is the child who consistently referred to her plastic fish as a "fis." An experimental observer engaged the child in conversation about it.

> "That is your fis?" said the observer.
> "No," said the child. "My *fis*."
> "Yes, a fine fis," continued the observer.
> "No, *fis!*" said the child.

Only when the observer said, "That is your *fish*," did the child agree, "Yes, my fis" (Berko & Brown, 1960). This example illustrates the concept of *linguistic competence* (or understanding before performance)—an important concept for early childhood educators to grasp. There is here an apparent tendency for language competency to outstrip language performance.

COMPETENCE VERSUS PRODUCTION

Thus, when linguists say that typically by the end of the preoperational stage, by about age six, most children have competence in most adult grammatical forms, the statement hinges on language *competence*. *Performance*, even at ninth grade, is another matter. Grammatical capacity (competence) matures faster than production. But even early in this stage children will correct ill-formed sentences presented to them (e.g., "Give me two shoes red?" or "Give me two red shoes?") Young children have competency in language; it's the early childhood educator's task to help them have chances to *use* language productively. Language performance is affected by nonlinguistic factors, such as missing teeth, indecision, and fatigue (Chomsky, 1965).

We need to uncover and have respect for children's language competence.

DEVELOPMENTAL FEATURES OF VOCABULARY

Features of vocabulary found in this preoperational stage include creative inventiveness, rapid growth, and beginnings of socioeconomic variance. With television acting as a great influence, size of vocabulary during this period ranges from hundreds to thousands of words. Children of about four years of age may invent words to meet their needs ("spit-get" for "spaghetti"), or they may employ words that they already have as amusing substitutions. For example, a child with cold hands called out that he wanted his "muffins" (instead of "mittens"), told a friend that his mother was calling at the back "scream" door (rather than "screen" door), and explained she was going to have a baby because the birth "patrol" hadn't worked.

Semantic levels of concreteness and abstractness

Typically, children understand and use words concretely before they use them abstractly. For example, they will use "deep water" before "deep secret," and "on a block" before "on Saturday" (with its abstract "time" dimension) (Feofanov, 1958). Ruth Krauss's book *A Hole is to Dig* (1952) is a delightful collection of preschool children's concrete definitions.* Research indicates children's progressively developing competency with abstract meanings for their vocabularies (Lundsteen, 1974).

Positional relationships of vocabulary

Children in this stage show increasing ability in using relationships. They will understand prepositions of spatial relation with reference to their own body (e.g., respond correctly to "place the hoop above *your head*") before understanding with relation to another object in space (e.g., "place the hoop above *the cow*."). From around three years children begin to use words that describe position (such as "on," "in," "over," "in front of," "beside"). If children can understand that an object is *in the corner*, they are aware of angles; if they can put the object *on the second shelf*, they are aware of sequential ordering; if they can place the object correctly *with the other toys*, they are likely to be aware of classification of like objects. These relational words—"above," "in," "on"—are descriptive of children's perceptions of their world and its many connections.

Children's speech marks out what is relevant in their environment and affects their thinking. Early childhood educators find that children who have little or no experience with words that qualify relationships have trouble thinking and performing in this way. In other words, lacking the contrastive experience to give them underlying and prerequisite competence, children cannot perform using relational vocabulary.

* Half the fun in this book is Maurice Sendak's frolicsome illustrations.

We can see that some ECE programs have segments designed to promote this competence and performance. *It is a mistake to drill children on these relational words in isolation without the meaningful context of experience.* Drill of this sort is a mistake not only in preschool oral language programs but also in early reading programs. The guiding idea is to *make sure that there is competence (or understanding) before any demand for performance is made.*

DEVELOPMENTAL FEATURES OF CHILDREN'S SENTENCES DURING THE PREOPERATIONAL STAGE

Much of what we have already described as occurring at the end of the sensorimotor period applies to sentence structure developing at the beginning of this, the next period (preoperational). The important feature seems to be that children apparently continue their experimental, rule-governed behavior.

At this time children do begin to refine their sentences, supplying inflections ("'s," "ed"). They embed and coordinate two or more simple sentences (e.g., a child's imaginative and empathetic sentence about a toy dog: "Mickey fell out of bed and hurt hisself so bad!"). But it is still generally difficult for children in this stage to combine sentences which are contradictory in meaning (e.g., "It is cold although the sun is shining"). Conditional forms ("if . . . then") may typically appear near the end of the third year.

INCREASE IN SOCIAL FUNCTION OF LANGUAGE

Given opportunity and encouragement, children increase in group communication (especially toward the end of this stage). That is, the amount of time children spend talking in social settings concerned with the interchange of ideas depends not only on the children's maturational stage, but also on the encouragement gotten from adults and early childhood educators. The more typical soliloquizing in the presence of others gradually includes a higher quality of interaction; children talk in order to communicate something to the listener.

Children who cannot express their feelings in words will be more likely to act them out—violently—like the child in Figure 5-6. But those able to use the social function of language can tell others what they want in the hope that they will receive it, instead of just tugging at another's property, or screaming.

An extreme case of the negative effect of an inability to express feelings in words was a Canadian boy whose grandparents demanded perfection in French while the parents pushed for his production in English. Both sets of elders were constantly critical. In the preschool setting, this boy would open his mouth to speak when his needs conflicted with those of other children, but nothing would come out. In frustration, he would bite hard, drawing blood on many occasions—and earning a

Figure 5-6

formidable reputation. (See the section on discipline in Chapter 14.)

Adults and early childhood educators need to assist and support a child's socializing speech (rather than to demand specific verbal behavior). The preoperational stage is the opportune time to model, reinforce, and otherwise support developing social uses of language. (See Chapter 10, a companion curriculum chapter on the language arts.) Moreover, it is plain that "pushing" children can result in pathological behavior.

THE PLACE OF LANGUAGE IN THE PIAGETIAN SCHEME OF KNOWLEDGE CONSTRUCTION

What about the role of language as a person oriented to Piaget's theories might see it? One investigator offers us some interesting findings (Sinclair-de-Zwart, 1969). She found that children able to perform certain tasks (e.g., seriation of sticks) and children able to conserve used comparative language. (An example of comparative language is "The boy has more than the girl"). Children unable to conserve used absolute terms instead (e.g., "The boy has a lot"; "The girl has a little"). Research has indicated that verbal training leads children who are unable to perform conservation tasks to direct their attention to relevant aspects of the problem, to focus on more than one attribute (e.g., tallness and width). *But* verbal training does *not* necessarily bring about the ability to conserve. The conclusion is that language is not the source of logic, but is structured by logic. (Bernstein, 1972; Sinclair-de-Zwart, 1969)

Trying to rush stages by simply giving labels results in empty talk, which has no meaning to the child. The child does not retain the idea. To illustrate, consider the following example. (In fact, try the activity yourself with children about five years old.) This task concerns dealing at the same time with a general class (in this case, fruit) and with subclasses (peaches and apples). The task is to conserve the whole when one has to compare the whole with one of the parts. Materials for the task include a girl doll, a boy doll, and pieces of fruit. The investigator has a child (who cannot conserve) watch as the investigator gives six pieces of fruit (e.g., four peaches and two apples) to the girl doll. Next the investigator asks the child to give the boy doll "Just as many pieces of fruit, so he gets just as much to eat; *but* give him *more apples*, because he likes them better than peaches."

The nonconserving child cannot deal with classes and subclasses at the *same time*. Such children will say, "You can't do it," or they will give an identical collection, or simply try to add more apples—so that the boy doll has too much fruit. Moreover, attempts to teach labels—such as "some," "more," "total class of fruit," and "subclasses of apples and peaches" (i.e., language related to the thought necessary)—apparently are useless. Children may be able to mouth the words, but this language performance will outstrip their underlying *thought*. Their construction of the necessary underlying process of thought *takes time* (Inhelder, 1972; Sinclair-de-Zwart, 1969).

Preoperational thought and reading

Does the evidence of a mismatch between language and thought say something to early childhood teachers about beginning reading instruction? We cannot assume that young children comprehend the instructional process used in teaching reading, which requires analyzing and synthesizing words as specimens (relationships of parts to the whole). Preoperational children have difficulty with rules (applying an abstraction to a concrete situation). Young children can show apparently correct behavior when they do phonics lessons as an end in themselves, *but they cannot apply the practice to reading. They may not see any connection. Such practice, then, is a senseless, time-wasting activity.*

In sum, what do these ideas about preoperational thought and reading mean to the teacher? (1) If children are in a stage when rules are difficult to apply, then do not be disappointed if such children cannot apply phonic rules. Spend the time to better advantage. (See Chapter 10.) (2) A page of phonics exercises out of the context of real-life reading is a meaningless activity at any time, but it is especially meaningless if the learner is still in the preoperational stage. The next activity illustrates an additional way to see if children have a match between language and thought.

Dual classification—Matching language to thought

Another illustrative Piagetian task you can try with children is the following. The task may show whether a child has mastered vocabulary without having mastered the underlying thought.

Ask the following questions. (Use the word "sister" or "brother" as appropriate.)

YOU   Do you have a sister?
CHILD   Yes.
YOU   Does your sister have a sister?
CHILD   No.

If you do get the "No" response, it is not just that the child is egocentric and cannot put himself or herself in another's position. The difficulty is that the child cannot think of *having* a sister (or brother) and *being* a sister (or brother) at the same time, i.e., as being in two relationships at once. It is as if the child is thinking, "You cannot be in two places at the same time, so you cannot be in two classifications at the same time" (Elkind, 1973).

In short, we are reminded to *tie up the child's verbal skills with their underlying thought processes.* School texts (including this one—though we *try*) are guilty of tossing out labels and assuming that learners have concepts that they don't have. This is a fairly common disease of teaching at any level.

In conceptualizing classroom instruction, one can stress the knower or one can stress the language (symbolization). Piaget stresses the knower. While developmental linguists (e.g., Chomsky, 1965) have stressed that performance is bound to appear poorer than language competence, Piaget would say that there is another side to consider. There is also the somewhat opposite danger. Apparent performance might cause us to overrate competence. That is, what appears to be advanced performance might represent only isolated instances of language bound to specific content, context, and imitation. Certain early childhood programs and measurement on certain tests have led us into this trap.

In any case, when children are at the stage when they really understand a basic concept, the language will come readily. If you just teach the words, you cannot guarantee that the child can do the mental operation necessary really to grasp the concept. *Language is an aid to thought, but not a guarantee of thought.* Just giving children language is like giving a bicycle to a child who can't reach the pedals. Mere language drill accomplishes little and robs children of time that might be spent on more valuable experiences. (Down with language drills!)

Section 2: AGES SIX TO EIGHT

We have seen that contrasts help the child to attain concepts within the area of language and thought. Similarly, contrasts among stages of children's growth help us to develop concepts needed as early childhood educators. With that idea in mind, let's examine Piaget's next stage, which takes us into later childhood—ages six to eight. Let us also contrast this stage, concrete operations (and its companion, language development), with the earlier stages.

Piaget's Stage 3: Concrete Operations—About Age Six Onward

Information about, perspectives on, and materials for early childhood education multiply alarmingly. Since ideas grounded in Piaget's work give us a carefully wrought set of measuring sticks, let's continue with Piaget's age-stage way of viewing children.

We have seen that knowing about a world of objects in earlier stages helps children to grasp a more and more symbolic world. Beginning at about age six, this more symbolic world with its rules and generalizations can be understood when the context is concrete—when it can be seen, touched, moved. In a later stage—formal operations—children will manipulate rules formally and abstractly.

Figure 5-7

For example, a boy in the concrete operations stage knows that when he is pulled in a wagon, other children will see a ball clutched in his hand as a moving object (Figure 5-7)—that they will see the event this way even though he is clutching the ball ever so tightly, holding it still. The grasp of this idea represents a concrete expression of a highly abstract and complex concept: relativity.

Of course, concrete-operational children cannot abstractly relate the measurements of observers who are accelerated relative to each other, nor can they grasp the formula $E = mc^2$. That kind of knowledge—which involves explanation by abstract logic—belongs in the next Piagetian stage, formal operations. But concrete-operational children *can* grasp the idea of relativity when it is presented in terms of actual objects.

DEFINITION

As a student of early childhood education, you meet the term "concrete operations" again and again. What does it mean? First tackle the term "operations." An operation is an organized mental action. Think, for example, of adding, subtracting, and conserving. (Recall that by the term "conserving" we mean recognizing sameness despite change in appearance or shape. For example, a strip of clay weighs the same even when cut into sections.) In a moment, you will find others examples of conserving and an example—putting sticks into a series according to increase in size (or the reverse, decrease in size)—of another operation, *seriation*.

A point to remember about operations in this stage is that they are still connected to actual (concrete) objects, to things the child can see and move about. For example, at this stage social studies requires manipulable materials, such as building blocks for miniature cities, representative dress, and other artifacts. One young social science student showed this need for concreteness when he said, "Geography is polar bears at the top and penguins at the bottom." In short, now is the time for logical thought linked to real objects.

The other key word in this stage is, of course, "concrete." Such concrete elements as sensory impressions of a particular moment, or manipulated materials (buttons, blocks, bottle caps, clay), help children to use logical thought.

NEW INTELLECTUAL FEATS: CONSERVATION

Children in the stage of concrete operations can accomplish many new intellectual feats. First, consider conservation—the basic idea that aspects such as quantity, length, and number are constant in the face of certain transformations. These children have attained the following concepts.

Figure 5-8

Conservation of number (Figure 5-8)

The number of pencils in a group does *not* change if they are bunched together, rather than spread out. Children in the earlier, preoperational stage do not take into account the spatial gaps between objects. They judge by overall appearance and therefore think that the number changes.

Figure 5-9

Conservation of substance (Figure 5-9)

The amount of a malleable substance (e.g., clay) does *not* change when its shape is altered. Children in the earlier, preoperational stage do not apply principles of *reversibility* (e.g., if you re-formed the two balls of clay, they'd be the same) or *identity* (you have not added any) or *compensation* (one is long and skinny, but one is fat). They think the amount has changed.

Figure 5-10

Conservation of weight (Figure 5-10)

When a ball of clay is made into a long snake, it will *not* weigh more. Children in the earlier, preoperational stage are unable to realize that the weight of an object remains unchanged regardless of how its shape is altered.

Figure 5-11

Conservation of volume (Figure 5-11)

A tall, thin glass and a low, flat one can hold the same amount of liquid. Children in the preoperational stage find it hard to believe that both containers (tall-thin and low-flat) could hold the same quantity of water—even when it is poured back and forth before their eyes. They fail to realize that the volume of an object (in terms of how much water it holds) remains unchanged regardless of changes in its shape.

Comments on conservation

According to Piaget, conservation hinges on a child's development of the concept of *reversibility*. That is, *for every action there exists another action that undoes it.* Examples: The water may be poured back into the tall glass from the wide container; the snake-shaped clay can be remodeled into a ball; twelve beads remain twelve beads whether placed in a row, a circle, or a heap and can be placed back as they were. Children in the concrete-operational stage can get away (or *decenter*) from the configuration of material at a given moment to see that amount or number remains constant.

Although most children have attained conservation of volume by age seven or eight, difficulty may persist for a few throughout the elementary school years. Conservation of volume remains one of the most difficult concepts. What happens is that the children concentrate on *one* aspect of the glass that stands out for them. They may say that this low, wide glass holds *less* (if concentrating on "tallness") or *more* (if concentrating on "wideness"). But—and here is the key—they do not consider the *two factors at the same time*. They lack "dual focus" and the ability to coordinate variables.

In spite of the old Chinese proverb "I see and I forget; I *do* and I remember," sometimes a child can do and do and do—and still does not *know*. In the case of the water being poured back and forth, a preoperational child (with wide eyes) asks, "Where did all that water come from?" As a further example, you show the puzzled child a weighing device called a "balance" with two balls of clay which balance each other, even after one has been pulled out to form a long strip. Some children will even deny what they see with their own eyes: "See, the weight *has* changed just a little bit." Some will accept the data confronting them with surprise, then repeat the weighing action, but still not understand. Others will simply act as if they had been defeated by the evidence: "I just don't understand!"

But as children reach concrete operations, they can attend to what they know is true rather than to what they see. That is, they can use parallel systems of information processing—*both* what they see and what they come to know as rules. Children in the concrete-operational stage will say some of the following things:

> "You didn't add anything; you didn't take anything away."
> "It's long but narrow or skinnier."
> "If I put it back, it would be the same."
> "Some things have to stay the same, even if they look different." (Duckworth, 1973).

Successfully manipulating objects in the world does not necessarily mean that children are making all the connections and grasping the rules involved. More mature ways of knowing take *more* than opportunities to manipulate objects in a rich environment. *Advances take a slow building and rebuilding of cognitive structures.* Children construct concepts layer upon layer. Teachers cannot hurry children who are just on their way to becoming concrete-operational.

What is the order in which aspects of conservation are learned?

Children can generally conserve number (a sock for every shoe; a roof for every house—even when one group is spread apart) before they can conserve substance and length. Next they learn conservation of area, then weight, and last of all volume.

OTHER NEW FEATS: CLASS INCLUSION, SERIATION, AND APPLICATION TO LIVING

What else can children in the concrete-operational stage do besides conserve? They can use simultaneous reasoning about a class and its subgroups. For example, they can see that ten white beads that are wooden and five wooden black beads (as in Figure 5-12) make fifteen wooden beads. *And* they can see that there are more beads *altogether* than there are of either color. The preoperational child who lacks a firm grasp of the concept of *class* and who lacks reversible thinking cannot shift attention away from the fact that there are more white beads than black beads.

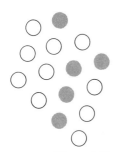

Figure 5-12

Children in the concrete-operational stage can respond correctly to the following question: "Are there more *wooden* beads than white wooden ones?" The question is designed as a check to determine whether they can think of white and of wooden at the same time, to see if they can grasp an inclusive class concept—wooden beads. Mastery of the inclusion relationship means that they can think of the whole and its parts at the same time. That is, the whole is not destroyed when it is split into parts. They can understand how, at one and the same time, all of one thing can be some of another. They can hold in mind the shifting parts and the whole. Not until children grasp this idea can they attain the genuine ability to *classify*. This simultaneous reasoning about a class and subgroups is crucial to beginning learning in reading, mathematics, and many other areas. (An example in reading is the match of not just one letter per sound, but of two letters standing for a sound and of letters standing for more than one sound.) It makes sense to delay formal instruction until a child can meet this prerequisite—that is, can classify. (See, e.g., Elkind, Koegler, & Go, 1964.)

What is another feat? One of the best examples is seriation (arranging objects according to some specified order). This feat is even more difficult than classification. Classification is easier, since children have simply to decide whether an object possesses a required characteristic. (Is it a stick? A blue stick?)

Example: Seriation

In the following example of seriation we can note a connection among stages as the child progresses gradually toward concrete operations—a progressive rebuilding of thought structures.

Seriation means putting unorganized objects or events into a series—each leading to the next—according to some principle. In the following task designed by Piaget, seriation consists of arranging a group of sticks

Figure 5-13

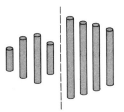

Figure 5-14

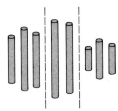

Figure 5-15

Figure 5-16

from the smallest to the tallest. Let us examine four ways of thinking about the task—going from less mature to more mature.

1 During the early part of the preoperational stage, the youngest children in Piaget's sample claimed that all the sticks were of equal length. They simply put them together in a hodgepodge (Figure 5-13).

2 Next, the children progressed to dividing the sticks into two categories—large and small—with no ordering of the various sticks (Figure 5-14).

3 Slightly older children talked of large, middle-size, and small sticks (Figure 5-15).

Following that step, the children did construct a true series, in a trial-and-error fashion. But they were not able to produce a perfect serial construction immediately. Perfect construction, including discovery of a method, did not appear until the Piagetian stage of concrete operations. Recall that children at earlier stages grouped the sticks into two parts (large-small) and three parts (large-medium-small), and then used trial and error to create a series.

4 Finally, they did discover a method. They chose the tallest of all the remaining sticks, placing this one beside the first selected stick. Then they took the largest of those remaining, and so on, until they put all the sticks on the table in order. Thus they constructed a progressive series (Figure 5-16). *Finally—at the stage of concrete operations—they created a perfect series without any trial and error.* Moreover, their reconstruction assumes a relation that is *reversible.* That is, one stick is both smaller than the ones before it and larger than the ones after it (Piaget, 1969).

The feat involved reveals that the children must have continually thought in this way: If stick A is taller than stick B, and stick B is taller than stick C, then stick A is taller than stick C. These children could switch from "smaller than" to "taller than" and back. That is, they could see that these relationships are reciprocal and reversible. They could say (while holding and manipulating the sticks) that the red stick was smaller than the yellow stick, and therefore the yellow stick was bigger than the red stick.

A COMPARISON OF THE SENSORIMOTOR, PREOPERATIONAL, AND CONCRETE-OPERATIONAL STAGES

By now it should be clear what Piaget means by the difference between sensorimotor intelligence and conceptual intelligence of the concrete operational stage. "Sensorimotor intelligence" refers to knowing through "real" objects—objects perceived through the five senses and coordinated with observable movements. Conceptual intelligence during concrete operations consists of entire rebuilding of structures of thought, as in the example of seriation given above. As a child's intelligence develops, more simple structures (e.g., big-little) become incorporated into higher-level structures (big-medium-small). These structures in turn become parts of other structures at an even higher level (bigger than this, but smaller than this—as in the case of true seriation), layer upon layer upon layer. According to Piaget, these structures do not replace, but are integrated into, one another. In Chapters 9 and 10 on developing cognitive and language abilities, we see how important this concept of intellectual construction is to classroom learning.

If children are not conservers, then symbols such as number words are just names to them. *Reciting the names of the numbers in order means about as much to mathematics as saying the alphabet means to reading—nothing.* When children have not achieved the feats of the concrete-operational stage and try to do school exercises that require the abilities characteristic of such a stage, distaste and apprehensions are likely to develop and solidify (Sharp, 1969).

Not only have children in the concrete-operational stage grasped the feats of conservation principles, class inclusion, and decentering (described in Piaget's experiments), but they can grasp these rules in real life—as in games. (Preoperational children have trouble applying even general rules in games.) Older children, accusing younger ones of cheating, may not realize that the young ones are having conceptual difficulties. (Young children do seem to grasp one egocentric rule: "I win—you lose.") Teachers need to try to understand the rules that young children think they are using.

THE CONCRETE-OPERATIONAL STAGE: SUMMARY

In sum, children do not pass from the preoperational stage of development into the stage of concrete operations all at once. Children *construct* these operations layer upon layer; transitions are gradual, boundary lines are blurred. If children still think in a preoperational way (e.g., as nonconservers of number), they will not understand much formal (abstract) schoolwork. And they will resort, if forced, to parrotlike memorizing.

Children do gain the ability to think in logical patterns (part-whole, series coordination, reversibility). This relational thinking is based on their *own actions on objects that they understand.* Concrete-operational children can grasp almost any concrete sequence of actions or events all at once—e.g., an inning of a baseball game, which involves past, present, and future. They can describe a sequence of events without having to actually act them out.

Regarding children who are at this stage, what does the early childhood educator need? He or she needs patience, understanding, and well-selected resources to provide manipulative materials at the right time to the right child.

Language Growth during the Years Six to Eight

These years bring not only new ways of knowing, but also refinements of language. During this "true" linguistic stage, some significant features of sound production, vocabulary, and sentence structure develop.

SOUND PRODUCTION AND RECEPTION

By the time they enter first grade, most children have control of sounds that characterize their dialect. According to Templin (1957) by age six, 75 percent of pupils in her study produced /t/, /th/ (as in "thin," unvoiced), /v/, and /l/; by age seven, 75 percent produced /th/ (as in "then," voiced), /z/, /zh/, and /j/. By age six, the only distinctive speech sounds not produced by at least 90 percent of the sample were /s/, /sh/ (as in "mission), /z/, /zh/ (as in "vision"), /th/ (as in "either"), /ch/ (as in "church") and /hw/ (as in "why"). A child's sound substitutions, such as "wady" for "lady" and "tat" for "cat," may mean not that the child is unable to say correct sounds, but rather that the child has failed to note differences in sounds made by others—i.e., the child is unable to listen. In the primary grades, children grow not only in speech production but in speech reception (listening).

VOCABULARY

As children continue in their schooling they develop specialization in vocabulary (e.g., words specific to science, to sports, to literature). Children in the primary grades not only widen their range of words (like the girl in Figure 5-17), but also improve in accuracy, depth of concept, the ability to handle multiple meanings, and the ability to think more abstractly with their vocabulary (Lundsteen, 1974). The vocabularies

Figure 5-17
Vocabulary development. (Source: Reprinted by permission of A. Johns.)

"Okay, Mom, I've done all the nooks. Now what's a cranny?"

which children listen to and understand continue to outnumber their spoken ones. (Even as adults we have a larger vocabulary of words we recognize than of words we actually use.) As primary-grade children develop, they begin to grasp different categories of meaning, such as object-nonobject, animate-inanimate, human-nonhuman, male-female. (See Katz & Fodor, 1963.)

SEMANTICS   It is interesting to note the growth that primary-grade children can show in reacting to the subtleties of *denotative* and *connotative* meanings. "Denotation" refers to the literal dictionary meaning: e.g., "pig"—the animal); it does not refer to colorations and imaginings. "Connotation" does refer to the colorations—images, pictures, and feelings—that a word produces: e.g., "pig"—a gluttonous, sloppy person. Even young children can begin to note the difference between the tone of words, sometimes referred to as "purr" words (words that have happy connotations) and "snarl" words (words that have unhappy ones). Note these examples: "I am slender"; "you are skinny" or "Mary wept"; "Mary blubbered."

The more abstract the meaning of a word ("love," "peace"), the more susceptible it is to various connotations. Carl Sandburg expressed the idea of connotation well when he said (connotatively) that a word has long shadows. The language of advertising makes an early assault on the ears of children with its use of connotations. We have already seen what overgeneralizers children can be. They are easy targets for advertising.

In spite of apparent development in grasping the subtleties of vocabulary, primary-grade children do tend to be very *literal-minded*. They have difficulty in grasping similes and metaphors. For example, hearing the line "like a diamond in the sky," a child may be bewildered and ask, "Is it really a diamond?" Or, in response to the line "My love is like a red, red rose," a child might ask, "Does she prick you?" Young children typically get a lot of joy out of the sheer fun of sound in language (e.g., "supercalafragilisticexpialidoshus") and should be guided to enjoy the sensory features of figurative language in children's literature. At the same time, they need help in searching for the truth in language that comes their way.

PRODUCTION OF SENTENCES AND LARGER UNITS OF LANGUAGE   In the period from kindergarten through the primary grades, children show gradual growth in: (1) the length and (2) the complexity of their language forms (Halliday, 1977) and (3) style (see, e.g., Opie & Opie, 1959). Primary-grade children may produce relatively long sentences strung together with "ands," "buts," "and sos," or "becauses."

The child's frequent use of "and" signifies that more is coming. The child uses an easy-to-follow grammar, which reflects the fast-moving activity of the typical young child who goes from one event directly into another. To the young child, a long series of "because" words conveys support of opinion, swiftly and directly (Smith, Goodman, & Meredith, 1976).

Thus, maturity is not represented so much by long sentences as by the complexity by which they are made longer or shorter. Examples: less mature—"The girl ran by and she was wearing boots"; more mature—"The girl who was wearing boots ran by"; still more mature—"The girl wearing boots ran by" (O'Donnell, Griffin, & Norris, 1967).

It is relatively unusual to find young children holding one idea subordinate while another related idea is being developed (again, Piaget's "dual focus" idea). Children throughout the primary grades are most likely to use a sentence pattern consisting simply of subject, verb, and predicate or direct object—e.g., "Joe threw the ball." Use of movable parts of sentences and subordination increases gradually—e.g., "Joe threw the ball when it was his turn"; "When it was his turn, Joe threw the ball."

SENTENCES AND DISCOURSE DURING YEARS SIX TO EIGHT: SUMMARY

Although by the time children leave the primary grades they may produce almost all the grammatical sentence structures taught in school, they do not use as many, at the same time, and within another as older children and adults do. Languages have rules for "rewriting" sentences (that is, for transformations). Skill in this rewriting and compression is one index of maturity. It is ill-advised to pressure young children to use such skills. The larger picture of growth is not just accumulation of vocabulary and progress toward more sophisticated sentence structure, standard usages, and accurate mechanics of writing. (By "mechanics," we mean conventions such as punctuation, spelling, and legible handwriting.)

Early childhood teachers can see important growth in the child's understanding of relationships among words, phrases, and the greater meanings within and among sentences, paragraphs, and the child's total experience. A teacher's supportive climate and awareness of developmental features assist children to cope with the difficulties of abstractions, to move out of their egocentricity, to find the joy and self-fulfillment of preserving shared experiences by expressing them in language.

How Does Creative Problem Solving Develop in the Early Years?

Ideas from Piaget are highlighted in children's creative problem solving, and it is here that they find an ultimate use. All the smaller mental abilities and language abilities feed into this larger, unifying process. Here is the area where early childhood teachers need to center their attention, rather than getting lost in a maze of details and never getting around to promoting this basic creative process. Much of the kinds of thinking encouraged (and investigated) in early childhood schooling presents only a minor subpart of creative problem solving.

DEFINITION What do we mean by "creative problem solving"? We mean a unified process with goals growing out of (1) felt needs, problem areas or blockage, (2) hypotheses for solution, (3) planned procedures, (4) testing of hypotheses, and (5) qualities such as uniqueness and originality associated with an attack on unknowns. Even at the beginning of children's long push toward knowledge, some probably have competence in making hypotheses. Many young children are testing ideas long before Piaget's stages of concrete and formal operations. Children may solve problems creatively when dealing with science and mathematics (cognitively), with art materials (esthetically), and with other people (socially).

The development of problem solving related to human relations ("people problems") may have a different schedule than Piaget's logical-mathematical problem solving. It may be more crucial for the well-being of the child to assist development of "people-problem solving" earlier than any natural, weedlike growth that may haphazardly occur.

PRESCHOOL CHARACTERISTICS OF PROBLEM SOLVING Although the major mental process of creative problem solving starts early in life, there are special characteristics related to the preoperational stage. For example, young children tend to solve problems by trying out all their hunches immediately, letting the consequences fall where they will. They can't keep from acting immediately; they can't remain calm while they formulate hypotheses, think out solutions, and follow their ideas through to completion.

Swf

Figure 5-18

This lack of inhibition is what makes the preschool child such a destructive experimenter in a household. This sometimes destructive play (as in Figure 5-18), however, permits children to explore combinations of things and acts that they would never explore if they just kept to reasonable problem solving (Bruner, 1973). Still, adults need to be advised that children as problem solvers do have a tendency to act rather than to think through. Typically, they fail to observe carefully and to vary their attempts and strategies for finding solutions systematically. (Such failings are not necessarily limited to young children.) The preschool child lacks information and experience (data) for solving problems. To be effective general problem solvers, children must somehow acquire masses of structurally organized knowledge that they can use creatively in new, complex ways. Productive solutions come to a prepared mind that knows how to use effective attitudes, strategies, and procedures.

As an example of preoperational problem solving, take the conversation about babies' teeth cited in Landreth (1967). The problem under discussion was whether or not babies have teeth. One child (volunteering the evidence from a close observation of a two-month-old brother) said, "No." Another child with a nine-month-old sister said, "Yes, my baby sister, Kathleen, has teeth." After several moments of silence, the eyes of another member of the group sparkled as he voiced his sudden inference, "I know, only babies called Kathleen have teeth!" This pronouncement, quickly approved and accepted by the preschool conversationalists, was an example of an intuitive conclusion based on insufficient evidence and characteristic of this stage. *But the inferential process crucial to creative problem solving was clearly there and developing.* We teachers forget that the child knows so much—and so little.

Summary and Conclusions

Why bother to learn about the developmental work of researchers? What is such knowledge going to do for early childhood teachers in the classroom? Is it going to make them more successful? Perhaps some answers to these questions are suggested by a touching letter a father sent to an editor of a journal dealing with child development. He asked, "Would you please organize a series of articles on the type of environment a child from birth on should be exposed to, so that he will grow up to be a thinking, understanding human being?" The content of this chapter provides some understanding that would guide teachers in providing such environments. Let's review what we have learned about cognitive development, language development, and that unifying process called creative problem solving.

In general we have learned from Piaget, who has theorized about how children acquire knowledge, that infants come into the world biologically equipped to make certain motor responses. These motor responses, in turn, provide the structure for mental processes to come later. Piaget concerns himself with connections that children develop within themselves—rather than with merely stimulus-response kinds of behavior. We have learned that little children instruct themselves by personal investigation. What they fail to perceive at first hand does not exist. They playfully explore and sample life's bits and pieces, close at hand, gradually extending boundaries of knowledge, disregarding what they cannot yet take in and use. Early childhood teachers can provide the rich environment for children's discoveries.

We have learned from Piaget about a framework of stages, characteristic of certain approximate age groups, in cognitive functioning. Piaget shows us that generally learners function differently in earlier and in later stages. Generally speaking, Piaget describes children as using gross unanalyzed relationships, as showing unawareness of conservation of substance, reversibility of operations, and classification by more than one feature at a time.

On the "plus" side, we can see the child's positive beginnings of symbolic representation, gigantic leaps in acquiring language (a highly creative process in each child), and an increase in social use of language and problem-solving processes. These beginnings are aided by alert, observant, pleasant, warm, educated adults who can stimulate children thoughtfully and appropriately with arranged environments.

Why use Piaget's ideas as a basic framework in which to accumulate and with which to compare your growing experiential knowledge of young children's achievement? His work is currently having great impact on early education. More than any other psychologist, he has opened eyes to intellectual growth and is changing basic ideas about instruction. His method was unique. He arrived at his conclusions about four major stages of development by putting himself into the world of children; he found out how children think. It is his empathy with children, together with true intellectual genius, that has made him outstanding. His finding that children learn best through their own discovery of how the world around them works presents a most valuable way of thinking about early childhood education. A brief review of his framework of major stages follows.

Children in the *sensorimotor* stage (first two years) begin to distinguish themselves from outer reality. They coordinate movements and repeat connective patterns. They begin to search for vanished objects, learn to use one thing to reach another that is desired, and begin to move beyond trial-and-error behavior.

Children in the *preoperational* stage show egocentric thinking and the ability to represent their world through language, dreams, and symbolic play. (See Chapter 12.) They do not usually form accurate concepts. Their logical reasoning is based on appearances (often misleading), unguided by reversible thinking. Children in this stage can handle only one attribute at a time. Thus, we note a private logic—reasonable to these young children, unreasonable to us.

Children in the *concrete-operational* stage can understand the logic of classes and relations, can coordinate series, grasp part-whole relationships, and use thought that is logical and reversible—*with concrete things*. But children in this stage do not think about thoughts or theories as they reason from a hypothesis to all its possible conclusions. They do not think about thinking. That ability comes in the next stage—*formal operations*. Analogies are not always appropriate, but let's try this one. In the concrete-operational stage, thought processes are speeded up somewhat like a movie film, as compared with a slow succession of slides in preoperational thinking. Like a film being wound and rewound, concrete-operational thought can project itself forward in time and can reverse itself.

Describing stages is one thing, deriving useful implications is another. Some important *implications* of Piaget's developmental work program planning in ECE are the following:

1 Sensorimotor experience serves as an important base for further cognitive learning.
2 New learnings grow out of older learnings.
3 Concept development takes time and many contexts.
4 Trying to accelerate learning of abstract concepts without sufficient experience and maturation results in no learning of any lasting value. (Readiness is needed.)
5 Young children are intensely, intrinsically motivated to learn. They don't need bribes.
6 The relations of language to thought are complex.
7 Teaching is an interpersonal, give-and-take process, with the teacher being a highly skilled listener, questioner, and environment provider.

Developmental linguists also offer us stages—of language development. Almost all children go through certain stages of sound, vocabulary, and syntax development; and all children show competence before performance. There is a biological basis and a social basis for language learning. At nine to eighteen months, children construct a language of their own in which certain vocal sounds are used again and again to express different needs. One sound (e.g., "da") might mean "give me"; another might reasonably be taken to mean "no."

Somewhere around twelve to twenty months, children make the breakthrough to letting words stand for things. These are the beginnings of symbolic representation and vocabulary. Children everywhere begin talking in one- and two-word sentences ("More cookie"; "Go store"). They don't (generally) use articles, prepositions, or word endings. Socioeconomic and dialectical differences are a negligible factor in these early grammars. Children tend to overcorrect, to overgeneralize their language principles ("I comed"). Such developmental errors represent a high degree of creative cognitive functioning. Next children start coping with things like time and the manner of doing things; and in many languages word order becomes important.

The pacesetter in a child's language growth is cognitive growth. Children use language to express what they already know. The young child, for example, may use the word "doggie" to refer to "dog," "cat," "horse," "cow"—any four-legged thing. Eventually the child refines and learns adult categories, putting aside preconcepts; and refinement in language use follows. By age six, children have a solid underlying *competence* in language. But mastery of more complex syntactical forms continues, and there is wide individual variation in *performance*.

Is there any ground common to the development of language and thought? It seems that the most important common ground in development lies: (1) in the child's ability to find the stable, as distinguished from the changing and the irrelevant, in both language and in thought, and then, (2) in being able to plan (through a developing sense of the future) and to make inferences (through a sense of the past). Thus, there is a common process of hypothesis testing for both language and thought (John & Moskovitz, 1970). Testing hypotheses is a part of the total creative problem-solving process. It is this common process that early childhood educators can make it their business to promote. In this way they can give assistance to language and to thought at the same time.

Piaget has said that the principal goal of education is to create persons capable of doing new things rather than just repeating what others have done, persons capable of verifying rather than accepting just any idea that comes to them. With these thoughts in mind, we can set about planning optimal environments for children's growth, for developing children's language and thought.

References

Berko, J., & Brown, R. Psycholinguistic research methods. In P. Mussen (Ed.), *Handbook of research methods in child psychology*. New York: Wiley, 1960.

Bernstein, N. T. Effect of training on the language deficit of disadvantaged kindergarten children. In J. A. Figurel (Ed.), *Better reading in urban schools*. Newark, Del.: International Reading Association, 1972

Braine, M. D. S. The ontogeny of English phrase structure: The first phase. *Language*, 1963, *39*, 1–13.

Britton, J. *Language and learning*. Coral Gables, Fla.: University of Miami Press, 1970.

Brown, R. *A first language: The early stages*. Cambridge, Mass.: Harvard University Press, 1973.

Brown, R., & Bellugi, U. Three processes in the child's acquisition of syntax. *Harvard Educational Review*, 1964, *34*, 133–151.

Bruner, J. On the continuity of learning. *Saturday Review of Education*, 1973, *1* (February), 21–24.

Cazden, C. B. *Child language and education*. New York: Holt, Rinehart & Winston, 1976.

Charles, C. M. *Teacher's petit Piaget*. Belmont, Calif.: Fearon, 1974.

Chomsky, C. *The acquisition of syntax in children from five to ten* (Research Monograph No. 57). Cambridge, Mass.: M.I.T. Press, 1969.

Chomsky, C. Stages in language development and reading exposure. *Harvard Educational Review*, 1972, *42*, 1–33.

Chomsky, N. *Aspects of the theory of syntax*. Cambridge, Mass.: M.I.T. Press, 1965.

Clark, D. C. Teaching concepts in the classroom: A set of teaching prescriptions derived from experimental research. *Journal of Educational Psychology*, 1971, *62*, 253–278.

Cromer, R. The development of temporal reference during the acquisition of language. Unpublished doctoral dissertation, Harvard University, 1968.

Dale, P. S. *Language development: Structure and function*. Hinsdale, Ill.: Dryden Press, 1972.

Donaldson, M. *Children's minds*. New York: Norton, 1978.

Duckworth, E. Piaget takes a teacher's look with Eleanor Duckworth. *Learning: The Magazine for Creative Teaching*, 1973, *2* (2), 22–27.

Elkind, D. *Piaget in childhood education*. Listener In-Service Cassette Library. Hollywood, Calif.: Listener Corp., 1973.

Elkind, D., Koegler, R. R. & Go, E. Studies in perceptual development, II: Part-whole perception. *Child Development*, 1964, *35*, 81–90.

Ervin, S.M., & Miller, W. R. Language development. *62d yearbook of the National Society for the Study of Education, Part I*. Chicago: University of Chicago Press, 1963.

Feofanov, M. P. On the use of prepositions in child's speech. *Voprosy Psikhol*, 1958, *3*, 118–124.

Halliday, M. A. K. *Explorations in the functions of language* (2d ed.). New York: Elsevier North Holland, 1977.

Inhelder, B. Information processing tendencies in recent experiments in cognitive learning—Empirical studies. In Sylvia Farnham-Diggory (Ed.), *Information processing in children*. New York: Academic Press, 1972.

Inhelder, B., & Piaget, J. *The growth of logical thinking from childhood to adolescence*. New York: Basic Books, 1958.

John, V. P., & Moskovitz, S. Language acquisition and development in early childhood. In A. H. Marckwardt (Ed.), *Linguistics in school programs: The 69th yearbook of the National Society for the Study of Education, Part II*. Chicago: University of Chicago Press, 1970.

Katz, J. J., & Fodor, J. A. The structure of a semantic theory. *Language*, 1963, *39*, 170–210.

Krauss, R. *A hole is to dig*. New York: Harper, 1952.

Landreth, C. *Early childhood: Behavior and learning*. New York: Knopf, 1967.

Lenneberg, E. H. *Biological foundations of language*. New York: Wiley, 1967.

Lundsteen, S. W. Levels of meaning in reading. *The Reading Teacher*, 1974, *28*, 268–272.

Lundsteen, S. W. Understanding new perspectives of early childhood: What does research tell us about children? (section on the child's oral language). In L. Ollia (Ed.), *Handbook: For administrators on beginning reading*. Newark, Delaware: International Reading Association, 1980.

MacGinitie, W. M. Language development. In R. L. Ebel (Ed.), *Encyclopedia of educational research* (4th ed.). London: Macmillan, 1969.

O'Donnell, R. C., Griffin, W. J., & Norris, R. C. *Syntax of kindergarten and elementary school children: A transformational analysis*. NCTE Research Report No. 8. Urbana, Ill.: National Council of Teachers of English, 1967.

Opie, I., & Opie, P. *The lore and language of school children.* London: Oxford University Press, 1959.

Piaget, J. The theory of stages in cognitive development. An address presented at the California Test Bureau/McGraw-Hill Invitational Conference on Ordinal Scales of Cognitive Development, Monterey, California, February 1969. Monterey, Calif.: California Test Bureau/McGraw-Hill, 1969.

Sharp, E. *Thinking is child's play.* New York: Dutton, 1969.

Sinclair-de-Zwart, H. Developmental psycholinguistics. In D. Elkind & J. H. Flavell (Eds.), *Studies in cognitive development: Essays in honor of Jean Piaget.* New York: Oxford University Press, 1969.

Smith, E. B., Goodman, K. S., & Meredith, R. *Language and thinking in school* (2d ed.). New York: Holt, 1976.

Smith, F. *Understanding reading: A psycholinquistic analysis of reading and learning to read.* New York: Holt, Rinehart & Winston, 1971.

Templin, M. C. *Certain language skills in children: Their development and interrelationships.* Minneapolis: University of Minnesota Press, 1957.

Wilson, J. A. R., Robeck, M. C., & Michael, W. B. Psychological foundations of learning and teaching. New York: McGraw-Hill, 1969.

CHAPTER 6

*"Intellect is to emotion as our clothes are to
our bodies: we could not very well have
civilized life without clothes, but we would be
in a poor way if we had only clothes without
bodies."*

—*Alfred North Whitehead*

BECOMING: AFFECTIVE DEVELOPMENT IN EARLY CHILDHOOD

Patricia Kimberly Webb

Two preschoolers were playing in the park when a Catholic nun approached with her nursery group. One child fled in terror from "the thing with the covers on her head," while the other child joined the nun on the park bench and craned her little neck to see "what happened to that lady's hair." What accounts for these differences that we note in the socialization of preschoolers? This chapter addresses that question and others:

- What factors are related to the development of trust, self-confidence, initiative, and creativity?
- How does cognitive growth affect social and moral behavior, and what factors are related to the development of aggression in children?
- How do personal, sexual, and racial identities combine to create the concept of the self?
- Why does the child identify with some people and not with other people?

We should state at the outset, however, that there is one question we do *not* address: "What is the influence of television on children's affective development?" Obviously, this is an area in which television is very important; but a discussion of its influence is beyond the scope of this book. We can recommend three studies to interested readers: Evelyn Kaye, *The ACT Guide to Children's Television; Or, How to Treat Television with T. L. C.* (published by Beacon Press, Boston, 1979); H. Lesser, *Television and the Preschool Child: A Psychological Theory of Instruction and Curriculum Development* (published by Academic Press, New York, 1977); and Mariann Winick, *The Television Experience: What Children See* (published by Sage, Beverly Hills, California, 1979).

Theories

Several theorists offer interesting explanations of affective development in children. Theories of affective development, like other ideas concerning a child's growth, differ in their emphases on the relative importance of various factors: for example, the child's inborn potential for development versus the influence of the child's environment; or inner control (construction) versus control from outside (instruction). Below, we discuss the ideas of three important theorists: Erikson, Piaget, and Skinner. Erikson and Piaget believe that all children go through certain developmental stages. Nevertheless, they stress the tremendous importance of the environment in determining the amount and direction of growth at any given developmental stage. By contrast, according to the behaviorist views of Skinner, the reward the child receives following an action determines whether or not that behavior is likely to be repeated.

Erikson believes that society plays a vital role in the development of the individual. He has enumerated eight stages of development; four of these relate to the young child (Erikson, 1973).

Basic trust versus basic mistrust

Trust or mistrust evolves during infancy as children note whether or not their caretakers are reliable in meeting their needs. Trust leads to inner security and a desire for affiliation with others; mistrust may result in suspicion and withdrawal.

Autonomy versus shame and doubt

The "terrible twos" are so called because at about age two, children begin to assert themselves. A nurturing caretaker will help a child to strike a balance between "I can explore and do things" and "I must let others have their way sometimes, too." A child who can achieve a good balance between self-assertion and self-control will feel goodwill and pride. Shame and doubt may result if the child fails to develop such a balance during this period.

Initiative versus guilt

From about three to five years, children thrive on initiating tasks. They may need reassurance or consolation when they try things for the first time and when they attempt to play competently with older children. Moral responsibility begins at this time, but children may exasperate their caretakers by doing exactly what was *said* rather than what was *meant*—that is, following the letter rather than the spirit of the law. This happens because the children's understanding has an "all or nothing" quality. Maladjustment at this stage may produce children who are shy and afraid to take a chance or make a stand.

Industry versus inferiority

During the elementary school years children are to learn new skills and do meaningful work. Greater independence and new responsibilities come with the physical and social skills. Feelings of inferiority arise if children feel that they are not capable of mastering valued skills or if others constantly criticize their level of attainment as not good enough.

If the children develop more trust, autonomy, initiative, and industry than mistrust, doubt, guilt, and inferiority, they should become healthy functioning selves.

COGNITION: PIAGET   During the preschool years the "self" develops throughout the sensorimotor and preoperational stages of cognitive development. (See Chapter 5.) Through sensory development, children learn to view themselves as separate beings capable of initiating actions.

During the preoperational stage (about two to six years), children are *egocentric* and can see the world only from their own point of view. When they act, they find it impossible to imagine how another person feels, since it never occurs to them that others are not feeling as they feel. Kicking, hitting, biting, and sharp words are common during this period. And no amount of "How do you think Jeremy feels?" will be truly meaningful to the child. According to Piaget, only with maturation, experience, and interaction with others will the child gradually move toward more social behavior. (Piaget's views on moral development appear in a later section; see page 161.)

BEHAVIORISM: SKINNER   Skinner observed that regardless of the cause of a behavior, whether it is repeated depends on what happens immediately following it (Skinner, 1938). If you feel that the response you receive from the environment is satisfying, you will repeat the action; if the response is unpleasant, you will tend not to repeat it. Children vary in the responses that they like. Some welcome attention, smiles, pats, and praise; others are embarrassed by such actions. A wise caretaker notes the child's reaction to adults' responses and gives to each child individually the feedback he or she enjoys and appreciates most. (In this regard, we should note that some behaviorists stress the importance of modeling. These theorists believe that children tend to copy the behavior of persons in their environment who they feel represent qualities or powers they would like to possess. Such emphasis on modeling is in a sense an outgrowth of Skinner's theories.)

Personality Development

Personality development may be described in both positive and negative ways. It emerges as a result of the experiences on which personal, sexual, and racial identity is based. A troubled self filled with fears, anxieties, and frustrations may be transformed into a "happy face" through nurturant guidance.

THE EMERGING "ME"   Children combine their personal, sexual, and racial identities into one "me" (Dill, 1978, pp. 247–248). Feelings about each of these components determine the amount of self-confidence and the degree of self-worth that each child develops.

Personal identity

Our personal identity is many-faceted. It includes our perceptions of how we look, how "good" or how talented we are, and how much others like and accept us. What we think we are may or may not be objective truth; this opinion is a reflection of the acceptance and respect we have received from others, particularly from parents (Coopersmith, 1967). No matter how inaccurate, this perception becomes a "self-fulfilling prophecy," as we become whatever we are believed to be. Two possible reasons for this are: (1) we act like the persons we believe we are; and (2) after others have stereotyped us, they see only what they expect to see and overlook anything we do that is not consistent with their present notion of us.

Sexual identity

When is sexual identity acquired? At a very early age children notice and begin to ask about sex differences. To trace the development of sexual identity, Slaby and Frey (1975) interviewed fifty-five preschool-age children, using dolls and movies. They found that by about age 4, children had achieved stable sexual identities ("Are you a girl or a boy?"), and by age 4½, they had achieved permanence of sex identity ("When you grow up, will you be a mommy or a daddy?") and constancy of sex identity (boys reply negatively when asked, "If you played girls' games, would you be a girl?").

How is sexual identity acquired? A three-stage process has been suggested (McDavid & Garwood, 1978). First is recognition of sex roles; children learn what their culture accepts as appropriate behaviors for males and for females. If one model is missing or the behaviors observed are not conventionally masculine or feminine, the child may have difficulty at this stage. Second is preference for sex roles; children associate positive or negative value with each sex role. If children are inconsistently rewarded for same-sex behavior or inappropriately rewarded for opposite-sex modeling, they may become confused. Finally comes adoption of sex roles; each child accepts the culture's role for his or her biological sex. Even though children accept their culturally assigned sex roles, they may or may not like them.

Sex roles are rapidly changing. Perhaps there will be less conflict in accepting sex identity if one can feel free to do or be anything one

Table 6-1 DIFFERENCES IN SOCIALIZATION BETWEEN BOYS AND GIRLS

DIFFERENCES INDICATED	NO DIFFERENCES INDICATED		FINDINGS VARY	
Boys more aggressive from age two on—both verbally and physically.	1	Equally social	1	Tactile sensitivity
	2	Equally imitative	2	Fear, timidity, and anxiety
	3	Equal in self-esteem	3	Activity level
	4	Equal in rote versus higher-level functioning	4	Competitiveness
	5	Equal in analytic reasoning	5	Dominance
	6	Equally affected by heredity and environment	6	Giving in to pressure
	7	Equal in motivation	7	Maternal behavior
	8	Equal in both auditory and visual skills		

desires. For this reason, the young child's teacher needs to avoid sexual stereotypes in classroom activities—e.g., housekeeping, woodwork, sports, and career models.

What sex differences are apparent at the preschool and primary levels? The findings shown in Table 6-1 were compiled from an extensive review of the literature (Maccoby & Jacklin, 1974). Table 6-1 suggests that many of the widespread beliefs about sexual socialization are unfounded.

Racial identity

Another difference noted early by children is race. Since the parent is a highly significant person in the child's life, the parent's own self-concept serves as a powerful model. If the parent is proud of his or her identity, the child will reflect this pride.

How do ethnically different groups feel about themselves? Kohn & Cohen (1975) studied 428 three- to five-year-old black, white, and Puerto Rican children and found that children from minority backgrounds showed neither more nor less socioemotional impairment than middle-class, white children. Many more studies dealing with racial self-concepts among preschoolers are needed: (1) to determine how children of different ethnic groups feel about themselves, (2) to identify the areas in which children from different cultures perceive themselves as superior and inferior, and (3) to find ways to enhance racial self-concepts in early childhood. Attempts at fostering better racial feelings can be made through arranged pleasant contacts with other races, vicarious learning experiences using books and shared cultural realia, understanding by the teacher of a variety of cultural value systems, and modeling by the teacher of acceptance of differences.

SELF-CONCEPT: EFFECTS ON BEHAVIOR

By recognizing that the child's self is made up of personal, sexual, and racial identities, the teacher may help the child to build positive feelings in each of these areas. How does the self-concept affect a child's behavior?

No self-image

Some preschoolers have not had sufficient experiences to develop concepts of themselves as separate entities. For these children, activities involving knowledge of body parts, exploration of movement, awareness of feelings, and positive "I like me" references are needed. Since the child will remain egocentric and self-focused during the preschool years, it is the crucial period for forming the positive feelings about personal, racial, and sexual identity that will serve as a foundation for later positive feelings toward others.

Negative self-image

If children do not meet success in many of the experiences they initiate during this period, they may begin to develop a sense of "I can't." This feeling may come from negative feedback from caretakers and peers, it may be related to racial or sexual identity, or it may stem from excessive competition with older children in the family. Negative feelings about the self may lead later to such behaviors as copying, clowning, aggression, and withdrawal, and eventually to the self-fulfilling prophecy "I am no good."

Positive self-image

Since our society places great stress on achievement, an important developmental task in child care is nurturing in the child both the self-confidence to initiate and the competence to achieve. Secure young children are active—exploring, questioning, and planning. But their enthusiasm about starting things rarely extends to finishing them. An understanding caretaker will encourage new experiences despite children's failures, frustrations, and tears. If standards are too high or if punishment for mishaps is too frequent, children will "play it safe" and not try things they are not sure will turn out well. The importance of preschool attitude to later school success was indicated by the finding that preschoolers who were rated high in apathy-withdrawal and anger-defiance scored low on task orientation in the first grade (Kohn & Cohen, 1975).

THE TROUBLED SELF

Fear

Young children have many fears because their limited knowledge of the environment makes many events seem strange, because they have trouble anticipating what will happen next, and because they can't determine what cause produces what effect.

"It's strange; I'm afraid!" Campos, Ende, Gaensbaver, and Henderson found that as early as five to nine months, infants evidenced a fear of strangers (1975). When the mother goes shopping, the child with little concept of time has no way to anticipate that she will ever return. The child's howling and screaming is not temper; it is terror. Strangeness creates many pressures for the young child that don't exist for adults.

"Can that thing hurt me?" Children's limited knowledge of reality creates many unfounded fears. "Will I go down the drain with the bath water?" "If the doctor gives me a shot, will I burst like a balloon?" "Will bad things chase me the way they do on television?" Aggression they have witnessed and threats they have heard may also be a source of terror. Miller, Barnett, Hampe, and Nable (1972) found that children's greatest fears were of physical injury, natural events, and emotional pressure. "Don't talk to strangers, and don't eat off the floor" fuel such fears. While fears related to such things as traffic and dangerous "nonedibles" provide necessary protection, the child needs constant guidance in distinguishing between necessary and unnecessary fears.

"What's going to happen next?" Since from children's egocentric point of view, everything is directly related to them, the loud clap of thunder is coming to get them. Such fears are related to lack of understanding about cause and effect and may therefore lessen with age as children become more familiar with and more trusting of their worlds.

A phobia is a special kind of fear apparent when a child shows undue fear or avoidance of a situation. Sometimes the reason for the fear is not readily apparent (a girl who is stung by a bee while riding her tricycle may fear the tricycle because she doesn't understand cause and effect). At other times the reason for fear is real (a trip to the dentist) but the reaction is disproportionate. Two techniques frequently used for eliminating phobias are conditioning (presentation of the thing feared without harmful results) and role playing.

Anxiety

Anxiety is a vague feeling of uneasiness that is not directly related to a present situation but rather stems from tensions from many sources. Some indications of anxiety in preschoolers are "show-off behavior," withdrawal, inattentive flitting from one activity to another, nervous habits such as lack of elimination control and twisting the hair, and radical change in usual disposition—from noisy to quiet, say, or vice versa (Hurlock, 1978).

Frustration

Frustration occurs when one is not able to gain success or control in a given situation. A child's reaction to anxiety and frustration is dramatically portrayed in the film *John (Seventeen Months) in Residential Nursery for Nine Days.** As his separation anxiety and his frustration with unfamiliar surroundings increase, he exhibits typical symptoms of frustration, such as withdrawal, aimless wandering, whining, thumb sucking, and aggressive screaming and struggling. Children whose previous experience has not prepared them for the requirements of school, and children from backgrounds that are socially or ethnically different, may be particularly susceptible to frustration.

Developing Secure Young Children

Since the preschooler is still in an egocentric state and just beginning to be aware of the opinions of others, the classroom teacher has a real challenge. How can the caretaker help the child to overcome negative emotions and develop a positive and realistic self-concept?

Encourage Acceptance of Self and Others
- Talk about feelings in order to discover that others experience many of the same joys and fears.
- Use heterogenous groupings to provide firsthand experience with others who are different: that is, mingle children of different races and sexes, and the handicapped with the nonhandicapped.
- Develop empathy through the use of such techniques as role playing and "bibliotherapy" (use of books and stories related to adjustments).
- Model acceptance both in words and in manner.

Relieve Fears and Anxieties:
- Help children to distinguish between real and imagined dangers.
- Don't tease or scold about fears, since anxiety will persist until the children have gained familiarity and understanding.
- Make the unknown familiar through experience (e.g., visit a doctor's office), simulation ("make believe"), or explanations (what causes the thunder).
- Plan routines to be followed in the event of a troubling situation (e.g., fire, new baby).

*New York University film library. (This film was made by James and Joyce Rovertson.)

Move from Frustration to Success:
- Provide many opportunities for success and approval.
- Use flexible standards to measure individual accomplishments.
- Select appropriate rewards for desired behaviors.
- Establish familiar routines so that the children will know what to expect.

Social Development

Several aspects of social development are considered in this section. Children become social beings through attachment, dependency, and identification. They then learn to relate to such significant others as parents, brothers and sisters, and peers. Sometimes all goes well; at other times social development is troubled by jealousy and aggression.

BECOMING A PART What is meant by attachment, dependency, and modeling? How is each important to the child and what environmental conditions contribute to the development of these characteristics?

Attachments

That sense of trust that enables an infant to become part of a family and later a member of society begins with his or her first attachment. "As a result of the original attachment, the child forms feelings, memories, wishes, expectations, and intentions that serve as a lens, coloring subsequent experiences with others" (Gardner, 1978, p. 41). What is this attachment? How and with whom is it formed?

Attachment is a mutual bond between infant and caretaker that is characterized by such behaviors as smiling, touching, and talking. Since all humans vary in kind and degree of responsiveness, it is most fortunate when there is a match between baby and caretaker in this regard.

How are these attachments formed? After an extensive review of research, the following six factors were found to be related (Rutter, 1972, pp. 17-22): (1) The child needs to have contact with the same person over a long period since forming attachments takes time. (2) As many as three or four caretakers will not impair attachment provided one of them is with the child over an extended period of time. (3) A dependable and quick response is necessary for strong attachment. (4) The person who is there at times of distress and anxiety becomes the object of attachment. *This fact helps to explain how small children may form attachments even to parents who abuse them.* (5) The strength of the attachment is not based on any particular activity caretaker and child do together; the only condition is that the behavior is mutually satisfying.

(6) It is the quality of time together, not the quantity, that determines the attachment (e.g., full, intense, undivided attention). There is also a seventh factor: (7) Timing is important; between six months and two years appears to be the optimal time for forming attachments (Bowlby, 1969).

When a working parent needs to leave an infant in a day care setting, will the child be hopelessly thwarted? When Moskowitz, Schwarz, and Corsini (1977) tested three-year-olds, they found no impairment of functioning in children who had received day care when they were compared with a matched control group that had had no group experience. Various studies of children reared on kibbutzim also showed that no deficiencies of attachment resulted from multiple caretakers (Kagan et al., 1976).

Dependency

Out of these attachments children develop dependent behaviors. Some of this dependency is related to things children cannot do for themselves; some occurs because children are seeking attention and affection. Little ones must satisfy certain needs and must know that they can count on their "significant others" to meet both physical and emotional needs. At the same time, children must be encouraged gradually to develop autonomy and independence. The following recommendations are made regarding dependency (adapted from McDavid & Garwood, 1978, p. 295):

- Provide opportunities and rewards for attempts to be independent, even if unsuccessful.
- Encourage children to seek necessary but not unnecessary help.
- Arrange scaled tasks, sufficiently difficult to challenge but not overwhelming.
- Help children to gain accuracy in estimating their ability.
- Be patient.
- Don't punish children for seeking assistance.
- Don't do things for children to save the bother of helping them do for themselves.
- Don't associate seeking help with being babyish and refusing help with being mature.

Identification and modeling

As children move toward independence, they develop a sense of security through identifying with significant persons in their world and copying the behavior of these persons. The significant people possess characteristics that children admire; and children believe that by imitation they can gain desirable traits and power (Parsons, 1955). Sexual identity, cultural mores, and morality, as well as personal characteristics, all result from identification. The results of identification may be appropriate, disastrous, or amusing. For instance, one five-year-old girl cut her own hair and proudly announced, "Now I look just like Farrah Fawcett!" (a glamorous star).

RELATING TO SIGNIFICANT OTHERS Many important people in the life of the child influence social development. Some of these people are parents, some are rivals called "brothers" and "sisters," and some are age-mates who enrich or infuriate a child. Let's consider each of these.

Parents

To what extent does a parent's behavior affect the personality of the child? Baumrind identified and described three kinds of parents—authoritative, permissive, and authoritarian—and discussed the effects of these three styles on the development of children (Baumrind, 1967). Authoritative parents were described as controlling and demanding, yet warm and receptive to their children's needs. The children of authoritative parents tended to be active explorers, yet content, self-reliant, and self-controlled. The permissive parents were also warm, but they ranked low in control and low in setting required standards for their children's behavior. The children of permissive parents were described as low not only in self-control but also in self-reliance and exploratory behaviors. The authoritarian parents, described as controlling but cool and aloof, had children who were discontented, distrustful, and withdrawn.

While all parents want to rear "good" children, their perceptions of what "good" means may vary greatly. To the active and asserting parent, an inquisitive and exploring child would be a real joy; a calm and methodical parent might greatly appreciate a little more "peace and quiet." Personal characteristics that tend to be valued in our society are self-control, independence, curiosity, affiliation, and a positive self-concept. The following parental behaviors seem to be related to the development of these characteristics in children, according to findings gathered by two research studies (Baumrind, 1972; Coopersmith, 1967).

- Clear and consistent communication of goals and ideas with clearly defined and enforced limits (See the section on discipline in Chapter 14.)
- Use of reason rather than "because I said so" to explain ideas and regulations
- Warmth and acceptance without permissiveness
- Greater emphasis on rewarding desirable behavior than on punishing wrongdoing

- High nurturance and support for children's initiative in designated areas
- Skilled judgment in determining which decisions the parent must make and which choices the child is mature enough to handle successfully
- Significant demands for academic achievement and appropriate, productive behavior
- Ability on the parent's part to model an active, self-assured adult functioning both in the family and in the outside community

An increasing amount of research is being done on the role of fathers in child development (Lamb, 1976; Lynn, 1974). Extensive surveys of the literature have indicated that effective fathers tend to be correlated with good social adjustment, popularity, assumption of leadership roles, high self-esteem, initiative in task situations, higher IQ, better scholastic achievement, and fewer learning disabilities on the part of their children.

Disturbances related to absence of the father seem to be correlated with several factors (Oshman & Manosevitz, 1976). Both boys and girls are more likely to have adjustment problems if the father leaves during preschool; if he is absent as a result of desertion or divorce rather than from circumstances beyond his control (death or illness); if no adequate substitute is available to provide a male model; and if the mother is unhappy with herself, is bitter toward the father, or both. Boys will be less likely to have trouble being assertive and independent if they have older brothers rather than older sisters (Santrock, 1972). A major problem of a girl without a father could be a tendency to be either overly shy or unduly assertive (Hetherington & Duer, 1972).

Siblings

Brothers and sisters in a family may serve as models in many areas of development. They may function variously as companions, teachers, protectors, or even adversaries. Both girls and boys who have older brothers tend to be more physically active (Smart & Smart, 1977). Older sisters tend to be particularly effective in giving explanations, answering questions, and aiding in vocabulary development with younger siblings, especially if at least four years separate the older child from the younger (Cicirelli, 1974).

Birth order also may affect siblings' interaction (Gardner, 1978). While individual cases will definitely vary, firstborns tend to be well-organized, highly motivated, and successful, though they may require more approval and encouragement. Middle children, while less conventional, are often eager for action, congenial with peers, and less dependent on adults. Youngest children may be more dependent and less mature than other children in the family.

Peers

Do children vary in their responsiveness to peers from a very early age? When do children begin to move out beyond family and into the world of peers? What effects do friends have on the development of social behavior? Recent research in this area merits attention (Elkind & Weiner, 1978; Fein, 1978).

Fein noted three distinct categories of social behavior in eighteen-month-old children: (1) some maintained spatial distance, moved away with a selected toy, and always stayed on the edge of the group; (2) some sought nearness to others though their socialization skills were limited; and (3) others constantly provoked commotions and were impossible to ignore. "The peer system that emerges is co-determined by predispositions that a child brings to the group setting, and by human and material resources in the setting that enhance, submerge, or modify those predispositions" (Fein, 1978, p. 213). Halverson found a positive relationship between a child's social participation and level of activity at two years of age and his or her sociability at age seven (Halverson & Waldrop, 1976).

A preference for the company of friends rather than the attention of a significant caretaker also develops quite early. The findings of two studies indicate that by eighteen months, infants were more interested in playing with peers than with their mothers (Eckerman, Whatley, & Kutz, 1975; Rubenstein & Howes, 1976). In another study, four- and five-year-olds regularly turned to other children rather than to adults for attention and praise (Hartup, 1970).

What behaviors cause a child to be more frequently chosen by others? Observers in a day care nursery found that at eight to ten months some babies were more popular than others and that peer preference was shown toward those children who were more responsive and adaptable (Lee, 1973). In a survey of literature concerning peer status, Elkind found that the best-liked children tended to be friendly, cooperative, adaptable, and capable of giving desired kinds of attention and approval. By contrast, children who were least-liked were described as being hostile, withdrawn or disruptive, and possessing a tendency to ignore or ridicule others (Elkind & Weiner, 1978).

Because of their importance to each other, peers can be very effective teachers. Preschoolers were found to be more successful in setting up categories of objects when helped by older children, particularly if they talked together as they worked (Cicirelli, 1974). Grouping children of different ages together can be developmentally beneficial, as more advanced children can share their expertise with those still learning a given skill. This allows more advanced younger children to benefit from interaction with older children. It also gives less advanced older children more status with younger ones than they enjoy with their own age-mates, since these older children possess some skills they can share with younger children.

Not all interaction of siblings and peers produces positive effects. Sometimes jealousy and aggression present problems. In recounting the story of Joseph for a Sunday school teacher, one preschooler said, "And Joseph's brothers took his new coat away from him, and they put him in a deep hole, and then they sold him at their next garage sale."

Jealousy

Jealousy naturally occurs when people feel that someone else has something of value that they don't have. This "desired something" may be the love of an important person, the ability to do well in a valued skill, or some treasured possession.

Reactions to jealousy are likewise varied. Some children simply give up and withdraw. Others act out by clowning, teasing, or ever-present overhelpfulness—for example, in expressing jealousy over a new baby, an older sibling may cover up the baby, oversolicitiously, almost as if to bury it in the blankets. Some children find solace in aggression, either physical (biting, kicking) or verbal (ridiculing, tattling). Some decide to even the score by fierce competition, perhaps frustrating and exhausting themselves or (if all else fails) by lying, cheating, or stealing (Hurlock, 1978).

Aggression

Not all aggression is unhealthy. Children need to be encouraged to strive actively for some of the things they want. Problems occur when children attack others in their determination to do as they please.

What conditions tend to increase aggressive behavior in young children? After reviewing current research, Robeck (1978) listed the following: observing the aggression of others, being denied a favored toy, being victimized by aggressive peers whose behavior goes unpunished, and being punished severely or frequently.

How can a teacher help young children deal with disruptive aggressive behaviors? Each of the following suggestions has been widely made by child development specialists and child care workers:

- Watch for signs of tension in the group, since some situations and some combinations of playmates regularly upset certain children.
- Realize that the "cause" of aggression may not be the present situation—it may be fatigue, excitement, or feelings brought from home.

- Ignore aggression only if it is hurting no one (and having no effect on the aggressor's social status), if the other children do not indicate that they may follow suit (since the aggressor gets by with it), and if the aggressor appears to have chosen this behavior in order to get attention.
- Suggest an alternative behavior rather than saying "Don't!"—give positive direction and divert attention.

Moral Development

Moral behavior may be defined as what is considered proper in a given society. A worthy goal of moral development is to help children understand the reasons for their society's rules and feel a commitment to select those behaviors that will, as much as possible, be fair to themselves and to others.

THEORIES Two major theorists in the field of moral development are Piaget and Kohlberg. Since Piaget's theory is basic to Kohlberg's investigations, we will consider Piaget first.

Piaget

Piaget used games and stories to explore the moral judgment of the child (Piaget, 1948). Through the use of games, Piaget discovered to what degree children are conscious of rules, where they believe the rules come from, and under what conditions rules might change. Piaget used pairs of stories in which one child engaged in a forbidden act that resulted in little damage while another child did extensive damage accidentally. From children's responses, Piaget determined whether "badness" was related more to the amount of damage or the intent to be naughty. (For example, in one story a child swings a door open and upsets a tray behind the door, breaking fifteen cups. Another child, reaching for a jar of jam, deliberately placed out of reach on a high shelf, breaks one cup. Which child has been "worse"? In both cases the breakage was accidental, but in one case the damage was greater while in the other case the child was doing a willful wrong. The preschooler probably would consider the first child more guilty, since more cups were broken.) Finally, Piaget investigated children's attitudes toward punishment by describing a transgression and letting the children select a punishment from a list of possibilities.

From such games and stories, Piaget (1948) discovered the following moral concepts in young children:

Rules
- Right and wrong are based on rules, and "goodness" is determined by the degree to which one follows the rules.
- Rightness is based on following the exact rather than the implied meaning of a rule.
- Rules are sacred and must not be broken or modified.
- Badness is determined by resulting damage rather than intention to do wrong.
- There may be considerable difference between saying what is right and actually behaving accordingly.

Punishments
- Punishment will be immediate, from God or from significant humans.
- A person who is hurt while committing a wrong is being punished by the act itself.
- Punishment should be severe. Penalties that young children dream up often are more harsh than a caretaker would advocate.

As children grow older they are better able to generalize the meanings of rules and apply them in context. Piaget also found that older children stressed the need for explaining the consequences of the wrongdoing as a deterrent to future misbehavior.

Kohlberg

Kohlberg used his research with children to delineate stages in the development of morality (Kohlberg, 1975). To determine an individual child's level of morality, an examiner reads the child a problem situation. The child then makes a moral judgment and explains his or her reasoning. The following is a brief summary of Kohlberg's hierarchy:

Preconventional Level (about Four to Ten Years)
- Emphasis is on obedience and avoidance of punishment (outside control)
- "What's good for me" is considered first; but there is *occasionally* consideration for "right" as determined by the welfare of others.

Conventional Morality (about Ten to Thirteen Years)
- There is a desire to be considered "good" by oneself and by others.
- The law is respected for its own sake, independent of personal desires.

Morality of Internalized Principles (over Thirteen)
- Rights and standards are supported by social consensus; rules can be changed for the public good.

- The individual is governed by principles chosen by himself or herself; individuals construct abstract, universal principles from their own experience.

From a study of Kohlberg's premoral level, caretakers of young children are further encouraged to help children build internal controls by understanding reasons, other than the threat of punishment, for choosing particular behaviors. Planned experiences related to perceiving the needs of others also will help children to outgrow their egocentric "me first" attitude. One concern related to Kohlberg's theory of moral development is that moral comprehension may or may not lead to moral behavior.

GUIDING MORAL DEVELOPMENT What strategies can a caretaker use to bridge the gap between moral understanding and moral behavior? Modeling, inductive discipline techniques, use of bibliotherapy, and involving young children in role playing and discussion sessions all may prove helpful in establishing moral behaviors in children.

Modeling

Modeling can be one of the most effective means for developing moral behavior. If the person whom the child has selected as significant consistently displays moral behaviors, the child often will imitate these actions. The model also may demonstrate attitudes and behaviors that are new to the child. Many children fail to exhibit responsibility, stability, and nurturance because such behaviors have not been present in their own experience.

Discipline

There may be a relationship between the type of discipline used and the moral development of the child. As a result of an analysis of research, Hoffman (1970) identified three commonly used discipline techniques and their relations to moral effect; see Table 6-2.

The external control involved in assertion of power is less effective than internal control because: (1) the controller may not always be present to enforce "good" behavior, (2) anyone (moral or immoral) may become the controller, and (3) there may be a greater tendency to find ways to circumvent rules if one is not internally committed to the principle involved ("You never put the puzzles away unless I'm standing over you"). Withdrawal of love, in addition to yielding inconsistent results as regards moral effect, also has the disadvantages of creating side effects such as a negative self-concept and mistrust ("If you don't

Table 6-2 DISCIPLINE TECHNIQUES AND THEIR EFFECTS ON MORALITY

TECHNIQUE	BASES AND EXAMPLES	TIME DURATION AND EFFECT
Assertion of power	Based on "parent power" Physical punishment Deprivation of valued resources Application or threat of direct force	Quick, direct, usually soon over Conformance if authority figure is present; otherwise "I can do it if no one is looking."
Withdrawal of love	Based on nonphysical expressions of anger and disapproval Ignoring child Expressing disapproval or dislike for child	Long-term effect Insecurity based on fear of permanent separa- tion or loss of affection "Please don't stop loving me!"
Induction	Based on explanations and reasons Citing requirements of given situation Describing effects of given behavior on self and others	Long-term effect Security based on "I can analyze and make a wise decision"

Source: Adapted from Hoffman, 1970.

put the puzzles away, I won't love you"). Since preschoolers usually view behavior egocentrically, it is of particular importance to confront them experientially with another point of view so that eventually they may be more aware of the feelings of others and more considerate of their welfare. ("If you don't put the puzzle away, John won't enjoy finding it all there as you did; and if John doesn't put it away, you won't find it all there. That's why we put puzzles away.")

Bibliotherapy

Use of books and stories enables the child to identify with the characters and copy their behavior, and exposes children to an endless variety of new ideas. A recent publication, *The Bookfinder*, supplies the teacher with a handy reference to over 1,000 children's books (Dreyer, 1977). Included are a topical index, age recommendations for books, and abstracts that are quite comprehensive. A caretaker may use stories to introduce and develop the meanings for such concepts as helpfulness, friendliness, sharing, and comforting. The teacher also may select stories to meet observed needs of a particular group of children. Not to be overlooked are the possibilities for extended participation by children in storytelling. Puppets stimulate retelling and may give shy children the emotional support they need. After all, if the puppet "goofs up," that's the puppet's problem. (See Chapter 10.)

Role playing

Role playing gives children the opportunity to try out roles that may not be available in real life. Rene, who barely speaks above a whisper in other class activities, may roar with delight as a make-believe lion. Susie, the youngest in her family, may develop some insights into how "pesky" little ones can be as she plays the role of older sister. Children also may benefit from seeing and hearing the reactions of other children to certain role behaviors without suffering the penalties of social censure that result when they try out these same behaviors "for real" with their peers. Role playing also may be used in relation to activities directed by the teacher in language, music, and social studies.

Talking out personal concerns

All children should develop the feeling that if they need to talk out personal concerns, someone will listen. The teacher may call the children together and explain that the group needs to share ideas about how to make life happier for each member. For about ten minutes twice a week, the children might be seated in a circle and allowed to talk about anything important to them. There are only two ground rules: (1) the use of anyone's name is avoided (speak of *actions* that are liked or disliked— not of *people*), and (2) only one person may talk at a time (they must listen to each other and help to think of helpful solutions). There also is one ground rule for the teacher: *Don't be judgmental.* If the caretaker speaks to the issues, the children will look to that person for the answers. The purpose of talking together is to get the children to help each other. While beginning attempts may deal with trivial matters, the children will come to look forward to this group support. The transfer of nurturant behaviors will soon spread to other classroom situations.

Creativity

Creativity is that quality of behavior which accounts for many human advancements and adds spice and variety to life. What are the components of creativity, what are some of the characteristics of creative people, and how may creative behavior be fostered in young children?

CREATIVE THINKING

Characteristics of creative thinking

Creativity is a process, not a product. It is an ongoing way of life, not any one behavioral characteristic. Torrance (1966), well-known for research in creative thinking and teaching, identified four criteria for creativity: (1) fluency (number of related responses), (2) flexibility (number of categories contained in the responses), (3) originality (novelty or infrequency of responses), and (4) elaboration (amount of detail in responses). Perhaps Dill (1978) summed up the creative process most succinctly when he wrote that to be creative one should see things in an unusual way, think unconventionally, and have a high tolerance for complexities, ambiguities, and uncertainties.

Convergent and divergent thinking

Convergent thinking involves selecting the most correct solution to a given situation. This type of thinking is very useful in some types of problem solving where a single particular answer is necessary (2 + 2 = 4, not 5 or 6; "when" is not spelled "whin"). In many instances, however, the best solutions come after a person has brainstormed, thinking of as many solutions as possible, and selected from among them the most appropriate and workable. This wide range approach is called "divergent thinking" and is a necessary component in the creative process. (For example, think of how many ways we can build targets that we can knock down.)

CORRELATES OF CREATIVITY When children are creative, certain personality factors seem to appear together—and so do certain behaviors of parents. When the research from a number of different studies is combined, the correlates shown in Table 6-3 emerge (Albert, 1971; Dill, 1978; Fein, 1978; Kogan & Pankove, 1972; Smart & Smart, 1977):

Intelligence

Creativity is not found to be related to IQ in most studies (Guilford, 1968; Wallach & Kogan, 1965). It appears that creativity may be one of many elements of intelligent behavior. It also is possible that intelligence may be related to some types of creativity but not to others. The similarity of format—paper and pencil, use of manipulatives—for both intelligence tests and measures of creativity could account for some apparent relationships found between creativity and intelligence (Fein, 1978). The caretaker should recognize that the highly creative child may give a novel or unique answer that is not on the scoring sheet and may be penalized as a result.

Stability with age

If a caretaker can foster creativity in children during early childhood, some research indicates that uniqueness and ideational fluency may persist throughout life (Kogan & Pankove, 1972). Persons who work with young children should take great care to facilitate, not stifle, the child's creative endeavors.

FOSTERING CREATIVITY In this section you will find some thoughts on enhancing children's creativity. Two questions to ask yourself are: (1) How can I promote, not

Table 6-3 PERSONALITY FACTORS AND PARENTAL BEHAVIORS RELATED TO CREATIVITY

PERSONALITY FACTORS

Attitude	Disposition
Openness	Empathy
Curiosity	Humor and playfulness
	Impulsiveness
Autonomy	"Wild ideas" and atypical schoolwork
Self-acceptance	
Self-confidence	Flexibility
Independence of judgment	Desire for complexity
	Ease with unclearness
Activity Level	Fluency of responses
High Drive	Seeing what others fail to see
High involvement	

PARENTAL BEHAVIORS*

Less	More
Authoritarianism	Encouragement of curiosity, adaptability, and
Possessiveness	flexibility
Status-consciousness	Emotional support, respect, and freedom
Stress on conformity	Encouragement of playfulness
Punishment	Age-appropriate materials
	Stress on creative use of materials
	Tolerance of fantasy
	Secure involvement of both parents in their own
	work or careers

* These could well apply to teachers, too.

crush, children's spontaneous responses? (2) How can I plan an environment to stimulate young children's creativity?

Spontaneous responses

Preschool children spontaneously exhibit a number of interesting creative behaviors. Dramatic play probably is the most common example. With few, if any, props, children soar into outer space as astronauts, cure the ills of doll and dog alike as doctor, and relive and replay the daily trials and triumphs of family living by "playing house." Few restrictions are placed on reality by their imaginations. Picture a young girl, complete with bridal veil and mothers high heels, roaring through the room on a fire truck, and watch a young boy in a football helmet checking groceries at the play market.

Children also have a wonderful capacity to breathe life into inanimate objects. A rock can be almost anything. It could be a dog chasing someone else's pebble; it could be food; it could be money; it could be a piece in a game. (See the section on symbolic play in Chapter 14.)

A charming aspect of spontaneous creativity is the proclivity of some children have for creating imaginary companions. One four-year-old girl gave daily reports on "baby brother." When asked by her father why the baby was never at home when he was, the girl explained that she and her mother were sharing the baby with a neighbor who had no children.

What needs to be done about such stories? Avoid accusing such children of fibbing. Tell them you enjoy their made-up stories, and spend some time sharing stories.

Planned facilitation

Children may avoid activities where they must compete for excellence with classmates. In order to be creative, children need time and fluid schedules. Deciding what use they want to make of their time and not being interrupted during a self-directed activity are essential parts of the creative process. Toys chosen for young children need to be easily adapted to various uses. For instance, a set of colored beads could be used for stringing (coordination), counting (number concepts), sorting (color names), and imaginative symbolic play (turned into cars or beetles). Selecting toys effectively involves determining how many ways and at how many levels of difficulty children can use the same object.

Several questions are frequently asked by teachers who are trying to manage a creative environment effectively.

"Should I try to stress creativity in all classroom activities?" Children need to realize that some experiences involve fact-finding—that sometimes it is important to look for particular things. Shapes of leaves, what the hamster does and does not eat, and how to brush one's teeth are examples. The wise teacher will strive for a balance between factual and creative learning. Even factual materials, however, can be presented in creative ways.

"What shall I do about the child who copies?" If one child puts four legs on her Thanksgiving turkey, you are likely to have an epidemic of four-legged fowls. Don't scold. One of a child's major avenues for learning is imitation. Also, some children may copy out of shyness or the desire to be identified with those whose creations they are copying. Try saying, "That's great. Now what do you suppose you could add so yours will be different from the rest?"

"What do I do when children want me to do their work for them?" In such a case, you might give a child confidence by saying something to draw out the child's own ideas: "I don't know exactly what your dog looks like. Could you tell me about him?" If necessary, mention the major parts of the dog to get the child to describe the particulars. Usually after such discussions, children have enough information in mind to feel more confident in tackling the project.

No discussion of creativity is ever complete. Creativity is a way of life, and the caretaker should be constantly alert to the new and different in life and find ways to share innovative notions with children. (See also Chapters 10 through 14.)

In our complex society anyone concerned with guiding the lives of young children must also attend to the intangible, multidimensional, and critical area of affective development. The skills of literacy are crucial— but so are a healthy personality, a positive self-concept, social and emotional development, a sense of morality, and creativity. One is humbled by the sense of responsibility to young children and to the future of society. The quality of life—of the individual child and of society—depends on how well we fulfill that responsibility. Chapter 11 will deal further with developing affective abilities.

Summary

In this chapter, an understanding of the various aspects of affective development—personal, social, emotional, moral, and creative—was combined with suggestions designed to foster optimal functioning in young children. We began with a look at the views of Erikson, the major theorist in the affective area, and described the stages operating in the early childhood years. The interrelationship was highlighted by a discussion of the affective correlates of cognitive development as seen by Piaget. Attention was also given to the role of reinforcement (Skinner) and modeling in the shaping of affective development.

The components of personality development (personal, sexual, and racial identities) were considered, and attention was given to how the children's behavior is affected by the self-concept. Ideas for helping children to develop positive and realistic concepts of themselves were presented.

Since even the youngest of children experiences instances of emotional stress, attention was given to the fears, anxieties, and frustrations that contribute to such stress. Children can be helped to work through negative emotions, and specific suggestions were presented to guide the adult in working with young children.

Social development involves becoming a part of a social setting through forming attachments, balancing dependence and independence, and identification through modeling. It also involves relating to significant others including parents, siblings, and peers. Problems in the area of social development, including jealousy and aggression, were discussed, and suggestions for dealing with both were given.

In tracing the moral development of children, the views of two leading theorists, Piaget and Kohlberg, were discussed. Strategies for developing moral behavior include modeling, inductive discipline techniques, bibliotherapy, role playing, and group discussion.

Creative development is related to such personality factors as curiosity, self-confidence, level of activity, divergent behavior, and flexibility. Related behaviors of parents are those that lend emotional support for flexible and fanciful use of the environment. Suggestions to caretakers for encouraging creative developments were offered.

Finally, we noted the multidimensional aspects of affective development and their significance to the lives of children and to the quality of society.

References

Albert, R. S. Cognitive development and parental loss among the gifted and exceptionally gifted, and the creative. *Psychological Reports*, 1971, *29*, 19–26.

Baumrind, D. Child care practices anteceding three patterns of preschool behavior. *Genetic Psychology Monographs*, 1967, *75*, 43–88.

Baumrind, D. Socialization and instrumental competence in young children. In W. W. Hartup (Ed.), *The young child: Reviews of research* (Vol. 2). Washington, D.C.: National Association for the Education of Young Children, 1972.

Bowlby, J. *Attachment and loss* (Vol. 1: *Attachment*). London: Hogarth Press, 1969.

Campos, J. J., Emde, R. N., Gaensbauer, T., & Henderson, C. Cardiac and behavioral interrelationships in the reactions of infants to strangers. *Developmental Psychology*, 1975, *11*, 589–601.

Cicirelli, V. G. Relationship of sibling structure and interaction to younger sib's conceptual style. *Journal of Genetic Psychology*, 1974, *125*, 37–49.

Coopersmith, S. *The antecedents of self-esteem*. San Francisco: Freeman, 1967.

Dill, J. R. *Child psychology in contemporary society*. Boston: Holbrook Press, 1978.

Dreyer, S. S. *The book finder*. Circle Pines, Minn.: American Guidance Service, 1977.

Eckerman, C. O., Whatley, J. L., & Kutz, S. L. Growth of social play with peers during the second year of life. *Developmental Psychology*, 1975, *11:* 42–49.

Elkind, D., & Weiner, I. B. *Development of the child*. New York: Wiley, 1978.

Erikson, E. *Childhood and society*. New York: Norton, 1973.

Fein, G. G. *Child development*. Englewood Cliffs, N.J.: Prentice-Hall, 1978.

Gardner, H. *Developmental psychology: An introduction*. Boston: Little, Brown, 1978.

Guilford, J. P. *Intelligence, creativity, and their educational implications*. San Diego, Calif.: Knapp, 1968.

Halverson, C. F., & Waldrop, M. F. Relations between preschool and aspects of intellectual and social behavior at age 7½. *Developmental Psychology*, 1976, *12*, 107–112.

Hartup, W. W. Peer interaction and social organization. In P. H. Mussen (Ed.), *Carmichael's manual of child psychology* (3d ed.) (Vol. 2). New York: Wiley, 1970.

Hetherington, E. M., & Duer, J. L. The effects of father absence on child development. In W. W. Hartup (Ed.), *The young child: Reviews of research* (Vol. 2). Washington, D.C.: National Association for the Education of Young Children, 1972.

Hoffman, M. L. Moral development. In P. H. Mussen (Ed.), *Carmichael's manual of child psychology* (Vol. 2) (3d ed.). New York: Wiley, 1970.

Hurlock, W. B. *Child development*. New York: McGraw-Hill, 1978.

Kagan, J., Kearsley, R. B., & Zelazo, P. R. *The effects of infant day care on psychological development*. Paper presented at a symposium, American Association for the Advancement of Science, Boston, February 1976.

Kogan, N., & Pankove, E. Creative ability over a five-year span. *Child Development*, 1972, *43*, 427–442.

Kohlberg, L. The cognitive-developmental approach to moral education. *Phi Delta Kappan*, 1975, *56*, 670–677.

Kohn, M., & Cohen, J. Emotional impairment and achievement deficit in disadvantaged children—Fact or myth? *Genetic Psychology Monographs*, 1975, *92*, 57–78.

Lamb, M. E. (Ed.). *The role of the father in child development*. New York: Wiley, 1976.

Lee, C. L. *Social encounters of infants: The beginnings of popularity*. Paper presented at the meeting of the International Society for the Study of Behavioral Development, Ann Arbor, Michigan, August 1973.

Lynn, D. B. *The father: His role in child development*. Monterey, Calif.: Brooks/Cole, 1974.

Maccoby, E. E., & Jacklin, C. N. *The psychology of sex differences*. Palo Alto, Calif.: Stanford University Press, 1974.

McDavid, J. W., & Garwood, S. G. *Understanding children: Promoting human growth*. Lexington, Mass.: Heath, 1978.

Miller, L., Barnett, C. L., Hampe, E., & Nable, H. Factor structure of childhood fears. *Journal of Counseling and Clinical Psychology*, 1972, *39*, 264–268.

Moskowitz, D. S., Schwarz, J. C., & Corsini, D. A. Initiating day care at three years of age: Effects of attachment. *Child Development*, 1977, *48*, 1271–1276.

Oshman, H. P., & Manosevitz, M. Father absence: Effects of stepfathers on psycho-social development in males. *Developmental Psychology*, 1976, *12*, 479–480.

Parsons, T. Family structure and the socialization of the child. In T. Parsons & R. F. Bales (Eds.), *Family socialization and interaction process*. Glencoe, Ill.: Free Press, 1955.

Piaget, J. *The moral judgment of the child*. Glencoe, Ill.: Free Press, 1948.

Robeck, M. C. *Infants and children: Their development and learning*. New York: McGraw-Hill, 1978.

Rubenstein, J., & Howes, C. The effects of peers on toddler interaction with mothers and toys. *Child Development*, 1976, *47:* 597–605.

Rutter, M. *Maternal deprivation reassessed*. Baltimore: Penguin, 1972.

Santrock, J. W. Relation of type and onset of father absence to cognitive development. *Child Development*, 1972, *43*, 455–469.

Skinner, B. F. *The behavior of organisms*. New York: Appleton-Century-Crofts, 1938.

Slaby, R. G., & Frey, K. S. Development of gender constancy and selective attention to same sex models. *Child Development*, 1975, *46*, 849–856.

Smart, M. S., & Smart, R. C. *Children: Development and relationships*. New York: Macmillan, 1977.

Torrance, E. P. *Torrance tests for creative thinking*. Princeton, N.J.: Personnel Press, 1966.

Wallach, M. A., & Kogan, N. *Modes of thinking in young children: A study of the creativity-intelligence distinction*. New York: Holt, Rinehart, & Winston, 1965.

CHAPTER 7

CHAPTER 7

*This was written by David Everett in 1791,
to be recited by a seven-year-old pupil:*

*You'd scarce expect one of my age
To speak in public on the stage;
And if I chance to fall below
Demosthenes or Cicero,
Don't view me with a critic's eye
But pass my imperfections by.
Large streams from little fountains flow,
Tall oaks from little acorns grow.*

ASSESSMENT

Jan Fish

Let us think a moment about the word "assessment." What kinds of images does it conjure up for you? Perhaps you think of taking tests, an experience that for all of us at some point has been an uncomfortable, anxiety-producing event: "What do they want to know? How will I do? What will my teacher and my friends think of me?" At other times, a test may present a welcome challenge: "Hey, this is sort of fun! Let me see if it will work this way!" Tests represent just one type of measurement device used to gain information about someone or something and to compare that information with a standard—an earlier performance of that person, perhaps, or the performance of other people.

To clarify the term "assessment" further, we consider some related terms: "measurement" and "evaluation." All these terms refer to some human judgmental process of assigning a value to the behavior of individuals or of groups. *Measurement*, the most limited of the three concepts, is the process and outcome of gathering and comparing information about someone or some group with the behavior of a similar group. The concepts of *assessment* and *evaluation* are often interchangeable. In assessing early childhood behavior or the effectiveness of a program, one goal is to gather information and compare it with a standard (measurement) and to evaluate (place a value on) that outcome. The context of the assessment or evaluation includes the setting and often a comparison of what has been done with what you think the child or group should be able to do (i.e., with your prior expectations).

What Is This Chapter About?

In early childhood education centers and classrooms, there are three main areas of assessment: assessment of children, assessment of teachers, and assessment of programs. This chapter focuses primarily on the basic concepts, methods, and tools of assessment, or evaluation, of children; with a brief discussion of evaluating teachers and programs.

Evaluation of children and programs can be analyzed in these terms:

- Who evaluates children and programs?
- Why do we assess the development and achievement of children and programs?
- What do evaluators evaluate?
- How do they evaluate?
- What tools can we use to evaluate children's growth and achievement and the effectiveness of programs?

This chapter seeks to answer these questions. Somewhat similar questions can be asked about assessment of teachers, of course; but we approach that subject by way of types of assessment and a brief discussion of accountability.

WHO ASSESSES? Evaluation can be conducted by all who are involved with young children and their programs—students, teachers, administrators, researchers, parents, children, and other community members. More important, we *do* evaluate children and their programs, whether or not we are aware of the basis of our evaluation. We form our concept of development from a combination of our own experience of growing up, the beliefs of our family and community, and the developmental theories that are presented to us in our academic training.

Theories of human development are based on knowledge and interpretation of human behavior. Each theory is developed to explain the human behavior that we observe. In addition to the recognized theories of child development, we each have our own "theories in use." Two teachers may be watching four-year-old Zelda playing in the yard. One teacher may think: "Zelda is very well-coordinated, so I'll bet she will do well in her academic subjects," while the second teacher may reflect: "Zelda is very well-coordinated, but I'll bet she won't do well in her academic subjects." Both teachers have definite concepts about the relationship between physical coordination and cognitive abilities, though they may not be aware of either the source or the potential impact of their "theories in use" on their interaction with Zelda.

In assessing children's learning and development, we need to be aware of our own points of view as well as the prspectives of other evaluators. Our points of view determine what kind of information we find important to gather, how we will gather it, and what uses it will have for us.

WHY DO WE ASSESS? Our planning for individual children and for the group as a whole should be guided by the results of assessment. These results serve as *blueprints for instruction.* Research studies show us that teachers often build expectations about a child's abilities on the basis of such characteristics as physical appearance, sex, and scores on past tests (Brophy & Good, 1970). The expectations we hold for children are powerful determinants of what type of experience we will structure for them in the center or classroom setting.

We need all the useful information about children that we can gather, and we need to use the information wisely. Assessment can give us *clues* about children's abilities and achievements. We must *not*, however, misuse results to label, pigeonhole, or compartmentalize children (Murphy, 1973). This inflexibility limits our expectations of children's potential and influences our treatment of them. Often, children from culturally different backgrounds have been mislabeled and placed in special classes on the basis of misinterpreted assessments. Many teachers choose to spend between a month and six weeks at the beginning of the year to become acquainted with the new children in their programs *before* looking at records of the children's past performance. In this way, teachers are able to combine their initial experience and understanding of the children with information regarding their past performances to assess children's abilities and to plan program activities better.

WHAT IS ASSESSED? In assessing children's development or accomplishments, program activities, and the impact of programs, evaluators focus on *processes* and *outcomes*.

Processes are actions involving the mind, e.g., associative thinking, concept attainment, evaluation, and problem solving. Processes include the development of children and adults, teacher-child interactions, and the development curriculum (see Chapter 9). *Outcomes* include the specific learning achieved by children and other "clients" of the program and the number of children served. Developmental processes are not visible; therefore, they cannot be observed and measured directly, and instead they are inferred from behaviors that we can observe. For example, at four months, Jane allows one of several caring adults to comfort her, but at six months she rebels unless her mother attends to her. We can infer from Jane's behavior that she has developed a strong attachment to her mother. Outcomes most typically include the results of tests and other measurements used to determine the relative effectiveness of a program. Whatever the focus of our assessments, it remains related to the goals and objectives of the program for children and other program participants. Again, it is important to remember that evaluators interpret stated program goals and objectives and evaluate outcomes on the basis of their own perceptions of the goals and implementation of the program.

HOW DO WE ASSESS? There are many methods used to assess development and achievement. First, we will discuss tests—standardized and teacher-made, norm-referenced and criterion-referenced—and the major controversial issues about testing. Second, we will consider techniques of observation. The most important points to remember are that: (1) tools for assessment (tests and observation instruments) must be appropriate to the focus of our evaluation, (2) results of assessment must be sensitively interpreted, and (3) results from assessment tools need to be combined with the information teachers gather from children, parents, and other program participants to provide the clearest possible picture.

The Tools of the Trade: Assessment of Children

Assessment tools, designed to measure a given aspect of development or achievement at one point in time, may be used to study both development and achievement. However, results are sometimes used in attempts to predict a child's performance. These attempts are not very successful because a trait or ability that we may observe and document at one stage in a child's development may not be observable at a later stage of development. This happens for two main reasons. First, a child may display the same trait at two different stages of development and yet display it in two very different behaviors. For example: as a baby, James may show his attachment to his father by crying when his father leaves the room; but at four years of age, James may show his attachment to and love for his father by wearing a belt just like his or drawing pictures for him. Second, it is also possible that traits and abilities are not always continuously present and observable in human development.

It is important for us to realize that human development is a very intricate and complex process. In longitudinal studies that have traced the development of individual children through adulthood, predictions of future achievement proved to be accurate in only 30 percent of the cases (Murphy, 1973). Although we realize that development is a continuous process, its course is both individual and uneven. Prediction of future behavior and achievement on the basis of limited and early assessment is far from trustworthy. With this caution in mind, we consider, first, various kinds of tests and then various observational techniques.

TESTS ### Types of tests

What are basic types of tests? Spodek (1978) outlines four different types: (1) developmental tests, (2) intelligence tests, (3) readiness tests, and (4) achievement tests. (Examples of each of these types are presented in Table 7-2 on pages 186–187.)

Developmental tests Developmental tests seek to assess a child's degree of maturity in a given area of cognitive, affective, or psychomotor growth (recall Chapters 4 through 6). The great majority of tests we use with infants and very young children are developmental tests, based on a variety of theoretical views of how children develop. Test items may include observation of a child's physical characteristics (e.g., height, weight). More often, these tests assess a child's ability to perform certain tasks which indicate the degree of maturation attained by the child. Note the following example (Uzgiris & Hunt, 1975):

Visual Pursuit of Slowly Moving Objects
1   Child follows a slowly moving object
2   Child notes the disappearance of a slowly moving object
3   Child notes partial hiding of the object

With regard to scoring children's responses, an infant who repeatedly notes the partial hiding of objects has developed further in this area than an infant who has barely begun to follow a slowly moving object visually.

Developmental measures also assist in the identification of developmental delays. For example, if a child starts walking three months later than the age indicated on a developmental scale, there is little cause for alarm. However, if the child still does not walk one year later, we would say we have a case of developmental delay. Developmental tests such as Uzgiris and Hunt's infant assessment (1975) and DeVries and Kohlberg's scale of Piagetian tasks (1977) may be used to assess a child's stage of cognitive development, to indicate a child's readiness for school, or both. For example, if infant Karen has not developed a concept of the permanence of persons and is not convinced that mother still exists when she walks out of the room, we may predict that Karen is not mature enough to be enrolled in an infant group program.

Intelligence tests IQ tests, a subclass of developmental tests, are the source of much controversy and confusion for teachers (and children!).

Part of the problem is that we do not know exactly what intelligence is. When Alfred Binet (the author of the widely used Stanford-Binet IQ test) was asked to define intelligence, he answered: "Intelligence is . . . what my test measures!" (DeVries & Kohlberg, 1977).

Although there are several ways of looking at intelligence, we will stress the Piagetian approach. The Piagetian approach is based on the following assumptions:

- Intelligence is to a degree inherited.
- However, the development of one's intelligence *is influenced* greatly by the environment.
- Intelligence includes both an innate element ("you were born with it") and the ability to use knowledge in new ways and in varying situations.
- Intelligence develops with maturation and experience.
- Levels and stages of developing intelligence can be assessed by observing how and when children perform *operations* (such as Piagetian tasks involving the conservation of number and volume described in Chapter 5).

Intelligence tests were originally designed to predict a child's level of success in school. In fact, intelligence tests do do a fair job of predicting success in school, but they do not do such a good job of determining levels of individual intelligence. Unfortunately, IQ scores are still being misused to predict future performance without regard to the effects of a child's home environment or school environment. Too often, IQ scores of young children are used to "track" them into different programs according to their supposed levels of ability. Items on tests often reflect concepts outside the realm of experience of children culturally or economically different from the children for whom the test was designed and thus penalize some children for having had different experiences. Further, as children grow and develop they undergo dramatic changes, and their scores are likely to fluctuate with time. Despite this variability, teachers and parents frequently think of a child's IQ score as an unchanging fact of life which determines that child's future ("Poor Jimmy, he has an IQ of 81" or "Shirley's really smart; her IQ is 158"). Studies have shown that both children's and parents' IQ scores can be raised by interventions at home and school (Gordon, 1973). We cannot speak of "an IQ"; we can speak of a child's IQ "score" on a given intelligence test taken at a given time.

Results of intelligence tests are only one indicator of a child's ability, and they need to be interpreted with caution. If we lower our expectations of children only because of test results, we may well find the children responding to those lowered expectations. Depending on the test, however, useful information, including a clearer idea of the child's strengths, may be gained from the results.

Readiness tests   Readiness tests are used to gauge a child's ability to profit from a certain sort of instruction in cognitive, affective, or psychomotor areas. Readiness tests may take the form of paper-and-pencil tests, performance tests, or checklists designed to assess a child's specific abilities in performing tasks. A teacher's informal observations of the child supplement the information gained from readiness tests.

Achievement tests   Achievement tests are usually standardized, norm-referenced measures of a child's or a group's level of achievement in a particular area of skill. (The terms "standardized" and "norm-referenced" are defined below.) Educators use such tests appropriately if the purpose is to compare the achievement of one group of learners with that of another group. Results usually appear as percentiles or grade-level scores. We would caution immediately that results of tests administered to groups apply to groups, *not to individuals*. The test score assigned to the group reflects a sizable measurement error in the case of any individual child in the group. Educators misuse group achievement tests when they use scores alone to determine placement of individual children (Lundsteen, 1976, chap. 11).

Some definitions

The phrase "standardized test" simply implies a test that is administered in a standardized manner (same amount of time is given to examinees, same format of testing is always used). A standardized, *norm-referenced* test is an instrument that has been developed and administered to a large number of children so that the score of an individual child taking the test can be compared with the scores of the children in the groups that originally took the test. Results from the original group (or groups) of children who took the test represent the standard (*norm*), which becomes the basis of comparison. Several different groups—differing, for example, in sex, geographical location, and ethnic background—may contribute to the development of norms.

What is a *criterion-referenced measure?* How does it differ from a norm-referenced measure? A norm-referenced test compares a child's performance with that of other children; a criterion-referenced measure assesses a child's performance in reference to mastery of the instructional goal that the test is constructed to measure. A criterion-referenced spelling test, for example, asks the question, "How many of the twenty words in our lesson can Patty spell today?" A norm-referenced test is designed to ask, "How many of the twenty words can Patty spell in comparison with the number of words that other children in her class spell (given one testing opportunity)?" The goal of a criterion-referenced measure is to assess the degree to which a child has mastered specific learning objectives.

The advantage of a criterion-referenced measure is that a child may continue studying and retaking the test until mastery is achieved: given all the time she needs, Patty can take the spelling test until she is able to spell the total of twenty words correctly. The value of the criterion-referenced test is dependent upon the appropriateness of the learning objectives chosen. (In contrast, the value of a given norm-referenced test is dependent upon the fairness of the test items.) If expectations are unrealistic, reaching mastery on a criterion-referenced test will take too long, causing much discomfort for children. (Let's hope Patty's twenty words were important and meaningful to her.) Criterion-referenced measures are tools that can pinpoint effects of instruction on each individual child.

Some basic issues involved in testing

Basic issues in testing revolve around the construction and interpretation of tests. In some instances, standardized, norm-referenced tests may be appropriate; in others, teacher-made tests may meet needs better. In some cases, standardized, norm-referenced, individually administered tests, assessing how well a child has performed at that moment in comparison with others, are adequate; in others, where eventual mastery of a skill is the appropriate goal, we want ongoing assessment of the child's progress. One of our tasks as teachers may be to choose a test normed on a group similar to the population of children with which we are working. The most common criticism of standardized tests is that it is easy to misinterpret test results of children who are very different from the children upon whose scores the test was normed. This is an issue particularly in the case of minority children, for whom test results may be invalid.

What are some possible sources of bias in the interpretation of test results? Test validity depends on a match between the sample of tested content or skills and the objectives of the instructional program. If the test measures skills to be developed later or skills developed in some other program, scores fail to show the effects of teaching. If the sampling of skills tested for, however, is *all* that is taught in the program, then test results become biased because of this "teaching for the test." When teachers are under pressure to show high achievement scores for their classes, standardized tests may be used in this invalid way. In addition, tests may present "irrelevant difficulties" to children, e.g., requiring them to *read* test instructions in a test designed to measure listening skills or mathematics skills. A child may be proficient in mathematics but unskilled in reading, and, misunderstanding the written instructions, may perform poorly on the test. The credibility of test results also depends on the reliability of the test: that is, its consistency in measuring whatever it is supposed to measure.

A further source of possible bias is the fact that test items may present something that is not written within the child's experience; for instance, even among children from rural areas, the word "waterfall" may not be universally understood. Children growing up in the wet northwestern part of the United States have a much greater opportunity to learn about waterfalls than children growing up in parts of the arid southwest. The construction and sequence of test items can also greatly influence how a child might answer the questions. Conditions of the testing situation are assumed to be similar for all children taking a standardized test, yet some factors are beyond control (e.g., unusual individual fatigue, atypical individual reaction to intruding noise). And it is simply more difficult for some children to cope with the testing environment than it is for others (Messick & Anderson, 1970).

How are test results misused? Test results are only as useful as we are skillful in interpreting them. Our potential misuse of test results stems from a lack of understanding of *what* the test measures, an exaggerated belief in the infallibility ("foolproofness") of tests, or an unwarranted use of the results to predict a child's future development or achievement.

Because of the pitfalls of standardized tests we describe above, some educators have suggested that we refrain from administering standardized tests until we develop better measures and an increased ability to interpret test results. Other educators have argued that the sensitive administration and interpretation of existing standardized tests represents at least an attempt to provide objective information regarding development and achievement. Alternative methods of assessment may pose an even greater threat of bias and misinterpretation.

Standardized and teacher-made tests

Standardized, norm-referenced tests contrast with teacher-made tests (it should be made clear that teacher-made tests may be constructed by the whole staff of a school, or by parents, as well as by individual teachers). We have all taken tests made up for us by our classroom teachers. These tests vary greatly in quality. Table 7-1 summarizes differences between standardized and teacher-made tests.

In this section, we have discussed aspects of those formal and informal assessment tools known as "tests." Table 7-2 presents examples of the four distinct types of tests and their uses. Who, you may wonder, administers these tests? Administering developmental tests requires some knowledge of behavior. Many behaviors on which these tests focus are ones that the classroom teacher would be capable of observing (e.g., determining whether a child can speak in sentences of two words). The group tests in Table 7-2 probably can also be given by the classroom

Table 7-1 CHARACTERISTICS OF STANDARDIZED AND TEACHER-MADE TESTS (AND IMPLIED ADVANTAGES AND DISADVANTAGES)

CHARACTERISTIC	STANDARDIZED	TEACHER-MADE
Relevance	Measures achievement based on *groups* deemed to be *similar* to this class.	Measures teaching objectives developed for this class.
Balance	Measures a large variety of learning objectives regardless of subject material or how much time is spent on this material *in class.*	Measures what was learned of a particular subject material *in proportion to the time spent teaching the material.*
Difficulty	Though the percentage may vary, each item is designed to be answered correctly by about 50 percent of the children.	Gears the level of difficulty to the group.
Reliability (consistency)	Normally, 0.85 (or 85 percent) reliable, or higher.	If carefully constructed, teacher-made tests have as high reliability as standardized tests.
Time parameters	Typically, there are rigid time limits.	Not usually timed; children have plenty of time to complete the test.
Discrimination	Attempts to discriminate between children doing well and those doing poorly on each item.	Each question might distinguish between children who are doing well or those doing poorly; in the case of a criterion-referenced test, this is meaningless.
Specificity	Attempts to measure specific learnings common to a large number of similar groups.	Measures specific learnings of material studied by the group.
Objectivity	Answers have usually been checked by experts.	Experts would agree on correct responses credited on each item.

Source: Adapted from Wall & Summerlin, 1972, p. 36.

teacher. The individual intelligence tests usually require someone who has been trained to give the test.

OBSERVATIONAL TECHNIQUES

Tests are important instruments of assessment, but there are other methods and tools of evaluation as well. Perhaps you can remember someone observing your performance in school—running the track in the gymnasium, giving a speech in class. Methods of observation, both formal and informal, provide valuable information about how we do something as well as about what we are able to do. When you were in elementary school, did the principal come to visit your class? The principal was observing the classroom environment and the performances of the teacher, and of you and your classmates. Techniques of observation are used to document both processes and outcomes of development.

In this section, the purposes and some of the methods of observing and recording observations will be discussed. Many educators and researchers who criticize reliance on paper-and-pencil tests for assess-

Table 7-2 A SAMPLE OF CHILD ASSESSMENT INSTRUMENTS AND THEIR PURPOSES

| NAME OF INSTRUMENT* | FOR AGES | WHAT DOES IT ASSESS? | | | | WHEN WAS IT DEVEL-OPED? |
		PURPOSE	TYPE	AREAS ASSESSED	HOW ARE RESULTS REPORTED?	
Gesell Developmental Schedules (GDS)	4 weeks to 6 years	To diagnose	Developmental	The maturity of the young child's nervous system in adaptive, motor, language, and personal-social areas	As a developmental quotient: DQ = maturity divided by chronological age	1934, 1940, 1941
Denver Developmental Screening Test (DDST)	2 weeks to 6 years	To diagnose early detection of developmental delays	Developmental	Areas same as those of the GDS	As DQ; reliability and validity high, widely used	1967
Griffiths' Scale of Mental Development	2 weeks to 2 years	To diagnose; (not with the pretense of measuring intelligence)	Developmental	Locomotion, personal-social, hearing and speech, eye-hand coordination, performance (achievement)	As IQ (intelligence quotient) but not conceived of as fixed	1954
Cattell's Infant Intelligence Scale	2–30 months (can continue with Stanford-Binet for older children)	To study development, used by research groups	Developmental	Areas revised from GDS; large motor and personal-social items altered or not included; benefit of short administration time: babies don't tire as with Bayley's Scales	Mental age (to one-tenth of a month); also IQ (same method as Stanford-Binet)	1940
Bayley's Scales of Infant Development	2–30 months	To study development	Developmental	Thirty behavior ratings of mental and motor development	Developmental assessment and mental scores	1969 (revision)
Uzgiris and Hunt's Infant Psychological Development Scales (IPDS)	1–24 months	To assess Piagetian stages of development	Developmental	Visual pursuit and object permanence, development of means, imitation (vocal and gestural), development of operational causality, object relations in space, schemes for relating to objects	As assessed step of infant on each of the seven area scales	1964, 1966, 1972

Test	Age	Purpose	Category	Description	Scoring	Dates
Engelman's Basic Concept Inventory (BCI)	Preschool and kindergarten	To assess understanding of basic concepts	Readiness	Repetition and completion of statements, awareness of patterns	As four subscores assessing each area	1967
Illinois Test of Psycholinguistic Abilities	2–10 years	To assess abilities	Readiness	Auditory, visual, verbal, and memory measures	As twelve subscores assessing each area (MA, PA)	1961, 1968
Metropolitan Readiness Tests (MRT)	Kindergarten and 1st grade	To assess abilities related to school performance	Readiness	Word meaning, listening, matching, alphabet, numbers, copying, total, draw-a-person (optional)	As seven or eight subscores assessing each area	1933, 1969 (revision)
Peabody Picture Vocabulary Test (PPVT)	2½–18 years	To assess vocabulary	Achievement and readiness	Vocabulary and matching a word to one of four pictures	As total score	1959, 1970
Caldwell's Preschool Inventory	3–6 years	To assess abilities	Achievement	Variety of areas included; standardized on disadvantaged child population	As total score	1965, 1970
Stanford-Binet Intelligence Scale	2 years and older	To assess intelligence	Intelligence	Individual intelligence	As IQ	1913, 1973 (3d revision)
Wechsler Preschool and Primary Scale of Intelligence (WPPSI)	4–6½ years	To assess intelligence	Intelligence	Fourteen areas related to verbal and perceptual performance	As fourteen subscores, verbal scale IQ, performance scale IQ, and full scale IQ	1949, 1967 (revision)
Wechsler Intelligence Scale for Children (revised)	6–16 years	To assess intelligence	Intelligence	Ten areas (two optional) related to verbal and perceptual performance	As ten subscores, plus verbal scale, performance scale IQ, and full scale IQ	1974 last copyright to date

* Information regarding these and other measures is available in Buros, 1974.
Sources: This chart was compiled from information presented in Buros, 1974; Lewis, 1976; Spodek, 1978.

ment suggest that we perfect our skills of observation in order to assess and document development more effectively.

When should we observe and record children's behavior?

The answer to that question is: "Continually." Observation of children provides us with invaluable information for planning programs, and observation needs to be an integral aspect of our planning as teachers. Whether we are aware of it or not, we are continually observing others and interpreting our observations.

What do we observe?

We observe specific behaviors and, over time, patterns of behavior. From our observations, we make inferences about the processes of development that we think are at work. We cannot observe Linda's mental processes involved in her dealing with the concept of conservation of volume, but we can observe her transfering liquid into and out of two beakers of different shapes that hold the same volume. We cannot observe Johnny learning to "talk out" his anger instead of hitting, but we can observe him on the playground asking for his turn in the game for the very first time. We interpret Johnny's behavior to mean that he has learned something new about interpersonal relations and about himself.

Who observes?

Formally and informally, teachers, administrators, researchers, parents, and children themselves observe. Observational clues guide the teacher's plans for working with each child. These clues alert us to special needs of children so that we can arrange for services to diagnose and work with these needs. The accuracy of our understanding of a child depends upon our *observation skills*, upon the *variety of situations* in which we have observed the child, and upon the *length of time* over which we have collected our observations. Over time, we begin to identify typical behavior *patterns* as well as typical bits of behavior. Behavior patterns must be interpreted in the context of: (1) the setting in which the pattern is usually recorded, (2) the stimulus that usually precedes the behavior, (3) the behavior itself, (4) the sequence of behaviors, and (5) the time period over which we have observed this pattern of behavior.

How do we observe?

Experienced teachers base many of their judgments on observations. How can we direct and refine observational techniques so that the value of observation is recognized and respected? Some suggestions follow.

Name of child _Sarah J._   Date _September 18, 1979_
Observer _J. Jones_   Time _10:02 a.m._
Setting _Housekeeping Corner with James_
Incident:

Sarah forced James into the high chair and insisted that he play baby while she played mother.

Is this report cross—filed?   Yes _✓_   No _____

Is supporting information available?   Yes _____   No _✓_

What is it?_____   Where is it?_____

Figure 7-1
Anectodal record.
(Source: Form from
C. Cartwright
& G. Cartwright,
1974, p. 145.)

Diary record   The diary record is a journal of experiences in the classroom setting. The diary record, in narrative form, may focus on a specific child or learning-center area, or on your own experience as a teacher.

Anecdotal record   The anecdotal record is used to document specific incidents. A sample form for recording anecdotes might look like Figure 7-1.

Selective record   Selective records focus on some specific aspect of program operation (such as children's conversation at snack time) or the children's choices of learning centers (see Figure 7-2).

Observer _____   Week of _____

Directions: Each time a child comes to the center and spends at least 5 minutes there, enter a tally mark in the appropriate space.

Figure 7-2
Learning center
interest assessment;
example of a selective
record. (Source: Form
from C. Cartwright
and G. Cartwright,
1974, p. 166.)

Learning center	Day					Total
	Mon.	Tues.	Wed.	Thurs.	Fri.	
Science area	ⅢⅢ Ⅰ	ⅢⅢ	ⅢⅢ ⅠⅠ	ⅢⅢ ⅠⅠ	ⅢⅢ ⅠⅠ	32
Book corner	ⅢⅢ ⅠⅠⅠⅠ	ⅢⅢ ⅠⅠⅠ	ⅢⅢ ⅢⅢ	ⅢⅢ Ⅰ	ⅢⅢ ⅢⅢ	43
Puzzle corner	Ⅲ	Ⅰ	ⅢⅠ	Ⅰ	ⅠⅠ	11

Behavior scales, ratings, and checklists   Scales and ratings serve to order observed behavioral responses. A scale may consist of points on a continuum, such as low-, medium-, and high-level behavior. In other words, you have a series of items progressively arranged according to value or magnitude of difficulty (see Table 7-3 for an example of scaled problem-solving behaviors). The profile of mathematical abilities for kindergarten through third grade shown in Figure 7-3 is another example of progressive scaling, though neither zero point nor equal increments are indicated. The key to effective checklists is the planning involved in their construction. Well-planned checklists enable rapid recording of behavioral information. Keep in mind, however, the words "Nothing in excess," and ask the question, "Are the results worth the cost in time and energy?"

Developmental histories   Developmental histories are records of a child's early development. They include such events as the pregnancy and birth process, the development of the child in early infancy, and the illnesses contracted by the child.

Home visits by the teacher   A visit by a teacher to the home serves several purposes. Visits can facilitate communication between teachers and parents. Since the teacher is visiting the family on its own ground, rather than at school, the parents may feel more at ease. Home visits give teachers an opportunity to observe children in a setting other than the classroom. In addition, teachers may meet other family members who are not able to visit the school. Records of home visits in narrative, or diary form, are appropriate. Checklists or ratings are not appropriate, because they imply that certain specific characteristics should be present in the home and shift the focus from the dynamics of the human relationships in the setting. However, an open-ended questionnaire, kept in the mind of the teacher, may increase the productivity of the visit. Table 7-4 is an example of questions from a longer interview.

Case studies   Case studies are in-depth analyses of individual children, typically including information gathered from several sources. They aim at discovering and forming explanatory concepts of complex relationships. Many important discoveries have been made through this intensive method of concentrating on a single case (e.g., the work of Piaget).

Cumulative records   Cumulative records include confidential data gathered by teachers regarding a child's past behavior and performance on standardized measures, accounts of conferences with parents, and information about the child's health. The records are usually passed on from one year to the next, following the child from level to level.

Table 7-3 PROBLEM-SOLVING OBSERVATION SCALE—MEASUREMENT

	Observer and/or coder _____ PROBLEM-SOLVING OBSERVATION SCALE
	Time _____ (Lower to higher behaviors;
	Context _____ for young children)
	Type(s) of problem(s) _____ Teacher number _____

CODE NUMBERS AND DESCRIPTIONS	CHILD CODE NUMBERS, TALLY, AND LINE NUMBER							
	1	2	3	4	5	6	7	8
STRUCTURAL/OPERATIONAL VARIABLES								
1 *Response Tendencies and Problem Finding*								
1.1 Ignores problems when they arise (No response or irrelevant response)								
1.2 Responds to problem directly affecting self but ignores problems affecting others								
1.3 Responds to problems affecting self								
1.4 Responds to problems affecting others as well as self								
1.5 Invents or seeks out problems to solve								
2 *Generation of Hypotheses*								
2.1 Generates no hypotheses (0)								
2.2 Generates partial ideas that might be worked into an hypothesis								
2.3 Generates one hypothesis								
2.4 Generates more than one hypothesis when prompted								
2.5 Generates multiple hypotheses with no prodding (fluency)								
3 Use of Resources								
3.1 Uses little or no resources either from self or others								
3.2 Uses resources from others (external)								
3.3 Uses own resources (internal)								
3.4 Uses available resources in novel ways								
3.5 Turns failures into successes								

Source: First three items from a 16-point scale by Sara W. Lundsteen.

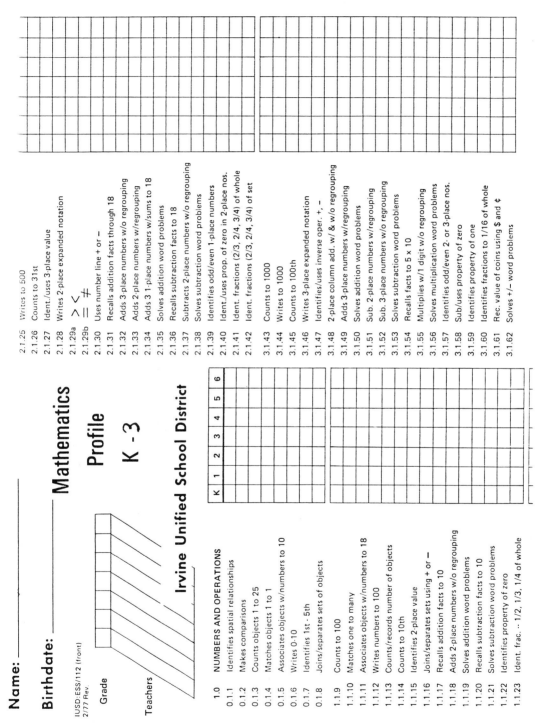

Figure 7-3 *Mathematics profile. (Source: Irvine Unified School District.)*

Name: _____

Birthdate: _____

IUSD:ESS/112 (front)
2/77 Rev.

Mathematics

Profile

K - 3

Irvine Unified School District

Grade

Teachers

	K	1	2	3	4	5	6

1.0 NUMBERS AND OPERATIONS

0.1.1 Identifies spatial relationships
0.1.2 Makes comparisons
0.1.3 Counts objects 1 to 25
0.1.4 Matches objects 1 to 1
0.1.5 Associates objects w/numbers to 10
0.1.6 Writes 0-10
0.1.7 Identifies 1st - 5th
0.1.8 Joins/separates sets of objects

1.1.9 Counts to 100
1.1.10 Matches one to many
1.1.11 Associates objects w/numbers to 18
1.1.12 Writes numbers to 100
1.1.13 Counts/records number of objects
1.1.14 Counts to 10th
1.1.15 Identifies 2-place value
1.1.16 Joins/separates sets using + or −
1.1.17 Recalls addition facts to 10
1.1.18 Adds 2-place numbers w/o regrouping
1.1.19 Solves addition word problems
1.1.20 Recalls subtraction facts to 10
1.1.21 Solves subtraction word problems
1.1.22 Identifies property of zero
1.1.23 Ident. frac. -- 1/2, 1/3, 1/4 of whole

2.1.25 Writes to 500
2.1.26 Counts to 31st
2.1.27 Ident./uses 3-place value
2.1.28 Writes 2-place expanded notation
2.1.29a $>$ $<$
2.1.29b $=$ $\neq$
2.1.30 Uses number line + or −
2.1.31 Recalls addition facts through 18
2.1.32 Adds 3-place numbers w/o regrouping
2.1.33 Adds 2-place numbers w/regrouping
2.1.34 Adds 3 1-place numbers w/sums to 18
2.1.35 Solves addition word problems
2.1.36 Recalls subtraction facts to 18
2.1.37 Subtracts 2-place numbers w/o regrouping
2.1.38 Solves subtraction word problems
2.1.39 Identifies odd/even 1-place numbers
2.1.40 Ident./uses prop. of zero in 2-place nos.
2.1.41 Ident. fractions (2/3, 2/4, 3/4) of whole
2.1.42 Ident. fractions (2/3, 2/4, 3/4) of set

3.1.43 Counts to 1000
3.1.44 Writes to 1000
3.1.45 Counts to 100th
3.1.46 Writes 3-place expanded notation
3.1.47 Identifies/uses inverse oper. +, −
3.1.48 2-place column add. w/ & w/o regrouping
3.1.49 Adds 3-place numbers w/regrouping
3.1.50 Solves addition word problems
3.1.51 Sub. 2-place numbers w/regrouping
3.1.52 Sub. 3-place numbers w/o regrouping
3.1.53 Solves subtraction word problems
3.1.54 Recalls facts to 5 x 10
3.1.55 Multiplies w/1 digit w/o regrouping
3.1.56 Solves multiplication word problems
3.1.57 Identifies odd/even 2- or 3-place nos.
3.1.58 Sub/uses property of zero
3.1.59 Identifies property of one
3.1.60 Identifies fractions to 1/16 of whole
3.1.61 Rec. value of coins using $ and ¢
3.1.62 Solves +/− word problems

Table 7-4 PARENT INTERVIEW*

CHILD'S NAME _____ DATE _____
PARENT(S) INTERVIEWED _____

Note: Frequently insert the child's name for the words "your child."
Introductory (Open-ended—following the lead of the parents' topics)
1 Tell me something about your child. (If parents mention no concerns, ask, "What are some of your concerns?")

Family relationships
2 Who lives with you and your child? (Try to get ages—or approximate ages—for siblings and other adults living with the child.)
3 Which member of the family would you say your child is most like? Why? (If parents are hesitant or say vaguely that the child is like all of us, you can ask, "If you had to choose, which one would you say?" or "In what way is he [she] like so-and-so?")
4 What member of the family would you say your child is least like? Why?
5 How do you make family decisions? (If you need examples, you might say, "If different members want to watch different TV programs, how do you decide which channel to turn to? Who decides what clothes your child will wear to school?")
6 Think of a time when your decision was different from what your child wanted and tell me about it. What happened in the end? Are you pleased with the results?

Typical day and responsibilities and discipline
7 Tell me about a typical day for your child. (If the parent describes a school day, ask, "What about on the weekends?" Conversely, if a parent describes a non-school day, ask, "What about on school days?" Pay careful attention to descriptions of various routines, such as rising, bedtime, and eating times. How does the parent describe these?)
8 Describe your child's chores and responsibilities at home. How does he (she) feel about them?
9 How does he (she) go about doing them? (Is the child planning? Rebelling? Complying? Getting both chores and fun accomplished?)
10 Does your family have a pet? If so, who takes care of it?

Source: Adapted by Carol Mason Wolfe from a 30-point parent interview compiled by graduate students at North Texas State University under the direction of Carolyn G. Maurer, Ph.D.

In conclusion: Observational techniques

Table 7-5 lists the observational techniques we have just described and poses questions that each technique may be used to answer.

Development and use of observation skills are important for several reasons. Observation tells us much about what a child has learned or accomplished and at what stage of development a child is reacting. Observation supplements test results and can provide invaluable insights into the causes of behavior and the emotional states of children that elude assessment by tests. Observations can be made by children, teachers, parents, and others. Each observer has a slightly different perspective (and probably is observing the child in a distinct setting). The decisions as to *who* records behavior, *what* behaviors are recorded, *where* the behavior is observed, and *when* behavior is observed are all

Table 7-5 METHODS OF OBSERVING CHILDREN

TECHNIQUE	QUESTIONS ANSWERED
Diary record	How does each day go for you as a teacher? How would you describe the center or classroom environment today?
Anecdotal record	What specific incidents are especially illustrative of child or program development in the educational setting?
Selective record	What aspects, e.g., of the snack time routine are continually observable? How does a particular child behave in a given school routine or area from day to day?
Behavior scales, ratings, and checklists	How well-developed is a child's large-muscle development? How well (measured on a continuum or in terms of scaled behaviors) can the child solve a problem? Ride a tricycle? These scales may be completed by teachers, parents, and other program participants to give added perspectives.
Developmental histories	What can others tell you about a child's early development (medical history, early child rearing, etc.) that will assist you in understanding the child's behavior in the present?
Case studies	What formal and informal measures and records can help you create the most complete picture of a child's development?
Home visits by the teacher	Can your relationship with a child's parents and family enhance your work in the classroom? Who are the significant people in the child's home life that you may never meet in the educational setting?
Cumulative records	What information have past teachers and school personnel gathered regarding an individual child?

factors related to our *reasons* for observing a certain child. The trained teacher (or parent) can use the recorded observations to design more individualized programs.

SOME CONCLUDING THOUGHTS ON TOOLS OF THE TRADE

A thorough documentation of broad dimensions is the approach to early childhood assessment currently advocated. Such documentation includes background history, medical records, anecdotal materials, records of contacts with parents, samples of the child's work in a variety of media, "draw a person" samples, curriculum records, interviews with children and their parents, sociograms (or friendship patterns), and records of cooperative reviews by the staff of case studies. In the past, we were carried away by the so-called objectivity of standardized, normed measures of achievement. We need to educate and sensitize our human judgments through intensive observation.

Assessment of Teachers

EVALUATION Evaluation is designed to tell us how well something is being done. Certainly, the teacher concerned with developing effective teaching-learning strategies, derived from a thoughtful educational philosophy, will also be concerned about how well he or she is succeeding. In almost all instances, teachers are subject to evaluation by others whether they like it or not. It is also advisable for teachers to evaluate themselves.

Evaluation by parents

Parents share information with each other about teachers' personalities, styles, and techniques. The grapevine quickly transmits information on "who the best third grade teacher is," or "how good the new teacher is." The criteria are varied: sometimes they have to do with personal qualities ("She has such a lovely smile and such an affectionate way with kids"); sometimes they have to do with technique ("He really gets those kids to give their all").

Open lines of communication between teacher and parents help ensure that, at the very least, such judgments will be based on accurate information.

Evaluation by children

Children also evaluate teachers. Older children actively share information with each other ("You can't get away with anything in her class"). Younger ones often transmit information to their parents or to the teacher in somewhat less direct ways ("Why is Miss Marston so mean to Suzie?").

Because younger children's interactions with their teachers give clues to their opinions, a teacher should notice these things:

- Do the children initiate contact with you?
- Do they show affection and trust?
- Are they eager to share their experiences with you?
- Do they accept suggestions or criticism of their actions and not construe these as put-downs?
- Do they look to you as a resource? (Hess & Croft, 1972)

Evaluation by colleagues

Teachers' gossip about children, parents, and colleagues is notorious. But your colleagues can also be a source of constructive criticism and guidance.

You can informally gage the opinions of your colleagues by considering how they respond to your suggestions, how they react to your opinions, whether they seek you out, and whether they are willing to share their ideas with you.

There are also more informal ways of getting evaluation from your colleagues. If there is mutual trust and respect, you can ask a colleague to observe you in your classroom. A checklist is helpful and increases objectivity. Welcoming each other into classrooms to observe techniques and share materials is extremely valuable. Modeling will always be an effective means of changing behavior, and it can be particularly effective for the beginning teacher.

Evaluation by supervisors

Most educational programs also provide for systematic observation and evaluation of teachers by their supervisors. In some cases, this is formalized into a set number of visits and written observations per year, sometimes by supervisory staff members at several levels. This type of evaluation has traditionally been the source of much concern, especially to younger teachers.

If such observations are truly designed to assist teachers in refining teaching skills, a copy of the observational instrument should be given to each teacher before the observation, and there should be feedback soon after the observation. Some teachers prefer to know in advance when observations will take place; others prefer not to know, so that they will not be anxious. If possible, their preferences should be taken into account.

Some programs separate the functions of personnel concerned with job security from those concerned with strengthening the teaching staff. Supervisors who serve the latter role function more as consultants, and teachers feel free to call upon them for help and suggestions, to acknowledge areas of weakness, and to obtain assistance in improving these areas. This can be most effective—if the goal is to develop a staff of highly competent teachers.

What criteria are used in supervisors' evaluations? Some supervisors use checklists, rating such things as "teaching effectiveness," "control," "rapport," "personal qualities," and "compliance with school policies and procedures." Others prefer to write a narrative report. Generally such a report includes:

- Descriptive information—subject, materials, grouping, etc.
- Comments—strong and weak areas
- Suggestions and recommendations

What do supervisors look for, or value? Principals have told us that they value:

- Feeling welcome in the room
- Being regarded as resource persons for teachers
- A positive attitude toward suggestions
- The teacher's ability to continue the class without frequent explanation to the principal
- Consistency in tone and attitude toward the children whether or not the principal is present
- Effective teaching-learning strategies

How can the new teacher reduce anxiety about supervision? It is helpful to plan carefully, to avoid transmitting anxieties to the children (who will probably fulfill your worst fears if you do), and to proceed on the assumption that since you are *always* doing your best, you do not need to do anything differently during a visit. It is also helpful to invite a supervisor, especially if you are trying out new ideas or want to introduce the supervisor to your own style and techniques of teaching.

Self-evaluation

The toughest evaluation the teacher should have to face is self-evaluation. Truly dedicated teachers are their own severest critics as they strive to perfect their skills; relate to other teachers, parents, children, and classroom assistants; and continuously grow and develop professionally. Ultimately, the only type of evaluation which will achieve these goals is self-evaluation. Information from all other sources has to be funneled through the teacher, to be assimilated and acted upon, in order for any change or growth to take place.

Some helpful techniques of self-evaluation include the following:

- Arrange to have videotapes made of you interacting with your class. Analyze the tapes and note areas to work on.
- Tape-record some of your interactions with children. Analyze these, particularly with reference to your own verbalization.
- Use a checklist which includes different teaching skills.
- Keep a diary of your experiences and reactions.
- Keep a list of experiences that made you feel uncomfortable. Try to understand why.
- Utilize information obtained from observations of supervisors.
- Utilize information from observation by colleagues or friends.
- Integrate the information you get from children, colleagues, supervisors, parents, and self-analysis to form a program for self-improvement. (Adapted from Hess & Croft, 1972)

ACCOUNTABILITY   "Accountability" is a frightening word for many teachers. It is not easy to make an account of a set of events as complex as a child's behavior and growth. Should teachers be held accountable for the specific content mastered by children? Combs (1976) has suggested that the responsibility of teachers lies in the *organization* and *communication of our goals* in teaching and in our supporting learning and development. All of us may choose to employ different methods and to present different content to children. The important thing, according to Combs, is that we know why we are doing what we are doing, why we use certain methods. It is important that we are able to communicate this to others and to design activities for assessing various aspects of child and program development. There is a relationship between accountability and program evaluation. Increasingly limited economic resources and increased doubts regarding the effectiveness of our educational systems have moved concerned community members and their legislators to demand proof of positive outcomes of our programs for young children.

Actually, the abstract concept of accountability is present in all ordered societies which hold their members responsible for the development of specified individuals. The important question about this concept is, "Who is accountable for what?"

One danger of accountability may lie within us. An abstract system is rarely bad or good inherently, but there may be something in teachers that is drawn to authority and conformity, something that causes us to take some pleasure in handing down a constricting influence. On the other hand, most of us realize that education is a social process of interaction with other humans—imperfectly measurable, unpredictable, cyclical. And like the submerged part of an iceberg, much human behavior and growth is not visible.

Who, then, is accountable in as humanistic a way as possible, and to whom? Teachers are accountable for providing optimal learning experiences matched to individual needs and interests. Colleagues, agreeing on their hopes for the welfare of children, learn how to trust one another, and how to use constructive criticism for mutual growth. Parents are accountable for supplying a nurturing environment for children and for helping to develop appropriate learning programs. Administrators are accountable for ensuring that the school climate is appropriate for the educational process. Wider communities are accountable for providing financial, cultural, and social support. Children are accountable for being active participants in the learning process. And we are all accountable to the children. We are learning to listen to them, to receive their messages discernible in movement—i.e., in their facial expression, in their dramatic play, and in their picturing (their art)—and not just in language. Their feelings tell us much about our programs— as we explore them next.

Assessment and Evaluation of Programs

Many people, including parents, teachers, and researchers, are interested in knowing what results are achieved by different early childhood programs. Program evaluation is an intimate part of program planning at all stages: when we are initially designing our program, while we are implementing it, and after we have completed it.

Evaluation may be said to fall into three types: diagnosis, formative evaluation, and summative evaluation. *Diagnosis* usually occurs before teaching, helping the teacher to fit objectives and instruction to particular children. *Formative evaluation* occurs during the teaching process. That is, if evaluation is ongoing *during* the implementation of our program, assisting us in making day-to-day improvements in our planning, it is called "formative." If evaluation seeks to describe the outcomes of our programs *after* completion of the program, it is known as "summative evaluation." Program planning needs all these types of evaluation. When we engage in formative and summative evaluation, we are gathering information about the operation and long- and short-term results of our program. Such information helps us to improve the programs we provide for infants and young children.

As teachers, we conduct formative evaluation in many ways in order to learn about the short-term effects of our program instruction. Most summative evaluation is initiated by people other than teachers. These people try to answer questions concerning the long-term effects of our teaching and the implications of our work for planning future programs. Teachers can help to contribute to the accuracy of information gathered and its interpretation when summative evaluations are conducted by outsiders.

DIMENSIONS OF PROGRAM EVALUATION

Program evaluations focus on a great variety of dimensions in addition to children's development and achievements. Methods used in evaluation need to cover and match the stated goals of the program. Our knowledge of strengths and limitations of various types of instruments for assessing children is central to our ability to assist in designing, implementing, and analyzing comprehensive evaluation plans. Figure 7-4 illustrates a few of the dimensions and appropriate tools for assessment that might be used to measure and document these program elements.

Some factors in early childhood programs make them difficult to evaluate. Preschool programs are often unique; they differ from each other in more significant ways than programs for older children do (Miller & Dyer, 1975). In preschool programs, there are multiple goals not only for the children but often for the parents, staff, and surrounding community as well. Recently, programs for children of all ages have included an emphasis on parent and community involvement (see Chapter

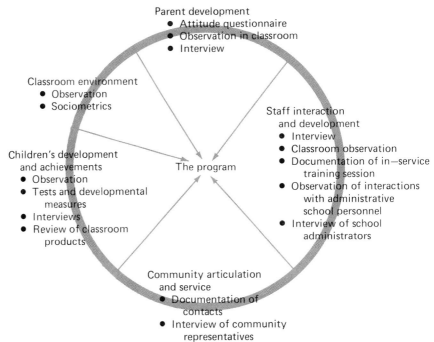

Figure 7-4
*Some elements in
program evaluation.*

15, which deals with such cooperation). The intimate relationship between development of parents and development of children is often integral to programs for infants and very young children. (See Chapter 3.)

Change of goals is another important consideration. Since young children are developing and changing at a very rapid rate, parents and staff often need to change their goals for both child and program. Thus, not only do early childhood programs have many goals, but these goals shift and change as children grow and develop. To use an analogy, the summative evaluation of a preschool program is as difficult as measuring a child's foot for a pair of new shoes when the child can't hold still long enough to be measured.

**SOME LARGE-SCALE
EVALUATIONS
OF THE PAST:
DIFFICULTIES
AND LESSONS**
Evaluation is often tied to the problems of funding. In order to justify the expenditure of public funds for early childhood programs, evaluations are frequently used to document the progress made by children as a result of their participation in the program. Evaluations indicating little or no progress may lead (rightly or wrongly) to cutting off funding, because the program fails to show results sufficient to impress the funding agency. And sometimes if children's achievement is much *higher*

than it was before the program was implemented, the program may fail to receive renewed funding, teachers and administrators having apparently done their jobs so well that they and the children are penalized by the discontinuance of funding necessary to the program. In such instances, personnel may occasionally attempt to skew results to indicate lower levels of effectiveness and thus retain funding for their program. Such actions associated with large-scale thrusts are, of course, highly undesirable.

If economizing is a concern, significant amounts of money can be saved by employing sampling techniques: sampling students tested and sampling items in tests. That is, not every child has to take every test or every item on the test. This practice applies when the goal of the assessment is a comparison among large groups (e.g., states and large districts). The achievement of those large groups gives an indication of the program's effectiveness.

In essence, it is our responsibility to understand the nature of program evaluation so that we may appropriately use and communicate the information it offers us. We need to prepare ourselves to comment regarding the design of the evaluation, the instruments, and the procedures used. The greater the knowledge we possess on types and methods of evaluation, the more integral the role we play and the greater our voice in the planning and evaluation of our teaching programs. Be informed; be articulate; be idealistic on the behalf of children.

Summary

In this chapter, we have presented important issues and aspects of the assessment and evaluation of children and programs. It was noted that through both formal and informal methods of assessment, teachers build expectations about children's potentials and abilities, and these expectations often determine the types of experiences teachers plan for them. Assessment gives clues about abilities and achievements that must not be misused to label children. Formal assessment is usually carried out with tests, and four different types of tests were described: developmental, intelligence, readiness, and achievement tests. Distinctions were made between standardized and teacher-made tests and between norm-referenced and criterion-referenced tests. Tests have sources of bias limiting their purposes and the interpretations of results.

Informal assessments are usually carried out by means of observational techniques, several of which were described (diary records, anecdotal records, selective records, behavior scales, ratings, and checklists, developmental histories, home visits, case studies, and cumulative records). We noted that observation (supplementing the results of tests), provides valuable insights into emotional and behavioral situations that elude assessment by tests. Although observation techniques tend to be more subjective than test results, this very subjectivity can be a positive factor allowing for highly valid and competent judgments. The tool of observation has served well a range of persons from the skilled and experienced practitioner to the distinguished researcher who has observed small, significant details of children's behavior, put them together to form patterns of development, related these to abstract concepts and to theoretical constructs, built systems to be tested, and provided us with significant advances in knowledge of early childhood. Observation—don't belittle its potential power.

The issues of evaluation and accountability of teachers were raised. Aware of their responsibility in the broad spectrum of "Who's accountable for what?" questions, teachers assess both children and programs as a means of improving programs for children. Careful planning and evaluation of activities involving young children represents a commitment to the continual improvement of early childhood programs.

As we have seen, programs for infants and young children vary according to a combination of factors, including the people who are being served, the curriculum and developmental philosophy that guides the teachers in program planning, the involvement of parents and the community as a whole. It is possible for all of us to read the same books and to describe our goals in similar words. Yet, when we implement programs, their content and style are determined by the unique contributions of program participants. Teachers are optimally involved in diagnosis of individuals as they search for strengths to build upon, and in both formative and summative program evaluation as they seek to increase effectiveness in meeting young children's needs.

References

Brophy, J. E., & Good, T. L., Teacher's communication of differential expectations for children's classroom performance: Some behavioral data. *Journal of Educational Psychology*, 1970, *61*, 365–374.

Buros, O. K. (Ed.) *Tests in print, II*. University of Nebraska, Lincoln, Nebraska: Buros Institute of Mental Measurements/Gryphon Press, 1974. Also: Buros, O. K. (Ed.) *Eighth mental measurements yearbook*, 1978.

Cartwright, C., & Cartwright, G. *Developing observation skills*. New York: McGraw-Hill, 1974.

Combs, A. W. Educational accountability from a humanistic perspective. *Educational Researcher*, 1976, *2*(9), 19–21.

DeVries, R., & Kohlberg, L. Relations between Piagetian and psychometric assessments. In L. G. Katz (Ed.), *Current topics in early childhood education*. Norwood, N.J.: Abley, 1977.

Gordon, I. J. A home learning center approach to early stimulation. In J. L. Frost (Ed.), *Revisiting early childhood education*. New York: Holt, Rinehart and Winston, 1973.

Hess, R. D., & Croft, D. J. *Teachers of young children*. Boston: Houghton-Mifflin, 1972.

Lewis, M. (Ed.). *Origins of intelligence*. New York: Plenum Press, 1976.

Lundsteen, S. W. *Children learn to communicate*. Englewood Cliffs, N.J.: Prentice-Hall, 1976. (Chap. 11.)

Messick, S., & Anderson, S. Educational testing, individual development, and social responsibility. *The Counseling Psychologist*, 1970, *37*, 80–88.

Miller, L., & Dyer, J. L. Four preschool programs: Their dimensions and effects. *Monographs of the Society for Research in Child Development*, 1975, *40*(5–6, Serial No. 162).

Murphy, L. B. The stranglehold of norms on the individual child. *Childhood Education*, 1973, *49*, 343–349.

Spodek, B. *Teaching in the early years* (2d ed.). Englewood Cliffs, N.J.: Prentice-Hall, 1978.

Uzgiris, I. C., & Hunt, J. M. *Assessment in infancy: Ordinal scales of psychological development*. Urbana: University of Illinois Press, 1975.

Wall, J., & Summerlin, L. Choosing the right test. In D. A. Payne (Ed.), *The assessment of learning*. Lexington, Mass.: Heath, 1972.

PART THREE

CURRICULUM AND DEVELOPMENT

Before you read the group of chapters on the real world of curriculum, we have several explanatory statements we consider crucial. We introduce them in the form of questions about four topics: curriculum, roles of teachers and learners, goals and objectives, and consistency in viewpoint.

How can the different curriculum areas be organized? *The chapters to follow on curriculum illuminate the developmental areas: psycho-physical-motor, cognitive, linguistic, and affective. Within each of our chapters on curriculum, organized by developmental areas, you will find illustrative ideas drawn from various subject areas. Play, for example, is related to development in all of the four areas listed above. Further, formal subjects (e.g., mathematics, science, social studies, reading) grow out of informal curriculum areas (play, sharing). This organization substitutes for the more traditional subject-by-subject or time-of-day organization. The intent is to demonstrate the prominence of development and of integration. Thus, a specific content area or activity (e.g., story time or reading) will not be a "be all and end all"—or a "tail that wags the dog."*

Is it more productive to focus on process for learning or on content to be learned? *The material to follow stresses a process orientation in the early years (rather than concentrating on isolated bits of content). We believe that if we give children chances to experience processes, they can keep on learning joyously, independently, and skillfully. Content in the early years is really the means through which children learn processes. Later they can apply these processes* (e.g., association, classification, problem solving) to any content. When we give Bobby in the primary grades the problem-solving processes of reading, we send him forth able to expand his world and able to find answers to many of his questions. When we help Susan, an infant, to distinguish between objects that she can and cannot place in her mouth, we are helping her learn to classify—a process she will use later, e.g., in classifying objects which bounce and objects which don't and (much later) in classifying countries which are democracies, monarchies, socialist states, and dictatorships. We generally reserve the word "skill" for rather automatic behaviors, such as holding a brush, automatically recognizing the letters of your name, and automatically writing them.

Which gives children the best opportunity for growth, a free program or a structured one? In our opinion, it is important to avoid confusing freedom with anarchy or structure with inflexibility. Children need freedom to explore, manipulate, question, and compare—but within safe, reasonable limits that do not constrain the rights of others. Most children appear to prefer a structure they can trust and move out from when they risk new adventures. For example, kindergartners like to know that they can generally count on a certain order in their day, that there will generally be a quiet time on the rug with the teacher after outdoor play, or that they can count on clean-up after work time and before any new activity. Toddlers are more comfortable when they know what is and is not permissible and do not have to find to their surprise that today taking out all the plastic toys from the cabinet is forbidden, when yesterday it was not only permissible but "cute."

Relational structure of goals, objectives, and activities.

How are goals, objectives, and activities related? *An early childhood program designed to enhance development in basic areas is structured by goals. These are few and have a long-range orientation rather than a short-range orientation ("Pass the test tomorrow and see how much we taught"). For example, the goal of developing the child's ability to communicate verbally pervades an entire early childhood program. For each goal, however, there are many related objectives, e.g., recognizing key vocabulary words or dictating stories. Growing out of these goals and objectives are the day-by-day learning activities. Again there may be many activities for each objective; for instance, informal games to build vocabulary, or sharing time for opportunities to speak interactively.*

The whole relational structure (goal, objective, activity) resembles a tree. The trunk might be the goals; the branches, the objectives; and the twigs and leaves, the varied activities. We like this analogy because we can add the further idea that any examples of such "trees" (which we give in the chapters to follow) can have new growth added to them, by you, the teacher, so that unique and additional material results.

Why not take a bit of this and that from many programs and points of view? *Early childhood teachers need to take a clear-cut position. We do not condemn eclecticism (borrowing bits of many differing programs) as long as the rationale behind these programs and the practices they suggest is consistent. For example, we suggest capitalizing on the best of several mathematics programs which proceed from similar points of view about children and learning. But the borrowing of activities and practices indiscriminately can lead to a chaotic or, at best, an inconsistent situation. For example, rushing into the use of pages of addition computation from one program before the child has succeeded at suggested experiences in one-to-one correspondence from another program seems to us a kind of professional irresponsibility based on superficial knowledge. By reading the chapters in this part of the book, we hope you will not only begin to achieve an intellectual hold on curriculum, relating it to what you have learned about development, but will also begin to form a consistent developmental viewpoint to guide your future selection of curriculum.*

CHAPTER 8

"We are underexercised as a nation. We look instead of play. We ride instead of walk. Our existence deprives us of the minimum of physical activity essential for healthy living."

—*John F. Kennedy*

CURRICULUM FOR PSYCHO-PHYSICAL-MOTOR DEVELOPMENT

Those concerned with the education of young children agree that a significant portion of the curriculum needs to be devoted to activities fostering perceptual development, physical growth, and motor skills. Teachers, administrators, school boards, and parents recognize the fact that these areas provide a foundation not only for mental and physical health but also for academic success. In practice, however, whenever we are faced with budget cuts, an outcry over the need to return to the three R's or a demand to remove the so-called frills from our educational programs, this is an area which becomes the scapegoat and is often reduced or slashed from educational programs. After having read Chapter 4, on psycho-physical-motor development, however, you now know how important an area this is. After reading this chapter, you will have had help in answering the following questions:

- What are the differences between perceptual-motor programs, physical education programs, and movement programs? What are the appropriate uses of each?
- What are the characteristics of movement education programs and some specific teaching techniques needed to implement them?
- What services can be provided for young children in the areas of health and nutrition?
- What is the nature of programs for infants?
- How can children's creative problem solving be included in a psycho-physical-motor development program?

Introduction

Current programs in psycho-physical-motor curriculum reflect a variety of theoretical foundations and major goals, historical trends, views of the complexity of the organism's interactions, and innovative approaches to curriculum.

The goals of any program in the psycho-physical-motor domain include these *areas:*

- Motor development
- Physical fitness
- Perceptual development
- Social and emotional growth

Since gross *motor* skills are fundamental, programs attend to goals related to development involving large-muscle control through running, jumping, climbing, and other locomotor skills. Programs also include goals related to small-muscle development accomplished through lacing, stringing, cutting, and drawing. *Fitness* can be developed through activities stressing strength, endurance, flexibility, ability, and balance. Activities that provide opportunities for children to judge similarities, differences, distance, height, and speed all contribute to the devolpment of the perceptual skills needed for success in physical as well as academic endeavors. Activities which foster sensory awareness—refinements of hearing as well as seeing, touching, and tasting—are all important in fostering *perceptual development.* Psycho-physical-motor programs also develop alertness, quickness of response, decision-making, and general self-confidence essential to mental development. We foster *social-emotional growth* through development of self-confidence, cooperation, leadership, democratic processes, and feelings of personal and group success (Hackett & Jensen, 1966).

Physical Education Programs

Until recently physical education programs have been directed at children from kindergarten onward; little or no attention has been given to programs for children below the age of five. Although physical education programs vary greatly from place to place, they typically have a specific time set aside for them. Often a classroom teacher (especially of young children) who does not necessarily have special training is responsible for conducting this type of class.

Instructional periods for younger children vary from those devoted entirely to activities totally directed by teachers to those devoted to activities undirected by teachers (i.e., "free play"). Most programs attempt to balance free play with teacher-directed activities aimed at developing specific skills. As a rule of thumb, it might be said that until recently, the younger the children, the more time spent in free play; the older the children (particularly those in the middle elementary school years), the more they engaged in teacher-directed activities. These activities have commonly consisted of competitive games, individ-ual activities designed to develop bodily and motor functioning, and dance activities. Calisthenics and exercises using small and large appa-ratus are common.

Until recently also, physical education programs appear to have been concerned mainly with working with the average child in groups and with developing skills required for competitive sports.

PHYSICAL EDUCATION: OUR POINT OF VIEW Although traditional physical education programs are theoretically de-signed for all children, in practice they appear to have benefited some types of children more than others. Teaching strategies have been directed at the *average* child; they do not challenge the talented or help the less able child. However, extracurricular activities are almost always geared to talented athletes. If the aim of physical education were to produce professional athletes, this would make sense. But we think it is more sensible to educate all children in use of leisure time for physical activities. In that case, we should pay greater attention to developing skills individually and give less emphasis to competitive sports such as baseball, football, golf, and tennis (Clifton, 1970). If we are also concerned with the development of girls, we need programs that do not inculcate a cultural bias in favor of passive pursuits for girls and more active ones for boys.

Perceptual-Motor Programs

Perceptual development has to do with the ability to receive sensory information from our sense organs (eyes, ears, tongue, fingers, nose)—an input system. *Motor* development has to do with the ability to respond to the information received—how we act in response to certain cues.

Perceptual-motor programs focus on input, or reception, and how it effects performance—in contrast to physical education programs, which focus on performance itself. Perceptual-motor programs are designed to lead to mastery of fundamental perceptual and motor skills by way of logical progressions; they received their impetus from the research and writings of people concerned with special education (Kephart, 1960; Cruikshank, 1963).

Programs receiving wide publicity were developed to work with special—that is, handicapped—children. Some of them were based on the rationale that all children go through universal perceptual-motor stages and that children with developmental lags need intervention programs to return to earlier or skipped stages (Delacato, 1959). Others were based on the rationale that improvement of learning skills would lead to direct improvement in cognitive skills—particularly reading

(Getman, 1962). However, neither of these claims has been adequately substantiated by research.

Often, before we are sure that there really are benefits for all children, new programs developed for a particular group of children are hastily extended to all. This has been the case in the area of perceptual-motor programs. Thus, they are used not only for remedial purposes (as they are in the case of special children) but also in what is deemed to be a preventative approach. The rationale seems to be that, extended to all children, such programs will prevent the appearance of many perceptually related disabilities. Since many psychologists and educators believe that basic perceptual-motor development has taken place by age five, most programs of this nature are directed primarily at the prekindergarten and kindergarten child (Fabricius, 1971).

COMPONENTS OF PERCEPTUAL-MOTOR PROGRAMS

What kinds of skills are stressed in most perceptual-motor programs? A review of many of the existing programs reveals that most of them emphasize:

- Body awareness and image
- Temporal and spatial awareness
- Laterality and directionality
- Form and figure-ground discrimination
- Eye-hand and eye-foot coordination
- Locomotor skills

Body awareness is the recognition of the ways in which the body or part of the body can be controlled, moved, and balanced upon. *Body image* involves knowledge of the physical structure, movements, and functions of the body and its parts as well as the position of the body and of its parts in relation to one another, to other people, and to objects. Awareness of the physical body is important in the development of the concept of oneself as well as in the development of coordination.

Temporal awareness involves an internalized concept of time which allows a child to integrate and organize sequential movement patterns. It involves sequence (order of movements in an action), rate (rhythm of activities), and timing—which is what makes a movement successful or efficient. *Spatial awareness* is the ability to perceive the position of two or more objects in relation to oneself and in relation to each other.

Laterality involves the internal awareness of the two sides of the body and their resulting differences. *Directionality* involves the awareness of, and distinction between, up and down, left and right, front and back.

Form and *figure-ground discrimination* involves discrimination of likenesses and differences and the ability to differentiate specific forms from background. These abilities are considered prerequisites for beginning reading.

Eye-hand coordination is involved in tossing, catching, rolling, bouncing. *Eye-foot coordination* is involved in kicking, leaping, hopping over, and climbing.

Locomotor skills include walking, running, jumping, hopping, sliding, skipping, leaping.

Carefully planned activities in each of these areas are based on the idea that motor development cannot be left to chance.

Motor development, in these programs, is considered to be a prerequisite for learning skills commonly taught in school, such as reading, writing, and numerical computation. Perceptual-motor difficulties are considered by the theorists in this field to block children's academic performance and to hinder their success in the playground skills that are most valued by their peers and themselves.

Since special children seem to learn best by doing, these programs provide a lot of physical activity. Three examples of the many different types of activities suggested for these programs follow.

EXAMPLES OF ACTIVITIES IN PERCEPTUAL-MOTOR PROGRAMS

One activity uses a ladder, and the others use objects for balancing one's center of gravity.

Coordination Ladder
Performance objective:
By moving through the openings of a ladder held on its side without touching it, student demonstrates space awareness, directionality, and body awareness. [See Figure 8-1.]

Challenges:
(1) Creep in and out the windows with ladder on side. (Ladder should be held.) (2) Student is challenged to demonstrate a different way of going in and out the windows. Example: moving backwards, or going through every other window, etc.

Stress:
Student attempts to go through openings without touching parts of ladder. If students are moving too slowly, have them skip every other space. (Capon, 1975, p. 41)

Figure 8-1

Center of Gravity

Blindfolded, try balancing your center of gravity directly over a walking beam, coffee can stilts, or a bench. Experiment with movements in which your center of gravity no longer falls directly over the surface on which you are balancing. Experiment with movements in which you raise and lower the center of gravity, as in walking on tip toes versus walking in crouched fashion. (Texas Education Agency, 1977, p. 21)

Precision

Play Pin the Tail on the Donkey and variations which demand precision while blindfolded. Play dodgeball with the stipulation that the ball must touch a specific body part to earn points. (Texas Education Agency, 1977, p. 21)

PERCEPTUAL-MOTOR PROGRAMS: OUR POINT OF VIEW It is our opinion that these programs must be recognized for what they are—programs to increase perceptual-motor efficiency. Grandiose claims that they increase academic success are not well founded. By giving children opportunities for both physical outlets and successful experiences, these programs probably have subsidiary effects on social and emotional development, including the concepts children have of themselves. They serve as an effective means of early identification of children with disabilities or developmental lag—*if* teachers are trained in careful screening. For children so identified, a concentrated perceptual-motor program is probably effective. For children who are functioning well, however, such programs probably serve no purpose. Although some would claim that they "do no harm and may do some good," such programs *do* take up most of the time usually allocated for attention to children's physical development. We believe this time could be better spent in a program that builds skills while encouraging creative responses, exploration, problem solving, and social cooperation. Such programs, called "movement education," are discussed in the next section.

Movement Education Programs

Movement education is that phase of the total education program having as its goal the development of effective, efficient, and expressive movement responses in a thinking, feeling, and sharing human being (Tillotson, 1970). In a movement education program, a child progresses from uncontrolled to controlled movement by means of opportunities for discovery of self and environment, freedom with safety, communication, enjoyment, and acceptance. Whereas uncontrolled movement can bring with it failure, awkwardness, and disgrace, controlled movement can give the child mastery, rhythm, and grace.

GOALS Movement education provides an opportunity for coming to know oneself through one's own body movements ("I can jump over that hurdle"). Its goals are to help the child gain and develop the following:

- A sense of self—through building of body image
- Gradually, more complex ways and new ways of using the body
- Differentiation and organization of sensory perceptions
- An ability to collaborate socially
- An esthetic sense—through sensory exploration and creative movement.
- An ability to think and engage in symbolic representation—using the body to develop such concepts as shape, weight, and distance
- Problem-solving abilities (Adapted from Gerhardt, 1976, p. 267)

The goals of movement education are attained most meaningfully through exploration and problem-solving experiences (Tillotson, 1970). Tillotson defines *problem solving* as a teacher-guided method involving:

- Presentation of the problem
- Provision of time for exploration with guidance by the teacher
- Refinement and selection of solutions
- Demonstration for evaluation, analysis, and discussion

For example, the teacher may present the problem thus: "Show me how you can support your body on just one point." The children will attempt a variety of ways to meet this challenge (e.g., supporting themselves on one foot, one hand, shoulders, buttocks—and even a head stand) with guidance and encouragement from the teacher. They may then select one position to demonstrate and all participate in observing, discussing, and evaluating various solutions to the problem. This method of teaching and organizing experiences through a *problem-solving approach* is consistent and ongoing throughout a movement education program. It encourages a variety of responses at levels each child finds comfortable.

Movement education also has a unique approach to *content*. The two main content areas are *expressive movement*—in which the body is regarded as a medium for the communication of ideas and feelings (dance and drama) and *objective movement*—to develop powers of body management and skill in the use of all kinds of apparatus (gymnastics, games, athletics) (Cameron & Pleasance, 1971). (Other authors combine athletics and games with dance and drama to develop a tripartite model involving gymnastics, games, and dance.)

In contrast to traditional physical education programs where the aim often is to develop skill in competitive sport and the activities designed to teach the skills involved in these sports, the *long-range goal* in movement education is to inculcate skill in body management. Thus, activities are designed to teach all children skillful use of the body in various situations through combinations of movements based on knowledge of the principles of time, strength, space, and flow. The emphasis, thus, is on what is *happening* to the child, rather than how well he or she can perform.

FACTORS IN MOVEMENT

This section explains and illustrates four major factors affecting movement:

1 Body awareness and actions (what is moved)
2 Space (where one moves)
3 Effort, or quality, of movement (how one moves)
4 Relationships (with whom one moves or what one moves)

Let's consider each of these factors one at a time.

1 Body actions and awareness

Awareness involves learning the capabilities of the body, moving as a whole or using various parts (independently or together). These capabilities are learned through exploration and problem solving. The following are examples of such capabilities:

- Any part of the body may initiate movement into space.
- Various parts of the body can bear body weight.
- Weight can be received from outside objects or from other body parts.
- Weight can be transferred.
- Locomotor movements may be developed from many positions. (Adapted from Gray, undated.)

Body actions can include the following: nonlocomotor skills (e.g., twisting, stretching, bending, lifting, and various combinations of these skills), locomotor skills (e.g., walking, jumping, running, skipping, and various combinations of these skills), bearing weight, receiving weight, transferring weight, and initiating movement.

2 Space

Two kinds of space exist, personal space and general space.

Personal space is the area an individual can reach or use while in a fixed position without intruding into the personal space of others. The nonlocomotor skills outlined above can be used within this personal space.

General space is the area into which the person can move using the locomotor skills outlined above. Through exploration and problem solving, children learn to judge the height from which a ball is approaching, the chances of evading an opponent, or the distance from a "safe" point in a game of tag. And, in learning this they learn that movement into space varies by *direction* (forward, diagonal, upward) and *level* (high, medium, low).

3 Effort or quality of movement

The body needs to adjust to these factors:

- *Time* (speed of the movement—e.g., fast, slow, sustained)
- *Force* (strength of the movement—e.g., light, heavy)
- *Pattern* (direction of the movement—e.g., direct or twisted)
- *Flow* (free, smooth, or hesitant movement)

4 Relationships

Movement can involve relationships with another person (in cooperation or apposition to this person) or an object (which can be used or overcome).

Partner or Apposition	*Objects or Obstacles*
Small group	Small equipment
Large group	Apparatus
Team or side	

ORGANIZATION FOR TEACHING With their stress on problem solving, exploration, individualization, and creativity in programs for children, most movement educators are committed to organizational procedures and teaching methods which place a high value on these characteristics. Both teachers and children are encouraged to be flexible and creative in their choice and implementation of activities. Normally, a teacher chooses a broad area of interest from the elements of movement (body awareness, space, qualities, and relationships). Then the teacher devises tasks appropriate to the stage of development the children have reached. This choice forms the basis of the individual lesson plans. For example, if the theme is "directions," the teacher will devise activities getting children to move forward, backward, sideways, upward, and downward (see Figure 8-2 for further examples).

Planning the individual lesson

The emphasis of an individual lesson is on one particular theme; the teacher, however, may include other elements of movement, supple-

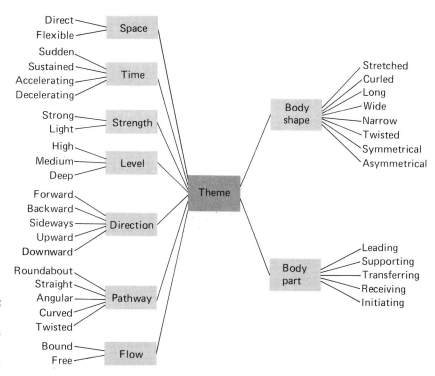

Figure 8-2
Theme development.
(Source: Cameron
& Pleasance, 1971,
p. 24.)

mentary ideas, or review activities. For example, the main focus of a lesson may be on direction (i.e., moving in various directions). But there may be review of work on the theme of time (movements that are sudden, sustained, or increasing or decreasing in speed). Instructional periods are usually divided into the following phases:

• Introduction (including free practice and warm-up)
• Skill development
• Practice
• Conclusion and assessment
• Closing routines (see Table 8-1)

Introduction Children are usually encouraged to start work immediately as they enter the movement education area. Small apparatus are to be set out by the first children ready. Children need to know what they are going to do and how to do it. By having established procedures which are clearly established the teacher can use this time to circulate, ensure that activities are purposeful, and offer individual guidance, coaching, and recognition. It is recommended that the children use only the small apparatus at this time. The teacher typically restricts practice

Table 8-1 SAMPLE MOVEMENT LESSON

A DANCE LESSON

Introductory activities	Development of a movement vocabulary and of a dance idea or concept	The dance—developed, assessed, and revised in several stages	Dance demonstration	Shower
Free response to selected music			Assessment	Dress
Warm up of body			Verbal summary	Return to class

Source: Stanley, 1969, pp. 25–26.

to individual movement skill with or without a partner (Kirchner, Cunningham, & Warrell, 1970). Small apparatus may include:

Balls	Stairs
Ropes	Stilts
Bean bags	Indian clubs
Wands	Tables
Hoops	Balance beams
Tires	Stall bars
Deck tennis rings	Climbing ropes
Scarves	Jump boards
Hurdles	Sawhorses
Mats	Chairs (Fabricius, 1971, p. 152)

The free practice period in the introductory phase will vary, but generally lasts about three to four minutes and leads right into the *warm-up*. During this period, the entire area is used; children are deployed in a "scatter" formation rather than in rows, and each child is responsible for finding and using his or her own personal space. Challenges are directed to the children which increase circulation and provide a burst of activity and an opportunity to practice various movements related to the theme (e.g., move quickly, move slowly, "freeze").

Skill development In this phase, new skills are taught; demonstration by the teacher is kept to a minimum; the setting is informal, with the teacher setting limitations and providing emphasis according to the needs of the children. Children may use small or large apparatus. (Large apparatus may include boxes, stage, benches, springboards, and climbing apparatus.)

Practice Children are encouraged to explore the activity which has been introduced at their own pace and at their own level. Teachers phrase their communication in the form of questions or challenges rather than commands, e.g., "Who can . . .?" "What can . . .?" "How can . . .?" "Show me . . ." "Can you find a new way to . . .?" "What can you do on the . . .?" The children are expected to do as well as they can but not to compete with others (Hackett & Jensen, 1966).

Conclusion and assessment This will give the children a chance to "wind down" and to assess their accomplishments. It should leave the child with an idea of where he or she wants to begin the next movement education session.

Closing routines These include putting away equipment, changing clothes and showering, if appropriate facilities are available.

Suggestions and techniques

The movement education approach places a great deal of responsibility on the children for establishing their own performance limits, disciplining themselves, caring for equipment, demonstrating experiences, and maintaining safety. The teacher needs to establish certain signals. Often just "Stop, look, listen . . . *go!*" is sufficient. The teacher needs to be willing to venture into new areas, to read signs of fatigue, to gage the level of interest, and to regulate the vigorousness or length of lessons appropriately. Talking and discussion must be kept at a minimum, with the emphasis on movement. Each child's progress should be observed and evaluated. While the teacher needs to awaken the critical and analytical powers of children, he or she must also encourage tolerance of others and respect for their efforts.

A note for the novice: If you are thinking of implementing movement education in your classroom for the first time, you may be feeling overwhelmed at this point. Although one of the basic tenets of movement education is that teachers creatively generate and adapt activities to specific children, to get started you may wish to use a fairly complete and well-thought-out teacher's guide. One such guide that has done much of the organizing for you is Gilliom's *Basic Movement Education for Children: Rationale and Teaching Units* (1970). Once teachers have built both understanding and confidence, they can adapt and expand the program. Table 8-2 is an example.

MOVEMENT EDUCATION: OUR POINT OF VIEW We have discussed three different approaches to the development of psycho-physical-motor skills: physical education, perceptual-motor education, and movement education. Which is the best one for you? In order to answer that question, you must consider the background of the children with whom you are working, the environment in which you are

Table 8-2 AN EXAMPLE OF ONE MOVEMENT EDUCATION LESSON PLAN: PATHWAYS

Introduction

(Children sitting on the floor.)

"Today we will work on making different pathways when we move. Have you ever noticed what you leave behind you when you walk in the snow or in the sand? Yes—footprints or tracks so that you can see what pathway you took. Right where you are, can you make different pathways with your fingers on the floor?"

(Start—stop.)

"There are two main pathways you can make—curved ones and straight ones. Or if you put two straight pathways together with sharp corners you can make a zigzag path. Can you make straight and curved and zigzag pathways on the floor with one hand or one leg?"

(Start—stop.)

"This time, try making different pathways in the air with a hand or a foot . . . curves, straight lines, zigzags.

(Start—stop.)

SIXTH SET OF PROBLEMS:
DEVELOPMENTAL PROBLEMS AND EXPECTED OUTCOMES

PROBLEM 38

BEGINNING GRADE	MIDDLE GRADE	LAST GRADE
"On the signal, move into general space to see how many ways you can make a curved pathway on the floor." ". . . If there were snow or sand on the ground, what kinds of tracks would be behind you? . . . All curved ones? . . . Can you make a big curve and then a small curve (change of range)? . . . Can you make a curve to one side and then a curve to the other side (change of direction)? . . . Have you tried making a high curve then a low curve (change of level)? . . . no collisions."	Repeat all material from Beginning Grade, and then add: ". . . Keep making curved pathways on the floor, but see on how many different body parts you can move." (Free exploration. Then . . .) ". . . Have you tried moving on hands and feet? . . . Tummies? . . . Backs? . . . One foot (hopping)? . . . Two feet together (jumping)? . . . Two hands and one foot? . . . no collisions."	Repeat all material from Beginning and Middle Grades, and then add: ". . . Try making *one side lead* on one curve and the *other side lead* on the next curve? . . . Do you find yourself *leaning into the curve* almost as if you were on a bicycle? . . . Have you tried moving backward to make a curved pathway on the floor? . . . Try making different shapes while you move in a curved pathway."

CHECKLIST OF QUALITY FACTORS FOR PROBLEM 38

Moving in a wide variety of ways in curving pathways.

Suggested minimums:
    B—6 ways (changing range, level, direction);
    M—12 ways (including locomotion on different body parts);
    L—14 ways (including moving backward and in different body shapes).
Avoiding collisions with others by using the space well.
Continuing to be well distributed over the floor space.

When children demonstrate these factors, go on to Problem 39.

Source: Gilliom, 1970, pp. 103–104.

working (physical facilities, educational setting, and community), and your own educational philosophy. We believe, however, that the goals and activities of movement education best fit the developmental-interactionist approach which we advocate, and also that movement education most appropriately meets the varying needs and interests of all children.

Of course we must stress that movement education—like any other program, no matter how praiseworthy—must be adapted by individual teachers for the individual abilities, interests, and goals of children in their own classes.

What Else?—Infants, Health and Nutrition, and "Setting the Stage"

What else is important in the psycho-physical-motor curriculum? We concern ourselves here with programs for infants, the role of assessment, attention to nutrition, health and safety, and setting the stage for optimal psycho-physical-motor development.

PROGRAMS FOR INFANTS How early should programs in psycho-physical-motor development begin? The answer to this question depends on how one defines "programs." If a "program" means providing the child with a variety of materials that stimulate sensory awareness and encourage movement, with an environment that encourages problem solving and exploration as well as physical growth, we believe such a "program" should begin in earliest infancy. If, however, the word "program" means a planned series of exercises for the parent or caretaker to perform with the infant, we not only question the value of such efforts but suggest that they have a detrimental effect. Parents and children are placed under undue pressure by many of the current "infant stimulation" programs.

When you are out observing programs for infants, here are some positive aspects to look for, contrasted with negative instances:

- *Opportunities for natural interaction between parents and children.* Too often, in some highly structured programs, precious time for interaction between parent and child is ineffectively used or lost. Rather than encouraging interaction between parent and infant, many infant stimulation programs place the parent in an *active* role and the infant in a merely *reactive* one.
- *Stimulation that encourages sensory awareness and movement.* Even today investigations have turned up instances of deprivation of most opportunities for stimulation (infants drugged or restrained by straps). Less startling are rather barren atmospheres.

- *Opportunities for free play.* Sometimes the activities of the infant stimulation programs displace the kind of play that fosters the development of sensory-motor skills. Furthermore, external stimulation must not interfere with the developing neural integration that allows infants to begin controlling random movements.

Bromwich (1977) points out that research does not support the assumptions upon which most infant stimulation programs are based. There is a wide variation in the ability of infants to control their own actions and to use environmental stimuli profitably. (See Chapter 13 for an example of an infant center program directed to identification of infants with developmental handicaps.) We turn next to a consideration of health services and health education.

HEALTH SERVICES AND EDUCATION Any efforts to foster psycho-physical-motor development of children must take into account the health services and education offered to children and their families. In order to implement such programs, there needs to be long-range planning involving a cross section of the professional health talent in the community and clear-cut goals. The goals established for Head Start and federal day care programs are appropriate for any early childhood program. The goals are two: (1) to improve a child's present functioning by finding and remedying health defects, and (2) to ensure a child's health by preventing health problems through activities such as immunization and health education (Project Head Start, 1967).

It is helpful for teachers of young children to have information on community sources of funding and services. Such information is important both in planning programs and for use in referring families to various health services. Services need to include screening tests (including vision, hearing, speech, and physical growth), medical and dental examinations, provision for keeping records, and treatment, follow-up, and preventative measures.

The environment

Good health is fostered by establishing an environment which promotes good health and safety practices. Attention must be given to:

- *Rest.* Young children need a daily rest period. Mats or cots with clean sheets need to be provided, a quiet, semidarkened place available, and variations in children's needs taken into account.
- *Heat and light.* Temperature needs to be controlled, and fresh air and adequate lighting must be provided.
- *Children's medical needs.* Teachers need to be aware of allergies, medication, and unusual reactions, and how to deal with them.

- *Procedures for dealing with sudden illness or emergency.* Teachers should know what to do in these situations. First aid equipment and someone trained in its use must be available.
- *Inspection.* All equipment and material should be checked periodically to ensure that there are no sharp edges, splinters, or other unsafe conditions.
- *Cleanliness.* Although there should be provision for "making messes," reasonable standards of cleanliness need to be maintained—both for the environment and for the adults and children in it.
- *Health of adults in the environment.* Everyone who comes in contact with children should be required to pass a medical examination and to undergo a chest x-ray.
- *Communicable diseases.* Adults with any communicable disease should be kept out of contact with children. Children with communicable diseases should be kept home. If they arrive at school, they should be sent home or isolated from the other children until they can go home.

Health education

Through health education programs, children and their families learn about many services and resources available to them. Health education programs also help establish greater consciousness of good general health and good dental health. It is important to help children and parents overcome resistance to medical examinations, to set healthful examples for children, and to provide opportunities for them to practice good health habits. Through health education programs, children learn about:

- Brushing their teeth by brushing daily in school
- Nutrition by eating and discussing well-balanced meals and snacks
- Personal hygiene by washing hands before meals and snacks and after using the toilet
- Pedestrian safety by going on neighborhood walks and field trips
- Accident prevention by eliminating safety hazards and developing new skills
- Environmental sanitation by using wastebaskets, trash cans, and clean-up procedures
- First aid procedures and healthy attitudes toward minor accidents by observing how the teacher handles them
- Appropriate attitudes towards physical handicaps by learning to interact with children who are handicapped
- Safety or fire prevention by visiting with police officers or firefighters

Formal presentations to both parents and children can also be useful. Doctors, nurses, dentists, and psychologists can be invited to discuss appropriate areas of concern (adapted from Project Head Start, 1967, p. 44).

NUTRITION SERVICES AND EDUCATION We are often exposed to statements like "You can't learn on an empty stomach" and "You are what you eat." These sayings deserve our serious consideration in guiding young children's learning. The professional and lay literature of the last few years is full of articles dealing with the effects of malnutrition and of food practices and attitudes on children's growth, development, and learning (see Chapter 4). Food and nutrition needs to be integrated into any early childhood program via the feeding program and the child and parent education program.

Snacks and meals planned for children need to ensure adequate nutrition, taking into account what the child generally eats for the rest of the day. Food needs to be served in a pleasant, well-ventilated, and clean area with equipment and utensils scaled for children. A relaxed climate needs to be established to eliminate tensions associated with mealtimes. Some suggestions for implementing a successful feeding program and nutrition education include ways in which teachers can implement Head Start feeding programs:

- Make mealtime an enjoyable experience by helping to create a favorable physical, emotional, and social environment.
- Use mealtimes as an educational experience for the children where they may learn:
  - To acquire taste for a variety of healthy foods
  - To develop a wholesome response toward all food
  - To eat and enjoy a variety of new foods, new tastes, and new dishes
  - To identify and talk about foods
  - To establish orderly meal patterns and healthy eating habits
- Develop helpful table techniques, such as:
  - Proper preparation for meals, including hand-washing procedures and restful activity just before eating
  - "Family-style" meals with warm feelings and pleasant conversation between teachers and children
  - Small servings, with second helpings available if requested
  - Gradual and careful introduction of new foods
  - Patience with individual differences in rate of eating and general deportment
  - Tolerance of restlessness
  - Flexibility as regards children's likes and dislikes
  - Balance in providing clearly understood expectations of behavior and casual handling of spilling, manners, and other behavior
- Be willing to set a good example by their own attitudes and reactions.

- Provide opportunities for growing and cooking foods.
- Build a bridge between the center and the child's parents by sharing ethnic or family dishes (adapted from Project Head Start, 1971).

Meals and snacks can be excellent learning experiences. Teachers can encourage children to learn about, and learn to enjoy, a variety of healthful foods; to develop good eating habits; and to regard mealtimes as a pleasant social experience. Children can experiment with growing certain foods and with cooking. Field trips to discover how food is grown, marketed, and purchased are worthwhile.

Food can actually be a bridge between home and school, and thus between cultures. Parents may participate in nutrition education programs or group meetings dealing with purchasing and preparing food. Parents may be invited to prepare foods for the children, to share recipes, and to suggest particular ethnic or family dishes. Food is often a very effective means of drawing parents into the activities of the center.

SETTING THE STAGE FOR PSYCHO-PHYSICAL-MOTOR DEVELOPMENT

Creating an environment for the optimal development of psycho-physical-motor skills requires attention to assessment, to the physical surroundings (both indoor and outdoor), and to the establishment of a climate that integrates mind and body.

A word about assessment

When your goal is the optimal development of psycho-physical-motor skills, you need to know the children's level of development and what they can do. You assess each child's achievement in relation to the level of development the child starts at and not in relation to the levels attained by other children. The role of assessment in a total program for young children has been fully discussed in Chapter 7. Even preschool children rapidly become sensitive to an evaluative climate, explicit or implicit. Try to analyze what your evaluative climate is or will be. Informal assessment can provide teachers with "blueprints" for instruction for each individual child in a perceptual-motor or movement program; this helps to provide challenge and success.

A word about physical environment

The physical environment is discussed in Chapter 14. Here, we would like to emphasize the value of "open-ended" equipment that allows for multiple uses, including exploration, creativity, and problem solving. We hope that the cement enclosure adorned with swings, slide, and teeter-totter in the playground will soon become as obsolete as the potbellied stove in the classroom. There are a variety of publications dealing with building creative playgrounds. Many items can be obtained free of charge (e.g., cable reels, concrete pipe, utility poles, tires, inner tubes) and utilized in a variety of ways (Hogan, 1974). Use of materials from the natural environment (i.e., water, sand, earth, stones, geological formations, trees) provides a total world to which the child can respond (Friedberg, 1969).

A word about integrating mind and body

Parents and caretakers of very young children have a unique opportunity to contribute to the children's outputs and inputs.

Here is an example of contributions to output. From birth onward, a baby has tried out many movements, repeating those that give satisfaction either directly or indirectly through approval and reinforcement. This tendency can be encouraged by use of imagery: "Let's walk with the wind at our backs. Let's dance with the breeze." "Let's reach up and bring down an armful of air. Can you sit on it? Carry it away?" (Shipley & Carpenter, 1962).

Sensory games are an example of contributing to input. Such games can help increase awareness.

- *Hearing:* "Close your eyes and listen to the world."
- *Seeing:* "How many circles can you see on the beach?"
- *Tasting:* Sweet, sour, spicy.
- *Smelling:* Scents of flowers, spices, foods (Liepmann, 1973).

The word "centering" has been used by the humanistic movement to describe a solid integration of mind and body—an integration considered by many to be as important as knowing how to read. Schools often emphasize the cognitive at the expense of the other aspects of development. We need to balance this emphasis on the cognitive with attention to affective, intuitive, and creative processes. Some educators have recommended helping children to *feel* centered—that is, to experience their own physical and psychological center of gravity. Hendricks and Wills (1975) suggest that teachers and children spend at least 15 minutes a day in a series of exercises: breathing, relaxing, picking up sounds, clearing the head of thoughts, stretching the body, and dissolving tensions Diskin (1976) suggests simple yoga exercises for children, to develop poise, stamina, and powers of concentration; to create a sense of well-being; and to recharge energy. Diskin recommends exercises to stretch the muscles, fill the lungs with air, and help the mind rest. She points out that the word "yoga" derives from a word meaning "joining things together"—in this case, mind and body. According to its adherents, "centering" helps establish a mood or set allowing for the optimal functioning of mind and body. It helps create a union of intellectual, social, emotional, and spiritual potential so that one can be more responsive to the environment. It provides for an interlacing of cognitive, affective, and psycho-physical-motor activity and development.

Summary

This chapter, after introducing the goals of psycho-physical-motor development, discussed three approaches: traditional physical education programs, perceptual-motor programs, and movement education programs. We explained their similarities and differences with regard to planning, teaching strategies, and objectives and indicated our preference for movement education, with perceptual-motor education reserved for children with special needs. We also considered the controversial matter of programs in sensorimotor training for infants; health services and health education; and nutrition services and education. Finally, we discussed recent attention to integration of mind and body and the concept of "centering" to ensure well-balanced human beings.

References

Bromwich, R. Stimulation in the first year of life? A perspective on infant development. *Young Children*, 1977, *32*, 71–82.

Cameron, W., & Pleasance, P. *Education in movement.* Oxford: Blackwell, 1971.

Capon, J. *Perceptual-motor lesson plans.* Alameda, Calif.: Front Row Experience, 1975.

Clifton, M. A developmental approach to perceptual-motor experiences. *Journal of Health-Physical Education-Recreation*, *9*, 1970.

Cruikshank, W. *Psychology of exceptional children and youth.* (2d ed.). Englewood Cliffs, N.J.: Prentice-Hall, 1963.

Delacato, C. H. *The treatment and prevention of reading problems.* Springfield, Ill.: Thomas, 1959.

Diskin, E. *Yoga for children.* New York: Warner Books, 1976.

Fabricius, H. *Physical education for the classroom teacher* (2d ed.). Dubuque, Iowa: Brown, 1971.

Friedberg, M. *Playgrounds for city children.* Washington, D.C.: Association for Childhood Education International, 1969.

Gerhardt, L. A. Movement. In C. Seefeldt (Ed.), *Curriculum for the preschool-primary child.* Columbus, Ohio: Merrill, 1976.

Getman, G. N. *How to develop your child's intelligence.* Luverne, Minn.: Author, 1962.

Gilliom, B. *Basic movement education for children: Rationale and teaching units.* Reading, Mass.: Addison-Wesley, 1970.

Gray, R. *Movement exploration: A discovery approach to elementary physical education.* Omaha: Nebraska Department of Education, undated.

Hackett, L., & Jensen, R. *A guide to movement exploration.* Palo Alto, Calif.: Peek Publications, 1966.

Hendricks, G., & Wills, R. *The centering book.* Englewood Cliffs, N.J.: Prentice-Hall, 1975.

Hogan, P. *Playgrounds for free.* Cambridge, Mass.: M.I.T. Press, 1974.

Kephart, N. C. *The slow learner in the classroom.* Columbus, Ohio: Merrill, 1960.

Kirchner, G., Cunningham, J., & Warrell, E. *Introduction to movement education.* Dubuque, Iowa: Brown, 1970.

Liepmann, L. *Your child's sensory world.* Baltimore: Penguin, 1973.

Project Head Start. *Health services: A guide for project directors and health personnel.* Washington, D.C.: Office of Economic Opportunity, 1967.

Project Head Start. *Nutrition-staff training programs.* Washington, D.C.: Department of Health, Education, and Welfare, 1971.

Seefeldt, V. Recent history and current status of perceptual motor programs. Paper presented at Perceptual-Motor Conference: Theories and Applications, Fairfax County Public Schools, Fairfax, Va., September 16–17, 1977.

Shipley, F., and Carpenter, E. *Freedom to move.* Washington, D.C.: National Education Association, 1962.

Stanley, S. *Physical education: A movement orientation.* Toronto: McGraw-Hill of Canada, 1969.

Texas Education Agency. *Approaches to programs of motor development and activities for young children.* Austin, Tex.: Author, 1977.

Tillotson, J. A brief theory of movement education. In R. Sweeney (Ed.), *Selected readings in movement education.* Reading, Mass.: Addison-Wesley, 1970.

CHAPTER 9

CHAPTER 9

*"If we give people a fish, we feed them for a
day. But if we teach them the process of
fishing, we feed them for a lifetime."*

HELPING CHILDREN DEVELOP COGNITIVE ABILITIES: EXAMPLES FROM SCIENCE AND MATHEMATICS

In this chapter we speak to the teacher in early childhood education who wants to help children to think. We use examples from areas of science and mathematics as illustration, although cognitive development certainly occurs in other areas, notably language arts, social studies, and spontaneous symbolic play (see Chapters 10 through 12). First we present some guiding ideas; then we talk about what the children can do; finally, we suggest what the teacher can do. Since we cannot deal with everything at once and we do not want to stress compartments of the subject matter, we focus on basic developmental processes, letting certain areas serve as illustrations.

Some of the questions this chapter answers are the following:

· What ideas can you use to guide you?
· What are some major goals for periods from infancy to age eight?
· What materials can you find in the classroom laboratory?
· What does the teacher do?

Although part of guiding young children's learning is helping them to think, that does not mean that we forget about their feelings or their social and physical needs. We keep the whole child in mind.

Note: Many ideas in this chapter are based on the research of Kamii and DeVries (1978).

Three Guiding Ideas

As we think about major ideas we would want to keep in mind for a long, long time, three stand out. These ideas represent our many years of reflection on how to develop children's cognitive abilities.

1 FOCUS ON PROCESS AND NOT JUST ON CONTENT

Recall the quote at the beginning of the chapter: "If we give people a fish, we feed them for a day. But if we teach them the process of fishing, we feed them for a lifetime." We advocate not throwing children bits of content ("fish"), but guiding their growth in thinking *processes* so that they can better learn how to learn.

Some curriculum practices for young children appear to stress content more than process. We are more interested in process. Though content may represent today's fact, it may turn into tomorrow's error. Of course, thinking does not happen in a vacuum; as children think, they do deal with content.

For example, a boy has collected three objects and wants to know whether or not they would float. He asks his teacher, "Will these float?"

The teacher responds, not with a "content" answer, but with a "process" question, "How can we find out?"

"We can put them in water," the child responds.

"OK. Try it out and let me know what happens," says the teacher. The child goes to the water table, puts the objects in, and watches. The child is going through the process of learning how to solve problems. The concrete objects (corks, pennies) serve as the content. We use this content merely as a means to developing children's learning processes. (And, incidentally, the closer the whole experience is to the child's natural interests and concerns, the better.)

What we are really saying to the teacher is "Help children to participate, even show them, but don't just tell them." The teacher shouldn't simply say, "The cork and the block float, and the scissors and the penny don't." When that happens, the teacher gives the child little or no chance to develop cognitive abilities—the focus of this chapter.

If the focus of teaching remains on process, children have the ability to recapture learning. Let's consider an example from math. When children are taught by rote that $3 \times 5 = 15$, all is well—as long as they remember that fact. If, however, they forget it (and have learned it strictly by rote), the only thing they can do is guess or ask, or—if they are taking a test—leave this item blank. If, however, they have understood that one of the things that "3×5" can mean is three groups of five objects each, they can use the process of addition or the process of counting beads, sticks, or buttons to arrive at a solution.

2 PROVIDE OPPORTUNITIES FOR CHILDREN TO CONSTRUCT THEIR OWN KNOWLEDGE

Knowledge is built up from within. Too often we spend too much time trying to *instruct* children rather than letting children *construct* their own knowledge. Children come to us with lots of knowledge they have constructed themselves—they are not just empty vessels waiting to be filled by us. And children can't be rushed. There are things, developmentally speaking, they just can't do. It takes a child some time to learn to walk. We can't speed up the process of learning to walk so that it takes just three days. It takes children some time to build a foundation and really learn concepts in science and mathematics, too.

Let's consider an example in which a teacher gives a girl an opportunity to construct her own knowledge. The child has a chance to "mess around" with cylinders (rollers), planks, and small, soft objects. Soon she wants to construct a catapult. She gets the idea that when she jumps on one end of the seesawlike construction, the small objects on the other end fly into the air. First, our child walks around to the "down" end of the catapult. We surmise, as the child hesitates, that she is thinking, "If I jump on the 'down' end, I don't think the objects will fly up." She puts a foot out tentatively, then walks around to the other ("up") end, jumps, and gratifyingly the objects go flying off. The child has constructed for herself a bit of knowledge about physical science. She was ready, the teacher had provided the environment, and the child had a chance to instruct herself. If you watch children carefully, know about child development, know the possibilities of your subject matter area, and allow plenty of chances for children to have autonomy in learning—then you set the stage for children to construct their own knowledge.

3 HAVE DEVELOPMENTALLY APPROPRIATE BUT HIGH EXPECTATIONS —THINK BIG

We have just said, "Don't rush children." But we also want to caution you not to underestimate them. Remember to "think big" about young children when setting goals and planning learning activities. We can forgive ourselves for making small mistakes as we instruct children. Children are amazingly resilient in the face of our small errors; they forgive us, too. The inappropriate word or activity we used last Monday counts for little. What we cannot forgive ourselves for is "thinking small" about children, lacking respect for them.

We are thinking big about children when we value them for what they are, use long-range planning, see long-term results, and help them to stretch to their fullest potential. We can think of our children's major accomplishments (or movements toward them) each morning as we start the day. We can think: "We have this fleeting time together; what big goals are we going to aim for today?"

If we think small about children day after day, cut them down to size, burden them with minutiae, make them dependent on us, coerce them with punishment or bribe them with rewards, we not only do them a disservice but can hold back the forward push for all humanity.

Thinking big should be easy for adults (in the stage of formal operations, supposedly). It is not. There are too many adults who think too small about almost everything almost all the time. They waste everyone's time scrounging for the "nickles and dimes," the trivia in education. Educators, just like children, need guidance and support in trying to think big. That is a large part of the function of this book—to help you to think big about young children.

Teaching at Four Developmental Stages

This section answers the question about teaching goals from infancy to age eight. We use some of Piaget's stages as organizing principles.

SENSORIMOTOR PERIOD: A COGNITIVE GOAL FOR INFANTS

We need to keep in mind that cognitive growth begins with sensorimotor growth. What kinds of experiences leading to cognitive development do we want for children in the sensorimotor stage? Our goals deal with fostering curiosity, and the freedom to explore, to manipulate, and to find problems.

The major cognitive goal at the stage of infancy is the preservation of the infant's innate *curiosity*. Curiosity is the basis for learning. What are some "dos" and "don'ts" when it comes to encouraging curiosity?

- To encourage an infant's curiosity, the caretaker may place the child in varied locations so that the infant is pleasantly surprised.
- Caretakers, intent on protecting children, need to be careful not to stifle curiosity. (Babies are more careful than some might think.) Similarly, caretakers (whether at home or in an institution) should not be overprotective of the environment. A little clutter is a sign of a healthy, curious baby. If children's curiosity is stifled, they can become overinterested (or underinterested) in their caretakers (White, 1975).
- Allow children 8 to 16 months of age to explore the properties of objects—detailed, interestingly shaped objects that move. (A word of caution—these objects should be large enough so that they cannot be swallowed.) Examples are table tennis balls bouncing on a wood floor, big hinges, bottles with big caps, plastic jars with covers, and a big plastic container filled with interesting objects. One of the best ways to let babies explore objects is to put them in a safe area filled with pots and pans, canned goods, and other household objects. One doesn't need elaborate toys and equipment. Avoid caging and confining

children, and placing them in a sterile environment. Cognitive understanding is based on accurate perceptions. Such perceptions require the development of adequate sensorimotor skills (recall Chapters 1 and 5). Optimally, the caretaker provides the child with many opportunities to stretch, move, touch, taste, feel, and manipulate the world of objects.

- Caretakers should interact with children; they should look at, handle, and talk to even the smallest infants as active, participating individuals worthy of respect. The caretaker tells the tiny infant what is about to be done (e.g., "Now you are about to have a bath") and waits for a response. Whenever the infant initiates interaction, the caretaker responds, talking to the baby from his or her point of view and with respect for feelings (according to Magda Gerber, Demonstration Infant Program, Palo Alto, Calif.).

What about systematic programs of infant training? The emphasis in this section does not mean that we advocate subjecting very young children to systematic training periods in climbing, balancing, or grasping (see Chapter 13 for discussion of children with special needs).

In short, then, the major goal of a "curriculum" for cognitive development in infants deals with making the most out of whatever potential the child brings to this world. This goal is accomplished through natural experiences during the child's first years. It helps when the caretaker provides as free and as interactive an environment as possible to serve as an aid to the child's natural curiosity.

PREOPERATIONAL PERIOD: GOALS FOR TWO- AND THREE-YEAR OLDS

The goals for infants (just described) remain appropriate for children of two and three: curiosity, exploration, manipulation. Because toddlers can move more freely, exploration becomes broader. And we are now able to encourage a child's symbolizing. As the child demands labels, we can move into the beginnings of vocabulary development for science and mathematics.

> "What's that?"
> "That's a duck."
> "What's that?"
> "That's another duck."
> "One duck, two duck; *two* ducks."

Children as young as 2½ can use the "how to count" principles (Gelman & Gallistel, 1978). Tending to use as many tags as there are objects to tag, children usually assign a unique tag for each object. Using a stable, ordered list of tags, they often use the last tag to indicate how many things there are. Some children of this age do not count in a conventional way. For example, a child might count a two-item array by saying, "two, six," and might count a three-item collection by saying, "two, six, ten." Interestingly, the same erroneous sequence ("two, six, ten,") may be used *each time* an individual child counts. And even more interestingly, the child uses only as many tags as needed for counting. Furthermore, if the child is asked "How many?" the chances are that the child will respond using the last tag. Thus we see a developing grasp of "how to count" principles and several developmental milestones.

The implications for teachers are that when they are helping children count real objects, they should not force children to be conventional in their counting immediately and should not overcorrect. But teachers can encourage the child to have counting experiences that will lead naturally to accurate use of word labels. Sometimes young children are not too successful in matching number words to objects in a one-to-one way. You can see children "double count" and skip. Again, be patient with the child's motor ability and with partially stabilized rules. If children are having trouble saying one number for each object, help them to separate objects as they count by picking the objects up and putting them someplace, e.g., in a box. In short, provide lots of meaningful counting experiences (Gelman & Gallistel, 1978).

The teacher helps children of this age develop science concepts by providing an environment worth exploring. For example, one teacher brought in a rock collection, a child's large magnifying glass, and a collection of primitive musical instruments—in addition to her usual sand, water, clay, and blocks. The children's "why" questions were encouraged—not squelched. The teacher made careful attempts to figure out what the children really had in mind when they asked questions. The teacher kept all answers brief and concrete—not long and abstract.

PREOPERATIONAL TRANSITIONAL PERIOD: GOALS FOR FOUR- AND FIVE-YEAR-OLDS

Again the goals for the younger children carry forward for those children in transition, the children who are not yet concrete-operational but are getting there. Teachers of children four and five years old, however, have additional goals, which are developed in this section.

Goals for this period relate to the children's ability to ask more complex questions for testing ideas and to their more complex symbolizing—e.g., as they draw pictures and talk about them and as they construct comparative relationships (big-little). As we examine these goals, we keep in mind a broad, process-oriented curriculum. But first, we consider a prerequisite.

A prerequisite for most of these goals is an attitude of *willingness*. Where there is a will there can be a way. If children are unwilling to observe, to manipulate, to compare, or to classify, the best-laid plans of teachers go astray. Thus encouragement of children so that they are open to new ideas and ready to respond is a necessary (though not a sufficient) condition for achieving any goal. A *willing* child will respond to a teacher's "What would you like to know?" or any of the other invitations illustrated below.

Observation

The child observes properties and changes. For example, the children come into their classroom one morning and notice that their bean seeds and nasturtium seeds have sprouted. Children comment on the size and the change.

We can see children learning the properties of wood through firsthand observational experience. We can see a girl observing that she can change the shape of wood by tools. Sawing her wood, she sees a physical change and the creation of a new form—sawdust. As she works, she is observing that force is needed to overcome the resistance of the wood. Observing while handling and smelling the sawdust, she extends her knowledge of this material. If she is given time to manipulate the materials and follow her own ideas, her learning is more meaningful.

Too often teachers demonstrate experiments for children of this age and think they are teaching a science concept. But what happens may look like magic to the child because the child is not getting a chance to act directly on the materials. Even when, for example, children use magnets and observe small objects being drawn to the magnet, they are not observing the effects of their own actions; rather, they are observing mysterious, invisible effects of the magnetic field. The child is not directly involved in creating the event. Other "magic" examples are cold making ice, heat making steam, and the physical change that creates crystals. There is nothing wrong with these "magic" activities, but don't think that the child is grasping scientific concepts.

Manipulation

The child acts upon objects, manipulating them, in order to learn about them. For an example, let's go to the block corner.

> "I can make my block towers tall now."
> "How?"
> "I stack them straight, not crooked."

This child has figured out how to do something by manipulating objects. The boy has not grasped an abstract concept of comparative size and principles of balance, but his manipulations are setting the stage for such development. We have seen him check and recheck his alignment of the blocks; such checking is the foundation of a scientific approach to problem solving.

Meanwhile, at the water table, a girl is acting on objects by blowing small things across the surface of the water. She is finding out how to make the objects move more quickly, how to change direction, and how to make bigger waves. By acting on objects she is beginning to experience principles of motion, speed, force, resistance, and movement of air and water. She is getting the time she needs to make her own meaningful discoveries, building a foundation for scientific inquiry.

Comparisons

Children notice similarities and differences. For example, a teacher and some children are inspecting a collection of fruits that have been cut open—a peach, a mango, a cherry, an orange, and a pomegranate. The children talk about how they are alike and how they are different—the skins, the pulp, and the seeds.

> "These seeds are smaller," comments one child.
> "The cherry skin is smoother than the orange."
> "There are more seeds in the pomegranate than in the peach."

Classification and categorization

The ability to classify grows out of the ability to make comparisons, so that children can place items into groups according to their common properties. Some ways of classfying are by color, shape, size, and general categories (such as furniture, food, and clothing). Classifying is the act of designating something by kind ("That's a duck and that's a duck"). Categorizing is the act of grouping similar things together or putting an item into an appropriate group ("These are all birds").

For example, some children are seated at a table sorting small items they have brought from home—buttons, spools, ribbons, scarves, nuts, and bolts. The teacher encourages them to make their *own* groupings and to collect the groupings they have made in paper plates. Children need time for making their own discoveries, developing their own category systems.

Activities of classification can make a contribution to development of both language and thought, since children classify according to some property. (A *property* is any quality or attribute that enables one to compare objects or concepts. Suitability for eating is a property of many green plants; buttons usually have holes or a shank by which to secure them to an article.) Teachers can encourage children to increase the number of properties—sizes, shapes, textures, colors, and degrees of flexibility—they use to describe objects. Children notice that there is no one correct way of grouping when they see that multiple materials suggest many different ways of categorizing.

One-to-one correspondence

The child can take an object from one group and match it to an object from another group so that a pair is formed, e.g., a brush for each paint pot, a penny for every doll. During snack time, we can see a child giving out one cookie for each child.

Many children at this age level will be able to count in a way that indicates that they are handling *sums* (addition) and *differences* (subtraction). The child in charge of giving out snacks sees that someone has too many cookies and takes some away or sees that someone has too few and adds some cookies. We say more about these operations below.

Seriating (or ordering)

The child places objects in sequential order. For example, in the music corner a child is arranging glasses filled with varying amounts of water and striking them to make a sound so that the glasses end up ordered in a series starting with the glass which makes the lowest sound and ending with the glass that makes the highest sound. In another part of the room, four children are being put in a row from the smallest to the tallest by a child who is staging a bit of dramatic play.

The concept of number is built up from the fusion of two earlier concepts: classification and seriation. A true understanding of number depends first of all on the development of these two logical operations, which underlie almost all types of analytical thinking.

Having discussed classification, categorization, and seriation, let's next consider some other operations that make up a portion of the goals and objectives of developing cognitive ability for this transitional age group. Some simple *measurement* activities for this age include, e.g., seeing how many steps there are from the block corner to the adjacent housekeeping corner, and putting 2 cups of water into the gelatin mix.

Other related functions are the use of *ordinal* numbers (first turn and second turn), and *space* and *time*. We can see children working with spatial concepts when they play "Simon Says" using parts of the body. "Simon says, 'Put your hand on your head,' 'over,' 'under your chin,' and 'to the left,' 'to the right.' " We can see time concepts at work as children begin and end an activity when so instructed, when they plan activities of the day, and when they estimate how long it will take to finish an activity.

One of the best and most simple tests to see whether children have made the transition from preoperational to concrete-operational thinking is seeing whether they have the spatial orientation necessary to copy a diamond. Copying a square is far easier than copying a diamond (in the case of the square, there is more of a match with the frame that a piece of paper makes).

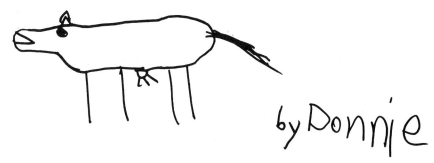

Figure 9-1
*(Source: Prepared by
Don Kingore.)*

Symbolizing

The goal of extending ways of symbolizing can be achieved as the child accomplishes the following objectives.

First the child uses gestures (*enactive representation*). For example, the child symbolizes "duck" by moving like one, making sounds like one.

Second, the child uses blocks, clay, wood, and objects (*concrete, three-dimensional representation*).

Third, the child uses paints, crayons, pencils, and other art media (*two-dimensional representation*). It bears repeating again and again that as children express themselves through creative art media, teachers need to allow them freedom and autonomy to *symbolize* in their own ways, without imposing standards of realistic representation. (For instance, a child's cow, like the one shown in Figure 9-1, does not have to look like the cow the teacher drew, or any real cow.) (Chapter 11 deals further with art curriculum.)

Fourth, the child uses words, numbers, and very simple displays with graphs for *abstract symbolic representation*. We have seen a class of five-year-olds who had made bar graphs to represent the number of children in the class with brown, blue, and green eyes.

Problem solving

When you focus on the goal of developing problem-solving abilities, the chances are that you are involving the child in a meaningful way in most of the other goals we have mentioned so far—at one time or another. The chances are that the goals are meaningfully interrelated and the child is self-motivated. The child can certainly be interested in seriating for the sake of seriating and in classifying for the sake of classifying. On the whole, however, it is when children have problems to solve, goals to reach, and events to explain in situations that intrigue them that such operations are most productively exercised (Piaget & Garcia, 1974).

For example, at the seed center, we see the teacher and children about to plant some seeds. A child speaks:

"Will the little seed make a little plant and the big seed make a big plant?"

Here we have an example of a child identifying a problem *autonomously*.

Teacher: "What's your idea?"

"The big seed will make a big plant."

"I think little seeds make big plants because my dad once showed me this big oak tree and this little acorn that started it."

Here we have examples of *making hypotheses*.

Teacher: "How could we find out?"

To which the children respond, "Let's plant them!"

Here we can see the children beginning to engage in *planning*. They plant the four kinds of seeds, one kind to each of four cups, with an identifying seed taped to the side of each.

For a few weeks the children engage in "observe-test-observe" operations, alternately looking and measuring with a piece of string, and trying to verify results by repeating their activities. As the children decide whether or not the biggest seed did make the biggest plant, we can see them *evaluating hypotheses*, another important part of the problem-solving process. We can see that classrooms are laboratories where children, through play, search for ways to understand their world.

CONCRETE-OPERATIONAL PERIOD: GOALS FOR SIX-, SEVEN-, AND EIGHT-YEAR-OLDS

Again, the goals for the younger children remain appropriate for these older children. We need to strive to protect that precious element, children's curiosity. By the end of the third grade, some children seem to have lost curiosity about anything that happens in school.

First, the teacher checks to see if the children of this age are truly concrete-operational, i.e., if they are conserving, have reversibility in thinking, and can hold more than one variable in mind as they classify (recall Chapter 5). Then, teachers need to give opportunities to children of this age to use these abilities. Operations such as addition, subtraction, multiplication, division, and the systematic testing of variables in science are appropriate. Concrete materials are essential at the beginning of these symbolic operations; workbook pages are not.

Children in this period can classify, extending their ability to hold more than one variable in mind at one time. For example, while reading a story about a doctor, the teacher asks, "Is a doctor ever also a mother?" Conservers have the ability to answer "yes" to this "double entry accounting." They can see a bird as one that eats and one that can be eaten. They can understand that numbers can have various characteristics simultaneously: position, labels, ways of being symbolized, total quantity, sequential order, and infinite progression. They don't confound the conceptual with the quantitative.

With their abilities at multiple classification, children can handle certain concepts which they are taught. "Taught" in this context involves a combination of three things: (1) the readiness on the part of the child (i.e., being concrete-operational), (2) the stimulation of the teacher, and (3) the stimulation of the environment in a context meaningful to the child. Given these conditions, children are stimulated to construct their knowledge and ideas. That is what we mean by "taught."

One of the examples that can be handled when thus taught is the concept of zero. Children are unlikely to attain this concept all by themselves just as a result of counting and other natural experiences. When they have had experience writing symbols for numbers, however, and "the moment" comes—for example, when a child had three grapes and gave them all away—the teacher can help the child symbolize the fact that there is now nothing left by using the word "zero." As another example, the concept of the infinite progression of numbers can have its beginning when the teacher asks, "What happens when you add 1 to 50? What happens when you add 1 to 51 . . . to that . . . to that . . . to 101? What happens when you add 1 to 1,001? Is there a largest number?" "Why?" This format, with many examples, can lead some children to begin to attain the concept of infinity (Gelman & Gallistel, 1978).

In the classroom scene, we can see older children handling money and making change, keeping many concepts, variables, and operations in mind at the same time. We can see them experimenting again with seeds, but now more systematically manipulating many variables; light, heat, water, various kinds of fertilizer, and media for growing. These children are ready for most of the traditional primary-grade subjects found in curriculum guides for districts. But we should not forget that children need to use concrete materials they can manipulate while they are beginning to master these concepts, and we should not just use Ditto sheets, paper-and-pencil tasks, and verbal abstractions.

Materials

It's helpful to see a list of typical materials found in classrooms for the areas of science and mathematics, materials that can, with appropriate guidance by the teacher, help stimulate children's cognitive abilities. (Note: Not all these materials are displayed at once.) A lot of materials are simple things you can find around the house or neighborhood, many of which would otherwise be thrown away, e.g., moldy bread, containers of all kinds, spools of thread, grains, and scraps of material. The following types of things have been found helpful. Each teacher can add specific items according to the interests of teacher and of children.

Some Science Materials for the Classroom Laboratory

Bird feeders
Insect cages
Prisms
Various seeds
Thermometers
Pulleys
Simple machines to take apart and put together
Wires
Magnets (bar, horseshoe)
Wood
Magnifying glasses

Various kinds of soil
Objects to smell, taste, hear, touch
Levers
Compass
Batteries
Plants, terrariums and aquariums
Various pets
Seashells and other natural objects

Some Mathematics Materials for the Classroom Laboratory

Scales
Geometric blocks (cones, cylinders)
Clock
Sticks or counting rods
Items to sort (e.g., by size, texture)
Patterns
Yardsticks
Flannel stories involving mathematics concepts

Geo boards
Cash register
Measuring cups and containers
Pegs and boards
Books with number concepts
Tape measures
Rulers
Stamp pads
Dominoes and bingo

What Does the Teacher Do?

Teachers need more than a basic knowledge of children and materials to be the kind of teachers we want our children to have. In this section we explore "teacher-proof" programs "trust the teacher" programs, and planning strategy. We emphasize the importance of orchestrating and interrelating methods and content that build children's cognitive abilities.

"TEACHER-PROOF" PROGRAMS VERSUS "TRUST THE TEACHER" PROGRAMS

Not all programs, even if they have everything on the lists just presented and much more, foster creative interplay between teacher and child. Programs vary on a continuum from the most "teacher-proof"—in which a script is followed slavishly—to those relying on the teachers' skills in observing and assessing children and abilities in evaluating and choosing learning activities appropriate to the goals and objectives. To trust the initiative, experience, and skills of teachers or to prepare elaborate "follow the recipe" directions—that is the question.

If one believes that programs should be "teacher-proof," the teacher's activities and the materials might look like this. The teacher's role is to *teach* facts, concepts, and principles in a didactic way through a carefully planned sequence of tasks. For example, in one program—DISTAR Arithmetic I—a teacher follows a script for 220 different plans (Engelmann, 1969). The teacher's material consists of 5 books, and the student's material consists of 170 take-home exercises.

Step into this "teacher-proof" classroom for a moment. A group of about seven children are seated in a semicircle around the teacher. The teacher holds the manual, scans it, and says his or her "lines" (which are printed in black). The children respond with the answering phrases (which are printed in green). The lesson is on subtraction.

TEACHER	I have ten and I want to take away four. How many do I have?
CHILDREN	Ten. (All responses in unison.)
TEACHER	How many?
CHILDREN	Ten.
TEACHER	I want to take away four. How many do I want to take away?
CHILDREN	Four.
TEACHER	(Pointing to ten lines she has drawn on blackboard) I have ten. Ready? Nine (point), eight (point), seven (point), six (point). How many did I take away? (The teacher holds up a finger for each line taken away.)
CHILDREN	Four.
TEACHER	How many do I have left?
CHILDREN	Six.
TEACHER	(Writing equation.) Right; ten take away four equals six ($10 - 4 = 6$). (Engelmann, 1969)

If one believes that programs should "trust the teacher," the teacher's activities might look like this: (1) The teacher is guided by the realization that a child's learning is a process of construction from the inside, rather than instruction from the outside. (2) The teacher uses a wide variety of materials (carefully chosen for their value in aiding children's learning). (3) The teacher provides the child with freedom to make choices and construct his or her own solutions through active manipulation. (4) The teacher realizes that children understand only those concepts and generalizations that they find themselves. In this situation, there is a maximum of activity, experimenting, manipulating, and comparing; and as far as possible the children ask the questions and find the answers.

In this informal laboratory situation, the teacher supplies direction when needed and has a clear concept of the purpose of each activity.

Children, working on different tasks, might be seated in small groups at tables using, e.g., abaci, Cuisenaire rods, counting frames, and hundreds boards. They are free to get up and get those materials they need. The teacher encourages the children to consult with one another; they might be recording mathematical operations and discussing solutions.

"How can we find out how many groups of five can be formed out of the thirty-five pencils in this box?" the teacher might ask one small group.

"Why don't you put the sticks in piles of five and see how many piles you get?" suggests one child to another.

In one set of materials encouraging this approach, the content begins with prenumber ideas (such as one-to-one correspondence), then moves to classification and seriation, set relations, and comparisons, operations of addition, subtraction, and multiplication, and also to measurement, geometry, and monetary exchange (Nuffield, 1967). The same concepts appear in increasingly complex form at different stages. Stress is placed on allowing children to manipulate, classify, and involve themselves in a variety of concrete experiences *before* introducing the more abstract ideas of mathematics. The teacher's guides cover the main topic, contain teaching suggestions rather than lesson plans, and deal with how the teacher can interrelate various mathematics topics in a project.

People develop different teaching programs because they bring to the process different assumptions about the nature of teachers, children, and learning. In our view, as trained professionals, the teacher accepts responsibility for observing children, assessing their current stage of development, being well aware of a variety of materials and approaches that could be used, and providing a match between material and child. We have no script, no computer, no teacher-proof materials that can do this nearly as well as a trustworthy teacher—enthusiastic, humanistic, and *prepared*.

How does one approach the "formal" teaching of mathematics as a subject area in the early years? One does not didactically *teach* mathematics. Rather it is the teacher's responsibility to capitalize on critical moments in children's learning by being ready with materials to help children grasp concepts. The teacher is just a step or so ahead of where the children are at any given moment (Lovell, 1971).

We have tried to paint a picture of a balanced classroom—not anarchy, not a room filled with lots of "cute" ideas to occupy children. We have tried to picture a room with activities that are there because they *serve a purpose* for some of the children in that room. Teachers have a responsibility to use their professional skills to observe their children and provide activities to meet their needs.

FOUR STEPS IN PLANNING   How can a teacher plan? If you accept the idea that children need to learn autonomously, then you need to put the idea into practice. Let us illustrate this with science. Teachers typically concern themselves with these questions:

1 How do I *plan* a science activity?
2 How do I *introduce* it?
3 How do I *interact* with the children during it?
4 What kind of *follow-up* is important?

1 Planning

In planning a science activity, teachers are concerned with setting up environments so that children can act on objects. Such environments make it possible for children to see how objects react and how and why they were able to produce a desired effect—recall the girl who was exploring the effects of blowing things on water across a water table. Here is another example: a child who has pens and crayons (fat and thin) and chalk. By letting them drop, the child finds out that the pens do not break like the thin crayons and chalk when they hit the hard floor. The child might try bending the pen, squeezing it, and making marks with both ends. *As the objects react consistently to the same actions, the child builds physical knowledge by recognizing this consistency.* The materials in the environment help to enlarge the repertories of actions children can apply to objects in order to explore their nature.

2 Introducing

In introducing the activity, the teacher needs to be concerned with fostering children's autonomy and initiative. The teacher can be a non-participant-observer or a participant-observer. The teacher can simply put out materials naturally attractive to children: e.g., for the water table, straws for blowing, table tennis balls, cotton balls, floating soap, and corks.

Or as participant-observer, the teacher can say, "See what you can think of to do with these things" (given that the children are familiar with the materials and can come up with some ideas). Or, as participant, the teacher might even propose a more specific problem; e.g., "Can you find something that you can blow across to the other side of the water table?" (Avoid being too specific.) The teacher can introduce the activity in such a way that cooperation among children is possible ("Take a partner, if you like"), but not necessary or demanded. In introducing the activity, the teacher is encouraging the children's initiative to come up with a problem of their own and to wonder. It's better, we think, for children to come up with one question of their own than to answer ten questions that they don't care anything about (Kamii, 1972).

3 Interacting

In deciding how you will interact with children during the activity, you need to watch, figure out what the children are thinking, and respond very briefly, without letting your mind push against theirs. For example, if you see a child blowing harder and harder through a straw down at the object, you might guess that the child thinks that force alone is the way to move the object in the desired direction. The child may not grasp the idea that it is the direction of force (the stream of air) that is also important. When to intervene, if at all, is the most delicate problem of the teaching strategy. You might ask, "What happens when you blow just on top?" or "What would happen if you tried blowing from the side?" *The child's process of trying to figure out the answer is far more important than arriving at the right answer.* Other sample, generic questions are:

"What would happen if you . . . ?" (Acting on objects and seeing how they react.)

"Can you . . . ?" or "Can you find anything else you could use?" (Producing a desired effect.)

"How did you do it?" or "Which works better?" or "Does it make any difference if you . . . ?" (Becoming aware of how desired effects are produced.)

"I wonder why it happened?" (Explaining causes.)

Remember: don't overinfluence the children, but be ready to ward off frustration when it gets too much for the children.

4 Following up

Follow-up can promote desirable reflection on the part of children. Follow-ups can help children think about what they did, what they observed, and what others noticed. It is *not* a time for the teacher to produce the one right answer. Some examples of follow-up questions are:

"What happened when you blew through two straws instead of one?"

"What might you try next time?"

The stress is on the *child's* actions and observations, the feedback the child has received, and the child's organization of this knowledge (Kamii & DeVries, 1978).

SEEKING CURRICULAR INTER-RELATIONSHIPS

Teachers can seek interrelationships among activities and different contents when they make their plans. For example, a teacher exploring living organisms with children may encourage ideas prompted by a walk out of doors that reveals a natural orchestra of katydids, woodpeckers, buzzing bees, and other natural noisemakers. The children discuss and imitate the sounds indoors with various percussive rhythm instruments— a tie-in to scientific concepts of sound and music. An alert teacher can seek transfers from scientific observational processes to children's more sensitively written (or dictated) compositions in the language arts area (see Lundsteen, 1976, pp. 235–316). Alert to interrelationships, the teacher of young children need not set aside a special time of day for science.

With the goals outlined so far in mind, with a teaching strategy, and with an ability to provide meaningful interrelations among learning, the teacher does not need fancy programs or materials. However, if you have been given texts and guides with highly structured "experiments" or activities in them, by your school district or private employer, you can adapt a traditional activity so that the children have more autonomy and are able to act more on objects. Luckily, there is a wealth of activities to redesign that are interesting and likely to capture the imagination of the young child.

HOW TO RECYCLE TRADITIONAL ACTIVITIES

If you have a collection of traditional activities to recycle, the following examples may be helpful. One is for younger children, one for older children.

A traditional activity for younger children: Shakers

Young children love to shake shakers. Save saltshakers, garlic-powder shakers, and various other shaker containers. Put rice, sawdust, or cornmeal in the shaker, and add some powdered tempera colors. Let the child make a design on paper with glue. Then shake the colors onto the design.

Note: Although the children get to make the design by themselves, they have not participated in the earlier steps of this activity. The following are some examples of activities that children *could* be doing:

- Finding containers that could be used as rattles, e.g., cereal boxes, juice cups, milk cartons, shakers, rolled-up pieces of paper secured at the ends.
- Finding contents for the rattles, e.g., blocks, cereal, different grains, small objects, leaves. (Note: Children could look at home, at school, and on walks for containers and what to put inside.)

- Figuring out ways of shaking out just a few of the contents at a time (e.g., putting hand with fingers spread over the top of the container, using a piece of paper with holes, fastening with a loose rubber band).

After the last step, introduce the concept of making pictures with glue and getting the contents of the shaker to stick to the design. Children can handle the shakers, varying their techniques. Encourage alternatives with questions such as "What is another way you could do this?" or "What do you think would happen if you added to your contents?" (The child is encouraged to act on objects and to note how they react. These actions are the beginnings of physical science.)

To encourage the child's own autonomous artistic evaluation (when a child is ready for this) you can ask, "Is this the way you want it to be?" "Why?" "What could you do to make it more like what you want it to be?" Thus in redesigning this activity, we see many more opportunities for developing cognitive abilities.

A traditional activity for older children: Materials that conduct electricity

Let's consider another example. This time it's for older children and a teacher with an adopted or required text featuring traditional science activities (see Figure 9-2). Frequently teachers with such materials start a science lesson this way: "On Thursday from 10:00 to 10:20, we'll do this experiment on page 25 of your book for science period and write the correct answer."

It's possible to be more creative and to be of more help in the development of more cognitive abilities and processes. Let a small group of children "mess around" with the materials listed in the text (plus a few others, perhaps, which you have gathered). Give encouragement: "See what you can do with these things." Then you can take advantage of children's questions (plus a few of your own if need be) to structure the experience.

While manipulating and experimenting with cells, bulbs, sockets, and wires in the lesson in Figure 9-2, a child might ask "Will the light shine if I use a string to connect it?" (predicting reactions and actions on objects).

If the children fail to ask questions and you feel the need for some added stimulation, you might use a puppet to make up a little story and ask questions.

PUPPET "The other day I wanted to turn on my little desk light, but it just wouldn't work, even when I tried a new bulb. I wondered . . ."

A. **Problem:** What materials will conduct electricity?

B. **Materials:**
1. One 1½ volt cell
2. Several feet of #20 wire
3. Several pieces of cloth, wood, glass, rubber, nails, pins, water, and paper
4. Flashlight bulb and socket
5. Knife switch

C. **Procedure:**
1. Connect cell to lamp, lamp to switch, and switch to cell (see diagram).
2. Throw the switch so that lamp glows.
3. Open circuit (as shown in diagram) for place to test materials.
4. Place a piece of cloth connecting the circuit and close switch. Record whether or not the lamp glows.
5. Do the same for the following materials:
   a. glass
   b. wood
   c. nail
   d. pin
   e. paper
   f. water
6. Record the results for each material placed in the circuit.

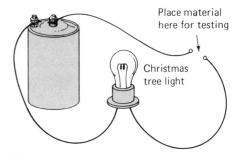

D. **Result:**
The lamp glowed when the nail and pin were used to complete the circuit. The lamp did not glow when wood, glass, cloth, or rubber were used.

Figure 9-2 *A traditional activity from a textbook. (Source: Nelson and Lorbeer, 1976, p. 102.)*

As the children attempt to answer questions, you can help them to formulate their own plans. You could ask: "How could you find out if the light will shine then?" or "What other materials might you need?" If the children mention something not actually found in your textbook, such as hooking up the bulb with a rubber band, be ready to help them and follow their lead (within the confines of safety, of course).*

As the children set up their experiments, you can ask questions related to thinking in terms of cause and effect, explaining causes, or becoming aware of how to produce a desired effect:

"Why do you think using the nail will work?"

---

* A note on safety: As a responsible teacher, you may well wonder if the children might get hurt "messing around" with electricity. Suggestion: Ask the children if they've ever had an electrical shock and how it happened. Ask: "Do you think human beings can conduct electricity? How do you know? What might happen to you if you put your finger in the socket?" Questions such as these usually get the point across, but add your own elaborations as necessary. Be sure, of course, that the materials and equipment you have on hand are appropriate and safe.

You might ask a question related to the child's acting on objects to see how they react:

"What do you think will happen if you connect the paper strip to the bulb?"

And afterwards ask:

"Did it work?" "How do you know?" "What did you do that made the light come on?"

Or if the light did *not* come on:

"How do you know it isn't just a worn-out bulb?" "What else do you think could be preventing the electricity from moving from one place to another?"

Acting on objects to produce a *desired* effect might be reflected in your question:

"Can you find something else that will work, that will make it light up?"

If enough interest is aroused, children may start scurrying around looking for materials to test. During their experimentation, they may wish to record results or simply make two groups: one for conductors and another for nonconductors.

With certain types of questions teachers can encourage comparisons:

"When I did this, did I get a brighter light?" Or: "Which way works better?"

Don't be surprised if such recycled activity leads to further and further experiments. You're setting an environment and a process of inquiry that might spark another Einstein or at least lead to genuine assimilation and accommodation, as children themselves act on objects.

In short, to recycle any traditional activity, use the materials listed, but do not follow the recipe steps. Allow time to "mess around," when you encourage children to come up with questions (asking a few yourself as necessary) and ideas, and to draw their own conclusions.

Once you are confident about recycling traditional activities, you are even ready to take on the impressive experts who hand you (via your school district) a curriculum, field-tested with statistical significances, and flanked by a constellation of published books and articles.

EXPERTS ON CONTENTS VERSUS EXPERTS ON CHILDREN

Suppose you are in a school where you have science materials fashioned by academic-area experts. We have mixed feelings. There are pluses and minuses. Too often these experts know their subject matter discipline but don't know children.

On the plus side, they do think big about children but sometimes too big—i.e., too abstractly for the actual developmental level the children have reached. Some of these programs have as their main goal the development of scientific literacy. They prepare teachers to avoid talking down to children. For example, the teacher moves from saying that "plants make food in the presence of light" to using the precise, brief term "photosynthesize." The idea is that as primary-grade children report their observations and classifications using precise terms, they begin to achieve the goal of scientific literacy. But (on the minus side) encouraged by the experts, sometimes teachers may make too much abstract vocabulary come too quickly, too soon.

On the plus side, the academic experts do know the discipline so that they can structure the knowledge, formulating hierarchies of interrelated concepts. It is appropriate for teachers to know this formal organization. They need to know more than they ever intend to teach children. Besides, when that highly gifted child comes along the teacher might have to use everything he or she knows (or knows how to find out about).

One program is hierarchically built around major scientific concepts of (1) *matter*, (2) *energy* in the physical science units, (3) *organism*, and (4) *ecosystem* in the life science units. ("Ecosystem" becomes clearer when you think of a forest with interdependent plants and animals, sun, air, and water.) These four large concepts give depth to the central concept—*interaction*. ("Interaction" refers to the relation among objects or organisms that do something to one another, bring about changes in one another. Think, for example, of a magnet picking up a steel pin; the magnet and the pin interact.) (Karplus et al., 1970.) But, as we said, too often the experts know the hierarchy, but don't know children. The teacher has been trained for five weeks, the beautiful materials are laid out, and the wrong children walk in the door.

On the plus side, the experts can help teachers to relate the children's findings to key concepts in science as the children "mess around," exploring the environment with various materials. The experts can help teachers to suggest beginnings, engage in discussion, and ask appropriate questions during processes such as observation, measurement, interpretation, prediction, and transformation. Helping children relate their findings to key concepts is something that knowers of children could add to what they do. And the experts will also help those who know children to add to their feelings of professionalism and scientific literacy. By studying the experts, teachers can gain skill in sharing with parents and school officials the significance of what is happening to children in the classroom. But again there is that caution: Subject matter experts may beguile teachers into pressing their minds too much on the minds of children (a common disease of teaching) and into "overcurricularizing."

The balance—taking the best of both worlds, rather than battling—therein lies the art and the science of guiding young children's cognitive development. You cannot make a viable curriculum for children just by sitting in an office and writing. On the other hand, those who only know (or think they know) children may think too small about them. We need a new breed of specialist who knows both content and children. When curriculum makers and teachers do not take the time to find out what and how children are thinking, many of our children in the primary grades become disabled by the curriculum. They have been immersed in confusing content too early, too quickly, and too abstractly.

"OVER-CURRICULARIZING"

In one of our educational pendulum swings (as a reflection of subject matter expertise), we began "overcurricularizing" almost everything (Elkind, 1979). To illustrate: A child expressed an interest in dinosaurs, and the next day the teacher had a week's worth of structured lesson plans with formal "musts" for observation, measurement of dinosaurs, classification of dinosaurs, drill on positional words "on," "above," "under," work sheets, word analysis "games," and twenty-five measurable objectives, all on dinosaurs—until almost all the children were exhausted and turned off.

Actually, the children may have taken a liking for dinosaurs because of a developmental need to associate themselves with something powerful and strong, when they were so small and weak. What the child needed was just symbolic play (that ultimately gives rise to poetry, art, science, and progress). (See Chapter 12, page 351.)

When we "overcurricularize," when we cut off symbolic play and its transformations which children find meaningful, we run risks. We risk the danger that children will not get a chance to pursue personal feelings and concepts and to express them in their own way. If children have become fascinated with dinosaurs, it is because they have *transformed* this difficult concept into one that makes sense to them. Should we start curricularizing and leave no room for the children themselves? Again, what we ask for is balance, some quiet corners, some time and space, some areas where children can symbolize and transform on their own.

Summary

This chapter began with three guiding ideas for the teacher interested in developing cognitive abilities: (1) focus on process and not just on content; (2) provide opportunities for children to construct their own knowledge; and (3) have developmentally appropriate but high expectations—think big. By the end of the chapter we added two more guiding ideas: (4) look for chances for interrelating the child's experiences, in part by letting children focus on problems or challenges of interest to them; and (5) leave time for play by not "overcurricularizing" everything.

The chapter continued with goals designed for four periods in the young child's life: (1) sensorimotor for infants (with a big emphasis on enhancing the child's natural curiosity), (2) preoperational for twos and threes (with chances for development of vocabulary added), (3) preoperational transitional for fours and fives, and (4) concrete-operational for sixes, sevens, and eights (not all children are concrete-operational in all areas at these ages).

Because of the emphasis of this book, we stressed the preoperational transitional period for fours and fives, paying attention to many goals for children. These goals were: observation, manipulation, comparisons, classification and categorization, one-to-one correspondence, seriating (or ordering), symbolizing, and problem solving. We stressed that as young children see objects reacting to their actions in regular ways, they build knowledge by structuring the regularity of this feedback; it is thus they come to learn and know their world. This is one of the most significant ways young children develop cognitive abilities. The goals are cumulative (more and more demanding operations are added). The goals are spiral. For example, problem solving can become more and more scientific as the child has chances to use this process again and again throughout life. We gave suggested lists of classroom materials appropriate to our stress on children's manipulating and acting on objects during the attainment of these goals.

Next we turned our attention more specifically to what the *teacher* does. Here we encountered the issue of "teacher-proof" programs versus "trust the teacher" programs. The teacher-proof program tries to make the steps so small and so spelled-out that the children are going to learn carefully sequenced bits of knowledge almost in spite of any teacher. Programs that trust the teacher, on the other hand, are guided by the principle that the children learn from the inside out; such programs provide children the freedom to make choices and construct solutions through their actions on objects. The classroom resembles an informal laboratory with children using different materials. The teacher in this kind of program watches children, knows children, and gives attention to four planning steps.

These steps are (1) planning, (2) introducing, (3) interacting, (4) following up. In *planning*, teachers set up environments so that children can act on objects rather than being mystified by "magic" in science or mathematics. In *introducing*, the teacher can be a non-participant-observer or a participant-observer doing the delicate balancing act of asking a productive question at a productive time. The teacher can encourage children to exchange ideas with each other, or not. In *interacting*, the teacher first watches the child carefully to try to figure out what the child is thinking. The child's process of trying to figure out is more important than question or answer. In *following up*, the children transfer what happened into word symbols for reflection in order to organize what happened, to assimilate and accommodate it—a most important way of developing cognitive abilities.

Since you will be teaching in the real world and will probably be supplied with much traditionally oriented material, we suggested ways for adapting such materials to a more developmentally oriented approach. Such adaptations would focus on the actions *the child* uses to construct knowledge. We maintain our view that in light of the rapid expansion of scientific discoveries, children need chances to use investigative *processes* as they interact with their environment. In this way, children build foundations for understanding the nature of our universe—for science and for mathematics.

We all want the best cognitive development for children, the "teacher-proofers," the "overcurricularizers," and the developmental interactionists. We suggest that we'll help children over the long term more solidly, with better long-lasting attitudes, a surer foundation, and with better curricular interrelationships, if we trust more and watch children with a "developmental" eye and see to it that they have environments in which they can learn processes.

References

Elkind, D. *The child and society*. Paper read at the Early Childhood Education Summer Workshop, Federation of North Texas Area Universities, Dallas, Tex., June 15, 1979.

Engelmann, D. *Distar arithmetic I, An instructional system*. Chicago: Science Research Associates, 1969.

Gelman, R., & Gallistel, C. R. *The child's understanding of number*. Cambridge, Mass.: Harvard University Press, 1978.

Kamii, C. An application of Piaget's theory to the conceptualization of a preschool curriculum. In R. K. Parker (Ed.), *The preschool in action*. Boston: Allyn & Bacon, 1972.

Kamii, C., & DeVries, R. *Physical knowledge in preschool education: Implications of Piaget's theory*. Englewood Cliffs, N.J.: Prentice-Hall, 1978.

Karplus, R., et al. of the Science Curriculum Improvement Study (SCIS). *Sample guide*. Chicago: Rand McNally, 1970.

Lovell, K. *The growth of understanding in mathematics: Kindergarten through grade three*. New York: Holt, Rinehart and Winston, 1971.

Lundsteen, S. W. *Ideas into practice*. Englewood Cliffs, N.J.: Prentice-Hall, 1976.

Nelson, L. W., & Lorbeer, G. C. *Science activities for elementary children* (6th ed.). Dubuque, Iowa: Brown, 1976.

Nuffield Mathematics Project. New York: Wiley, 1967.

Piaget, J., & Garcia, R. *Understanding causality.* New York: Norton, 1974.

Plowden, Lady. *Children and their primary schools: A report of the central advisory council for education.* London: Department of Education and Science, Stationery Office, 1967.

White, B. L. *The first three years of life.* Englewood Cliffs, N.J.: Prentice-Hall, 1975.

CHAPTER 10

*"No! Don't punch him in the nose!
Use words instead."*

HELPING CHILDREN DEVELOP LANGUAGE ABILITIES

Beginning Literacy 288

The statement on the opening page of this chapter ("No! Don't punch him in the nose! Use words instead"), from a five-year-old responding to a puppet show, brought a smile to the face of the teacher sitting unobtrusively in the background. One of the goals of teachers in this day care center was to guide children to use language to solve problems—instead of hitting, biting, and kicking.

In this chapter you will find other aspects of what the child can do with the help of the teacher. More specifically, this chapter answers the following questions:

- What are some major goals teachers of the language arts should set for themselves? For the children?
- What is the teacher's role in developing competence in listening and speaking?
- How does a teacher develop appreciation of literature in very young children?
- How does a teacher introduce children to beginning reading and writing?

We mentioned in Chapter 5 that there was one question we could not deal with; it concerned the influence of television on affective development. A similar situation exists here: "How does television affect linguistic development?" is an important question, but it lies beyond the scope of our discussion. We recommended three studies which certainly bear repeating now: Evelyn Kaye, *The ACT Guide to Children's Television; Or, How to Treat Television with T. L. C.* (Boston: Beacon Press, 1979); H. Lesser, *Television and the Preschool Child: A Psychological Theory of Instruction and Curriculum Development* (New York: Academic Press, 1977); and Mariann Winick, *The Television Experience: What Children See* (Beverly Hills, California: Sage, 1979). In addition, we recommend an article by J. S. Busch, "Television's Effects on Reading: A Case Study" (*Phi Delta Kappan*, 1978, *59*, 668–671).

Why do we stress helping children to develop language abilities? One reason is that language is used in the total early childhood program and is crucial to it. Listening and speaking processes are prerequisites for reading and for written composition. Children are unlikely to read and write better than they can speak and listen. Before we say more, however, we should define what we mean by "language arts."

Some Definitions

"Language arts" usually refers to four interrelated, progressively developing processes—listening, speaking, reading, and writing. These processes are made up of many components ranging from simple motor skills to the use of complex relationships. Behind all these language processes lie many intellectual processes. These processes (such as perceiving, classifying, forming concepts, fantasizing, evaluating) can be meaningfully integrated into activities of creative problem solving, and children can be motivated to use them when they engage in creative problem solving.

For example, five-year-old Don finds a creative problem in kindergarten when he wants to write a sentence about the boa constrictor that he saw at the zoo. He has *listened* to his teacher's instructions about requesting and filing key words he wants and he knows that several words he needs are there for him to copy and *write*. He can *speak* and ask for one that is not there. And he can *read* what he has written to himself, to his teacher, to his friends, to anyone who will listen. In solving his creative problem, he has productively used all language areas. (See "Problem Solving" in Chapter 12.)

Goals

In talking about Don, we touched on one of the major goals of the early childhood program in language—the goal of keeping language *use* as creative and as autonomous as possible. The next sections look further at some major goals to give our programs a sound sense of direction.

MAJOR GOALS FOR THE CHILD
In general our goals for children include: (1) use of and respect for their own language; (2) use of and respect for the language of others; (3) interactive and interrelated use of language with others and in many curriculum areas; and (4) development of language concepts.

Let's examine these goals in more detail:

1 Children are to *use* language, more and more, from the inside out. They are to use their own experience as a resource. For example, they come to use it to express their *own* needs and feelings. They come to use language to report what they see, e.g., by naming, describing, classifying, and narrating. They come to use it to entertain themselves and others or to persuade others. They may come to use it in the housekeeping corner, during a puppet show, or while dictating a story to someone. (It is a fact that children learn language by *using* it. For example, children do not learn to read by phonics. They learn phonics by writing their own invented spellings and by reading what they and others write.)

2 Children are to understand and relish the language of *others*. They may come to respond to a story another child has produced or to one by a famous author and illustrator. They come to respond to the communications of a teacher or parent. They come to use the language used by others as a resource and ask questions of others.

3 Children come to *interact* with messages given them by others. Children not only come to use language to send their own egocentric messages and to receive authoritative messages, but also come to communicate together in a reciprocal give and take so that new wholes are created by mutual influence.

4 Children are to *respect* language. They come to respect their ability to use it (and present a positive picture of themselves). They come

to respect the ability of others to use language to make experiences memorable; they come to respect its power and they come to grasp some of its limitations.

5 Children are to learn *language concepts*. Children come to grasp certain specific concepts: words, letters, sounds, conventions of writing, and many other aspects of our system of language. (Some of the general concepts about what they can do while listening, speaking, reading, and writing are developed in the section "The Language Experience Approach" later in this chapter.)

6 Children are to *interrelate* their experience with these goals. They come to interrelate the various forms of language (listening, speaking, reading, and writing). They come to interrelate by transferring uses among these forms, among contexts, and among subject matters (e.g., literature, science, mathematics, the arts). And they come to interrelate many forms, contexts, and subject matters by focusing on a creative problem and solving it.

Children cannot accomplish these goals very well all by themselves. They need the help of teachers. Thus we have some complementary goals for the teacher.

SOME GOALS FOR THE TEACHER Goals for the teacher parallel the goals for children. Let's start with goal 6, interrelation, since it combines or touches upon many of the children's goals, and then consider goal 3, interaction.

How can a teacher help to interrelate children's uses of language while they are listening, speaking, reading, and writing?

Sometimes interrelatedness happens by chance, especially in a rich environment. But we're suggesting that it be deliberately planned. A one-at-a-time, eye-dropper fashion of pouring separate bits of language knowledge into a child is impractical and obsolete, except in programs trapped in minimal competencies ("Now everybody mark and color this worksheet for the 'a' sound; and when you finish that one, there's another one for you to do"). The several language arts areas are like a closely knit family with a common heritage, common purposes, and a strong, natural unity.

How do you go about accomplishing the goal of exploiting interrelationships? Some examples follow.

Use the children's *own* interests, purposes, and problems in promoting the ongoing and continuously creative use of common language and thought processes. Incorporate the arts (music, art, drama) where appropriate. Recall Don and the boa constrictor. Don heard about a boa constrictor in a little song, visited the zoo, was read to about the

The boa constrictor is having his lunch

Figure 10-1
*(Source: Prepared by
Don Kingore.)*

boa, wrote his own one-sentence story, read it, and illustrated it with
dash and fervor (Figure 10-1).

Interrelating the language arts also requires that the teacher plan
to develop children's comprehension through *experiences*, followed by
interactive talking about the experiences and listening to others talk
about them. Thus, when Donna finally looses a tooth, the teacher (as a
resource person) may have arranged experiences for the class so that
they have used the whole gamut of speaking, listening, reading, written
composition, and depiction in the arts—attaining and applying concepts,
classifications, and empathy.

How does a teacher facilitate interactions among children and adults environmentally?

Promoting *interaction* is a goal which has a very general scope. Almost
all of the early childhood teacher's desirable verbal behaviors can be
related to this goal. We examine this goal in some detail, starting with
infancy. This section focuses on the environment; the next section focuses
on the teacher's *words*.

Did you know that babies and their mothers "converse" with one another when infants are about three or four months of age? They do this in a smooth, rhythmic pattern that is different from the kinds of communicative interactions that babies have with their fathers (more staccato), and still different from interactions between babies and strangers. Fathers tend to punctuate and jump rhythmically in tune with their babies as they poke them with their fingers (Brazelton, 1969, 1972). Infants (only three months old) apparently express themselves (their intents) to the mother and then allow time for back-and-forth exchanges of nonverbal messages. Once caretakers are aware of the possibilities of this interactive "dance" with infants, they can look for and encourage it.

Does this idea of interactively communicating with babies surprise you? It's a fact that within a few months of life an infant's noises already show patterns: a cry followed by a pause to listen for reactions, then another cry. Apparently the child communicates partly because it is stressful *not* to communicate—another thought that caretakers should keep in mind. Brazelton has shown us dramatic films of mothers remaining stony-faced—pretending indifference—while infants run through their repertory of communicative devices in attempts to elicit a response. Learning to talk takes about two years of practice by the child and by the principal caretaker, whose every word represents a lesson in what sounds and tones work best. Teachers of the very young share this responsibility (Brazelton, 1969).

In short, interactive communication (the base for all the language arts) begins at birth. Careful observation of and communication with infants (or children of any age) is important because caretakers and teachers provide models for behavior and reinforce certain behaviors. While language production appears innate, language development is dependent on interaction with users of a language, their environment and culture. Language communication (later including reading) is a *social* process.

As children grow older, interactive dialogues and eventually small-group discussions are a key means to development of language. Such activity includes vocabulary development, an important base for learning to read. Teachers can develop the ability and desire of children to speak interactively (with one another) by providing learning experiences having to do with (1) room arrangement, (2) use of equipment, (3) scheduling, and (4) activities.

1 *Room arrangement.* Arrange the room with centers of interest according to where materials are put away (e.g., blocks, paints, books, musical instruments, listening materials, housekeeping equipment). Room arrangements can encourage interaction among class members—whether they are pairs or groups, children or adults.

2 *Use of equipment.* Provide equipment for *role playing.* Trying on

grown-up lives for size and talking about them with one another is stimulated by grown-up clothes, costumes, props and accessories— and a full-length mirror so that children can see themselves in various roles. Other kinds of equipment for interactive talking might include telephones, puppets, flannelboards, cozy seats for two to sit in and share a book, and water or sand tables. Once the children understand how to use the equipment, leave, and let the children interact and handle it autonomously. (See "Play" in Chapter 12.)

3 *Scheduling.* Schedule time for cooperative planning and reviewing with individual children, small groups, and the whole class. Schedule a walk around the building grounds or neighborhood. Before going, discuss and make plans for experiencing certain sights, sounds, smells, and feelings. After the walk, recall the planning. Discuss what the children saw or what they gathered. Next respond to the real-life experience in representational ways (e.g., drawings, photos, stories or sentences dictated, dramatic play) that the children can share interactively. Help children to associate word meanings with experience ("We saw it go *fast;* we saw it go *slow*").

4 *Activities.* Arrange to play interactive games, especially for the sake of relatively silent children. For example, two or three children can gather around a box big enough for them to step into and (with the teacher as language guide) can take turns saying what they will do and asking *others* what they will do. "I can step *in;* what can you do?" "I can walk *around* it; what can you do?" "I can jump *over* it; what can you do?" (Stop while the children are still interested.) In order that children have something significant to communicate and interact about, provide the class with as many *memorable events* (e.g., interactions with pets, experiments, trips, visits by others, making films) as possible.

How does a teacher promote interactions verbally?

Although environment and activities certainly can help to set the stage for interaction, there are specific things that teachers can do with their words. Caretakers and teachers need to learn how to talk with children. An inexperienced person may reach out with words to a child and get no place at all.

> "How are you today?" (No response.) "Would you like to dictate a story to me?" (No response.) "I'll write it down for you. Tell me something to write." (Nothing.)

Establishing a free flow of communication takes some know-how. The experienced person knows that for some "shy" children the most nonthreatening kind of communication is that which requires no verbal response on the part of the child.

> "I'm glad to see you, Louisa. Your bright smile shows that loose tooth." In this case shy Louisa does not feel pressed to speak until she is ready.

Many times during the day teachers have a chance to make their words count in children's language development. In this section we examine: (1) arrival time, (2) problems, (3) elaboration and expansion of children's words, (4) asking questions, (5) giving directions, and (6) involving parents when they come to collect their children. Try using these activities and suggestions during the day in order to improve verbal interaction.

1 *Try to give each child a personal greeting upon arrival.* "How is that loose tooth, Sandra? Still wiggling about? What does your mother say about it?"

Comments about how children feel or look or personal touches can help them to feel accepted and comfortable. Greeting children with comments about clothing, for instance, can help children to classify colors, differences, similarities, and changes. Again, give special greetings to shy children. Asking personal questions (e.g., about pets)— queries that need more than a yes-or-no response—can help these children to make the transition between home and school. (The intention is not to discourage yes-or-no interchanges altogether; they are better than no interchange at all.)

As you verbalize children's actions as they enter the room (or at other times), you are helping them to attain concepts.

"That's really a struggle to carry in that big sombrero!" The teacher can elaborate upon and *help the child to elaborate upon* these early conversations later in the day when the children are gathered in a group.

> "Sally told me this morning that her grandmother had brought her some presents and that one of them was a puppet. What else did she bring you, Sally? . . . What else do you think she brought, Salvador?" (Pause for responses.) "If you could have wished for one special present, what would it have been?" (Pause for responses.)

Find time each day to converse with children about important events in their lives.

2 *Let children solve their own problems through language.* We mentioned this idea at the very beginning of this chapter. It bears repeating. Especially during free play, the teacher can give children an uninterrupted opportunity to talk with one another without adults

jumping in. If on occasion they quarrel at the swings, or at the block corner, avoid imposing adult solutions.

Here's an example. Toward the end of the kindergarten year Donnie and Jeff had become close friends. After juice and crackers, Donnie pounced upon a favorite book and settled into a corner hugging the book to himself in a tantalizing manner. Jeff soon asked Donnie to share the book with him, and they snuggled down to turning the pages. Then Jeff gave Donnie a friendly little kick, to which Donnie responded with a much stronger kick.

"You didn't have to kick so hard," complained Jeff, tears welling.

"You kicked me first," replied Donnie.

"I just gave you a little kick. You kicked real hard," snapped Jeff.

"Don't tell Miss Adams," responded Donnie.

(Pause.) "Would I tell on my best friend?" said Jeff, and the two went peacefully back to looking at the book—the problem settled.

This situation might have had a much different ending if an adult had interrupted and admonished the boys for kicking. When teachers allow children to solve their own problems in relating to one another, children can use language to understand feelings and relationships.

3   *When appropriate, elaborate and expand children's language.*

Billie (a toddler) comes with a shoe in her hand and says, "Shoe."

"Do you want me to help you put it on?" asks the teacher, elaborating. Billie nods her head to indicate, "Yes."

Expanding a child's language is a matter of taking a word or a phrase that a child has used and using it in a sentence which expresses the child's meaning more completely. You take the child's bit of language and "stretch it out." During snack and juice time, opportunities often arise for elaborating children's language and concepts about taste, texture, color, and of food ("tart and juicy, satin-bumpy, orange tangerine").

What are some suggestions for body postures? Sitting down with children at eye level makes communication easier. (Cut the legs off an old stuffed chair.) Let them see your face, mouth, and eyes. Your nonverbal communication complements and elaborates your verbal messages.

Here is another thought on elaboration: Accept a child's attempts to articulate a word. If Donna says "lellow," say, "Yes, the paint is yellow." Donna's articulation will improve as she develops and observes more mature speech models. Her sentences will become more complex, too. Reward the child's imitations with smiles, touches, or words. Show the child that you appreciate efforts.

Help the child to talk about and elaborate feelings and to use already learned words ("mad") in connection with new words ("angry").

"I mad," quivers Thad.
"You're mad and angry because he took your toy."

Instead of ostentatiously correcting speech errors such as "wented" or "goed," repeat them, unobtrusively employing the correct form. "So yesterday you went to the store, did you?" When you say this, you have modeled correct usage; in time (maybe not at this moment) the child will copy it. (Recall from Chapter 5, on language development, that such language errors—e.g., overgeneralizing past tense markers—are a healthy sign of developing prowess in language abilities.)

"Joann," says Kristie to her teacher, "I'm afraid of snakes."
"Why do snakes make you afraid, Kristie?"

Finally, sometimes, in order to help children who are less verbal than their classmates, you model language without elaborating. You have children carry simple messages to another staff member who has been alerted to the child's need for verbal-memory practice and self-confidence.

"Oliver, please go tell Mrs. Adams. Say 'It's time to bring the record player, please.'"

Another time when teachers can use their words interactively to assist the development of children's language is during outdoor play. You may have opportunities to participate in children's playful chants. Dan is chanting when he sees his teacher, Joann, approaching.

"Look, Joann; look, Joann. Look-i-look-i-look, Joann!"

Joann chants back. "I'm looking, Dan. I'm looking, Dan. You're high. You're high in the sky."

This exchange goes back and forth quite a few times.

In essence, having your words interact with a child's words helps in many ways. Children tend to speak more if their speech is attended to and rewarded with responses and smiles, when they are talked *with* and not *at*.

The following are other suggestions about the ways teachers can use words to promote children's interactive use of language through expansions.

- Paraphrase children's words and actions ("I see you've *chosen* to peel an apple and cut it carefully. You will *create* an attractive dish"). Use of verbs showing that you recognize actions initiated by the children indicates your respect for their work.
- Use personal pronouns to enhance children's sense of themselves ("You're carrying that book carefully; it must be important to you").
- Help children to take risks as they creatively solve problems in new ways ("You say you feel sad now. But you're cutting out very well, even if you did manage to cut the tail off your cat. What do you have in mind to do next?").
- Use the same tone of voice and choice of words whether you are speaking to children or to adults. Avoid talking down to children. Indeed, "talk up" to them. Young children love big words and relish using them ("I see the gigantic dinosaur you're painting"). Use your best quality of voice and language, for this is the language they will learn (Lundsteen, 1979a).

4 *Use interactive questions.* Sometimes you can expand a child's language and thought through your interactive questions. For example, ask questions that help a child to identify a significant attribute for a concept.

> "How are the plate, the wheel, and the juice lid you've collected like the Frisbee?" (They're all round, or circular.)

Ask questions that help children to see what is alike and what is different.

> "You can pour this milk and this water. What will this clay do if you try to pour it?"

And a more complex or abstract example:

> "This line you made is straight, and this line is too. But this mark you made curves a little. I think you found the difference I asked about."

Try modeling language and adding a question so that a child who is less verbal has a chance to copy a language pattern while it is still fresh in memory.

"I think this puppet looks funny. How does this puppet look to you?

Your questions can guide children toward discoveries as you answer a question with a question. For example, when five-year-old Jeremy asks, "What does a frog eat?" you might reply, "How might we find out?"—and then set up some experiences that would lead to answers.

We had better insert here a word about developmental levels of *children's* questioning. Recall that when four-year-olds ask questions, they are not usually asking for adult explanations. Many 2½- to 4-year-olds aim their "why" questions at getting and holding an adult's attention. Sometimes children at about age four are asking rhetorical questions, in the hope that caretakers will ask for their opinions. Such children are ready to venture responses to their own questions which reflect their beliefs that events and things in the world have a purpose (sometimes magical, animistic, and egocentric).

Four-year-old Teddy, after a windstorm, when the lawn is littered with mulberry leaves, speaks: "Do you know why the grass is green? . . . To make the leaves feel at home when the wind blows them down." An adult who tried to tell Teddy about chlorophyll would be missing the point: Teddy is not really asking for an explanation; he is simply expressing his own idea. Eventually, of course, children will go beyond their important misconceptions and arrive at accurate explanations. At this level, it is more important that they feel that their caretakers understand their questions than that they get strictly accurate answers. At any level, however, a child's questions deserve the same attention that you would give to a friend asking a question—polite consideration. (It should be noted that questions asked by five-year-olds are typically less rhetorical and more to the point; see Elkind, 1978.)

Returning to teachers' questions, we find that they can elicit various levels of thought and speech. Some questions asked by the teacher call for only yes-or-no answers from children. (Examples are: "Do—or did—you?" "Can—or will—you?".) "Who," "what," and "when" questions are less provocative than "how" or "why" questions. Other provocative questions call for identifying problems ("What's the matter here?") and making hypotheses ("If the egg falls off the table, what will happen?"). Even more provocative are questions that call for prediction, comparisons, cause-effect thinking, identification of consequences, and planning procedures ("How could we find out?").

May we suggest as a motto: "Look to your questions."

5 *Keep directions to a minimum and be sure they are well-reasoned. (Don't turn off interaction.)* Instead of running on and on, repeating

directions over and over, explain your requests and cautions so that children will understand and grasp your reasons. Note these two contrasting examples.

> "Ann, I've told you five times to wash your hands. Wipe the bowl out with your paper towel. Don't use too much soap. Don't let the water drip. Clean off the mirror, too. Don't drop the soap."

> Ann's memory is overloaded by this time.

> "Ann, please go wash your hands; it's time to eat." (More effective!)

Children turn you off, if you're "on" too often (and future interactive communication may go down the drain). Decide which ideas you genuinely want children to listen to. Use simple gestures and touches to show meanings with your hands as well as with your eyes. As cues are reduced during the year, children need help only in identifying what is to happen next.

Nap time is another part of the day when teachers need to watch their words. Rather than shouting across the room for a child to be quiet, the skilled teacher moves close to the child, whispers, plays soft background music, and understands that children often practice their language skills just before sleeping. Consequently, quiet murmurings are natural. It helps to give a child a familiar toy with which to "interact." Again, concise cues and polite, well-explained requests serve better than loud nagging. (Note also that it is a good idea to have more than one adult on hand.)

6   *To increase a child's language-rich experiences, share conversational ideas with parents about what the child has been doing during the day.*

> "Donnie had a fine time painting a paper poncho to wear during our fiesta today. I bet he can tell you which part he liked best and how he made his poncho."

Now the parent has something to converse with the child about and can bring school talk and home talk together.

What we've been saying about the teacher's goals and roles can be adapted for children of various ages. (See, e.g., Weir & Eggleston, 1975.)

In summary, let's review these six ideas that teachers can practice during the day to promote the goal of enhancing children's interactive communication. In order to assist children's language development:

1   Try to give each child a personal greeting upon arrival.

2 Let children have a chance to solve their own problems through language; assist them by encouraging the use of a supply of words needed to express feelings.
3 When appropriate, elaborate and expand children's language.
4 Use interactive questions.
5 Explain your directions concisely so that children will understand you. Justify your demands with appropriate reasons. Don't turn children off to language in general.
6 Feed parents ideas about the child's day so that school-related communication can continue in the home.

USING LANGUAGE: SOME ACTIVITIES TO PROMOTE GOALS FOR CHILDREN

In this section we examine areas and activities that can promote children's language use and abilities: finger plays, dramatic play, puppet shows, flannelboard shows, listening experiences, and last (*but by no means least*) children's literature. Many teachers and districts are attracted to the many prepackaged language programs because they think they've found an easy solution. But no school workbook, kit, or Ditto sheet can take the place of the day-by-day flow of conversations, the child's own compositions, artistic literature, and other natural uses of language in allowing children's language abilities to reach their full functioning.

Finger play

Recall the goals related to use of language and to interaction. Among commonly found activities supportive of those goals are finger plays. See to it that you have some in your repertory.

What is a finger play? Usually finger plays are verses with accompanying actions (usually finger motions, but often including the whole body). For the child, the actions may come before the words; but the rhymes give pleasure. The activity helps children to join a group and experience feelings of accomplishment in the group's activity quickly. A well-known example of a finger play is "Here is the church; here is the steeple; open the doors and see all the people."

When do you use finger plays? Use them at almost any time of the day for language development, to provide a change of pace, to help children through moments when they must wait for something, as a transition between activities, or when the children need to be calmed down.

A word of restraint—a teacher can overuse finger plays. ("What is kindergarten?" "Five finger plays a day.") Finger plays should not be used so much that they become mindless gimmicks. So watch it—nothing in excess.

Dramatic play

Dramatic play has to do with several goals: using one's own language and that of others, interaction, and interrelation of learning in various areas.

Dramatic play is the activities of young children that involve make-believe. It is spontaneous and plotless, needs no audience, and has no set sequence. Early in life children act out, repeating the words and actions of others. Early childhood teachers plan for this activity by designating an area for such play. Then they construct kits for dramatic play, collecting items that will serve in different situations. As children momentarily assume roles (a family member, an animal, an object), they may shift suddenly, according to impulse. Some dramatic-play areas are permanent and elaborately furnished; some are simply improvised temporarily (say, by marking off a corner with a few easels) and provided with simple props (a few breakfast utensils, a grown person's jacket, a briefcase, and car keys, for instance, can encourage children to play at "getting off to work"). Children actually work hard at such play; and they have an amazing ability to slide easily from the real world into make-believe. (See also Chapter 12.)

Some previous experience is a prerequisite for dramatic play. Children would be unlikely to act out a wedding or a visit to an aquarium if they had had no experience with these things. Accordingly, the early childhood teacher may provide field trips, films, filmstrips, slides, guest speakers, and books, as well as kits, equipment, and settings for dramatic play.

Dramatic play serves the child in many ways, besides being a prime developer of conversational abilities, vocabulary, concepts, and relationships. Dramatic play helps children to understand the feelings, roles, and work of others, to connect actions with words, to develop creative and evaluative thinking through problem solving, to learn social interaction skills, and sometimes to act out troubling events (e.g., the doll gets the spanking, instead of the child). Moreover, dramatic play allows children to try out different modes of behavior in a socially acceptable way. (Quiet Laura who had never given herself permission to be loud and rowdy may pretend she is the "bad guy" and act up a little.)

Kits for dramatic play might contain the following: "pretend" cake, candles, presents, balloons, hats (birthday party kit); stamp pads, stampers, Christmas seals for stamps, shoe boxes to represent post boxes, scales for weighing (post office kit); cash register, play money, pads and pencils, bags, empty food cartons and cans, wax fruit, grocer's apron (supermarket kit). Consider the following example.

Discount store. A discount store kit would be closely related to the supermarket kit. Dramatic play involving a discount store has many uses and fosters many interrelations. Young children can practice not only their spoken language skills, but also their beginning mathematics skills. Children can call out special sales on a make-believe loudspeaker from the kit and staff an information booth. They can keep a lost and found department and a complaint department. They can set the price of items, sell them, and draw pictures of the items for sale.

Children can use the pictures they've drawn in the following game. First, they categorize by the department of the store the pictures drawn or collected. Then they hide one picture from view and, with a partner, try to guess what it was a picture of. They can use a "twenty questions" technique—i.e., the child doing the guessing gets feedback on which category the picture is in, rather than just making random guesses.

Many other productive activities can happen in connection with the discount store activity. Shoppers can have conversations about products and service. Managers can hold training sessions for their personnel on courtesy and how to help customers (social learning). Not only does much productive use of language go into the planning of the discount story activity; it also involves the beginnings of social science concepts, such as the specialization of labor.

Puppet shows and problem solving

Another activity conducive to most of our goals for children involves puppets. You can use puppets for many purposes.

A puppet can hold a child's attention. (That is an understatement!) Confront a child with a puppet, and it is as if something magical happens. Children slide right out of the here and now to participate wholeheartedly in the fantasy. In this section we suggest interactive uses in order to develop children's language and thought through creative problem solving. One of the domains of problem solving is the social domain—the domain of "people problems." Puppets can be your ally in assisting the development of the use of language to solve "people problems."

What is the first step? Have in mind a few selected points in the creative problem-solving process that you think your children can handle. Some of the points that we have used with kindergarten children are:

- Identifying problems
- Finding causes
- Finding solutions
- Identifying consequences

Identifying problems is a matter of increasing sensitivity to a problem area ("I think the problem with Elwood—the puppet—is that he doesn't have any legs"). *Finding causes* involves relational thinking, becoming aware of events which may cause or influence behavior ("That's why he's crying"). *Finding solutions* is a matter of generating and exploring alternative hypotheses ("You could take some of the felt off his jacket to make some legs"). *Identifying consequences* requires realizing the effects of alternative behaviors and making plans to test the success of the behavior that is chosen ("Then I bet he would be happy").

Some other aspects to have in mind during a creative problem-solving discussion with young children are qualities of empathy (caring) and autonomy (self-directedness). Finally, you will also be interested in getting the children to interact among themselves and with the puppet characters.

Guidelines The following are a few guidelines that we have found useful.

1 *Avoid dramatizing any problem that isolates one child.* That is, avoid embarrassing a child in front of others.
2 *Avoid using the name of any child in the group as a name for a character in the dramatization.* If the other children identify the puppet character with that child, they may transfer the problem and the personality of the puppet character to the child with the same name. If the puppet acts in *undesirable* ways, this transfer could be a problem.
3 *Be conscious of the attention span of children.* Plan your puppet presentation and discussion to meet the children's limits of attention spans. Keep a careful watch on nonverbal reactions. Stop while the children are still interested.
4 *Do not moralize and avoid the goody-goody approach.* Keep in mind, however, how quickly young children copy behaviors. Let your puppets' actions reflect realities ("Sometimes you just don't feel like sharing") and *not* a "Pollyanna" attitude.
5 *Be flexible. Use the children's ideas as much as possible.* Avoid imposing your mind on the children's minds. It's all right for children not to know and it's all right for them to be wrong (according to adult standards) in this exploratory situation. There is no one right answer during this activity.
6 *Have a wonderful time!* The chances are that the children will enjoy themselves more and interact at higher levels of language and thought if you are enjoying yourself. Remember the importance of dramatic play for children's development.

Management: A few hints Sometimes young children will get a little aggressive toward a puppet. Pointing out to children that this is a kind and gentle puppet and that we need to respect its body will help to counter aggressive behaviors. Also, calming words such as "If you sit down, we can see your faces better" will help when eager children crowd the stage too closely.

What will you need in the way of *materials?* You will need one puppet, yourself, and some children. You will be referring to two other characters, but not using them. Try to have a big pocket for the puppet to retreat into. (Or the puppet can retreat under your jacket or a loose smock.)

Roles of the teacher What is your role? You will be playing three roles: the puppet, a facilitator of interaction between the children and the puppet, and the first person the puppet confides in. You will want to keep in mind a simple plot and the kinds of children's thinking that you might like to guide. You also need to be ready to respond to those unexpected moments when the children surprise you with fresh responses. Roles can also be taken by a trained parent, an aide, or an older child.

A sample plot Your puppet first appears preceded by the sound of crying, and you encourage the children to speculate about why the puppet is sad. You and the puppet gradually help the children to clarify the problem. Then you encourage the children to offer possible solutions.

Here is one plot you could use. (It's better to make up your own, close to the children's interests and needs.)

The story in a nutshell: Elwood (your puppet) has been told by his best friend, Andrea, and her new friend, Hector, to get out of the sandbox because they don't want to play with him. That, basically, is the problem and the data. From there you follow children's leads, working for interactive communication and identifying choices to be made during the problem-solving process and qualities of productive problem solving. Here are two possible ways of concluding. (1) The puppet chooses one of the children's ideas, *confirms* the positive aspects of the discussion (the accomplishments), and goes back into the pocket (or wherever). (2) The puppet thanks the children for talking the problem over with him, confirms the positive processes and qualities exhibited, says the children's concern makes him feel better (and he's glad to have them as new friends), and goes back into the pocket. (You could use the last alternative if none of the children come up with a solution—something that is not likely to happen.)

The following dialog took place in Sweden (hence the Swedish names). We enter in the middle, after the teacher has warmed the children up, had them explore the problem, and had them make several hypotheses.

PUPPET   (To children) What am I to do then?
TEACHER   (To children) Yes, what could he do? (To puppet) Ask Anna, Joakim,

Josefin, Karoline, Maria, Edvard, and Simone. They might know what to do.

PUPPET (To children) What am I to do?

MARIA Play. Play by yourself. Play with someone else.

PUPPET But I want to play with Stina.

ANNA You can *tell* her that you want to play with her.

CAROLINE What is he doing?

TEACHER (To puppet) You are pondering aren't you? Oh, you are certainly pondering. What did Anna tell you to do?

ANNA (Not waiting for the puppet to answer) *Talk* to her.

PUPPET What am I to tell her?

JOSEFIN (Usually a very shy, noncommunicative child) Tell her that you want to, to, to play with her!

This sample gives you something of the flavor of what can happen.

Implementing the goal of interrelating   An occasion like the example just given gives teachers many opportunities to implement the goal of interrelating the language arts. For example, you might want to have an adult act as a recorder and write some of the children's advice on a large chart as they discuss the puppet's problem. Then use some of the phrases collected for a language experience approach to beginning reading (details are given in the section "The Language Experience Approach"). Even if the children can't read the words recorded, they are developing important concepts about language, writing, and reading as they watch the recording process.

Another possibility is to have someone make quick sketches ("chalk talk") of the children's solutions. If a child says, "Put some apples in a bandanna and give them to him," have the adult make a quick sketch of that solution. And invite the children to respond to the puppet show by using art media themselves. Or invite the children to respond by dictating or writing about the experience: "My Ideas for Elwood" or "The Day I Invited Elwood Over to Play with Me." Sometimes a character is adopted by a class and a whole series of writings is generated.

Flannelboard

The various phases of a puppet show (or any story) can be transferred to flannelboard pieces. One board can represent the past, one the present, and one the future. Pieces made from felt or pellon can be stored in large boxes with felt glued to the lids (which can then serve as instant display boards). If you are adept, cut out simple items for the flannelboard on the spot as the story and ideas unfold. If possible, videotape (or audiotape) the discussion. Memory is assisted, the strength of children's responses is increased, and children are more likely to be confirmed in productive behaviors once the discussion is in some permanent, visible fashion (quick sketch, piece of flannel, one or two key words, or on videotape). Children, in a position to examine the past from the perspective of the present, can reflect more skillfully, interact better with one another's ideas, and make predictions more easily.

Listening to oneself and others

One of the goals for children is use of the language of others. This goal implies the ability to *listen*. An integrated approach to language arts for young children means that listening is not separated out for instruction or drill. But a few thoughts seem worth emphasizing separately here.

Among the key aspects of listening to which teachers should pay attention are developmental and individual differences among children, their own abilities as listeners, and their choice of techniques for creating optimal listening experiences for children.

Hearing (a prerequisite for listening) and comprehension vary even at birth, and both environment and native endowment affect children's abilities to hear and comprehend. Developmentally speaking, who listens? Children are naturally much more interested in "sharing" their own thoughts (really in listening to themselves, an important learning activity for them). A willingness to receive while actively interpreting the messages of others and while resisting the temptation to follow their own free thoughts—it takes time, effort, and practice for children to develop that kind of discipline. It is important to remember that the teacher is a model of effective listening who will be copied by the children. Listen intently yourself, and avoid worrying (as we all tend to), "How do I get them to listen to *me*?"

We do, of course, want children to be willing to receive the language of others. But listening is more caught than taught. Take the example of four-year-old Susan, whose mother always welcomed her home from preschool with "Now, tell me about your day." Then Susan's mother started working; and one night she arrived home rather late, when Susan was already in bed. "Hello, Mom," ventured Susan, sleepily, "Now, tell me about your day."

Here is an example showing the difference between a nonlistening teacher and a listening teacher.

NONLISTENING TEACHER   OK. It's time to put the paints away. (No response.) Time to put the paints away now! Right now, not a minute later. Paints away! You don't really want to make that picture or you'd have finished by now. I've got other things we need to accomplish today."

LISTENING TEACHER   I know you want to finish that picture for your mother's birthday. I should have given you more warning. Before you go home today, we'll try to figure out together how you could have some more time to finish your picture. But now it's time to put the paints away. (This opens chances for further communication.)

Which kind of teacher will you be?

We'd like to leave the idea with you that your program ought to have the best possible listening experiences for developing youngsters. Have the best language, the best (and most appropriate) music, and the best in literature for young children. (Literature is discussed in the following section, "Literature for Young Children: A Must.") If listening experience is fun and well-paced, with some relaxed, undemanding times for tired ears, you're likely to be providing a superior program. If children hear only mindless trivia that provides them with few opportunities to set their own purposes, development is unlikely to be optimal.

Here is an example of words that children like to hear and say.

From the rippulous pond
Came the comfortable sound
Of the Humming-fish humming
While splashing around. (Seuss, 1971)

Here is an example of how a teacher seeks more listening responses to the preceding verse. "Who will try to imagine and make a sound like a rippulous pond?" . . . (Pause for responses.) "Now who can imagine and make a sound like a Humming-fish? Can you include its splashing noise?" (Pause for responses.) "Whose sound do you think would belong to a *big* Humming-fish, and whose sound do you think would belong to a *little* Humming-fish? Listen again." The idea is to try to give children listening experiences that matter to them and that are appropriately challenging to them. (For more than you ever wanted to know about listening, see Lundsteen, 1979b.)

If you agree with the idea of high-quality listening experiences for young children, then the next section, on children's literature, has some thoughts to offer. Experiences of quality listening and quality literature help children achieve the goal of using the language others use. Experience of literature also helps children develop respect for language.

Literature for young children: A must

If we were parents looking for suitable education for our children, we would ask: "Is good children's literature used in the program? Where is it located in the room? When and how is it used? How is it selected?"

Importance of literature in relation to goals for children   Why would we set such a high priority on the use of children's literature? Our reasons have to do with living life fully, being committed to a developmental approach to reading, gaining a lifelong respect for language, and developing the imagination (which is essential to higher levels of thinking and reading).

1 *Fine literature helps us to live life more fully at any age.* Fine imaginative literature helps us to live more fully by engaging our affective, emotional, creative side and by bringing about greater cognitive growth. Literature frees children from being confined to living just their own lives and lets them sample the lives of others. It prepares the way for lifting them out of egocentricism.

2 *Fine literature enhances children's listening, speaking, reading and writing experiences.* It has been found that children who read early have persons who read to them a lot and who answer their questions about language; such children have enhanced listening, speaking, reading, and writing experiences (Chomsky, 1972; Durkin, 1966). This kind of evidence is useful for those of us who are or will be pressured to go "back to the basics" (meaning narrow, formalized schooling). The studies show that influential books are those read and reread at a child's request. Such repetition leads to open curiosity about the identification of written words. When the child points to a street sign or a cereal box label and asks, "What does that say?" someone answers the question. The environment contains a potential reading and writing vocabulary.

Children who read early see important people in their lives reading, and they show interest in putting pencil to paper and in making visual distinctions in signs and labels. When these children play school with siblings, they benefit from opportunities to read and write. Their families value reading. A high mental age is not necessary (for early readers, the median is 5 with a range of 3.2 to 8.3 years). These children profit from television shows where symbols and words are read and repeated, e.g., commercials and weather reports. (Needless to say, we do not find children with these characteristics in remedial reading classes.)

Children who learn to read early have *not* necessarily received formal instruction in reading, e.g., decoding-skills training (phonics or matching sounds and letters). Early readers are "taught" in ways that are only *rarely* similar to traditional methods used in schools. Learning to read through long, gradual induction more closely approximates the way children learn to speak their native language (Lundsteen, 1977). (We should point out, however, that early reading will be a natural development for some but not all children.)

In short, there is evidence that children who read early have had these advantages: (1) They have had books read to them, some at their own request. (2) Their curiosity was fostered because their questions were taken seriously. (3) There were people in their environment who valued language. (4) They had chances for a gradual, inductive approach to reading.

Providing children with lots of attractive books for looking at and for listening to when read aloud offers strong motivation for development in all the language arts, including reading.

3   *Fine literature can help to develop children's respect for language.* Children gain respect for language when they see the power of literature to move us, to make us aware of beauty, and to make us think and experience vicariously. For example, when you read aloud the poetic prose in Tresselt's *Hide and Seek Fog*, the words help you feel the moisture and cold while they create an eerie mood for playing in the mist and fog.

If children receive formal training in reading in the primary grades that gives them nothing of importance, they can "turn off." Not only must material have meaning when the child decodes, but it also needs to deal with something of *importance to the child*. We need to provide reading that not only *means* but *matters*, material that engages the child's respect.

4   *Fine literature can help develop children's imagination.* Much of respect for language depends upon children's capacity to have their imaginations stimulated. For reading to matter to children, they need to be able to visualize, to close their eyes and see and feel, to bring their experience to bear on the words. Children frequently use the make-believe images in fairy tales in constructing their own daydreams and stories. One child said in connection with television, "My imagination is bigger than that screen." We wish more children could say that. It is important for teachers to encourage extension of ordinary ideas into make-believe situations in order to develop productive thinking and problem solving. An example follows:

> Teacher: "We've been reading a story about a kitten stuck up in a tree. If *you* are stuck up a tree without a ladder, what make-believe way could you imagine to get down?"
>
> Literal-minded child with little imagination and little autonomy: "I would call for my daddy."
>
> Imaginative child, with twinkle in eye: "Well, I might make some big wings out of leaves and fly down." (A bit of Peter Pan is detected here.)

Either answer, of course, is accepted by the teacher. It is those who insist on one and only one way of responding who are finally responsible for the death of children's imagination. And wouldn't you think that the child who has literature and imagination enjoys life a lot more?

In sum, imagination helps children to summon up images, feelings, memories, and intuitions. Imaginative children rearrange the mosaics of their world to create new relationships. Imagination transforms the child's outlook so that persons, places, and events take on beauty and continuity.

Selecting children's literature Given that teachers are convinced of the importance of children's literature in early childhood education, they are faced with selection. Some sources of good books are these.

- A list compiled by Cullinan and Carmichael (1977) of 100 best books and authors for young children.
- Your local children's librarian.
- The list of Caldecott Award winners (and runner-up books).*
- Reviews of new books. (For sources, see Lundsteen, 1976a, p. 225.)

Select from the many kinds of literature for young children: the treasure house of simple picture books; books of objects to name (e.g., Anno's *Alphabet*, *Brian Wildersmith's ABC's*); series of pictures in wordless picture books (e.g., Mayers's *Frog, Where Are You?* and Hutchins's *Changes, Changes*); and the uncomplicated images of the nursery rhymes (de Angeli, *Book of Nursery and Mother Goose Rhymes*). If children miss this stage of their literature, they lose much that needs to be introduced early and carefully: *Pictures convey reality; and books are windows on the world.*

You miss out on a valuable source if you don't know about and use *wordless picture books*. In these books, the story is told entirely through illustrations. Some of the stories are simple; some, for older children, are complex and sophisticated. The first time through, an adult and a child usually look together in order to discover and tell the story to each other. Then they practice "reading" these books—e.g., to themselves, to another child, to a puppet, or into a tape recorder. When several children (separately) tape their individual renditions of the story as they interpret it from the pictures, sharing these renditions provides valuable language and thinking activities. Such activities implement most of our language goals for young children. Each taped rendition will be individual, with its own insights and oral literary style. Many children over a wide age range who thought they didn't like books or could not tell a story (or write one) have bridged the gap by using wordless picture books.

Though a lot has been said about books, one thought to keep in mind

* Examples of a few children's favorites: McClosky, *Make Way for Ducklings;* Bemelmans, *Madeline;* Krauss, *A Very Special House;* Yashima, *Umbrella;* Keats, *The Snowy Day;* Lionni, *Inch by Inch* and *Swimmy;* de Regniers, *May I Bring a Friend?;* Emberly, *Drummer Hoff.*

is that literature is not just books. Films, recordings, a few television programs, and combinations of filmstrips and cassettes are examples of nonprint media that can serve as literary materials to enrich a child's life and language.

One thing that the teacher can do is to develop personal criteria for distinguishing good children's literature from "junk." Many books published for young children are simply not good. The plots are poorly crafted and the thought is expressed tritely or sentimentally. Check out such items as characterization, appropriateness in art style, discernibility of author's purpose and its fulfillment, validity of concepts, interest, use of a child's point of view, timeliness, and esthetic appeal (see Lundsteen, 1976a, chap. 5).

One responsibility the teacher has when selecting children's books is watching out for *stereotypes*. The idea is to include in the children's environment books which include, and treat equally, all sorts of people. Race and sex are particularly important. What can the teacher do? Provide a balanced selection of books. Avoid the impression that demeaning any person or group is socially acceptable. If you come across a stereotype in a book, provide time for discussing it.

Finally, as you select books, keep in mind those that give opportunities for *creative problem solving*. As you read a story, you can stop at various points and encourage children to discuss it. For example, in the book *Nobody Listens to Andrew* (Guilfoile, 1957), stop when the problem becomes apparent to the children. Ask then how they can get people to listen to them. (See "Creative Problem Solving for Young Children" in Chapter 12.)

Teaching techniques Teachers have responsibility for collecting various techniques for using literature (the language of others) with young children. It is especially important to develop basic techniques for telling stories and for reading stories and poetry aloud (including techniques for stopping before the children become restless). Some of the techniques for the storyteller to acquire are ones which facilitate expressive variations of tone, pitch, pauses, and gestures. Your voice and manner can provide an intimacy that intensifies the experience. By substituting the children's own names for those of the main characters, a storyteller can adapt the story to young children's egocentric interests. It's also useful to change the story and setting so that they correspond more closely to the children's own world. Last, but not least, a final technique: When choosing books or telling stories, wise adults select ones that they (as well as the children) really enjoy.

To get children *settled down* for storytelling, establish a "listening atmosphere." To stress the importance of this atmosphere, you might use some ritual as a signal—a certain finger play, a song. It may help to gather the children at some distance from the site of previous activities, in a place where there are as few distractions as possible. Eye contact and whispers can help.

Some advice on how to handle picture books for sharing: With the book upright and in front of you, turn the pages from the top with your left hand. Hold the book open and keep it centered with your right thumb, the base of your right hand supporting the bottom of the book.

How often do you read to children? *Every day.* How long throughout their schooling is it appropriate to read to children? *Always.*

A delightful storyteller, delightful pictures—what better introduction to books and to reading? What better way to establish readiness than by a warm relationship—a loving adult, with child on lap and a book to share? The child comes to connect reading with warmth and closeness and real-life experience. Gather all the adults you can find for this "lap method" of learning to read. Such one-on-one interactions are characteristic of the experience of children who learn to read early. (See Chapter 15, on using aides and volunteers.)

How do you get children and books together? Surround the children with books. Have books on open shelves (with covers facing out) at the children's eye level. Take books outside in special, attractive book boxes. Encourage one-child-to-one-book relationships at quiet transition times. Organize books into units of interest where they are stored (e.g., books about pets near the hamster cage). Coordinate books with picture files, tape cassettes, records, artwork, cooking, and music (e.g., for a book about Jack and the beanstalk, plant beans, cook, and eat them; make bean collages). Start the very youngest children on cloth, plastic, or all cardboard books. Promote respect for books by making sure that they are not thrown around or walked upon. Keep mending tape handy and use it to help children learn to turn pages at the upper corner.

Many children will join a reading session when they hear the sound and rhythm of repetitions and alliterations. The process of successive enumeration appeals to young children as they explore their capabilities in reapplying a basic language pattern: for example, "This is the cat that ate the rat that ate the malt, that lived in the house that Jack built." Children enjoy joining in on refrains such as the one found in Wanda Gag's *Millions of Cats*, where children are charmed into gleefully repeating, "Millions and billions and trillions of cats."

We can, in sum, do much to help children appreciate language besides presenting them with superior language models ourselves. We can be discriminating in our selection of books for children. Literature is a valued resource: *It is not just a toy; it's a tool for life.*

Literature for young children is another area where the early childhood teacher needs to have professional expertise. And literature is an indispensable ingredient in reading readiness—the next topic.

Beginning Literacy

In this section you find key ideas on reading readiness from a developmental, Piagetian perspective. We give suggestions on planned reading instruction (generally for the primary grades). We include a number of approaches: "key words," "language experience," "individualized reading," and others. Although the section focuses on reading printed material, the point of view calls for the integration of the other language arts, especially written (or dictated) composition. Children's progress in the mechanics of handwriting, spelling, and punctuation follows easily when developmental, natural methods are employed. The basic content of the beginning literacy program is the children's own written (or oral) composition and the treasure of real books, real literature we have for children. Texts are the reference materials only. Mechanics follow naturally out of highly motivated *use*. Children need to see that communication through the medium of print is for real. If you limit children to texts and work sheets, you kill motivation, stunting development of a long-lasting appreciation of the value of literacy.

Much of what we have said before in this chapter bears strongly on the topic of reading readiness. Since provision for readiness for literacy is one of your major responsibilities, let's approach it as intelligently as possible. If using language of oneself and others is one of the major goals for children, then we need to find methods that will make the accomplishment of this goal as easy and as rewarding as possible for children.

READINESS

Definitions

A first step is to define "readiness" for reading. The term implies a best time for initiating a specific task—in this case beginning reading instruction. Reading instruction typically involves grouping of children by their abilities, using published materials and lesson plans, teaching for a prescribed, preestablished amount of time daily—in short, formal reading instruction. Many children are not ready for that (sometimes traumatic) experience. Consequently, teachers need to establish reading readiness.

But, more specifically, what is *reading readiness?* Actually, it is easier to ask and answer the question, "What *isn't* reading readiness?" By understanding some basic components, the creative early childhood teacher can turn almost any experience that is important and enjoyable to children to the service of reading readiness. When you provide environments that promote *relational thinking*, you simultaneously provide a "reading environment." (Illustrations follow soon.)

Reading is a thinking process that depends on concepts and operations. The following are prerequisites:

- Perception of shapes, symbols, and detail
- Awareness of spatial relationships (directional order), configuration, and figure-ground distinctions
- Awareness of whole-part relationships (coordinating more than one relation simultaneously)
- Awareness of sequence and order
- Eye-hand and hand-hand coordination
- Language background and facility
- Auditory discrimination
- Classificatory abilities (multiple and simultaneous)
- Experiences of autonomous problem solving (sense of power, curiosity, and self-confidence)
- Reversibility of thought
- Familiarity with conservation and transformation
- Ability to accept discipline

Examples of readiness in an open classroom

In order to explain each of these prerequisites, let's use a classroom scene. Walk into Mrs. Bower's kindergarten and note the many creative activities going on—all are promoting readiness for beginning literacy.

Painting and drawing Janie is painting at an easel. Because she is free to experiment, Janie tries different ways of holding her brush and applying paint. As she tests materials, she is refining motor operations she will need for writing—which goes hand in hand with learning to read. Also, Janie refines her *eye-hand coordination.*

As Janie paints, she concentrates on straight lines and slanted lines, on curves, and on the thickness or thinness of her brush strokes. That's all part of how letters—letters found in reading and writing—are made.

Janie is creating shapes and symbols, recognizing what they are in relation to her world. She is engaging in a form of communication with herself and with others. And communication is what reading is all about.

Janie is now making features for the face, five fingers on each hand, even hair, ears, and a purse—all showing her ability to pay attention to detail. Paying attention to detail is important when learning to read.

Next Janie proudly paints her name on her picture. She knows that when she paints these shapes (these letters in order), those who read it will know it is her name. In order to see her name, she must discriminate the *figure* (or letters) from the *ground* (background). Janie gets this same perception of shape whether finger painting, using clay, or other art media. (See Williams, 1977.)

Across the room is Ted. He finds it easier to use crayons than paint. He will hold a pencil as he holds crayons, to copy words from a favorite book. His partner has chosen to copy some words from a wall chart. As they copy letters in sequence from left to right, they are learning that they can use letters to make words. They are in the process of indirectly beginning to learn to read and to write.

The block center   At the block center, Loretta is using a three-dimensional medium full of opportunities for employing perceptual abilities needed for reading and for writing. Blocks, like letters, have predetermined shapes and are made up of lines and curves. While building, Loretta experiences relationships of parts and wholes and of sequence and order—relationships which letters exhibit when they are put together to form words. She sequences her blocks (right—left, up—down, backwards, and so on). Such directional understanding is called for in reading and writing.

As Loretta sequences the blocks, she refines eye-hand and hand-hand coordination. She will use such coordination when she writes words on paper.

Now, Loretta is experimenting with her own patterns with blocks. Developing an awareness of pattern making in block building may serve as readiness for pattern making in language. ("Brown bear, brown bear, what do you see? I see a blue bird looking at me." The *pattern* of the answering sentence remains the same, but the subject, verb, and object may be changed.)

Loretta's block structure (modeled on the Dallas–Fort Worth airport) takes on many different *configurations.* The ability to see word configurations, e.g.,:

airport

is a word-attack skill that develops early. Loretta has asked for help in describing her structure. She is experiencing a *use* of language that is important to her. Close by, her friend Marilyn is matching blocks to color patterns. This is another form of visual discrimination that bears a similarity to the activities of matching units involved in reading.

Loretta is now doing another prereading experience useful to her—*classification*. As Loretta puts her unused blocks away, she practices classification by size and shape, identifying and matching several different levels of features. Each of Loretta's experiences—not only the one which involves words—may be called "reading."

1　Loretta may match by comparing the blocks she wants to put away with the three-dimensional blocks that are already on the shelf.
2　She may match by comparing the blocks with the two-dimensional picture that marks the storage spot.
3　Loretta may compare the blocks with what she reads on the label— LONG BLOCKS—that also marks the spot.

The science center　Victor is also engaging in *classificatory* activities. He has taken apart a discarded record player. Since Victor's curiosity is continuously encouraged, the chances are that he'll be curious about the world of books and signs. As he takes parts off the old record player, he groups them in ways that make sense to him: "All nuts here. All bolts here. All springs here." When Victor reads, he will be classifying upper-case and lower-case letters, consonants and vowels, and word families ("bomb," "bombardier," "bombing"). There is a stage in young children's conceptual development when they cannot see that groups stay the same but believe that they change magically. A child in this stage, without the conceptual skills to handle conservation will make no sense of letter groups.

Attaining the concept "letter"　Let's think a bit more about the concept "letter" and what it means to us in regard to readiness. From a child's point of view, the concept "letter" poses many problems. Most preschool children lack a true concept of units (whether letter units or number units) because they cannot coordinate two relations simultaneously. (See Chapter 5, on cognitive development.)

Each unit (letter or number) is like all other units but also different from any other unit. (1) Letters have an ordinal property—their position in the alphabet. (2) They have a cardinal property—their name ("A," "B," "C," . . .). This name is shared with all other letters of the same name (all "a's" are "a."). (3) In addition to its name, each letter also has phonic (sound) properties in context. (4) And (to complicate matters even more), a single letter can be sounded in more than one way, and a single sound can be represented with different letters ("a," "ai," "ay," "ey"). Thus, to understand phonics, children must be able to perform logical operations on letters and sounds and understand all possible combinations. The concept "letter" is a complex logical product, and its construction requires the ability to reason (relational thinking) (Elkind, 1975).

Consider one more thought. *Reversibility* is what allows the child to follow an operation from its conclusion back to its beginning and vice versa (e.g., addition-subtraction). A preoperational child who cannot use reversible thinking will be unsuccessful in converting letters to sound by memorizing the sound that goes with the letter, and vice versa.

Attaining the concept "word"   Moving from letters to words (as challenges to young children's thought processes), we see that children have another difficulty. Young Patty in Mrs. Bower's room is able to focus on only one variable at a time, and has difficulty discriminating between, say, the words "wash" and "wish." Patty can perceive the whole but not the parts and the differences between the words but not, at the same time, their similarities. Patty also cannot handle transformations from one state to another. For example, Patty can anticipate a cause-effect relationship, but she cannot at the same time grasp all the steps in between ("I watered my plant, but it died." Patty cannot fill in other possible causes—leaving it out in the burning sun, leaving it too long without water the, giving it too much water). In some formal reading situations we try to teach children associations between letters and sounds and then expect them to use a multistep process. We expect them to: (1) transform the sounds together into a word; (2) coordinate words into a meaningful sentence; and (3) relate sentence to sentence. Without the ability to hold various aspects of a word in mind at one time, the child is in trouble.

What to do about the child who is not ready   What does Mrs. Bower do about children who are not ready? Stand back and wring her hands? No! She engages them in the same sort of activities we've just been describing. Let's watch again.

What's all that noise? Look at Patty in the art center pounding clay, putting pieces of clay together, making a dog, sharpening her idea of shapes, her concept of whole-part relationships. Being able to keep the part and the whole in mind at the same time is important to reading and writing.

Mrs. Bower approaches, "If I called your dog, could he hear me?" Indirectly she is encouraging problem solving and an eye for detail.

"Oh, I forgot ears," says Patty.

José is cutting shapes in dough and lifting the shapes out. Because when he lifts out his figures he creates a negative space, José is gaining experience of figure-ground relations. (Negative spaces lie between words in reading and writing.)

Earlier, José was performing almost the same operation while working with puzzles, matching shape with empty space, correcting himself when necessary. Children seek and use clues as they try to recognize different configurations of letters, words, phrases, and sentences when they read. Such activities involving matching shapes to spaces is productive for almost any child who is not ready for formal instruction. (See the sections in Chapter 13 concerning the special child.)

Helping the ears to attend   Mrs. Bower has gathered a small group (Marta, Ned, and Tim) in the listening center. *Auditory discrimination* (essential to any sound-to-letter correspondences in reading) is indirectly readied as children follow creative rhythmic patterns, e.g., CLAP, clap, clap; CLAP, clap, clap. Children can construct their own creative patterns besides following the patterns of others. Preserved on tape and played back, the patterns are recognized by Marta, Ned, and Tim as their own. Children can use drums or other rhythm instruments.

Next they sing. Singing not only helps auditory discrimination but develops *facility with language.* Learning songs requires abilities to recall, to order in sequences, to make predictions, and to recognize repetitions of patterns—all basic to reading comprehension.

"I had a cat and the cat pleased me, and I fed that cat under yonder tree. And the cat went fiddle-i-fee . . ." Musical sounds can be an enjoyable way to tune into the differentiation of spoken sounds—phonics.

We have already devoted an extended section to dramatic play and storytelling. These activities are great helps to the ability to discriminate sounds, the facility with language, and the experiential background that are important to reading. In using literature, children match what they hear with what they see on the printed page, especially as the favorite story is read again and again.

Conservation   In the water area, Mark is pouring water into variously shaped containers. He is building his concept of conservation. Conservation is important to reading. With conservation, Mark will grasp the idea that a word can be in more than one place at the same time, even look a little different (uppercase, lowercase, larger, smaller, a few optional curlicues), and still be the same word:

AN   an   an   AN   an   An   AN

Mrs. Bower knows that at first a child will not recognize the same word in a new place.

Problem solving and autonomy   Andy is building dams with sand and water. He has a "set" for autonomous problem solving, as he messes about, comprehending the situation and the attributes of his materials. After Andy invents solutions, he develops some mastery over them. He can make the dam do what he wants it to do—"What I do will make a difference." His focus of control contributes to intellectual excitement. With such confidence, he may be ready to "mess about" with words and then develop a sense of mastery over them. He can realize that he is in charge of the act of reading and writing. Andy feels that he is a competent, worthwhile individual. He is eager to learn and to meet new challenges. Before long this adventuring may include reading and writing. We can imagine him asking, "Where does it say that?" "What does that word say?" "How do you make a 'B'?"

Putting tools of reading and writing in the environment   One more thought to keep in mind—though there is some transfer, children learn concepts in the medium in which they are working. For example, if children learn conservation of substance through working with substance, it is equally important to provide experience with tools of reading and writing so that children may conserve, seriate, and classify in those realms. That means the child has opportunities for using many tools such as magnetic letters, word games, sandpaper letters, crayons, pencils, large paper, smaller paper, paper stapled in booklets, cut-up sentences, rhyming words, letter-sound games, key words filed in personal boxes, and individual and group experience charts.

Building language background for readiness   We can hear a typewriter pecking away in another spot. Mrs. Bower displays news about the children on a bulletin board. She (or an aide, a volunteer, or an older child) takes dictation, and both child and recorder read it back. This writing is treated as material of great importance. "Teddy's grandfather brought him a baby duck. They fed it together last night." After Teddy sees the story translated to the printed page and bound in a volume, it is read many times. Mrs. Bower helps reading comprehension by having children make their own efforts to represent their own experiences. The more opportunity they have for this, the better prepared they will be for interpreting the representations of others. *The more children write, the more they will get from their reading.* Writing about their own experiences helps children build linguistic background and facility. (And the typewriter is one of the best aids for building the concept of left-to-right progression in reading and in writing.)

Readiness: A summary

"What is reading and writing readiness?" Let's hope it is *not* (as one child put it) "They find out what I can't do, and make me do it all day long!" We want children to like the idea of going to school! While waiting for specific reading and writing interests to sprout in the fertile environments we provide, we can keep developmental constraints in mind as we provide children with many interesting situations to comprehend and many opportunities to invent creative solutions to problems. That is, we give children many interesting opportunities to *learn relationships*. As we saw in Mrs. Bower's room, reading and writing readiness is often "hidden" in other favorite activities, and these activities are often like games. We can also provide tools in the environment.

"Readiness" refers to a combination of understandings that grows slowly. It is not a single package consisting of specific skills in specified quantities. Children become ready for instruction both through natural growth and through nurturing, planned environments with which they can interact. Lasting understandings come *slowly* for children, layer upon layer, forming a solid foundation on which a child can build securely. Teachers and parents become more patient in their eagerness to have their children gain reading and writing skills when they realize that children need time to attain certain abilities: multiple classification, eye-hand coordination, seriation, reversibility of thought, conservation, and transformation. In fact, most of the information in this section could be usefully shared with parents. (For more on communication with parents, see Chapter 15.)

If you are in doubt as to whether a child is ready to learn to read and write, try some teaching to find out. Do this not because you are under external pressures, but because of your own best judgment. Be humanistic, be enthusiastic, and *be prepared!* (Knowing different methods of teaching reading is the topic of the next section.) Keep Piagetian stages related to reading readiness in mind, but do not use them as excuses for inaction. Keep in mind that reading and writing are complex processes from the child's point of view. Adults forget how difficult and complicated it was to learn to read and write. Readiness, then, implies a slow and gentle introduction to reading itself. By "reading itself," we refer to the ability of a child to pick up an unfamiliar book and read it enough to respond to it and to tell you what it's about. By "writing itself" we refer to the ability of a child to mark down thoughts on paper and read them back, using "invented" spelling if necessary. Usually when a word a child has written has three accurately rendered consonants it is stable enough to be read and reread by the child—if the child is given encouragement and the chance to try. If children have a minimum of about eight sound-letter correspondences (consonants) under control, they can be in the writing business.

With reading in mind and with reference to the preceding section on readiness, we wish to stress a major point: It is crucial to resist any steps toward making early reading a standard for all children (McGinitie,

1976). As we stated in Chapter 2, reading readiness in kindergarten is a much-debated issue. Now it appears that beginning reading instruction in kindergarten is also an issue. To the question "When should we begin to teach reading?" the appropriate answer is another question, "What do you mean by 'begin to teach reading'?" We need to specify instructional programs (the topic of the next section); and then we know more about what kind of readiness a child might need.

APPROACHES TO BEGINNING READING

The following are some brief descriptions of current approaches to reading instruction (with developmentally oriented approaches emphasized). These approaches may be used in combination.

Typically in the United States we expect children to learn to read in first grade. Children who don't are in trouble, sometimes for the rest of their lives. Part of the problem has been giving much the same instruction to all children. In a usual first grade in the first month of school, some children will be 6¾ years old; some will not reach 6 for another two months. The range of IQ is likely to be extensive—say, 85 or less to 125 or more. A usual first-grade class contains children with mental ages ranging from 5 to 8½ years—3½-year range (MacGinitie, 1976). *It is professionally irresponsible to select one time schedule and one approach and try to make each child fit that approach.* When a teacher sees that a child does not conform to the typical approaches, the teacher needs to respond creatively and find other ways to meet that child's needs. (The teacher might even try asking the child.) With this in mind, it is important to know many different reading approaches.

Suppose you have selected a promising approach that just is not working. You want to change; what do you do? Trial and error? No. Instead, *try to utilize the strengths and interests the child already has.* Some approaches may make teaching a bit more difficult for you in the beginning, but they do make learning easier for children. When you don't have to push, pull, and prod the children, they give energy and enthusiasm back to you. The "key words" approach and the "language experience" approach discussed below are examples of methods that fit in with the egocentricity and language background of the child—and thus are in tune with children's motivations. They are natural methods which allow children to build their *personal foundations for learning to read.*

The "key words" approach

Key words are words which have a *strong personal meaning* for the child. It is these emotion-laden words (e.g., "mother") that help children to bridge the gap between their inner thoughts and feelings and the world outside. The "key words" method is useful in many grades, and teachers can use it in conjunction with other reading methods, especially the language experience approach discussed in the next section. (For more on written composition, see Lundsteen, 1976a, chaps. 6, 7, and 11; 1976b.)

What are the basic stages and steps in this reading-writing method?

Stage 1: Vocabulary (1) The child volunteers a word to the teacher. (2) The teacher writes it down on a card in the child's presence. (3) The child reads the word card, traces it with a finger, and copies it.

The child volunteers about a word a day on the average. All the child's words are kept together in a collection. Once a day the child reads the collection of cards to the teacher or to an aide. Any words the child does not readily recognize are quietly discarded. Because those unrecognized words do not have intense meaning for the child, no attempt is made to teach them.

Stage 2: Reading and writing Once a child has eight to ten word cards mastered, the teacher may offer to add a word card to the child's collection. Well-chosen, the added word may be of great help in allowing the child make short sentences. For example, if a child has only nouns in the collection, the teacher might add a verb. (If the child's collection includes many names, the teacher might add the verb "loves"; if it includes many words for objects, the teacher might add the verb "saw.") Then, the teacher and child take the word cards and place them so that they can make simple sentences and read them together. After that, the child reads them alone. Next, the teacher asks the child to make a sentence alone, offering help if needed. Teacher and child repeat this procedure over and over as long as the child shows interest and indicates an understanding of what is happening. Finally, the child will start writing and reading sentences on strips of paper. (Expect great individual differences in development. Some children will be making word cards only for a long time, some will be making simple sentences, some will make several sentences at a time, and some will be totally uninvolved.)

Once the child is comfortable in writing sentences, the teacher asks for at least one sentence a day to be shown to the teacher and filed. The teacher encourages the children to share words and writing with each other—this reinforces symbolic communication. The prerequisites for moving into the third and final stage of this method are, again, interest, success, and an accumulation of word cards *and* sentence strips.

Stage 3: Independent reading and writing Children start spelling out their words. The teacher may give some incidental phonics instruction. As children write more and more sentences, the teacher encourages the making of simple "books." The teacher introduces individual children to the idea of a "book" as a series of sentences about the same idea to be illustrated and shared with family and friends. Children are not required to make these books but rather do them voluntarily. The book belongs to the maker, and the teacher accepts all subjects. These stories, like the key words, will most likely revolve around the child's family, friends, fears, wishes, individual experiences, and observations and perceptions of the world.

Children can begin to use picture dictionaries under their own direction, and make their own word cards autonomously. When children leave the class, they can take their key word cards with them; and they will be coming to realize that words can have intense meaning. This realization is a key to the love of reading.

The "language experience" approach

This method, which has gained much recognition since the 1950s, also uses the child's own language as the teaching medium. It lends itself well to use with beginning readers of any age, including those learning a second language and older children with difficulties. The material collected from the child usually consists of units larger than words.

Concepts for children   This approach is known for a certain "credo" that has undergone some linguistic variations. Here is a late version. It indicates that the language experience approach can produce a pattern of thinking about reading that is internalized by each student:

- What I can think about I can talk about.
- What I can say can be written.
- What has been written in my language can be read.
- What other people have written can be read because they use many of the same words and sentence patterns and they say some of the same things but in different ways (Allen, 1978).

Allen adds other concepts for children:

> As I talk and write, I use some words over and over and some not so often. As I talk and write, I use some words and clusters of words to express my meanings. As I write to represent the sounds I make through speech, I use the same symbols (letters) over and over. Each letter of the alphabet stands for one or more sounds that I make when I talk. And, as I read, I must add to what an author has written if I am to get full meaning and pleasure from print. (1976, pp. 53–55)

Concepts for teachers   There are concepts for the teacher, too.

- The basis of children's oral and written expression is their sensitivity to their environment.
- Freedom in linguistic self-expression leads to self-confidence in all use of language (including grammar, punctuation, and spelling).
- If a program is based on children's personal language patterns and vocabulary, there will be a natural flow of language production and a high degree of independence in writing and reading.
- It takes multiple activities to promote interaction, a process through which language matures (adapted from Allen, 1976).

One advantage of this approach is that it reduces the "comprehension load," since material produced by the students is used to introduce them (when they are ready) to word-recognition skills.

The following are examples of word-recognition skills:

Word Recognition Skills

Rhyming—understanding that language can be characterized by patterns of repeated sounds

Blending—understanding that certain combinations of letters represent sounds not represented by any of the letters alone or combined differently

Sight vocabulary—understanding that certain words, especially words of structure (e.g., "of"), occur so frequently that they must be recognized at sight if a person is to read independently

Form-class vocabulary—understanding that in all communication by language people tell the names of things (nouns), tell what things do (verbs), and describe them in various ways (modifiers) (adapted from Allen, 1978)

A distinction between the key words approach and the language experience approach is that rather than draw language samples solely from individuals, the teacher uses different groupings. Sometimes, especially at the beginning, a story may come from the entire class, stimulated by an experience; but sometimes a story may come from a small group. Small-group dictation helps in encouraging interaction of ideas; individual dictation is valued by children and allows the teacher to watch for specific learning needs.

Some questions and answers   Here are a few questions typically asked about the language experience method.

What should I know about a child before embarking on the language-experience approach?

It is sensible to make some assessment of a child's language production, background experiences, and interests before using this approach. Before incorporating any language study or word-attack skills demanding more than one-to-one correspondence (e.g., more than one letter standing for a sound), see if the child is concrete-operational. Abilities for language production will bear on the children's abilities to make up stories. Knowing about interests gives the teacher clues to the child's sensitivity and hints for providing further usable experiences. Children may find stimulation for their stories from their own paintings and slide sequences made from them, their own lives and families, school itself, audiovisual materials, field trips, and books that they read or that are read to them. First-graders generally have little difficulty in finding things they'd like to write about, once the contagion starts. Older children may need a bit more enticement.

What are some steps I would go through in using the method?

1 Encourage the child to share ideas and experiences.
2 Help the child clarify and summarize the ideas and experiences.
3 Record the child's story.
4 Ask the child to share the written ideas by reading them back.
5 Design skill-development and extension activities based on the child's story (if the child is ready for this).

How does the word collection or "word bank" work?

Every word that a child marks as known in a story is printed on a card and placed in the child's personal "word bank." When children are ready, they can use the cards to practice spelling out words, improve directional sense (by putting words together from left to right), and use phonic analysis (by placing together words belonging to the same family). Words transcribed by the teacher and placed in the word bank can serve as ingredients for stories the child will write independently of the class.

What kind of records do I keep?

You can keep account of both stories written by the children and stories read by the children. (Provide good children's literature by the bucketful.) A child might have a notebook or file folder containing all the stories dictated to the teacher (or to an aide or an older student). Another file might contain stories the child has transcribed. Each week, check the concepts listed above (pages 298–299) and select activities appropriate for the three major ideas: use, study of language, and relating communication by others to oneself.

Individualized reading approaches

Given the start provided by the key words and language experience approaches, many children are ready to move naturally into appreciating independently the words and thoughts of others, especially the wealth of easy-to-read but good and well-illustrated children's literature (referred to as "trade books"). In individualized reading approaches, the instructional material is not limited to those in the language produced by the child; it encompasses a wide variety of reading material of all types, including children's literature. (There should be at least five reading items from which each child can choose.) The teacher guides the children by means of *individual conferences* for checks on comprehension, diagnosis, instruction in skills, help with selection of reading material, and ways of responding to the reading or independent activities. Record keeping by pupils and teachers and flexible grouping for skill development are also features of this approach. (See Veatch, 1968, and Scholastic Book Services, n.d., for help in getting started.)

Other approaches

We have just described methods of teaching reading which take the child's interests and oral language as a starting point. Now we will briefly mention some other approaches and some aspects advantageous to any program.

The *basal readers* are a set of textbooks organized in progressive levels of difficulty and designed to provide a sequential program in mastering word identification and comprehension. The best way we can think of to use basal texts is as reference books or sources of stories that the teacher can cut up and bind separately.

Some children's books are based on *repetitive, dependable language patterns*, such as rhythms and refrains. Because of the repetition, children can predict much of what is to come. Children enjoy reading these patterns in unison or in chorus. Since the children are reading together, no one child feels "put on the spot" and required to read perfectly. Moreover, because of their exposure to literature, the quality of the children's dictated stories generally improves.

Another way to promote reading is to group materials around areas of interest. In the *problem-oriented* or *theme* approach, the material the teacher cooperatively selects for each child revolves around a central area of class interest (e.g., "animals" or "how animals live") or a central theme (e.g., characters who wanted to be something they were not) or a problem ("helping to save our land"). The children may be grouped in "family style," with all ages or levels of ability together and each child contributing to the endeavor in some way. Teachers use varied media (including tapes) and many ways of learning (including asking) to provide material related to the theme under investigation. The method can promote a sense of unity in the group (rather than "bluebirds" versus "redbirds" versus "buzzards"); but it can also foster feelings of personal identity as each child pursues goals and makes a contribution. The teacher and children can meaningfully interrelate content areas of the curriculum, such as literature, social studies, and science.

Some approaches start with trying to get the child to master the relationships between sounds and letters. The idea is that the child will then put these parts (i.e., individual letters and sounds) together to make wholes (i.e., words). *Phonics* approaches emphasize teaching sound-letter relationships at the very beginning of reading. Not all beginning readers get the phonic information they need when they need it; and sometimes the phonic information they get is *not* what they need. Children can learn phonics informally when they need it as they are learning to read (and write) through other approaches. Furthermore, children need to apply skills in unlocking the sound-letter code and in identifying words in *context* (not: "mat," "fat," "spat," "rat"). It is important that children understand the meaning of the words with which they are working. It is our feeling that a *little* phonics is a useful tool for a child ("a little dab will do you"). Some phonics programs, however, load children down with such excess baggage as rules (for which they may lack the necessary concrete-operational thought) and many more workbook pages of practice than they really need.

Summary

This summary lists the most significant ideas of the chapter for ready reference. You could use this collection as an observation checklist for others and for yourself.

Formulating Goals

1 Some major goals for language development are interrelating the language arts, meeting individual needs, and fostering language interactions. Key concepts in goals for children are (*a*) use of one's own language, (*b*) use of the language of others, (*c*) interaction in communication with others, (*d*) respect for the positive—even exciting—aspects of language, (*e*) formation of concepts of language systems, and (*f*) the interrelation among the child's uses of language.

2 Interactive communication is an important goal in which the teacher's role, the environment, and the materials provided play a facilitating part. (Talk *up* to children, not *down* as you interact with and elaborate their language.)

3 An integrating, motivating force for your communication program for young children is creative problem solving.

4 Help young children to use words in a positive fashion to solve problems.

5 Children deserve a program in which the language arts, listening,

speaking, reading, and writing are integrated and guided without pressure.

6 Nourish children's imaginations. The affective experiences—art, drama, other esthetic experiences, emotional stimulation—interact with and produce growth in the child's cognitive experiences.

7 Help children gain a lasting respect for language. (Be a superior language model yourself and provide high-quality literature.)

Oral Language Development

1 Children's interactive communication begins at birth.

2 The child's oral language base is important. Children are unlikely ever to read and write better than they can speak and listen.

3 Children learn language by using it. Uses of language need to be the focus of the program. (Look to your questions. Learn to use puppets.)

4 Language is a child's means of survival. Accept the language the child brings to school.

5 Children need to discover language relationships autonomously, on their own, in a rich environment, solving their own problems with as little direct assistance as possible.

6 Share your know-how with parents. They are teachers, too. And they need education as much as any of us. Draw them into the educational enterprise, especially where oral language is concerned.

7 When children make sense of their environment by means of speech, they sometimes chatter away in monologue, uninterested in interacting with listeners. When children enter school they are still using this way of knowing things by talking about them; often to quiet these children's tongues is to quiet their minds.

Listening

1 However much we want to help children become willing to receive the language of others, we must remember that it is more important for teachers to listen to children than for children to listen to teachers. And though both hearing and listening abilities crucial to receiving the language of others are highly valuable, fascinating material is always helpful in capturing children's interest in the language others use.

2 By and large, effective listening is modeled or caught, rather than taught.

Literature: A Must

1 Literature for young children is not just a toy; it's a tool for life.

2 Fine literature enhances children's listening, speaking, reading, and writing experiences.

3 Become knowledgeable and develop criteria so that you are expert at selecting all kinds of literary materials.

4   Be wary of materials and actions that promote racial, sexual, or any other types of prejudice.

5   Read to your children every day. (People enjoy and profit from being read to all their lives.)

Readiness for Reading and Writing: A Developmental Perspective

1   An early childhood professional knows the difference between the concept of general readiness (for any learning) and specific factors that play a part in reading readiness, but understands that reading begins at birth. (And don't forget the "lap method"!)

2   Reading is thinking. Reading material should not only "mean" but "matter."

3   Piaget's ideas on the development of ways of knowing have much to say to us about reading readiness. (Recall the Piagetian concepts—conservation, reversibility, seriation, part-whole relationships, multiple and simultaneous classification. All are needed for the reading process.)

4   The more children represent their own experience by means of written compositions, the more they will get from their reading. Teachers need to observe both the process and the product carefully and keep individual files for each child. (And don't go scribbling corrections all over children's compositions. If you must comment, interact with the content, participate in the communication.) Writing is something we do *with* children, not *to* them. Enjoy writing yourself and model this joy in and respect for writing. Encourage children to explore and invent their own spellings in the beginning. Writing is play, if it is allowed to be play.

5   Children become "ready" both through natural growth and through nuturing, planned environments with which they actively interact.

6   Lasting understanding comes slowly for children, layer upon layer of taking in and applying, resulting in a solid foundation upon which a child can build securely.

Beginning Literacy: An Introduction

1   As a teacher, be humanistic, be enthusiastic—and be prepared. Being prepared means being able to select from a large repertory of experiences and concrete materials for inviting spontaneous and creative use of listening, speaking, reading, and writing skills (do not isolate reading from these other activities). Being prepared means knowing a lot about teaching reading (for the sake of the child who is ready).

2   Plan a reading and writing program which provides for success of *each* child—no wholesale instruction for all. There is no one best system. Teach to the developmental strengths and interests of each

child. Group children "family style" so that individuals of different ages and abilities can help one another.

3 Some goals of a reading program for the primary grades are:
- Ability to relate reading to personal life
- Enjoyment of reading
- A basic sight vocabulary (associating meanings of words with experiences)
- Use of contextual reading with comprehension
- Use of word-recognition strategies in connection with contextual reading with comprehension
- Opportunities to interrelate listening, speaking, and written composition
- Ability to read orally for the benefit of an audience (and for the joy of it)

The overall goal of the language arts program is to give children the opportunity to experience themselves as thinking, communicating human beings. Learning to communicate is a lifelong process—a marathon, not a sprint. Our goals need to be long-range. Learning to communicate is a creative problem you can enjoy continuing to solve yourself, especially as you now learn to interact with young children. First learn to know them, then orchestrate your classroom environments, and you will guide young children to learn to communicate.

References

Allen, R. V. *Language experiences in communication*. Boston: Houghton Mifflin, 1976.

Allen, R. V. Personal communication. 1978. (Mimeo)

Brazelton, T. B. *Infants and mothers*. New York: Delacorte, 1969.

Brazelton, T. B. *Toddlers and parents*. New York: Delacorte, 1972.

Brazelton, T. B. Development of the infant in different cultural environments. Workshop presented for the Sixth Annual Summer Workshop, Federation of North Texas Area Universities, Dallas, June, 1980.

Chomsky, C. Stages in language development and reading exposure. *Harvard Educational Review*, 1972, *42*, 1–33.

Cullinan, B. E., & Carmichael, C. W. *Literature and young children*. Urbana, Ill.: National Council of Teachers of English, 1977.

Durkin, D. *Children who read early: Two longitudinal studies*. New York: Teachers College Press, 1966.

Elkind, D. We can teach reading better. *Today's Education*, 1975 (November–December), 34–38.

Elkind, D. *A sympathetic understanding of the child: Birth to sixteen* (2d ed.). Boston: Allyn & Bacon, 1978.

Guilfoile, E. *Nobody listens to Andrew.* Chicago: Follet. 1957.

Lundsteen, S. W. *Children learn to communicate: Language arts through creative problem solving.* Englewood Cliffs, N.J.: Prentice-Hall, 1976. (a)

Lundsteen, S. W. *Ideas into practice.* Englewood Cliffs, N.J.: Prentice-Hall, 1976. (b)

Lundsteen, S. W. On developmental relations between language-learning and reading. *Elementary School Journal,* 1977, *77,* 192–203.

Lundsteen, S. W. Give your speaking voice a home improvement course. *Instructor,* 1979, *89*(1), 120–127. (a)

Lundsteen, S. W. *Listening: Its impact on reading and the other language arts at all levels* (2d ed.). Urbana, Ill.: ERIC/RCS/National Council of Teachers of English, 1979. (b)

MacGinitie, W. H. When should we begin to teach reading? *Language Arts,* 1976, *53,* 878–882.

Scholastic Book Services. *Individualized reading.* (Scholastic Inservice Training). (Audiotape cassette and filmstrip). New York, N. Y.: Scholastic, n.d.

Dr. Seuss (T. S. Geisel). *The lorax.* New York: Random House, 1971.

Veatch, J. *How to teach reading with children's books.* New York: Citation Press, 1968.

Weir, M. K., & Eggelston, P. J. Teacher's first words. *Day Care and Early Education,* 1975, *3,* 17–21.

Williams, R. M. Why children should draw. *Saturday Review,* September 3, 1977, pp. 11–16.

CHAPTER 11

CHAPTER 11

*Art is a human activity having for its
purpose the transmission to
others of the highest and best feelings to
which men have risen.*

—Leo Tolstoi

HELPING CHILDREN DEVELOP AFFECTIVE ABILITIES: EXAMPLES FROM SOCIAL STUDIES, ART, AND MUSIC

Katheryn Sampeck

Music Experiences for Young Children 327

In this chapter we continue our practice of using relevant aspects of the curriculum to illustrate how teachers may foster development. In the sections to follow we focus on curriculum goals that assist affective development using illustrations from social studies, art, and music. Certainly there are affective and ethetical aspects to other areas, such as science; and certainly social studies, art, and music have cognitive aspects. And naturally, different kinds of development do not occur separately; they are intertwined. But here we do not go into the cognitive aspects of social studies, art, and music. Our purpose is to show how a teacher might work to promote affective abilities in these areas.

In the early years children who are finding out about the world they live in are also deciding who they are. They are increasingly interested in knowing about others—what they do; where they live—and in having relationships and interactions with them. We bring you ideas about facilitating the wholesome development of the child as a creative, well-balanced individual, and as a social being. These elusive concepts having to do with the quality of life are the warp and woof of the affective curriculum. Some of the questions this chapter answers are:

- What are some major goals of affective curriculum?
- What are some aspects of the social studies which are important to affective development?

- What is an enriching art experience?
- What can enhance the young child's musical development of music?
- When does esthetic awareness and appreciation begin? Hstimulated?

Major Goals of the Affective Curriculum

Curriculum can be broadly defined as everything that the child experiences in school. Thus, the *affective curriculum* encompasses an important relationship between the child and the school.

The major goal of the affective curriculum is the social, emotional moral, and creative development of unique persons. To meet that goal, the learning environment is planned with the whole child in mind and the interrelatedness of the curriculum areas becomes evident. The communication among all the subjects of the curriculum can be fully appreciated and used.

The following example illustrates that goal:

> Bill Adams came to school early to hang the *piñata* his class had made. He was well into the project (standing on a ladder) when Jennie came through the doorway, making circling turns—her full-skirted costume creating a splash of red. "It's finished! My dress is beautiful, isn't it, Mr. Adams?" Her eyes were shining and she laughed as she came to a stop below him to inspect the piñata. With appropriate "oohs" and "aahs," she danced off to share her excitement with other children who were arriving. In his mind's eye, Bill Adams could see an earlier version of this child—a well-developed, attractive, but hesitant, uncertain, afraid-to-chance-it six-year-old. He could fully appreciate Jennie's glowing enthusiasm and joy. Her volunteering to dance—in costume—for the Spanish fiesta was one of those hoped-for great moments.

For Jennie, the growth of self-confidence and feelings of assurance—the involvement and participation in the group project—served to open the way for spontaneity and creativity to emerge. The process was one of activating a learner, giving her, in Bruner's words (1971), a "full sense of intent and initiative."

Interweaving of art, music, and self-expressing; evidence of a positive self-concept; and learning about the world around her and the people in it—all these were the result of Jennie's being an interested, involved child in a responsive environment. Mentally, physically, emotionally, and creatively she extracted relevance from the interactions,

and ideas of the affective curriculum. The social studies and
ts are highly suitable disciplines through which to approach
'elopment. Now, on to a closer look at each of the areas
amples—social studies, art, and music.

Experiences for Young Children

t studies is an evolving and growing area of the curriculum—
evidence of our response to a world that is changing vastly both socially
and technologically. The school's growing role as a socializing institution
is reflected in the scope of ideas and concepts currently on the social
studies scene.

SOME GOALS FOR SOCIAL STUDIES

The following list is representative of current affective goals in social
studies. Let's consider them in terms of the teacher's supportive role:

- Engendering good feelings in children about themselves (positive self-
  concepts)—that is, instilling a sense of personal uniqueness, individ-
  uality, and self-value in the child
- Promoting effective interactions among children, and between children
  and adults
- Helping children to turn their interests outward, and developing a
  growing sense of social responsibility through personal involvement
- Helping children to realize the infinite possibilities of their _creative_
  potential
- Creating a learning climate that encourages activities which are both
  inviting and satisfying

Although goals need to be translated into daily specific objectives,
they are the necessary starting point to give us perspective.

With respect to content, we suggest five themes for selective
application: (1) broad ethical issues (e.g., pollution), (2) personal values
(e.g., self-improvement), (3) social action (e.g., assisting in a school
cleanup project), (4) moral development or social values (e.g., individual
integrity and group responsibility, (5) community research (e.g., identifying various voluntary and official efforts to reduce pollution in the
school and the community.

GUIDING EARLY SOCIAL LEARNING

Long before children enter school, they have begun their "study" of the
social studies. Consider these examples.

David, at two months, has begun to learn to expect that daddy appears
around bathtime, chucks him under the chin, and tosses him in the air before

mommy gives him his bath, cooing lovingly as she gently fondles, strokes, and supports him in the soothing water. Susie, at two months, smiles gleefully as daddy completes her evening bath, settles into his reclining chair, cuddles her close, and offers a bottle. Each of these babies is learning about family roles. No one had planned a social studies unit on "The Family." They didn't need filmstrips, story books, or class discussion to begin to form very basic concepts and attitudes about family roles.

Tommy toddles off with the teddy bear that Rickie brought to the children's center this morning. Rickie howls and makes a lunge for his teddy bear. The teacher intervenes and Tommy throws a tantrum typical of the "terrible twos." Eventually the teacher helps the children to solve their problem. The teacher didn't write a lesson plan or introduce a related art activity. But Tommy begins to learn about the concept of individual property and how to deal with frustration. Rickie begins to learn how to communicate to a peer.

Freddie, Gloria, and Ricardo are building a city in the kindergarten block corner. As Freddie builds higher and higher, Gloria helps to keep the columns straight to prevent them from toppling. Richardo's face beams as he shares with them the three hard hats that his contractor father has allowed him to bring to school. The teacher didn't have to follow a guide in some prepackaged kit. The teacher did not have to distribute a worksheet. Once the environment was established, in fact, the teacher had to be perceptive enough to stay *out* of the situation and *let the children learn.* These children developed understanding of increased efficiency through cooperative endeavors. They naturally increased their positive self-concept in an enriched environment guided by a sensitive teacher.

Every year teachers find new roomsful of children who need to be helped to rediscover for themselves the basic principles of human relations—principles which have evolved through the ages. Teachers need to set the scene and provide the nurturing that will encourage children in timid exploration of and experimentation with the self and others. We stand in awe of the tremendous responsibility of the teacher of these young children. *This is the one place where the content of learning is the process.* The teacher of these young children is expected to send on to kindergarten well-adjusted, cooperative human beings comfortable with themselves and able to function in a group setting as they move into their school years.

It is important that teachers think through the objectives to be accomplished during the year that they and the children will be "living" together. The activities to accomplish these objectives will be the ongoing practices, techniques, and experiences that permeate the day. Chapter 9 showed you how content in mathematics and science grows out of cognitive development fostered in the earliest years. In a similar way, *the formal study of social studies grows out of the discussions and social relationships that are nurtured in the preschool and kindergarten.*

What are some teaching strategies for getting across the goals and themes mentioned earlier? Several are discussed in the next few sections.

Individualization

The act of *individualizing* fosters affective (as well as cognitive) development. We have just talked about the younger child. Let's consider the older child. Have you ever seen the boredom in a classroom where twenty-nine children are listening to one child stumble through his or her turn at reading from the social studies text adopted by the state or district? To add insult to injury, when the children have finally suffered through the lesson, they are supposed to answer the questions at the end. Obviously there are more productive and less productive ways to use social studies texts. Consider these reservations: (1) Using the same textbook with the whole class might appear to be a simple method, but it certainly does not provide the child with attitudes and behavior recommended in this chapter. (2) If we acknowledge that children's reading levels can vary by as much as five grades in almost any third grade classroom, we certainly cannot expect all children in a class to benefit from a text written at one particular grade level.

How can you deal with these considerations? Individualization helps to maintain interest as each child makes meaningful discoveries. As different children seek out a variety of sources, they can help each other understand that more than one point of view is possible. Tolerance of differing opinions can be encouraged. Individualization also means allowing for different reading levels (and for nonreaders) and being able to go to different types of resources (e.g., books, atlases, films, and tapes). In this way the teacher helps to avoid frustration and children can maintain a healthy self-concept, particularly as regards their ability to learn. As part of the picture, the teacher who makes allowance for differing ways of expressing learning is enhancing a child's self-concept. For example, some children find it easier to communicate their findings through the use of oral reports, while others prefer to make dioramas. A key idea here is that individualization implies an acceptance of children as they are.

Involving children in the learning process

As was stated in Chapter 9, effective teaching methods actively involve children in the learning process as they search for information, cooperate with others, and make decisions. A culminating activity emphasizing themes and goals generally helps to provide evaluation of content and process for each social studies unit. For example, at the end of a unit on Asia, a Japanese family might visit the group to share their culture (food, values, clothing, games, and literature) and to answer the children's questions raised during their study.

Implementing the goal of improved self-concept

When teachers approach social studies with an eye to helping the child to know and to value the importance of the world and the people in it—an effective first step is to set the scene for the children to know and to value *themselves* as important persons. An initial step in planning your strategies is the realization that the teacher and the environment (the atmosphere of the school) affect the self-concept of the child.

For instance, the teacher we met earlier, Bill Adams, finds opportunities throughout the day to reinforce positive feelings, to promote the children's positive self-images. The first experience of the morning—a warm, personal, intimate greeting—given with true respect and interest, honestly meant just for Jennie, lets her know how important she is and how the day looks brighter because she is there. (This practice of greeting children individually was mentioned in Chapter 10 in connection with language development.)

Bill Adams realizes that his *body language* (or physical cues), coupled with the words he uses in the initial encounter of the day, gives a real message. Eye contact, a touch on Jennie's hand, Bill's total interest (if only for a moment)—all let Jennie know that she has something to contribute to the day.

This message is echoed by the environment, a pleasant, welcoming, inviting, interesting, and warm place. Jennie's self-concept is enhanced if her activities help her to realize she is capable and valued, that she is important as an individual and as member of the group to which she belongs. Sensitive teachers know that as they interact with children it is important to promote positive self-concepts. Teachers can approach self-concept through the "unwritten curriculum." They do this by creating a climate throughout the school that is supportive and by scheduling activities (e.g., celebrating the children's birthdays) that say in essence, "You're a very special person."

Avoiding sex-role stereotypes is another important area when considering the development of self-concept. Awareness of the subtle but real influences exerted by books, toys, stories, adults' expectations and exhortations, and the general climate ("Boys do this"; "Girls do that") is at last increasing and leading to long-needed action. Children are influenced at very early ages by ideas about limitations and restrictions based on sex. Bardwell and Seitsima (1978) found that even three-year-olds have already formed ideas about limitations and restrictions of interests and activities according to sex.

The Women's Action Alliance (Sprung, 1975) has developed a

nonsexist early childhood program. Katie can hammer and saw and build a train, as well as sing to the doll; Jim can sew on a button or iron the clothes, as well as climb to the top of the tree! Each child is encouraged to follow interests with no fear of being branded "sissy" or "tomboy," thus allowing each child in school to develop to his or her fullest potential.

Implementing the goal of turning interest outward

Once the children know themselves to some extent and have positive ideas, realistic expectations, enthusiasm, and interest—that is, once development is coming along well and the children are ready—then their interest in the world around them grows. Activities in support of this can stem from suggestions offered by actively participating children. Indeed, the interests of children are one of the most reliable guides to curriculum content.

For example, when a child from Vietnam enters the class, the teacher (after consultation with the child's parents) sets up a storytelling session in which the American children share a tall tale of Pecos Bill (a current burning interest) and the Vietnamese child shares a legend about the origin of firecrackers (another typical interest of this group). This is a springboard to collecting and sharing tales from other cultures. The children's interest is thus helped to expand outward to encompass other cultures and the question of how emotions (like fear) and the triumph of good over evil are expressed in stories belonging to various cultures. What better way to get into social studies?

Whenever and wherever possible the children need to accumulate firsthand experience. As we have mentioned, sometimes such experience can be arranged by having visitors come to the classroom, sometimes by having the children go out on a field trip. Take the ideas thus generated and *build* on the enthusiasm that results. Experiences and interactions that can later be used as references in explaining concepts, ideas, facts, and values are basic to early learning. Doing something and then talking about what you did helps make sense of things, and it's a sensible thing to do. Not only is memorizing unrelated facts dull, it's most often unrewarding. In essence, you, the teacher, can give children opportunities to appreciate themselves and others and gain knowledge of other times, other places, other people and other views of the world in a variety of effective ways in your classroom.

If you incorporate the creative arts when presenting such opportunities, you will add vitality, meaning, and understanding to the social studies activities of the children. And teachers benefit also when a focus on creativity is incorporated. They experience greater variety in their program, are better able to recognize the uniqueness of each child (and thus feel closer to each); they even find that they have fewer behavior problems in their classrooms.

Young children are naturally creative and curious. This statement means that children behave in ways and do things that are unique and valued by themselves or by others. Important elements of creativity can find expression in the affective curriculum through two avenues discussed in the next sections, on art and music. First, we will consider art.

Art Experiences for Young Children

Young children, given possibilities for creative development, respond naturally as "artists." That is, apparently the techniques of young children who are deeply involved in creative activities may be more like those of professional artists than those of older children are (Torrance, 1965). Observers suggest that the poetry, songs, and stories composed by young children are more creative than those of older children. And even the vocal behavior of young children is more like that of great vocal artists than is the vocal behavior of older children.

What happens? What can we do? First of all we need to look to the strategies and techniques we use that enhance the natural curiosity and spontaneity of the very young child. Then instead of being diminished and extinguished as the child gets older, natural curiosity and spontaneity can be not only kept intact but encouraged to grow. How can this feat be accomplished?

The thinking, planning, and preparation you do make it possible for children's spontaneous and creative responses to be used in meaningful ways. Too often, teachers have the feeling that art is effective only if presented by an "expert." It is important to realize that *you* are the best teacher there is to guide young children in their art experiences—because you know the *children*. Of course, you will take advantage of the expertise of others whenever and wherever it is useful, but do retain your role as the central person in the children's learning about art and their experiencing it. You will thus be able to take advantage of opportunities to design and implement such esthetic experiences in ways that suit the development, experience, and interests of each child. You can use art to clarify other areas of the curriculum. Art activities need not always be scheduled in some specific, limited time, but can flow through the day as the desire or need arises.

SOME GOALS FOR ART EXPERIENCES When it comes to goals for young children's art experiences, again, we need to think in terms of developmental and long-range goals. Three important goals are (1) to let children *use* the environment, (2) to let children *symbolize* through form, (3) to raise children's *awareness*.

1 *Using the environment.* We know that children progress from scribbling to artistic representation, showing a great deal of knowledge and information about the world by the time they reach kindergarten.

Our first goal, then, is to give children chances to actively extract information from their environment (by touching, listening, tasting, pushing, pulling), thus abstracting important and usable concepts. But to have goals beyond the artistic understanding of young children is to make the program meaningless. For example, having a child color in outlines of objects on duplicated sheets is a ridiculous waste of time (especially when the child has not experienced the objects depicted). Other examples of activities antithetical to this goal are making ashtrays from clay when, developmentally speaking, the children just need to experience rolling and pounding; and making flower baskets from egg cartons—a procedure that simply has too many steps and is directed toward too specific an end product.

2 *Symbolizing through control of form.* Provide the opportunity for children to control two- and three-dimensional forms in order to express through their art emotions, symbols, concepts, values, and thoughts that are a part of them and a reflection of their environment. ("My art is me!") Provide the opportunity for children to manipulate, change, or alter the materials and feel that what they are producing is uniquely theirs. Materials on which a child can imprint personal impressions include clay; durable paper of satisfying quality (to be used with brushes); charcoal to be used on a sidewalk; sticks for drawing on a smooth stretch of mud or wet sand. Process is more important than product. This process can bring a child great joy.

3 *Raising experience to a level of awareness.* Provide the opportunity for children to talk with someone as they create and become expressive; don't let their activity become mindlessly mechanical. For example you might ask a child hesitantly applying a felt tip pen to paper, "Suppose your pen were to walk around this piece of paper, just as you walked around this room a minute ago; how do you suppose it would go?" Teachers can confirm what the child seems to feel and know.

DEVELOPMENTAL STAGES IN ARTISTIC COMMUNICATION

Since our goals tell us that knowledge of development is important, let's take a closer look at some things we know about it.

Knowledge of how the child develops in this artistic mode of communication and expression is basic to incorporating art successfully in the early childhood affective curriculum. Children are not miniature adults; and children's artistic expressions are unique and meaningful, especially when looked at from the developmental point of view. As with all developmental guidelines, the ages mentioned below are approximate. These developmental sequences furnish the basic structure for the design of the art program for young children.

Understanding developmental sequences implies respecting children's artistic productions at any age (rather than trying to make them conform to external or adult standards). Teachers and caretakers can do much to help a young child's artistic development by providing ample

Figure 11-1
*Michael, age 2½: "My
rocket ship. It's
leaving." Scribbles
typical of age 2 to 4.
(Source: Collected by
B. W. Kingore.)*

opportunities for experimentation and practice, and being accepting of the results.

Between the ages of two and four, children typically draw "scribbles." These are lines drawn in various ways—by fingers on a steamed window, for instance, or with crayons, watercolor, or tempera on paper. These scribbles deserve our respect, for they are the foundation of drawing. Figure 11-1 is an example.

With practice and repetition these scribbles become symbols which form the elements of drawing sometime between the ages of four and seven. These drawings often are not clearly recognizable to adults but have a stable meaning to the child. During this time large heads and sticklike arms and legs make their apperance. (See Figures 11-2 and 11-3.) With further practice children draw in more conventional ways.

Drawings of seven-, eight-, and nine-year-olds (Figure 11-4 is an example) often have easily identifiable elements (such as houses, cars, suns, and rockets). But most children in this age group have not acquired the techniques of realistic representation that will be attempted by children in the upper elementary grades (Lowenfeld, 1947).

All through these developmental stages children need adults who will encourage and understand that the process is more important than the product. They need opportunities for solving their own artistic problems and for evaluating their own work.

Figure 11-2
Caroline, age 3½:
Scribbles become
symbols. (Source:
Collected by B. W.
Kingore.)

Figure 11-3
Thomas, age 5: "Me
and my house."
Symbol development.
(Source: Collected by
B. W. Kingore.)

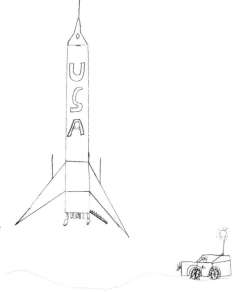

Figure 11-4
Don, age 8: "Blasting down on the moon." Easily identifiable elements typical of ages 7 to 9. (Source: Prepared by Don Kingore.)

AN ACCEPTING AND PSYCHOLOGICALLY SAFE CLIMATE FOR ART

One of the best strategies you can use to elicit positive response and active participation in art activities from children is to create an accepting and approving climate in the classroom. Jim should not feel timid or hesitant about going to the art area, choosing the color or colors he finds most appealing today, and putting his own idea on the paper before him. Careful planning and skillful guidance are necessary if such a creativity-supporting climate is to be a reality. (See Chapter 14.)

The arrangements you make for the children you teach will depend on a number of variables. What kind of space can you set aside permanently for art? Which materials will be most appropriate for the age and development of the children? Is there a low sink near the area to facilitate cleaning up, or must other means be planned? Some basic ideas on materials, techniques, procedures, and guidelines (to follow) can be useful in any setting.

Materials

The children will benefit from a variety of unstructured materials. Tempera paint, crayons, finger paint, felt-tip markers, large sheets of appropriate paper, real clay, collage materials and colored pencils—all fit into this category. It is essential to have a sturdy table, scissors that really cut well, and glue that can be managed by children and will really hold materials in place. Try each item yourself with the child's point of view in mind before you put it in the room. It may surprise you when you find that many inviting-looking materials really are ineffective.

If we avoid using baby talk with young children, why don't we avoid using babyish materials for their art? Why always give them cheap newsprint that develops holes, tears easily, and falls apart? Moreover, we need to avoid letting gimmicky materials be the tail that wags the dog. We need to keep in mind our goal of fostering the child's own construction, of fostering children's own symbolizations as they control the form of the media.

Teaching techniques

Give as much control over events to the children as makes good sense. Offer only the guidance and help that is needed so that the children can learn to control the media in which they are working. As the children gain experience, even less help will be needed. The environment is designed so that ultimately the children become quite *self-sufficient*. If this goal is to be attained, the physical environment needs to be carefully designed and the materials carefully organized so that the children will not encounter useless frustration. (E.g., paint can be thickened, so that it "runs" less. Or better yet, mount paper on the floor instead of on an easel.)

Learning to control the media effectively is an important first step. When the child can feel confident with the media, then truly creative work becomes possible. Young children enjoy simple activities, such as mixing clear, bright basic colors and observing the results. It can seem almost like magic as the blue and yellow combine to make green—right before their eyes! The world is filled with wonder; let the children experience it.

With Lowenfeld's developmental stages in mind, we can understand that it is important not to demand or expect realism in children's art. "What a beautiful airplane you made!" meant as a compliment, is anything but to the child who never intended an airplane in the first place. It is far better to ask children if they would like to tell you about their picture. "It's just a red picture" is a perfectly good reason for creating it—and having it valued.

It's to be hoped that most teachers have moved far from the idea of teacher standing in front of a room of thirty children demonstrating how to do a "winter scene," hanging her creation on the board, and then circulating to watch thirty pairs of hands "create" a winter scene, all of which end up looking remarkably like the teacher's. We would still, however, like to caution against creating a "model" for the children to copy. Even if not intended that way, leaving your product on display, in effect, sets up a "copy the model" situation.

Cleaning up is important in the sequence of events. When one child is finished, the space and materials should be ready for the next child. This management takes some gentle reminders for a while. But if you have shown the children how to do the cleaning up in a way they understand, it is accepted as a part of their personal responsibility and contribution to the art program.

Disciplinary guidelines

Another important factor in this creative art program is the effectiveness of *discipline* in the sense that there is a genuine respect for the worker and the work being done. The children can work more securely and more freely if there is no threat of interference by others. This important development is something to be carefully nurtured in all the activities of the classroom, for little can be accomplished in the way of true creativity without this well-established mode of conduct. (See Chapter 14.)

Time

Time is yet another important element of the creative process, whatever the media. Kellogg (1958) suggests that time be allowed for each child to paint as long as he or she cares to. Enforced "taking turns" in rapid succession never produces satisfied painters or satisfying paintings. When children must take turns, allow fewer turns of longer duration, rather than frequent turns of short duration. A "turn" should mean time enough to make several paintings if the child wishes to do so. Careful consideration of the time spans required by the various activities included in the environment is important. Do engage wholeheartedly in those activities that are possible; but if there is not sufficent time for the activity to be a fulfilling experience, it is better to omit it. The goals suggested imply sufficient time.

VARIETIES OF ACTIVITIES   Generally the classroom can accommodate at least three approaches to art activities.

1   The teacher can choose among the activities involving the variety of unstructured materials listed earlier, (e.g., clay, finger paint, tempera, collage). These are always available for the children to use. The space you have and the children you teach will determine which and how many of these materials you can use effectively.

2 Another class of art projects is done in a *block of time*—e.g., a large permanent mural. If the mural is not to be permanent, it can be done on long sheets of butcher paper and hung. Such a painting can be displayed for a satisfying period of time, and then it can be rolled and stored. Such a project requires careful attention to details. Small planning copies of the proposed work are usually a helpful idea. This sort of thing would *not* be appropriate as an initial effort in a new class. However, when the working atmosphere is established and children are able to cooperate well, something of this nature is worthwhile. Marshall (1963) describes many ways her pupils implemented such projects in all areas of the curriculum. Model cities or large detailed maps can make ideas come alive in social studies. (But take care not to become so involved in *product* that *process* is sacrificed.)

3 Other processes or activities, especially for younger children, require closer instruction and supervision. Examples are batik, spatter painting, and sculpture. Demonstrating a technique early in the week and then setting up a center to be used throughout the week is a successful approach. You can make up a *rotation system* so that the materials are available and in use for a satisfying period of time and each child that is interested has ample opportunity to work with the process or media. This plan will preclude the frantic atmosphere that seems to infect the art activities of too many classrooms!

Ideally, you will have a great enough variety of materials and ideas to create continued interest, but few enough projects or activities so that the children have real opportunities for many experiences in the same media. Then genuine growth can be accomplished.

SUPPORTING ARTISTIC DEVELOPMENT

How can you offer support to the developing artist? In any creative endeavor at school, you, the teacher, are the person who builds the structure for creativity. However, structure does not teach creativity; it is the framework, the occasion, or the place in which creativity can occur.

One caution: Children need to have the time and space in which to function within the broad guidelines of productivity and self-discipline—but with the freedom to make mistakes, to carry ideas through. They need some exposure to the fact that there are many steps to a final accomplishment—whether it is painting a picture, writing a story, or making a vase of clay. Children often do not witness the series of steps involved in the making of a product. They see only the finished product. They can build a false impression that if something does not work out rather quickly and easily, there's no use in keeping at it. Mistakes are important as indications that there are other ways to try—"This didn't work; what else might I do?" If we evaluate only those things the children are ready to have evaluated, they will be more willing to make mistakes and then continue along the way to their successes.

Another thing you can do to help children express their own ideas is accepting a child's decision on when a work is finished. The child's concern is initially centered on the process rather than on producing realistic works or specific and recognizable works. When the media are mastered, mistakes are accepted and reworked, and when the child has developed sufficiently, products will become important. Until then, there is the joy of doing.

Your *comments* on the works the children produce will be guided by your concept of what you are really observing. Lowenfeld and Brittain (1970) present a clear idea: "The picture that a youngster draws or paints is much more than the markings on paper. It is an expression of the total child at the time he or she was painting. My art is me" (p. 21). Sometimes children can become very engrossed in art, and the product may have a real depth of feeling and completeness. At other times the product may be merely an exploration of a new material. But even in this case, the product will reveal the youngster's eagerness or hesitation in attempting a new task. Although it is stating the obvious, it is true that of thousands of drawings by children, no two are ever alike. Each drawing reflects the feelings, awareness, the creative involvement, the esthetic tastes, and even the social development of the child who created it. Not only is each of these areas reflected in the art that youngsters produce; changes are also clearly seen in their art as they grow and develop.

Use your comments to share the unique quality of each child's work. Value judgments are unnecessary. If every picture is "marvelous" or "fantastic," the child begins to doubt either your sincerity or your taste. Why bother with "Oh, what a beautiful picture!" when you can honestly say, "You really made your crayon dance around that paper to the music." Enjoy what the child does with a sincere comment that lets you share in the creation or the experience.

The child as observer and consumer of art

Athough children spend much energy and time on the processes and activities of art, we must also consider the role of the child as observer and consumer of art. No classroom is complete without well-displayed paintings of the great masters, both ancient and modern. (One such learning center, described below, was called "Picasso's corner.") Luckily, many fine prints are available through the stores in larger museums (and mail-order lists are also available). Libraries are wonderful sources of prints, that can be checked out just as book are. The need to return them is a reminder to change the display often enough to keep interest alive. In a very natural way, ideas about the artists and their works become a part of what goes on in the classroom.

We tend to underestimate children's taste in art, often assuming that children will appreciate only what we consider "children's art." These items are generally all "cute" or "sunshine and light" pictures, "looking at the world through rose-colored glasses." Could young children really be interested in serious themes? An interesting experiment conducted by Meron (1976) with kibbutz children indicated that when children were permitted to choose the art they wanted to live with, they exhibited what is considered rather sophisticated taste. When these pictures were tastefully framed and given to the children, they hung them in their rooms, talked and wrote about them, and appreciated and related to them in the fullest sense.

One teacher has had great success with "Picasso's corner," a learning center in his kindergarten–first grade that is filled with activities related to the artist of the month. After a while, the children were able to identify new paintings by familiar artists; moreover, their own artwork reflected the various schools to which they were exposed! We suggest that you bear in mind these two examples as you think about what kind of art you wish to introduce to children and how you want to "decorate" your room.

Another enjoyable activity is a carefully planned museum visit. Seeing an actual painting after having seen a print of it in the classroom adds an important dimension for children. Just remember that several short and interesting visits are best suited to the developmental stage reached by the children you are working with. Early exposure to the wonders of the museum is well worth the careful preparation and work that is necessary to accomplish the trip.

An issue: "Back to the basics" versus the arts

A problem that sometimes occurs when all is going well in the integrated art program is the sudden sense of mistrust of your own positive responses. The work the children are doing is really exciting. In fact, quite a lot of time is spent in art activities on some days—with great satisfaction. But, what about the "basics"? Should you reconsider your whole approach? A look at some supportive statements may give you added reassurance:

Some researchers are now saying that it "seems clear that the arts have far more than an 'enrichment' role to play in the schools. They appear to stimulate a child's natural curiosity and—perhaps literally—to expand the capacity of his or her brain. The arts even help children discover their own worth and identity" (Williams, 1977, p. 11).

Furthermore, the time spent in creative experience each day has a high positive influence on and is a crucial element in the reading program in the early years (Allen, 1978). You can find many other ideas (e.g., therapeutic advantages) to add to these statements that uphold the value of a creative approach in your classroom. (Also see research in Brittain, 1979, and our Chapter 10.)

Music Experiences for Young Children

The creative approach also includes music as one of its vital components. Accordingly, we now turn to some suggestions for your music program.

As a general rule, the early childhood teacher has not benefited from a broad approach to music training during course work. Unless music is already a part of your own background, you may have feelings of uncertainty when you approach the teaching of music. Even programmed material (abundant in the areas of mathematics, science, social studies, and reading) is difficult to find. Does this lack mean that music is relatively unimportant? On the contrary, "music for every child and every child for music" needs to be one of the high priorities in any early childhood setting.

Fortunately, the technical material, techniques, and strategies of music for children can be learned along with the children if you are not yet familiar with them. The key ideas are these:

- Simplicity
- Following the natural instincts and interests of the young child (developmental music)

How can you begin to plan for the music program in your classroom? Stop and listen; the basic ingredients are all around you. Andrews (1976, p. 34) writes:

> Clearly, there can be no recipe for a musical expression. There can be no goal other than helping children discover the creativity that is inherently theirs. Experiences with internal and external outcomes, which are as varied as the children, are preferable to teacher-planned activities with the resultant finished products. The time allotted for music is *all time*, for who can impose a stop/go on children freely swinging and leaping in the play yard or imitating fall leaves or gusty March winds or singing their "babies" to sleep in the homemaking area or singing their own songs as they paint at the easel?

Music permeates the lives of young children and interrelates with all aspects of the curriculum. Music is, therefore, not an adjunct to the "business of learning," but an integral part of social, emotional, physical, and cognitive development. (For example, one teacher we know tapes children's spontaneous songs, transcribes them, and uses them as reading material for the children.)

The following section offers you suggestions for materials, techniques, and programs. As a preface, consider this important reassurance: even if music did nothing more than bring joy to the world, it would justify its existence. If you, the teacher, find *joy* in music, you *can* convey that to your children. If you do nothing more, you will still have made a valuable contribution. And if you don't do that, nothing else you do matters very much. Now let's look at our overall goals.

The goals of a music program fall into three major areas relating to: (1) appreciation, (2) performance, and (3) therapeutic aspects.

1 Appreciation

In this age of blaring stereos, television sets, and massive sales of records, tapes, and tickets to concerts and festivals, attention needs to be paid to the development of esthetic awareness. Young people are indeed "consumers" of music. What they consume is largely determined by the exposure they have had, their sensitivities to melody, harmony, rhythm, and tone.

2 Performance

We have a twofold responsibility in this area. First, we must develop a general level of competence in children's singing, in their instrumental music, in their own original songs and dances, and in their moving to music. Second, we need to be able to identify children with unique talent or ability and assist in providing the means to develop their special competences.

3 Therapeutic aspects

Music provides many opportunities for children to express ideas and feelings about themselves and their world. Music can soothe and calm or stimulate. It can provide a release for strong emotions, anxieties, and frustrations, and a chance to build positive self-concepts and social relationships.

Being soothed by a lullaby in the earliest days of life marks the *first* response of the child to music. The lullaby is a part of the cultural heritage of music around the world. Rhythmic movements of rocking, swaying, or dancing are used universally to soothe and calm the fretful child. Infants not only respond to song and rhythm, but begin cooing and making rhythmical movements of their own. Young children are tuned in to the rhythms and melodies of life. A developmental early childhood music program is designed to take advantage of this fortunate situation.* Some suggestions for parents or others caring for infants include the following. They are listed according to age levels:

For Infants under Six Months of Age
- Talking expressively to the baby or humming, singing or chanting as you carry out all the rituals associated with his or her care (bathing, feeding, changing)
- Providing opportunities for the baby to hear sounds—the ticking of a clock or metronome, a music box, wind chimes

For Older Infants
- Continuing to talk and sing to the child
- Using musical records occasionally (not constantly)
- Making sounds with a bell tied to a bootie
- Producing sounds with various kinds of colorful rattles
- Clapping for the baby and clapping his or her hands
- Demonstrating the ringing of a doorbell, the ringing of a telephone, the gushing of water from a faucet
- Playing melodies on a piano, guitar, harmonica, or even a simple kazoo
- Telling or reading stories involving sounds of objects or animals and making the sounds
- Giving the child objects that create various sounds—pot lid and wooden spoon, keys, measuring spoons, dinner bell
- Moving the baby's arms, legs, and body to music

For Toddlers
- Limiting musical experiences primarily to individual or small-group activities with time and space to experiment
- Providing simple instruments and props such as scarves and feathers
- Singing and chanting for and with the child, helping distinguish different sounds in the environment

LATER MUSICAL EXPERIENCES

Now we turn to children of preschool, kindergarten, and primary-school age. What kinds of musical experiences do we need to provide for them? First, we note four well-known systems of teaching music. Then we offer some suggestions for teachers who prefer to develop their own developmental music program.

---

* Bayless and Ramsey (1978) provide some excellent suggestions for capitalizing on the natural interest and daily opportunities for building a musical foundation.

Some systematic approaches to music

Although the many different systematic approaches to the teaching of music are directed to the same goals, each employs somewhat different means to reach them. For example, Suzuki (1969) begins at birth and stresses involvement by parents, the use of a musical instrument (a small violin) almost as an extension of the body, and capitalizing on the child's ear for music. Orff (Landis & Carder, 1972) stresses *rhythm* and the child's natural, "elemental" music, combining music (often using specially designed percussion instruments), movement, and speech. To make it easy to produce tunes, only the black keys of the piano are used at first. Kodaly (Nye, 1975) places emphasis on the *voice* and on developing literacy in music much as we develop literacy in language.

Developing your own program

You, the teacher, may identify with one of these approaches. If so, you should avail yourself of the many materials and workshops designed to develop skills in implementing such a program. You may want to adapt some of the ideas or practices and add them to your own ideas. You may want to build your own program. We next turn to some basic techniques that may help you to do so.

Teaching techniques You will want to ensure a balance of opportunities to *make* music (using the voice and other instruments) and to *respond* to music (using listening and body-movement skills).

Following are some suggestions adapted from Bayless and Ramsey (1978) for techniques related to *making* music.

Using the Voice
- Introduce new songs in a natural situation—at times to a small group, at times to the whole class. Capitalize on spontaneous situations.
- Memorize both words and melody before you teach a song, so that you can maintain eye contact and provide nonverbal cues.
- Use the voice rather than the piano for introducing a new song, as it is easier for children to match a human voice than a piano.
- Keep the introduction short. Children want to sing, not discuss a song.
- Action songs or songs calling for props will usually draw in the more timid singers. (Sing "Old MacDonald Had a Farm" with various toy animal props, for example.)
- Use the "whole" method: that is, sing the whole song through several times for several days, encouraging children to join in on key words or phrases until they can sing the whole song.
- Encourage children to improvise and sing about everyday activities.
- Select songs for children that have a narrow range (from middle C to

A) and a limited number of pitch leaps. Gradually broaden the singing range.
- Include songs that have repeated words, phrases, or rhythms.

Using Instruments
- Have as few rules as possible for handling instruments and many opportunities for children to select and even to create the most appropriate instrument.
- Encourage children to use different parts of their body to produce varying sounds.
- Use many objects in the environment to create sounds: spoons, jar caps, boxes (empty or filled with various beans), beads, and buttons.
- Encourage children and parents to make instruments.
- Introduce instruments in a manner that encourages explorations of the possibilities of each.

Responding to music What other ideas about music are important? As a general rule, the more simple the instrumentation in music, the more suitable it is for young children's listening. Records with a single piano or guitar or a solo voice seem more understandable for the young child. As their interest in music grows, children enjoy more complex instrumentation, and they will want to know more about the kinds of instruments they hear on some of their favorite records. If it is possible to have a series of visitors come to the classroom, perhaps the children could see and hear several instruments over a period of time. In addition, many records illustrate the sounds of the different instruments. The children enjoy knowing and eventually being able to identify the various "voices" of the many instruments. The following are some suggestions (adapted from Nye, 1975) for techniques related to *responding* to music.

Listening
- Provide short listening experiences using bells, recorder, piano, flute, and string instruments.
- Help children to discriminate between loud and soft, heavy and light, fast and slow, happy and sad, high and low.
- Provide opportunities to listen to orchestral instruments. You can use real or pictured instruments with recordings. Older children or adults may perform for children.
- Play recorded classical and contemporary music for the children, who will soon develop favorites they want to hear again and again.

Movement
- Help the child relate familiar experiences and responses to music.
- Encourage expression of feelings derived from music.
- Provide opportunities for the child to discriminate and respond to various rhythms, tempos, and dynamics. (See Chapter 8.)

Teachers can use recordings of various kinds of music in the outdoor area. More outdoor activities, especially expressive activities, will be welcomed by the children. Find an appropriate place for the record player outside and use rhythm instruments with a favorite record. How about marching, doing folk dances, or just moving with the music? Have you tried doing an art project to music? The creative arts can be an enjoyable addition to the environment in many ways each day.

Esthetic Awareness

Throughout our discussion of the creative arts, you have probably identified an unstated theme: developing the esthetic sense in children. Let's turn now to consideration of what people mean by children's "esthetic sense."

What do we mean by esthetics? In the narrowest sense, esthetics refers to the perception and appreciation of art, but that is only one element of what we are talking about.

Children who have a background rich in sensory and tactile experiences have a basis on which to build esthetic perception. If this perception comes so naturally to young children, why go into such detail about it? Margolin (1974, p. 377) states the case well:

> Technological processes, computer programs, and the product orientation of industrial efficiency is finding its way into various educational processes. For this reason, the humanistic element must be guarded continuously especially where young children are concerned. Their development in the aesthetic as well as the intellectual sense must be held in high priority. This development can easily be lost in goals of product efficiency.

In a rich and responsive learning environment, the curiosity, spontaneity, and eagerness of the child will be valued and nourished as the experiences and knowledge are enlarged and grow. This method is a way to give esthetics a high priority.

The Central Midwestern Educational Laboratory (CEMREL), has undertaken the monumental task of upgrading the nation's esthetic values and stimulating a greater awareness of both environmental blight and beauty. The educational goal of CEMREL's esthetic education program is to bring esthetic subject matter—music, literature, theater, dance, film, visual arts, and artificial and natural environments—within the grasp of all students.

Esthetic education needs to avoid cultivation of just one model of taste and judgment. Instead, it should educate an individual's senses to varied esthetic responses, judgments, and actions. It should also make individuals responsible for their esthetic environment ("Don't litter; add touches that beautify"). To the extent that education can broaden a student's capacities for esthetic experience, extending such capacities becomes the primary concern for esthetic education. (Can we increase children's pleasure in painting, in music?) These ideas sum up the CEMREL philosophy for esthetic education.

Earlier in this chapter, we mentioned Jennie's excitement over dancing for the Spanish fiesta. Music and art are to some extent international languages, and they can speak to all ages. The early years present wonderful opportunities to use children's natural capacities, abilities, and interests. This stage is the time to begin building esthetic awareness and enjoyment. Some strategies and techniques in the area of art and music can exert positive influence on the creative efforts of the child. Everything you do makes an impression on the child—from making an interesting arrangement of the daisies that Jim brings to playing favorite classics as a background of the morning activities to just noticing the bright red cardinal in the magnolia tree. You create the environment for esthetic growth!

Summary

Children are naturally curious, hungry for knowledge, and eager to learn. They are ready to reach out, touch, and experience with their minds the results of their interactions with their environment. The affective curriculum is essentially a design to enhance the social, emotional, moral, and creative development of children in the early childhood setting. The teacher not only arranges an interesting, inviting environment, but creates a climate fostering the search for understanding. This environment enhances self-concepts, social responsibility, and cooperation.

A major goal of preschool and kindergarten programs is the development of well-adjusted, cooperative human beings who are comfortable with themselves, their peers, and the adults with whom they interact. Specific social studies objectives and activities grow from this goal of positive self-concept and the turning of interest outward. A selection from among basic themes (e.g., ethical ones such as pollution) can add a further perspective and help integrate activity for social studies. Children can learn to appreciate the richness and value of cultural diversity early on and start to understand the ever-widening brotherhood and sisterhood that can unite us all.

The field of art offers many avenues for the development of affective abilities. With an eye to social, emotional, and creative development, this chapter provided some guiding clues for viewing and responding to children's art. It emphasized a developmental point of view. In this chapter you found emphasis on children's own symbolization of their experience through control of artistic forms (e.g., clay, paint), on the interactive, communicative role of teacher and children, and on creating an environment and climate that invites children's participation in art activities. Materials, techniques, and guidelines for art activities were presented. Teachers are encouraged to view children not only as producers of art but also to be aware of their potential as consumers and of their capacities and taste in observing and appreciating fine art. The teacher also needs to be aware of the worth of art as an integral part of the curriculum in the face of "back to the basics" pressures.

Another curriculum area just as critical to affective development is *music* (which also sometimes has to be defended—not a "frill" but an integral part of the curriculum). Goals for a music program relate to the child as (1) a producer (in the performance of vocal and instrumental music), (2) a consumer (in listening to and appreciating music), and (3) an individual in need of the therapeutic aspects of music as a release for emotions and a help in developing positive self-concepts and social relationships. The music "curriculum" begins when the baby hears the soothing tones of the mother's voice. You found, in this chapter, suggestions for providing opportunities for the baby to listen to a variety of sounds—the basis for early musical experiences. We mentioned several systematic and highly developed systems of teaching music to young children. But we stressed developing your own individual, developmentally oriented music program and gave many suggestions. Finally, this chapter discussed building children's esthetic sense and awareness and the importance of valuing the curiosity, spontaneity, and eagerness of young children.

This chapter has continued the emphasis of all chapters in Part Three. This emphasis stresses the intermingling and interaction between our knowledge of child development and our knowledge of curriculum goals, content, and processes. Applying your developmental know-how to the early childhood curriculum is one of your most important roles.

A Look Ahead

What does Part Four of this book hold in store for you? It provides some specific strategies designed to enable you to be the kind of teacher who sets a growth-oriented tone through managing people and resources, guiding children in self-discipline, planning, improving your teaching methods, meeting needs of the special child, and working with parents and the community.

References

Allen, R. V. A learning environment to develop language for reading. Paper presented at Reading and Early Childhood Conference, East Texas State University, Commerce, Tex., 1978.

Andrews, P. Music and motion: The rhythmic language of children. *Young Children*, 1976, *32*(1), 33–36.

Bardwell, J., & Sietsima, M. Bardwell-Sietsima sex-stereotype scale project report number one. Dallas: East Texas State University Metroplex Center, 1978.

Bayless, K., & Ramsey, M. *Music: A way of life for the young child.* St. Louis, Mo.: Mosby, 1978.

Brittain, W. L. *Creativity, art and the young child.* New York: Macmillan, 1979.

Bruner, J. S. The process of education revisited. *Phi Delta Kappan*, 1971, *53*, 18–21.

Kellogg, R. *The how of successful finger painting.* Belmont, Calif.: Fearon, 1958.

Landis, B., & Carder, P. *The eclectic curriculum in American music education: Contributions of Dalcroze, Kodaly, and Orff.* Washington, D.C.: Music Educators National Conference, 1972.

Lowenfeld, V. *Creative and mental growth.* New York: Macmillan, 1947.

Lowenfeld, V., & Brittain, W. L. *Creative and mental growth* (5th ed.). London: Collier-Macmillan, 1970.

Margolin, E. *Sociocultural elements in early childhood education.* New York: Macmillan, 1974.

Meron, C. *The child as a consumer of art.* Unpublished manuscript, Pacific Oaks College, Pasadena, Calif., 1976.

Marshall, S. *An experiment in education.* London: Cambridge University Press, 1963.

Nye, V. *Music for young children.* Dubuque, Iowa: Brown, 1975.

Sprung, B. *Non-sexist education for young children.* New York: Citation Press, 1975.

Suzuki, S. *Nurtured by love.* New York: Exposition Press, 1969.

Torrance, E. P. *Rewarding creative behavior.* Englewood Cliffs, N.J.: Prentice-Hall, 1965.

Williams, R. M. Why children should draw. *Saturday Review*, September 3, 1977, pp. 11–16.

PART FOUR

MORE INGREDIENTS FOR SUCCESSFUL PROGRAMS: WORKING WITH CHILDREN AND PARENTS

Parts Two and Three to this book have given you a thorough introduction. This introduction clarified what children are like and, thus, what goals and curriculum are appropriate in developmental areas—cognitive, affective, and motor. We selected examples from various subject and content areas appropriate to developmental abilities. In Part Four we complete the picture with four chapters concerning how to put together ingredients for successful and satisfying programs. The ability to select and implement the most appropriate curriculum on the basis of an understanding of the developmental needs of the child is what teaching is all about. But in addition, we need to attend to the needs of special children (Chapter 13), consider the tone of the classroom (Chapter 14), and involve parents and draw upon community resources (Chapter 15).

"Putting it all together" (the aim of this part) involves selecting, knowing, and feeling comfortable with your own philosophy, theory, and style of teaching (the deliberately created environment and you yourself as teacher, compatible with the child as learner and with the child's ways and styles of knowing). Putting it all together also involves an understanding of the role of processes (such as play and problem solving) as vehicles for learning (Chapter 12). In this introduction we examine three questions concerning learning, roles, and planning.

What is learning and what is the nature of the learner? *We conceive of learning as construction from inside children as they assimilate and accom-*

modate their natural life experiences. We do not conceive of learning as instruction from the outside with the teacher "pouring" knowledge into passive recipients. The process of construction takes place continuously with or without formal educational experiences. But the "teacher artist," who is prepared to assist the "child artist," can guide and arrange the learning environment. We have profound respect for children, whom we view as astonishingly capable and autonomous as they go about constructing their world.

What is the teacher's role? We need to avoid role confusion. Teachers are the professionals. We have the responsibility, based on our years of preparation and experience, to structure the learning environment to include activities and materials to meet the needs and interests of all our children.

We make certain crucial assumptions about teaching roles. Teachers need to stay alert, generate positive feelings, provide children with relevant experiences, encourage autonomy on the part of children, and (often by encouraging creative problem solving) assist them in synthesizing their experiences.

Is the teacher a technician or an artist? We strongly suggest the point of view that teaching is an art. Teaching is not a robotlike activity of carrying out exact recipes or parroting scripts. Teaching does use available scientific knowledge, e.g., about development, learning disabilities, and about preventative and remedial techniques that build upon strengths.

How much planning goes on in the open classroom? In our opinion the "open classroom" seems to foster and to help us reach goals of creativity and autonomy. The open classroom, however, needs to be well-planned—even more so than the traditional classroom. For every "lesson" planned in a traditional classroom, the teacher in the open classroom may plan three to five alternative activities to meet the needs and interests of different children (Chapter 14).

The teacher needs to have goals and objectives clearly defined in order to relate activities and learning centers to these aims, in order to be able to capitalize upon spontaneous situations, and in order to find the "match" among the nature of the child, the experience, and the time (the right experience for the right child at the right time). Plans need to include large-group, small-group, and individual activities.

What are other considerations for "putting it all together"? Putting it all together includes responding to the special needs of individual children (Chapter 13). You will find information on children with special needs and issues of bilingual education and of "mainstreaming."

Putting it all together involves creating an environment conducive to learning, setting a tone in the classroom based on mutual respect between teacher and children, and encouraging children's growth in self-discipline (Chapter 14).

Last, putting it all together means building a sense of worth and trust on the part of parents and making a team effort with them and the community to meet a common goal—"the best of all possible worlds" for young children (Chapter 15). In Chapter 15 you will find useful information to assist you with involving parents and the community.

CHAPTER 12

*"Teachers affect eternity;
they can never tell where their influence
stops."*

—*Henry Brooks Adams*

TEACHING AND LEARNING STRATEGIES

This chapter deals with several important questions:

- What are some of the philosophies and theories that influence teaching strategies?
- What strategies and styles do learners employ?
- What is the nature of such critical learning processes as play, discovery learning, and creative problem solving?
- What does play do for children as learners?
- What attitudes and procedures are appropriate for handling goals and objectives?
- What goal structures are appropriate in an early childhood setting?

Introduction

How does an early childhood teacher determine what teaching-learning strategies to use? Is it a matter of recalling how one was taught? Trial and error? Following recipes given in classes on "how to teach"? We believe that the strategies one uses and the style and role of the teacher come from the interaction between (1) an educational philosophy, (2) a theory of teaching, and (3) a theory of learning. This introductory section discusses these three topics, since they are important influences on your teaching strategies.

EDUCATIONAL PHILOSOPHY
When you apply for a job, you will sometimes be asked to explain your educational philosophy. This idea may surprise you; but if you consider, you will see that it makes good sense. Unless teachers want to accept a completely predetermined sequence of activities implemented by merely turning to the next page in a manual, they need to understand the *why* of what they are doing at least as much as the *how*. To understand the *why*, it is important for you to consider your own educational philosophy.

An "educational philosophy" is a systematic approach to educational goals and values. These are related to the basic political and sociocultural goals and values of the society.

If the community wants to produce obedient, conforming, single-minded citizens who absorb preselected content, there are effective means to such an end. The educational systems of China and Russia are examples. Closer at home, there are some highly structured, "teacher-proof" systems which are designed to ensure mastery of certain content but pay little attention to encouraging lifelong learning processes, curiosity, self-direction, or critical and creative thinking. (See Chapter 3 for discussion of the Engelmann-Becker model.) If this is our approach, we can readily accept the scientific model as *the* model for education. That is, we can assume that we can break all learning down into its component parts and program instruction for everything we want children to learn. We might possibly even be able to save all the money we spend on teachers by replacing them all with teaching machines!

If, however, we believe that the function of education includes leading society toward different goals and values such as lifelong learning, curiosity, independence, and creativity, as well as transmitting the culture of the past, then our task is not so simple. If our goal is to produce individuals who are self-directed, lifelong learners, capable of thinking and challenging, then our philosophy of education defines teaching as an art, with the tools and techniques of science contributing only a part. Then we see ourselves also as *educators*, not just as teachers. *Educators* help children to become educated. *Teachers* just teach—or impart knowledge. The artist-educator uses many materials and also sensitivity, judgment, and intensive observation. Such a person's philosophy is based on a broad interpretation of the role and function of educational goals and values.

THEORY OF TEACHING

Of the three topics in this introduction—educational philosophy, theory of teaching, and theory of learning—theory of teaching is the least developed. No generally accepted single idea of what teaching is or should be exists. We are, however, much concerned with how teachers behave, why, and with what effects. We do know that whatever it is that the teacher does is more important to the effectiveness of any educational program than curriculum, materials, or facilities, even though it is primarily such things as curriculum, materials, and facilities that researchers typically study (Klein, 1973).

Any consideration of what teaching is, or should be, must deal with the *role*, *style*, and *technique* of the teacher.

The teacher's role

The "role" of the teacher is the totality of his or her duties, responsibilities, and functions. In a well-defined program or model, roles are clearly delineated. A Montessori teacher or an Englemann-Becker teacher, for example, has a highly defined conception of exactly what to do. A Montessori teacher has a precise way to introduce new learning materials. An Englemann-Becker teacher has a precise format for grouping children, scheduling, and teaching. In other words, roles of teachers may be largely dependent on expectations inherent in programs in which they work. While some programs involve teachers in most of the major decisions, others expect teachers merely to carry out decisions made by others.

The teacher's role is also related to the major emphasis of a program. In the past, programs for young children were concerned more with child *care* than with an educational component. Only after children entered kindergarten did the teacher's role actually include responsibility for their "education." In recent years, however, many child care institutions have involved teachers in fostering cognitive, affective, language, and psycho-physical-motor development. Beyond providing love, comfort, and support, the teacher helps children to feel secure as learners and guides them in making decisions, in using play and problem solving as learning processes, and in providing a rich environment for learning (Spodek, 1978).

Teaching style

In performing the teacher's role, teachers have their own personal styles. Style depends on traits and attitudes that are highly individual and not easily influenced by training. For example, a teacher should have a positive and outgoing disposition, and be a natural leader; we think of such traits as being inborn, not taught.

There has been considerable research on teaching styles; but most teaching styles do not fall into the extreme categories sometimes used to describe them (e.g., authoritarian or permissive, structured or open). Bennett and Jordan (1975) identified twelve different teaching styles along a continuum from formal to informal on the basis of questionnaires filled in by teachers about themselves. Most teachers appeared to adopt intermediate styles combining elements of formal strategies (lectures, recitations, and drills) and informal strategies (open classrooms, learning centers, team teaching).

Teaching technique

"Technique"—unlike style—is a matter of reactions or attitudes that can readily be learned and thus can become part of the planned components of any program. Teaching techniques may well determine the success or failure of any program, yet they are often left to chance. Preservice and in-service training can increase the effectiveness of various instructional techniques, such as effective use of children's group processes (Chapter 14), assessment tools (Chapter 7), use of volunteers (Chapter 15), and use of appropriate goal structures (to be dealt with later in this chapter).

THEORY OF LEARNING What is a theory of learning? It is a set of interacting principles accounting for the conditions under which learning occurs for most people in most places. Unlike theories of teaching, learning theories are relatively highly developed; but there is no agreement on a single learning theory.

Associationist versus phenomenological theory

Since the middle of this century, learning theory has appeared to be dominated by two schools, associationist and phenomenological (Spodek, 1978). According to associationist theory, one learns by simple associations. According to phenomenological theory, one learns by total interaction with a large environment (or "field"). Let us examine each of these two schools in turn.

Associationism (or neobehaviorism) assumes that learning starts with small elements and the process of learning consists of combinations of these. We connect ideas in memory simply because they were connected in our early experience. Briefly, these connections are aided by paired repetitions called "conditioning" or "reinforcement" (a process that strengthens a response).

How do associationists see a child as a learner? It might be helpful to use an analogy. Since associationists see a child's learning as influenced by events outside the child, they might see the child's mind as it if were a camera (Figure 12-1). This "camera," initially filled with unexposed film, keeps taking pictures of reality. These pictures are stored in the child's memory.

What kind of teaching-learning strategies grow out of associationism? In general, associationist theory entails programmed instructional material (with short associated increments and immediate reinforcement in terms of feedback), behavior modification techniques, and behavioral objectives. (A section in Chapter 14 explains behavior modification techniques; see page 443.)

Many psychologists who react to what they consider overly simple and mechanical interpretations of human learning have been loosely labeled "phenomenological" theorists. They are convinced that human learning requires develoment of an organizing framework, of an understanding of all the varied events, conditions, and "things" (phenomena) in a situation. In essence, they share a common emphasis on development of an organizing mental structure and the process of understanding.

How do phenomenological theorists see the child as a learner? Again, an analogy is useful. Since these theorists see learning as influenced by the learner's own active information processing and logic (understanding), they do not see the child's mind as a camera or any other mechanism. Instead, they see the child's mind more as a creative artist, using its own impulses and inner vision combined with phenomena from the outer world (Figure 12-2). Children's creation takes from the outer world and from the inner world. The child's mind fashions a unique product, working from previously assimilated experiences. Children's ideas are not just stored snapshots. Phenomenological theorists oppose the stimulus-response straitjacket of the associationists. The mind of the learner is not

Figure 12-1

Figure 12-2

merely a passive receiver of impressions. The child notices what works and what doesn't, and then selects.

What kind of teaching-learning strategies grow out of phenomenological theory? Instructional strategies include discovery learning, inquiry learning, and problem solving (all discussed later in this chapter). Forming the basis for learning under this framework are concepts, generalizations, insights, and understanding—cognitive structures instead of habits.

Two significant offshoots of phenomenological theory are developmental interactionism and cognitive developmentalism.

Developmental interactionists stress the interaction among each of the developmental areas (cognitive, affective, language, and psychophysical-motor) and the interaction between maturation and learning. "Development" here refers not only to bodily growth and an increasing amount of knowledge, but also to qualitatively different and increasingly complex ways of organizing and responding to experience. (See Chapter 5.) "Interaction" has two aspects: interaction between maturation and learning, and interchanges between emotional, cognitive, and motor development. Developmental interactionists believe that the cognitive and the affective are inseparable. Examples of cognitive functions are acquiring and ordering information, judging, reasoning, problem solving, and using symbols. These functions cannot be separated from growth (Cuffaro, 1977).

Cognitive developmentalists stress different *ways* of knowing. Bruner, Oliver, Greenfield, and their associates (1966) have described three ways of knowing and have demonstrated their relevance to how children's concepts are organized and stored: "enactive," "ikonic," and "symbolic." Teachers need to understand these ways of knowing and to realize that at any given moment a child may need to use one as opposed to another of them or may use them together:

Enactive knowing. The enactive is a way of depicting events by movements—that is, by doing. Examples are demonstrating a motor skill such as catching a ball, or moving objects in order to show the concept of addition without talking about it. Hughes (1973) gives a particularly interesting example: A two-year-old girl was taken by her grandmother to see some hens. The child was fascinated by the way the hens drank water—bending their heads down and then tilting them back. Later, when the grandmother prompted the child—"Tell mommy about the hens"—the child went into a detailed enactment, making head motions remarkably approximating the drinking hens. Enactment was her way of knowing. For some children, enactment is the best approach to the meaning of words. For example, if the teacher's aim is to develop concepts of safety in boats, then the experience might best begin by playing boat, or by actually getting into and out of a real boat (rather than using less direct and more symbolic learning experience).

Iconic knowing. The iconic involves imagery, or "picturing." In this way of knowing, images in the individual's perceptual field are used as representations. For example, a teacher might have children play with a toy boat copied from a real one and then have them examine related pictures, charts, and diagrams.

Symbolic knowing. In this way of knowing, things and events are depicted by arbitrary gestures. The outstanding example is language—not only our own daily language but also codes, symbolic formulas, logical propositions ("if . . . then"), mathematics, and computer languages. (This way of knowing corresponds to two of Piaget's stages: concrete operations and formal operations.) Going back to the example given for iconic knowing, the teacher might substitute a paper plate for the boat and then use signs such as KEEP HANDS IN BOAT.

The ways of knowing listed by Bruner et al. have important implications for teaching and learning strategies. Teachers can use these concepts again and again as they evaluate programs, materials, their own teaching, and children's learning. They help teachers recognize a need for balance among the ways of knowing that they make available to young children: Is there too much symbolism and not enough enactment, or vice versa? We never discard any of these ways of knowing. (In fact, we could use a greater awareness of them in college courses.) Materials for children that rely on only one mode—as certain workbooks and practice sheets rely on the symbolic—are highly questionable. It should also be recognized that without some special guidance in symbolic knowing, children may continue throughout life depending largely on visual images for representing and organizing the world.

Children's learning styles and cognitive styles

Learning styles   Researchers have looked for individual differences among children showing consistent patterns in *approaches* to learning. Such patterns are important for teaching-learning strategies.

Note the way children approach materials and problems. Are they eager or fearful? Are they alert or indifferent? Are they irritable or satisfied? Some of these traits start becoming evident in earliest infancy. A child's "learning style" is not a specific or one-time way of responding but a consistent pattern.

Cognitive styles   A way of categorizing children's cognitive styles is in terms of their responses.

"Reflective" children tend to analyze and seek out details in scanning their environment. They reflect on a problem to the extent of spending considerable time on it and thinking deeply about it. They are capable of becoming absorbed in tasks and oblivious to distraction.

"Impulsive" children tend to respond to a field as a whole, and to respond quickly. They can be as intelligent as analytic, reflective children, but they are likely to be more active, impulsive, and distractable (Kagan, Moss, & Siegel, 1963). (See Chapter 13, "Children with Special Needs.")

Witkin, Dyk, Faterson, Goodenough, and Karp (1962) described two distinctive styles utilized in problem solving and related to cognitive processes. "Field-independent" (or "analytical") children are better able to perceive items as separate from their backgrounds and better able to reorganize an organized perceptual field or even to impose organization where there appears to be none. "Field-dependent" (or "global") children are less able to disengage elements from their surroundings, tend to accept the organization provided by the perceptual field, and experience their environment in a global fashion.

Rosenberg (1968) has classified cognitive styles into four different categories. The "rigid-inhibited" child has a need for structure and adheres to absolutes in dealing with the environment. The "undisciplined" child is aggressive, competitive, and critical and considers only immediate gratification. The "acceptance-anxious" child is excessively concerned with the opinions of others. The "creative" child is open to his or her own feelings, to the feelings of others, and to the environment and has highly developed and abstract language skills.

Rosenberg's styles are identified in two basic ways: by the location of information (from inside oneself or outside oneself), and by the child's level of symbolization (concrete to abstract). When thinking about these styles as approaches to learning and problem solving, we can often identify similar styles in parents and suggest appropriate intervention techniques so as to move the child toward more autonomous, sensitive, and creative means of dealing with problems or challenges. For example, if a child shows a rigid-inhibited style, the teacher or caretaker may at first provide the child with limited alternatives, to avoid confusion, and later ask the child to suggest more alternatives. Children whose style is creative are likely to be ready to cope with many alternatives much sooner, think of them more quickly, and evaluate them more readily. With such children, assisting adults should offer less guidance and more opportunity for independent action. Table 12-1 summarizes Rosenberg's four styles, the location of the child's information, behavior of children and parents, and suggested treatment.

Summary: Learning and cognitive modalities Ms. Jones has been working with the children on the concept of telling time. Mary grasped the idea as soon as she *heard* the teacher's explanation. Susan caught on when she *read* the textbook selection. Terry got the idea when he was given a cardboard clock to manipulate. The differences among these children relate to preferences for specific sensory modalities—e.g., auditory, visual, kinesthetic.

What do we know about modalities, or styles, of learning and cognition? A survey of the literature in the field leads to the following conclusions.

Different approaches that learners exhibit when introduced to new materials, new situations, and new problems are referred to as "learning styles," and "cognitive styles." Another widely used term for "style" is "modality." A teacher, working with children on a long-term basis, will probably be able to observe a preferred style or mode of a child. This information is useful because it allows instructional techniques to be matched to the child's own style. We need practical instruments to help determine preferred styles, or modes, and more conclusive evidence about interaction between these modes and matching instructional approaches. (See Lundsteen, 1980.)

Processes of Learning

The introduction to this chapter has suggested how teaching strategies are influenced by educational philosophy, theories of teaching, and

Table 12-1 FOUR LEARNING STYLES

LEARNING STYLE	LEVEL OF SYMBOLIZATION	LOCUS OF INFORMATION	TYPE OF PARENT	CHILD'S BEHAVIOR	SUGGESTED TREATMENT TECHNIQUES
Rigid-inhibited	Concrete	Very little internal (from trusting self) or external (from trusting others)	Authoritarian (constrictive and controlling)	Rigidly follows rules, cannot get job done unless helped; submissive to authority	Encourage ability to function independently. 1 Give concrete explanations, but develop ability to generalize gradually. 2 Provide structure, but encourage child to develop own alternatives (structure). 3 Explain why and encourage child's ability to understand reasons. 4 Use simplification techniques.
Undisciplined	Functional and moderately abstract	More internal than external	Inconsistent (total direction or none at all)	Disrespectful or negativistic with authorities; breaks rules says, "I won't"; attempts to manipulate; aggressive	Encourage child to control behavior within socially accepted limits. 1 Set limits; use logical and natural consequences. 2 Maintain a personal relationship, without rejection. 3 Provide feedback on child's behavior and use peer group to provide feedback. 4 Provide opportunities for independent, creative projects of child's choice.

(Continued on page 350.)

Table 12-1 (CONTINUED)

LEARNING STYLE	LEVEL OF SYMBOLIZATION	LOCUS OF INFORMATION	TYPE OF PARENT	CHILD'S BEHAVIOR	SUGGESTED TREATMENT TECHNIQUES
Acceptance-anxious	Moderately abstract (anxiety interferes with functioning) Verbalizes conventional concepts	More external than internal	Child-centered (main goal is child's happiness *at price of pleasing the parent*)	Looks for constant reinforcement; tries hard, meticulous; does something because you want him or her to	Encourage child to set his or her own goals, plan procedures and evaluate results. Help the child achieve emotional independence. 1 Give child support and acceptance. 2 Remove external sources of evaluation; child evaluates *self*. 3 Provide feedback in an unemotional and impersonal manner—reflecting on achievement, not on person. (Child sees value of self.) 4 Give some leadership roles.
Creative	Abstract	Both internal and external	Creative problem-centered (structure, warmth, respect, fostering independence)	Works independently; uses adults as resources; learns from mistakes; thinks for self; sensitive to others; enjoys learning	Encourage child to continue in problem-solving process. 1 Provide maximum opportunity for creativity, independence, divergent thought, and use of intuition. 2 Be ready to accept uniqueness, unusual ideas, and new solutions.

Source: We are greatful to Dr. Earl J. Moore, Associate Professor of Education, University of Missouri—Columbia, for his adaptation of Rosenberg's ideas (Rosenberg, 1968) and his incorporation of related styles of parenthood and related treatment techniques; and to Carol Mason Wolfe for her work in developing this table.

theories of learning. We will now consider how teacher and child interact in appropriate learning processes: play, discovery learning, and problem solving. We consider each of these learning processes in turn (plus some other ways of learning less attractive to us), and we discuss how teachers can handle them effectively.

PLAY   It is important for all of us to recognize and understand the significance of play in the lives of children. What is play? What categories does play fall into, and what developmental stages does it go through? What does play do for children? What should adults' roles be with respect to play? This section provides some answers to these questions and considers play as a transformational process.

What is play?

First of all, play is symbolic *transformation*. As such, it serves children's present and future development. Children transform materials in their environment into symbols meaningful to them. When they play symbolically they are personally working through who and what they are—now. A stick becomes a doll when a playmate is needed. An acorn becomes an elf's cup. A dinosaur becomes a symbol of power and strength that the child lacks. The symbolic transformations of play start in early childhood and should never disappear. Play as symbolic transformation can eventually give rise to poetry, art, and even science.

True play is spontaneous—not compelled. Children can play with no end in mind but enjoyment. Characteristics of playfulness may include freedom (physical, cognitive, and social), and also joyfulness and a sense of humor. In children—and adults—there is often laughter, or sometimes just a glint in the eye that says, "I'm playing." But the descriptive phrase we consider the most essential is "symbolically transformational." While children are freely manipulating clay, paint, sand, and other materials, play is serving as a means for growth, helping to create a well-balanced individual—cognitively, socially, emotionally, and physically.

What categories does play fall into?

Categorizing play helps early childhood educators to understand it. Piaget, for example, divides play into function play, symbolic play, and play with rules; we like to categorize play as (1) manipulative (2) physical, and (3) dramatic.

Materials for manipulative play in school may include puzzles, parquetry blocks, pegboards, materials for construction, materials for exploration in science and mathematics, and natural materials such as sand and water.

Physical play, which generally requires more space than manipulative play, usually takes place outdoors. There you may find sand pits for digging, playhouses, wheeled toys, equipment for climbing, and balls. The preschool child is sometimes called the "climbing-wheel-toy child"—preschoolers usually love motor gratification.

Dramatic play is of particular value as symbolic transformation. It is discussed in more detail in the section on stages of play. Here we will give just one example: blocks, which span the categories of physical play and dramatic play. Children use smaller blocks for miniaturizing the world and larger, hollow, blocks for building large structures which become sets for dramatic play.

What developmental stages does play go through?

Social stages   The various social *stages* of play point up its role in social development. Early egocentric play changes, as the child matures, to parallel play, then to associative play, and later to true social-group play (Millar, 1968).

Egocentric play is observable during the solitary activities of the young child. We might see a toddler gathering a bunch of paper scraps and manipulating them. Apparently, in this case the child is relating more to things than to people and is thinking just from his or her own point of view.

Parallel play is observable when young children play side by side, but with little or no apparent communication. Evidently, it doesn't matter who plays by the child's side, just as long as there is another body. You have probably seen two-year-olds side by side in a sand pile, each engaged in his or her own activity. Nonetheless, what they are doing is important. As they build, they are using materials (sand) to make an impression on their environment, an impression that did not exist before. This is a powerful and creative experience. And we believe that there is an attunement to the other human body nearby, even though the children may not yet know how to make their play interactive. Sometimes one of the parallel players may move to *onlooker play*, observing another and learning while standing by.

Associative play is observable when four or five children join or leave a group at will. You might see groups of four-year-olds climbing on free-form structures, visiting a garden area, and walking balance beams, each child dropping into and out of these groups from time to time.

True social-group play is seen when children are genuinely interacting—socially and cooperatively—during an activity; trying to deal with and understand their peers. This kind of play, evolving into cooperative play, might, for example, take place at the home center with one child ordering groceries on the play phone from another child—a typical activity for five-year-olds. Later we see an evolution to actual games, rule-governed group play (baseball, for instance).

The concept of the "generalized other," typical of mature socialization, develops in this stage. We can observe children autonomously beginning to formulate their own rules ("Let's take turns— first *we'll* be the wild animals chasing the children, and then *you* be the wild animals chasing the children. OK?").

What do these developmental stages imply for early childhood teachers? It is important to realize that children need experiences with all these levels of social interactions. Prekindergarten and kindergarten programs are excellent environments for social play experiences. Teachers can manipulate the environment to set up opportunities for these different kinds of play, considering each child's individual needs. There can be table games for solitary or parallel play and dress-up materials for group play. The teacher should allow children to experience social interaction at their own pace. For example, a three-year-old may need plenty of time in solitary or onlooker play before engaging in interactive social play.

Chronological stages   In this section, we discuss briefly some characteristics of play at different age stages and purposes which play serves at these stages. In general play helps to advance motor, emotional, social, and cognitive development.

Play in infancy. Piaget suggests to us that play in the very young is just a matter of "taking it all in"—assimilation. A familiar activity (e.g., sucking the toes, waving the hands in front of the eyes) is likely to be repeated almost indefinitely. The motivation here is the satisfaction derived from the activity itself. Recall (Chapter 5) that in the process of assimilation the child abstracts information from the outside world and fits it into what he or she already knows. Piaget believes that through play the outside world is made to fit the child's present organizational schemes. This kind of play is crucial to early intellectual development.

Sometime during the first year of life, the child combines several play activities so that repetitions include variations (e.g., banging plus loading and unloading a container full of small objects). Apparently, the pleasure gained comes from "ordering" the activity autonomously. But variation is not necessary for satisfaction: for example, a child who has learned to open a cabinet door or flush a toilet will repeat these actions again and again, apparently getting satisfaction each time. Piaget describes child's play between twelve and eighteen months as active, systematic exploration of the environment.

Play during the toddler stage. During toddlerhood, symbolic play emerges. An example of symbolic play was given in Chapter 5: a child who put two potato chips together to make butterfly wings. We see symbolic play when a toddler pushes a box around the floor, pretending that it is a truck. Symbolic thought is a prerequisite for dramatic play, which is closely linked to intellectual growth. Symbolic play may occur during egocentric, parallel, associative, or true social-group play.

Between ages two and three, dramatic play emerges as children imitate sounds and movements of things like planes and trains.

Play beyond toddlerhood. Children three to six years old are very much involved in dramatic play. They engage freely in "making believe"—which is in fact individual or group symbolization. This kind of play is fundamental to creative thinking.

But "let's pretend" and "make-believe" activities will not necessarily happen automatically, according to some cross-cultural studies (Smilansky, 1968). Where children are extremely economically disadvantaged, to the extent that the adults in their lives are simply struggling to exist, Smilansky has found that sociodramatic play is lacking. The play of such children is only sensorimotor in nature; there is little evidence of imagination. Smilansky did find, however, that skilled, interactive adults could teach these children how to play dramatically. At first the adults modeled ("let's pretend"); gradually, they provided more and more open-ended opportunities until sociodramatic play became spontaneous. Smilansky found apparent benefits in terms of both cognitive and social development.

In addition to its importance as symbolic transformation, dramatic play has another significant aspect: it prepares children for the future. It represents a way of rehearsing real-life situations. During dramatic play, children can change their attitudes toward people and things. For instance, by "playing hospital," a child may make an impending actual hospitalization less terrifying.

A good example of dramatic play is a kindergarten class where a locomotive has been constructed in the large-block corner. The children will of course pretend that they are getting on and off the train, buying and exchanging tickets, saying goodbye to their families, handling luggage, and eating in the diner. As they do all these things, they are learning and rehearsing—socially, emotionally, and cognitively. Another example is puppets: children may use puppets in an informal way to represent themselves. (See Chapter 10.)

To summarize, sociodramatic play has symbolic and social elements. Teachers should encourage many dramatic-play situations so that children can play many roles.

What does play do for children?

We have been suggesting all along how play advances children's development. But parents do sometimes object to play: "I don't want my children just messing around; make them learn; work them." This is especially likely to happen in communities with a strong "work ethic." It may be necessary for teachers to point out that play is the "work" of children. During play, children are actually learning skills: play develops vocabulary and concepts of number and color, for example, and games give children practice in following instructions. Parents can often see such learning happening at home—for instance, as children play at cooking, they learn mathematical concepts and practice manipulating materials. Another example is puzzles: as children's curiosity leads them to solve puzzles, they are learning how to concentrate, and this will help them reach long-range goals that teachers set for them. (See Chapter 10.) It might help to remind "work-addicted" parents that adults also play, and need to play. (The primate psychologist Harlow has said that "The path to passion is paved with play"; Aldis, 1975.)

But teachers must also maintain their own perspective. When we try to "sell" parents, saying that play is work, the danger arises that we will "overcurricularize" play, to the extent that it loses its value. For example, when third-graders' reading becomes a playful way of putting themselves into the lives of others, it is tempting to start asking for highly structured book reports. If all children's play is seized upon and curricularized, children have no room left for themselves. We need to remember that play is valuable in and of itself. When room is left for free symbolic play, children perform better in both social and academic settings. Not all imaginative activity should be geared to the external world and to the service of growing up. We need to save plenty of playtime just for the children, to pursue their own personal feelings, concepts, and challenges in their own way.

What roles are appropriate for adults with respect to play?

Should adults simply see to it that the children are safe from injury and otherwise get out of the way, letting play be completely natural and spontaneous? Or should they intervene? We believe that there are some things adults can do to assist play, and also some things they should avoid doing. Educational intervention can appropriately include environmental design, consulting, and social facilitating (particularly in the case of children with special needs). Following are some general principles to consider.

The teacher should be involved, but not overinvolved. Adults can enrich children's play by being involved in it. Get down on the floor with them, for instance; see what's happening from *their* point of view—e.g., as they explore what a toy car can do as it moves up and down a ramp. Play period is not the time for hovering; but neither is it the time for taking care of administrative chores.

Satisfying play can take place spontaneously in almost any class. But *preparation increases the probability of productive play.* For example, a teacher can change some materials daily in order to increase children's interest: change the accessories in the block area; replace three-piece puzzles with some five-, seven- and nine-piece puzzles; add some beads for children to string; add spools to be sorted and matched.

Sometimes the teacher's involvement entails "social engineering"— e.g., easing children who are often left out of group activities into dramatic play and suggesting contributive roles for them. From rather direct intervention, you can move to coaching: for instance, encouraging left-out children to think up and initiate contributive roles for themselves. Each teacher needs to decide on the spot when to become directly involved and how far to go in extending play. Occasionally, the teacher will actually join in play: e.g., play a role in the home center in order to encourage some new ideas. But adults should not get so involved in children's play that the children have no options, no chance to try things out independently, no choice of materials, no chance to learn from mistakes, and no chance to symbolize and invent. The *children*, not the adults, should introduce the transformations.

Play materials should leave something to the child's imagination. Visualize with us a child, fashioning a boat from scraps (brimming with private symbolism), and putting it "out to sea" on a small pond, blown about by a soft breeze. Into the picture come two others: another child, accompanied by, say, a father, carrying an expensive store-bought boat. The second child cannot make an imprint on the boat and is robbed of the chance to project a fantasy. (It may well be that the father really bought the boat for himself, anyway.) Let's draw some implications from this picture.

In the classroom, relatively open-ended, flexible materials lend themselves to long-term, imaginative uses. (Examples are paint, sand, water, and building blocks.) One study suggests that children engage in a greater variety of "make-believe" games when playthings are not too realistically detailed (Pulaski, 1973). Resist the fancy, commercially made kit, the coloring books, the wind-up toy (totally structured—and useless), and the streamlined models that rob children of the chance to transform symbolically and thus to create.

The teacher should be a skilled environmental designer and consultant. The father who bought the expensive toy boat was deficient not only as an environmental designer but also as a consultant. How can adults guiding children of various ages best fill these two intertwining roles?

In his research, White (1975) found that mothers who had "nicely developing" infants and toddlers performed these functions excellently, nurturing curiosity and enthusiasm. The mothers did this by making the environment of the home available. They provided interesting items to look at and manipulate—household items such as plastic refrigerator containers, bottle caps, shoes, and some purchased playthings. They made the environment safe, and then allowed their children freedom to explore and create clutter. These mothers did not remain aloof but shared in the pleasure of their children's discoveries.

In day care centers, what can caretakers do to encourage private symbolic play? First, they can be sure that there are plenty of unstructured materials (e.g., sets of blocks that children can put together in their own way). Second, they can provide quiet corners (small enough for one or two children)—places to climb on or under (tablecloths thrown over furniture will do). Third, they can see to it that they do not switch time frames too rapidly; they should allow large blocks of time for children to become engrossed in exploration. Fourth, they can avoid continually imposing their own goals and allow the children to express themselves.

For older children, early childhood teachers may withdraw some materials and add some new ones from time to time to provide diverse environments. (Two examples are rubber bands for pegboards, with which children can create varied shapes; and props for depicting many roles and events in dramatic play.) The teacher should provide enough time so that children can go beyond the initial aspects of activities. For example, after a field trip to the post office, the teacher can place in the block center envelopes and mailboxes to encourage play that will go beyond simple block building. The teacher can act as a consultant by suggesting forms of play or dramatic themes (like the post office), and may provide information ("telling," informational books, field trips, resource persons).

In essence, being involved with children and being a skilled designer and consultant means being involved just long enough to enrich the play without letting your mind push against the child's mind and take over. Using materials that leave room for the child's imagination means avoiding expensive toys that look good on the shelf but do not lend themselves to imaginative manipulation (instead, use sand, water, clay, paint, blocks, and scraps).

The teacher should be a careful observer of children's play, gleaning needed information about the children. Teachers have long studied children's spontaneous play in order to get information about: (1) what goals the children are achieving or what needs they are satisfying; (2) what motivates the children; (3) how the children cope with problems; (4) how children's self-concepts are developing; (5) how the children feel about others; (6) what cultural variations exist; (7) how curious the children are; (8) how the children solve problems; (9) what information the children have and how it is categorized; and (10) how ready the children are for more complex activities. The more teachers know about the ways in which each child functions during play (e.g., the child's personal temperament, meekness or aggressiveness, and ways of getting into a group), the more appropriately they can balance spontaneous play and structured, educational play. It is not sensible to limit play to activities structured by adults: this denies children the opportunity to initiate and test their own ideas and consolidate their own past experience.

As a careful observer, however, the teacher can set the stage for children's play, opening new cognitive possibilities and using words that encourage autonomous problem solving (e.g., "How can you make the roof high enough so that you can crawl into your house?" "How could you make the shadow change or go away?")

The teacher should learn how to play. Early childhood educators need to learn how to play imaginatively themselves and how to teach (and allow) others to play imaginatively. If children play imaginatively, it is because they have lived in a playful environment. When the school defines its role as the promoter of teaching and learning in an inflexible, constricted way, children are deprived of developmental opportunities. Optimal early childhood education requires adults who bring not only playfulness to the classroom but also respect for children and their play. To play is to develop.

In summary: Play

Early childhood educators can enrich the quality of play and help parents and others accept its intrinsic value. The following list should be helpful.

What Does Play Mean for Little Children?
- A chance to transform materials into meaningful symbols
- A chance to develop an inquiring mind and explore personal feelings
- A chance to work through who they are and what they are
- A chance to kindle curiosity; to create, imagine, and experiment
- A chance to express and to reveal themselves, develop a self-image, and make an impression on the world of materials
- A chance to understand and enjoy the world of meanings
- A chance to solve problems
- A chance to learn how to make friends with children and adults
- A chance to learn to live with groups, small and large
- A chance to respect the rights of others
- A chance to take some hard knocks and cope with them
- A chance to learn about others' feelings
- A chance to assert themselves and to be important
- A chance to develop hobbies and broaden their interests
- A chance to develop the body
- A chance to develop the mind, consolidate experiences, rehearse life, and widen horizons

DISCOVERY LEARNING

We now briefly consider discovery as a learning process. Discovery—like problem solving, which is discussed in the next section—sometimes does occur in higher forms of play; it is worthy of special consideration. As you read these two sections, try to recognize the distinctions between discovery and problem solving.

Discovery learning requires an environment in which children are free to explore and investigate. Even before the age of one, a child can participate in discovery learning. Obviously, play offers many opportunities for discovery learning, particularly when the environment is not restrictive and a variety of materials are available for investigation.

In discovery—or "inductive thinking"—one starts from an assortment of cases and arrives at a general rule (not a single certain or uncertain fact). For example, through experience of many particular instances, a child discovers that words stand for things, that mixing all colors results in mud color, that people are friendly and helpful. When the child goes on to apply such rules to new instances, the process is called "deduction," or "inference."

For further examples of discovery learning, see Chapter 2, which explains the historically significant Montessori toys designed for self-discovery, and Chapters 5 and 9, on developing cognitive abiilties. One third-grade class was challenged to discovery learning when the teacher used a common incident. Wiping off the chalkboard with water, the teacher asked, as the water evaporated, "Where did all the water go?"—thus prompting a lot of searching for explanations.

PROBLEM SOLVING

We find the beginning of goal-oriented problem solving at ages as early as seven months. For example, a seven-month-old child will shove one thing out of the way in order to get something else—using means "A" to get "B." Another example is crying: the infant begins to *cry deliberately* ("A") in order to get *attention* ("B") (White, 1975).

By age three, children may not be able to solve a great many problems, but they have learned some tools and strategies for problem solving. Here is an example:

> When a turtle was brought to one center (becoming the most popular item of the day), one of us observed a three-year-old problem solver who wanted the turtle very badly. Soon we saw that he had a *plan*. Standing watchfully with a bucket, he edged in closer and closer. He waited until a child tired of holding the turtle and let it drop. This three-year-old was ready with his bucket to catch it, and scooted away.*

Creative problem solving is perhaps the most important learning process. What is this process? How is it used by children and teachers?

---

* Thanks to Velma Schmidt, North Texas State University, for this anecdote.

How can teachers guide it? These are questions to be explored in this section.

What is problem solving, and how do children and teachers use it?

The questions "What is creative problem solving" and "How is it used in early childhood education?" are best approached through certain key descriptive ideas. These include the degree of "unknowns" in the problem situation; kinds of problems; social strategies; important elements of the problem-solving situation, such as open-endedness; and certain qualities, such as the ability to plan.

Unknowns   The unknown is an element of every problem-solving situation. In making problem solving *creative*, we find that the degree of unknowns—for both teacher and child—is critical. If both teacher and child know what the problem is and what the right answer is, we have noncreative problem solving: the child just goes through a reinforcing practice, or ritual. This is the situation with drill learning.

However, as soon as the child does not know what the answer is, we have some room for *divergent* thinking, and this is an important part of creative problem solving. "Divergent thinking" is thought that goes out in many directions to seek and explore and does not immediately reduce itself to (or converge on) one right answer. Teachers' questions can elicit either divergent thinking ("How many ways can you think of to use a brick?") or convergent thinking ("How do you spell 'brick'?")

Problem solving becomes even more creative when the child does not know what the *problem* is. Then "problem finding" can take place.

The chances for creativity are further increased when the teacher does not know what the answer is—or even what the problem is—and is willing to explore interactively with the children. Table 12-2 summarizes these possibilities.

Kinds of problems   Pinpointing *kinds* of problems is important, because when you know what kind of problem you are dealing with, you can match teaching methods to it.

Broadly, problem solving in early childhood settings can be described

Table 12-2 A CHART FOR CREATIVE POSSIBILITIES IN PROBLEM SOLVING

	PROBLEM	ANSWER
Teacher	Knowns or unknowns?	Knowns or unknowns?
Child	Knowns or unknowns?	Knowns or unknowns?

Table 12-3 EXAMPLES OF PROBLEM AREAS

SOCIAL	COGNITIVE	ESTHETIC	MOTOR
Environment Rules (violations of) Taking responsibility Following directions Interpersonal conflicts Racism Sexism	Physical science Biological science Mathematics	Art Music Drama or movement Composition: oral, written	Decision making in movement education, "adventure"-type playgrounds, and physical movement entailing autonomous decisions in any of the other problem areas

as (1) social, (2) cognitive, (3) esthetic, and (4) physical, or motor. Table 12-3 lists examples of problems in these broad areas. In any of these areas, problems can be just for children, just for adults who deal with children, or for both children and adults.

For example, under "Social" we list seven problems. (1) Some shared problems stem from faulty environments. Teachers can often remedy the environment, and thus solve the problem, swiftly. (E.g., if children are always getting into the animal pen when they're not supposed to, simply put a lock on the door to the pen.) Other kinds of problems may stem from (2) breaking school rules; (3) failing to take responsibility (e.g., spilt milk is not wiped up); and (4) being unaware of directions for certain activities or games. (5) Interpersonal conflicts, (6) sexism, and (7) racism create problems also. Children *can* become genuinely concerned about such problems, and their genuine needs can be satisfied by participation in problem-solving processes in these social areas.

At one child development center* several years were spent observing and categorizing kinds of preschool problems. The next step was to think carefully through matching alternative strategies for solutions. The staff found it important to have many different strategies to fit different problems. Some of the teachers would naturally use their own power—domination—to solve everything, so that the children never got a chance to grow as problem solvers. It was found that in the case of most kinds of problems children respond better to much less "power" strategy on the part of adults. Problems should be treated in ways that will encourage children to take responsibility for themselves. In most types of problems, teachers do need to give guidance to children, to remind them as necessary, to help them work things through. But teachers can still leave children choices. ("You don't always have to give in to me. We can find ways for both of us to meet our needs.") For that matter, so can parents. ("If I can't take noise from you, I can go to *my* room sometimes, instead of you always having to go to yours.")

* Isabel Patterson Child Development Center, Long Beach, California. Thanks to Helen Posky, Associate Director, for many ideas and examples.

Social strategies   Some social problem-solving strategies for teachers to use with children (after careful watching) are active listening, group discussion, negotiation, and setting limits. Setting limits is generally for adults' use only; it is discussed in more detail in Chapter 14. But adults can work toward getting children to use the other strategies with each other.

The scene described below illustrates social strategies. Suppose that you notice some young children in the school environment who are apparently in a most unhappy situation. Rather than make snap judgments, *watch*. Wait to see if the youngsters can solve the situation by themselves; often they can. In this case you finally decide that the situation is stalemated, and you step in. You want to:

1   Help the children understand how they are feeling.
2   Clarify the problem.
3   Help the children decide what they want to do about it (this involves active listening).

Here is the scene:

TEACHER   (Having listened carefully and actively to an "unknown" problem, and with the intent of helping the children verbalize) It looks as if you both really want that truck. Is that right? (Children nod. The problem is known.) That's a real problem. (The teacher is clarifying and reflecting.) What can you do so that you can both be happy? (The answers are *unknown*. Note how the teacher facilitates children's problem-solving processes by moving toward solutions with questions and trying to encourage discussion.)

CHILD   (To teacher) Well, I had it first.

TEACHER   I really don't need to know that. Tell *him*. (The teacher tries to get the children to explore the problem with each other. The teacher is *not* the judge and therefore does *not* need the facts. The children do need the facts, so that they can *discuss* and *negotiate*. Too often, teachers walk into a situation and quickly say, "Now, what happened?" What is happening is that children are upset. You can see that. You don't need to ask. Let's continue with the scene.)

CHILD   Well, I want the truck first.

TEACHER   (Delighted that the children are communicating, and not judging the comment as selfish) Hey, that's an idea; then he could have it when you're finished? Have you got another idea? How about you?

The teacher helps the children put their comments into the form of some sort of answer or solution and encourages alternative solutions, keeping them talking about it with each other until they can both agree on a solution (this involves negotiation). The teacher turns over to the children the responsibility for solving the problem ("What are you going to do about it?") When teachers give children opportunities to develop competence in problem solving, children do not always have to run to adults for solutions. In an open situation, with many unknown problems and unknown answers, the teacher facilitates and builds children's ability to solve problems creatively and autonomously.

The more opportunities children are given to solve problems autonomously, the better problem solvers they become. Hold to that idea: If you solve everything for a child, don't be surprised later, when he or she can't handle life. The more children solve problems and hear and talk about ways of solving problems, and the more aware they become of strategies other children and adults use, the more they expand their repertories as problem solvers.

Important elements of the problem-solving situation   In the following paragraphs we discuss several important and interesting aspects of problem solving situations: language, open-endedness, avoidance of "predicaments," and being "wrong."

Language of problem solving. Early childhood educators can help to give children words with which to express feelings, social relationships, and the beginnings of negotiating strategy. In fact, having the right words—vocabulary development—is an important aspect of problem solving for young children. Judging from their research, Spivack and Shure (1974) suggest, e.g., that young children need the word "and" in order to generate multiple alternatives. They also need words such as "some," "same," "different" (these are related to others' preferences); "happy," "sad," "mad" (these are related to feelings); "why" "because," "if," "then," "maybe," and "might" (for evaluating consequences and alternative solutions).

It should be noted that in the context of art most young children lack language for problem solving. We need to decide what the important words are here and then develop children's concepts of these words during interesting experiences (e.g., "light," "shade," "rhythm," "color," "space," "vertical," "line," "horizontal," "curve").

Open-endedness in problem solving. Creative problem solving does not require people to have every problem wrapped up with a "happy" solution. For example, the choices may include simply walking away from a stalemate ("Oh, you've decided to let him have it"). Choices may also include choosing to deal with a problem later or choosing to get someone else to handle it. With young children, participating in the process is often more important than the product. (Analogously, not every composition or piece of art has to be brought to the point of public display.) What is most important is that children realize the power and responsibility they have in a situation and recognize that they are not simply washed by the tides of fate. They can *choose* to act or react in certain ways.

Avoidance of "predicaments." Realizing that creative problem solving should be open-ended, the effective teacher takes care that problems do not become "predicaments." In a predicament—as opposed to a problem—the child lacks the freedom to leave a frustrating situation, or to leave a question unanswered, without serious consequences.

For example, a group of children in one program were making paper figures of the kind that are cut folded and remain whole when unfolded. One boy could not get the idea of leaving an uncut edge so that the figures wouldn't fall apart. In spite of the fact that the program was keen on developing persistence, in this case the teacher avoided creating a "predicament" for the child who wasn't developmentally ready for this task. Pursuing his own course, he turned his project into a part of a collage. Here is another example, which we observed. Two children became verbally abusive to a third. The third simply terminated her part in the dramatic play by saying, "Well, bye, bye. I'm going off to England," and left the confrontation. An adult might have created a predicament for this girl by insisting that she stand up for her rights.

Sometimes, then, it is better to let go, to step back and give yourself time and space to grow a little. If the problem is really in you rather than in someone else, you'll have another chance at it.

Being "wrong." There are two dimensions to the saying "It's OK to be wrong." One has to do with development, and the other has to do with the idea of building victory out of defeat. Let's see what we mean.

It is not only acceptable to leave a problem unsolved; it is also acceptable to come to a wrong solution. Just as preoperational children are "wrong" (according to adult standards) in their reactions to conservation tasks, young children will also go through stages of perceiving social relationships in ways that are "wrong" from the point of view of socialized adults. An example is solving a social problem by punching someone in the nose—and getting punched back. It does not help much to "explain" the conservation tasks to children who are not yet conservers; similarly, simply telling children about appropriate social solutions will have little lasting effect. Developing social ideas takes time, too.

To build victory out of defeat, individuals can use initially inadequate solutions to redefine their goals. This redefining helps them to better solutions. After having jumped in, tried a solution, and found it wanting ("Hey, that's not working!"), they build upon and refine the first attempt. This attempt becomes a part of the process, rather than merely a failure. The key idea here is not to be discouraged by inadequate solutions but rather to use them as part of the process of finding more successful ones (Klein & Weitzenfeld, 1978). The following example illustrates evolving "goal-orientedness."

Situation: Elwood (a puppet) is crying.

Ill-defined problem (for a child observing the puppet presentation): Stop Elwood's crying.

Goal (or solution 1): Hit Elwood.

Evaluate solution: It doesn't work. He cries harder. We want to . . .

New goal 2: . . . make Elwood happy. What will make him happy?

Solution: Ask him what would make him happy.

Evaluate solution: He says he wants Andrea (another puppet) to be his friend.

New goal 3: Think about how to help Elwood be friends with Andrea again.

Solution: Ask Andrea.

Result: Andrea says she is Elwood's friend, but she wants to play with someone else right now.

New goal 4: Think how to help Elwood find another playmate, or help Elwood play in a threesome. Etc.

In sum, it's OK to take a risk, to be wrong, and to build from there. Be like the turtle, who makes progress only when it sticks its neck out. In order to be right a lot of the time, you've got to risk being wrong some of the time.

Qualities of problem solvers   In the next paragraphs we take up some important qualities of problem solvers. Teachers should be able to recognize these qualities and help develop them.

Planning. Creative problem solving is organized and structured. That is, it lends itself to planning, to the sequencing of alternatives leading to a goal. Planning usually includes four major steps: (1) recognizing a problem, (2) generating hypotheses; (3) predicting consequences or planning evaluation, (4) (possibly) resolution.

One way to encourage children to become planners is to give them opportunities for role playing. According to one study, role playing was the single best teaching-learning technique with regard to long-lasting results and application (or transfer) to other situations (McClure, Chinsky, & Larcen, 1978). When a child is planning, we can usually note some assignment of priorities to steps. For example, a boy has broken his friend's truck, and the friendship is in danger.

FIRST CHILD   Look, I can just put the wheels on.
SECOND CHILD   What about the paint?
FIRST CHILD   And then I'll get some paint and paint it. OK?

Many young children, however, simply have not developed to the point where they can hold more than one variable at a time in mind; and these children will not be able to plan.

Elaboration. Elaboration includes the ability to give details and examples and clarify events and conditions. (As an example, recall the children who were faced with the problem of sharing a toy truck.)

Uniqueness, or freshness. Another term for this quality is "originality." For example, a child who has the problem of a broken vase might come up with the unique solution of making a mosaic out of the pieces.

Cause-effect thinking. Being able to think in terms of causes and effects is crucial to problem solving. Here is an example: Child, with reference to puppet, says, "He is crying because he misses his mama." This child is giving a *reason* why something has occurred. Here, the child is able to recognize that the reason has to do with something that has happened in the past (the mother has left).

Recognizing consequences. This is another important ability. An example: Child, with reference to puppet, says, "If his mama comes, he'll stop crying." This child is projecting thought into the *future* and considering possibilities. The child recognizes that a certain action may lead to a particular result in the future.

Autonomy. "Autonomy" is the quality of doing as much for oneself as possible. We stress this quality repeatedly not only in this section but throughout this book.

Here is an example: a toddler who just can't seem to get those pants up. Guidance might start out with verbal support: "You can do it." Specific steps might include these: "See if you can grab it over here"; "Don't forget the back"; "Try sitting down." The last resort is physical help; and such help should be confined to the absolute minimum, so that the child can do as much as possible. (Older children have a similar problem—those tough snaps on jeans.)

What is problem solving? A final word One last thought about the nature of problem solving in early childhood education is that creative problem solving can take place only in the presence of *genuine children's problems.* Too often "problems" are really tasks thrown at children like stones. This is especially true of cognitive problems: "Do this puzzle." "Mark which picture does not belong." It is crucial that problems in the classroom environment reflect interests, goals, challenges, decisions, or concerns that are genuine from the *child's* point of view—not something the teacher has manufactured without reference to children's developmental levels and interests.

This does not mean that the teacher can never set the stage for a problem. A skilled teacher is able to motivate and facilitate so that a task *becomes* the child's problem—i.e., the child understands it and has a desire to solve it. For example, one boy who had social problems looked through a series of pictures depicting various emotions and then shared his responses with the teacher: he felt like this picture, not like that one. Eventually, both had some insights to be shared with his parents. When the child "owns" the problem, the adult plays the role of a skilled listener and responds to the child's viewpoint. (The teacher is teaching, not preaching.)

How can teachers guide problem solving?

What does the teacher need to be able to do, then, to foster children's problem solving? The following are important aspects of the teacher's role.

Promote children's autonomy The role of the teacher is not to tell children the answers to problems or to help children remember answers, or to serve as an unquestioned, powerful authority. The teacher's role is to set up environments that will let children perceive problems and solve them with the least help from the teacher. The skilled teacher provides plenty of opportunities for autonomy.

Model The skilled teacher is able to model a large repertory of strategies for problem solving. Children need to see the teacher acting as a creative problem solver. Modeling is a powerful impetus to learning. For example, the teacher says aloud, "The cookies are stuck to the cookie sheet, and I don't have a spatula. I've got a problem. Let me think what I can use instead."

Pace children sensitively The skilled teacher is sensitive as regards timing. That means not intervening too quickly. The effective teacher does not rush problem solving, but gives children time. It takes *time* for children to become sensitive to social cues and to learn to adjust their responses continually to social feedback. (See the research of McClure, Chinsky, & Larcen, 1978.) The teacher needs time, too. It takes *time* to individualize instruction and to provide different modes of presentation— auditory, visual, and kinesthetic. Some children, for example, need to start with three-dimensional objects (say, in esthetic problem solving) and then move to two-dimensional objects. For instance, a child might be helped to tackle the problem of line by "drawing" first with yarn, then with crayon or paint.

Ask planned questions The skilled teacher knows how to ask productive questions of children—for example, questions that address different points of choice in the problem-solving process. After the children have had sufficient exploration with materials, a teacher might ask:

- What do you think the matter is? (focusing on problem area)
- Is there anything else you need to know? (seeking missing information)
- How could you find out? (seeking methods for searching)
- Do you want to do something about it? (eliciting willingness to hypothesize)
- Is there a small part you could handle first? (planning)
- What else? . . . Where else? . . . (seeking alternatives and multiple ideas)
- What might you try first? . . . Next? . . . (planning for hypotheses)
- Do you think that idea would work out? What might happen? (eliciting consequences)

Build on children's strengths and successes   There has been too much emphasis on children's deficits. When we think in terms of what children *can't* do, we immediately communicate to them only their weaknesses, not their strengths. The skilled teacher works from children's *strengths* in problem solving to help them build positive self-concepts ("I'm a good problem solver").

Studies suggest that a teacher can look for successful problem-solving behaviors in one area and try to help the child carry these over to another area—from mathematics to reading, for instance (Dworkin & Dworkin, 1977).

How can the teacher build strengths? One strategy is *confirmation:* expressing awareness of the strengths that children exhibit ("Oh, I see you have figured out how you can both play at the water table at the same time"). When teachers confirm strengths so that children understand, then the children begin to generalize problem-solving strategies and transfer them—that is, use them appropriately in new situations. Too often, children get feedback only on problem-solving strategies that apparently do *not* work. As a result, they view themselves as poor problem solvers. They lose confidence and can begin a lifelong habit of depending on others—teachers, parents, etc.—to solve their problems for them. When teachers do look for strengths, by the way, they usually find them.

Individualize instruction   All the preceding aspects of the teacher's role lead to this one: the ability to individualize instruction.

To individualize instruction, the teacher needs to know and understand as much of a child's background as possible, including the child-rearing practices of parents. Here is an example:

> One boy apparently was able to tackle only one kind of esthetic problem (cutting and pasting) because the other media were messy, and the restrictive child-rearing practices in his past forbade all kinds of messiness. The teacher,

therefore, helped the child by letting him guide her hand to make a painting, thus initially avoiding all "messy" contact with paint, but still creating a picture. Eventually the child overcame his constricted reaction and was painting freely and joyously.*

In summary: Guiding problem solving We are not suggesting that creative problem solving is the only learning process: we have already discussed play and discovery learning and noted their importance. But problem solving appears to be most important, and despite this it is unfortunately neglected in many early childhood classrooms or settings. Children use their problem-solving abilities to cope with their internal and external worlds. The following list summarizes ways in which teachers can guide problem solving. (See also Lundsteen, 1980, and the section in Chapter 10 on puppet shows and problem solving.)

Teaching Creative Problem Solving
- Welcome unknowns; seek open-endedness and divergent thought.
- Encourage planning and the setting of goals.
- Use genuine children's problems in a variety of contexts: social, esthetic, cognitive, and physical.
- Encourage autonomy, empathy, causal and consequential thinking, and evaluative thinking.
- Be tolerant of children who solve problems in different or even unique ways (even if these ways are less efficient).
- Model problem solving, and use a wide variety of strategies to fit various problems (including expressing feelings, negotiating, and role playing).
- Confirm children's successes with words they understand, so that you make children aware of their strengths.
- Use feedback. (For example, you might use videotapes so that children can see themselves as problem solvers.)
- Value children's ideas (hypotheses) and products.
- Be sensitive about pacing or timing. Don't rush children. Individualize instruction in problem solving.
- Allow children to leave problems unsolved sometimes. (E.g., let them stop playing a game before its conclusion or leave a project uncompleted.)
- Provide materials that are appropriate for children's developmental levels in order to avoid frustration and failure.
- Be prepared to provide more and more challenging environments and materials.
- Develop language needed for problem solving.

*Thanks to Deborah Hanschen, Arts and Ideas Foundation, Dallas, Texas, for this example.

- Keep a diary or log of problem solving in the classroom.
- Recognize that it's all right to be wrong in your problem solving. Make positive use of inadequate solutions.

Conditions for Effective Learning

Thus far in this chapter we have introduced you to modern theory of teaching and learning and examined three important learning processes: play, discovery learning, and problem solving. To a significant extent, teaching strategy revolves around three components of the teaching-learning process: readiness, reinforcement, and transfer. These components are conditions of effective learning; we now consider them in turn.

READINESS
When teachers are dealing with the concept of readiness, they need to keep several "subconcepts" in the back of their minds.

One should try to identify the abilities that the child brings to the learning situation. Much observation and questioning by the teacher is designed to check on these boundaries. A teacher may be interested in vocabulary, concepts, stage of thinking, or stage of social development.

If a child isn't ready to deal with a problem or answer a question, simplification may be in order. A particularly handy technique is restructuring a task to highlight specific components so that the problem will be clarified.

TEACHER Why do you think we couldn't fit this sponge into the small cup, and we could fit the marble?
CHILD Because it's a sponge.
TEACHER Okay, I'll cut this sponge into two. Now it's still a sponge. Why does it go into the cup now? (Blank, 1977, p. 223)

Motivation is a part of readiness. Children have a natural tendency to want to be accepted as they are now, to be competent, to model admired adults, to relate socially to their peers, or at least to *hope* that they can do these things. These are powerful intrinsic motivators a teacher can rely on. Add to them children's natural curiosity, and you can see that there is no lack of motivation under normal conditions. Children don't need bribes, gold stars, and other extrinsic motivators except in very special cases—and such cases require very special handling and shaping.

REINFORCEMENT
"If you don't use it, you lose it." This statement expresses one aspect of reinforcement and its role in learning: *practice.* We noted earlier that children need practice in solving problems if they are to be effective problem solvers. This is true in all other areas of learning as well.

Another aspect of reinforcement is the concept of *reward*. In fact, "reinforcement" is often used to mean "reward." A reward can be extrinsic or intrinsic—that is, external or internal. Although reinforcement is often thought of as external rewards, we are committed to the principle of internal, or intrinsic, rewards. An intrinsic reward is the inward satisfaction that comes from a sense of direction, from knowing where you are going and how you are coming along. When positive— even joyous—feelings accompany learning, they tend to create lifelong habits and attitudes of learning and growth.

TRANSFER *Transfer* is using learning acquired in one context by applying it to another. Transfer is crucial to learning: if what a child is learning in school is never usable anyplace else, we might as well close the school doors.

How does a teacher get children to transfer learning? First, the learning experience has to be understandable and meaningful. Unfortunately, much "learning" in school is nonsensical to children; either they do not understand it or they understand it but consider it insignificant. In order to transfer, children must understand what they are learning and consider it important.

Another aspect of transfer is perception, or recognition, of similar elements in dissimilar situations. Teachers can help to point these out. Some children, for example, meet the same problem over and over; but because they encounter it in different contexts, they never realize that it is the same problem. A teacher can help children to extract similarities ("Now it's still a sponge" in the example above).

A third aspect of transfer is mental "set." The teacher seeks transfer, and the child *knows* that the teacher seeks it. "How can you use this someplace else?"—an important question—makes "set" explicit. Transfering *in* of past experience and transfering *out* to new experiences are crucial; seek them. (See Lundsteen, 1968.)

Organization for Effective Learning

Earlier, we noted that problem solvers can use initially inadequate solutions to redefine their goals. This section develops the concept of goals. Do your goals remain wandering generalities, or do they become meaningful specifics? For instance, you may say, "I'm going to save money," but until you make that goal specific—"I'm going to save a dollar a day"—nothing much happens.

In order to organize effectively for learning, the teacher must establish goals and objectives clearly, use appropriate goal structures, and use individual or group processes to achieve the goals and objectives.

GOALS AND OBJECTIVES

In the introduction to Part Three of this book, we introduced the subject of goals and objectives and used the analogy of a tree. The trunk corresponds to broad, long-range goals, the branches to the multiple objectives needed to attain each goal, and the twigs and leaves to various learning activities that collectively accomplish the objectives.

Goals

Goals are broad and long-term and are formulated with reference to values. They should never be so broad that they are impossible to assess. "Developing the ability and skills needed to become a contributing member of society," for example, is certainly a worthy goal, but it cannot be assessed during the period of an early childhood program (Spodek, 1978). "Developing the ability to communicate through the skills of speaking, listening, reading, and writing" is, on the other hand, a long-range goal which can reasonably be accomplished, to some degree, during the early childhood years. In general, goals should be relatively few, significant, assessable over a period of one or two school years, and attainable through various shorter-range objectives.

Gagné (1965) indicates that there is a relatively high degree of agreement about the broad goals of education. He notes almost universal agreement on three major emphases:

- Enabling the individual to participate in, and share with others, a variety of *esthetic experiences*
- Developing responsible *citizenship*
- Developing individual *talents* leading to achievement of satisfaction in a life work or vocation.

(He acknowledges that behaviorally stated objectives are most helpful in attaining the third goal, which involves acquiring intellectual competencies and power to deal with and master the environment. Behavioral objectives are discussed below.)

Objectives

Objectives, as we have noted, are the steps leading to goals. There was a tendency in the past to state objectives in terms of "understanding" or "appreciation" which children were expected to gain. But since these could not be assessed directly, success or failure in achieving them had to be based on inference. "The child will *appreciate* the contribution of people of many cultures to the creation of this country" is an example of such an objective. You can see how difficult it would be to determine if it had been accomplished—how can we measure appreciation?

GIVEN	PERFORMANCE
Given two sticks	the student will rub them together to produce fire
MINIMAL ACCEPTABLE PERFORMANCE.	
eight out of ten times.	

Figure 12-3
Task description.

Behavioral objectives

In the 1960s a strong reaction to vaguely stated objectives and the rise of a movement for accountability of teachers resulted in the widespread acceptance of behavioral objectives. These are based on the idea that "learning is a *change* in capability which is inferred from differences in an individual's *performance* from one time to a later time" (Gagné, 1965, p. 9). Notice the emphasis on *change* and on judgment by *performance*.

Behavioral objectives state specific performances that students acquire through particular instructional procedures. They involve explicit statements of *terminal performance*—that is, an exact description of what the student will be able to do at the end of the instructional procedure.

Examples of behaviorally stated objectives are: "The child will name ten parts of his or her body." "The child will read aloud the fifty words on the word list." "The child will demonstrate the skills of running, jumping, and hopping." Note that in each of these examples the key word is the verb. In behaviorally stated objectives, the verb must indicate *action*. Thus, the child will *name, read aloud, demonstrate*. The child is not being asked to *understand* or *appreciate*, because there is no way to measure understanding or appreciation.

Some educators carry behavioral objectives a step further. For them, the statement of expected performance is not enough. There must be, in addition, a description of the conditions under which the behavior is expected to occur (often stated as the *given*) and a description of how good a student's performance must be to be acceptable (Mager, 1962). Figure 12-3 is an example of a task description. If the objectives are for a group or class, a behavioral objective may be given, as in Figure 12-4, when the teacher has stated:

- The performance
- The conditions
- The description of how good the performance must be to be acceptable

Figure 12-4
Behavioral objective.

Given two sticks, 80 percent of the students will succeed in rubbing them together to produce fire.

De Cecco (1968) refers to such a statement as a "task description" rather than a behavioral objective.

Advantages of behavioral objectives. One of the advantages of behavioral objectives is that they help the teacher or curriculum developer to plan. If you know what you expect the student to do, you can help the student take the steps to achieve the objective. Programmed instructional materials are based completely on behavioral objectives.

Another advantage is that such objectives simplify assessment procedures and direct the attention of the student to exactly what needs to be accomplished. Obviously, educators with a strong behaviorist philosophy (recall Figure 12-1) will favor stating objectives in this manner. Many insist that *all* objectives must be stated behaviorally.

Disadvantages. Among the disadvantages of stating behavioral objectives and imposing them upon schools as minimum competencies is the devaluing of subjective judgment of teachers and children. Subjective judgment (in the sense of disciplined introspection and personal meaning) is a central and essential part of evaluation and education. Subjective judgment can be cautious, deliberate, reasoned, and accurate. The worth of an early childhood curriculum is seldom indicated by the objectively measurable achievement of the children. Rather, it depends on the relevance of the curriculum to the environment, its effect on teachers' and children's morale and long-range attitudes, and its agreement with the highest goals held by the community it serves. Such matters have many dimensions and are subject to differing perceptions. Practioners using competency and behavioral objectives to the neglect of these nuances are potentially irresponsible.

It is also true that behavioral objectives can oversimplify assessment.

Another disadvantage is that using behavioral objectives tends to lead to relatively trivial objectives, since these are most easily measurable. In addition, limiting ourselves to predetermined behavioral objectives narrows education and discourages, rather than encourages, divergent thinking. If attainment of performance objectives is *all* a school attempts, learning will be severely limited (Shane & Shane, 1973). Humans can learn many things that transcend overt performance objectives.

Humanistic objectives Although we do acknowledge that it is important to achieve certain skills and habits, we see these as low-level building blocks in the learning process—not as the end of learning. If they are useful, it is as a means to an end. We can accept behavioral objectives as appropriate in the learning of low-level skills, particularly motor skills (e.g., handwriting, typing, mechanics of mathematical computation, punctuation). We believe, however, that educational programs can legitimately direct their attention to concept development, problem-solving behavior, creativity, responsibility for oneself and others, positive self-concepts, and desirable values and attitudes—that is, to *process*, not just content. With some important humanistic objectives (e.g., concepts and attitudes), we may not see the full benefit for many months or years.

One advocate of humanistic objectives suggests that professionals be held responsible for demonstrating some rational basis for whatever they do (Coombs, 1976). Coombs recommends that accountability be achieved through assessment of *process* on the part of the teacher rather than through achievement of some mechanistic learning on the part of students.

A moderate approach Because we recognize the significance of humanistic objectives, we do not find it necessary to insist that objectives be stated behaviorally. We would suggest that once broad goals are delineated, teachers state objectives in terms of:

- Skills
- Concepts
- Attitudes

which they would like to develop. Once these are carefully thought out, learning activities can be planned to develop each of them. Here is an example:

Goal: Acceptance of oneself as a member of a family
Objectives: Concepts, skills, and attitudes
>   *Concepts:* (1) Different members of the family play different roles. (2) Each member of the family contributes to the welfare of the others. (3) Older family members assume responsibility for younger ones.
>   *Skills:* (1) Assuming and carrying out family chores. (2) Writing the names of all members of the family.
>   *Attitudes:* (1) Feeling comfortable about being the oldest or youngest in the family. (2) Being willing to help younger siblings.

Some of these objectives can be assessed in terms of overt behavior; they therefore lend themselves to measurement and can be stated behaviorally. Attainment of other objectives can only be inferred. And for still others, our only realistic aim is to progress *in the direction* of the objective, rather than actually to attain it.

GOAL STRUCTURES The preceding section described approaches to stating goals and objectives for teaching-learning strategies. This section deals with the structure of goals—individualistic, competitive, and cooperative.

"Goal structure" refers to how children relate to each other and the teacher while working toward certain goals. We have pointed out that as children move from early, solitary play into more advanced forms of learning, there is an increase in activities involving cooperation and competition. Three types of goal structures are distinguishable: (1) An *individualistic* goal structure exists when attainment of a goal by one child is completely unrelated to the success or failure of other children. (2) A *competitive* goal structure exists when children realize that they can attain their goals only if other children *fail* to attain theirs. (3) A *cooperative* goal structure exists when children realize that they can attain their goals if the other children with whom they are linked also attain *their* goals (Johnson & Johnson, 1975).

None of these goal structures is "right," and none is "wrong." There have been emphases on different ones at different periods in educational history. We believe that there is a place for all three—and that the teacher's skill in selecting and implementing the appropriate goal structure is one of the most important components of effective teaching. Recent trends—emphasizing problem-solving skills and process learning, humanistic education, and open education—indicate the need for greater attention to cooperative learning, which is the least utilized of the three goal structures.

There certainly are conditions under which competition is desirable and effective. These generally are situations that produce little or no anxiety: games like chess, backgammon, and concentration, simple drills, and speed-related tasks (arithmetic tables, for instance). There are also conditions when an individualistic approach may be most effective. These include situations in which a specific skill must be mastered (e.g., learning to tie shoelaces, to jump rope, or to read), and there are enough materials, adequate space, and sufficient guidance to permit individual work. Cooperation (the least used goal structure, as we have noted) is most appropriately used when social development is a major goal, when problem solving and creativity are valued, and when the task is relatively complex (like building a block city or writing a class newspaper). Table 12-4 summarizes the appropriate or ideal conditions for use of each goal structure.

Recent emphasis on "individualized education" has led to the erroneous assumption that all children should be working at different places and different activities and perhaps should even be taught individually. This is neither desirable nor efficient. In fact, it can be chaotic. What should be individualized are the teacher's *expectations* for each child, based on a knowledge of the child's interests, needs, and capabilities. In many instances, this will mean that even on the basis of individualized expectations, several children would profit from the same instruction at the same time (so that the teacher works with a group) or from the same

Table 12-4 APPROPRIATE OR IDEAL CONDITIONS FOR THE THREE GOAL STRUCTURES

	GOAL STRUCTURE		
	COOPERATIVE	INDIVIDUALIZED	COMPETITIVE
Type of instructional activity	*Problem solving:* Assignments can be ambiguous. Students clarify, inquire, make decisions.	*Acquisition of specific skill or knowledge:* Assignments should be clear. Behavior should be specified.	*Recall and review; skill practice:* Assignments should be clear. Rules for competing should be specified.
Perception of importance of goals	Goals are important for *each* student. Students expect the group to achieve goals.	Goals are important for *each* student. Each student expects to achieve his or her goal eventually.	Goals are not important to each student. Students can accept winning or losing.
Students' expectations	To have positive interaction with others. To share ideas and materials. To contribute to group efforts. To divide tasks. To capitalize on diversity among members.	To be left alone by others. To take a major part of responsibility for completion of tasks. To take a major part in evaluation.	To have an equal chance of winning. To enjoy the activity (win or lose). To monitor the progress of competitors. To compare ability, skills, or knowledge with peers.
Expected source of support	Other students.	Teacher.	Teacher.

Source: Adapted from Johnson and Johnson, 1975, p. 62.

experience (so that the children work together). At other times, they will be working alone. Bearing in mind the individual differences in the classroom, the teacher will plan for a large-group, small-group, and individual activities, and for competitive, individualized, and cooperative experiences. The teacher will plan to meet the needs, abilities, and interests of the students while guiding them to become self-directing lifelong learners. (Chapter 14, on setting the tone of your classroom, gives more organizational information.)

Summary

In this chapter we have talked about teaching and learning strategies, stressing our own preferences.

We first explored influences on teaching-learning strategies: educational philosophies, theories of teaching, and theories of learning.

Next, we discussed some important learning processes: play, discovery learning, and problem solving. Play was presented as a crucial symbolic-transformational process. We discussed important teaching roles and principles for play and for creative problem solving, focusing most on creative problem solving, since it includes almost any other kind of learning and mental process. Autonomous problem solving is a highly motivating experience that stimulates much learning. Teachers are well-advised to become knowledgeable about it and proficient in its use with young children.

We also took up three conditions for effective learning: readiness, reinforcement, and transfer. General guidelines for almost any teaching strategy include these three elements. For higher mental processes and developmental, humanistic teaching, as opposed to behavioristic contexts, these terms have special meanings. We discussed setting goals and objectives, cautioning against trivializing education in the name of accountability.

Finally, we discussed goal structures—competitive, individual, and cooperative—stressing cooperative goals. Carefully considered goals, expressed in terms of meaningful, specific objectives, make it possible to evaluate the effectiveness of teaching-learning processes.

The following list sums up our beliefs about teaching-learning strategies (the format follows that of Dorothy Law Nolte's "Children Learn What They Live"):

Teachers Teach What They Live
If teachers value equality, they will not treat all children equally but will teach to each child's strengths and needs.

If teachers lead children to believe that they have choices, they will avoid manipulation and honor this commitment.

If teachers would understand children, they must understand developmental patterns in every domain.

If teachers want children to develop as whole persons, they will provide challenging situations in which children can be successful.

If teachers want children to develop as whole persons, they will also allow them some time just for themselves.

If teachers believe children can learn from mistakes, they will let them know that it is all right to be wrong.

If teachers want citizens who are secure and responsible, they will help children see the limits of acceptable behaviors.

If teachers respect children, they will avoid self-defeating ridicule, sarcasm, and favoritism. They will not find scapegoats but will treat each child with dignity.

If teachers want children to become self-sufficient, they will avoid doing what children can do for themselves.

If teachers want to help children become competent learners, they won't have days filled with so much teaching that there's no time for learning.

References

Aldis, O. *Play fighting*. New York: Academic Press, 1975.

Bennett, S. N., & Jordan, J. A. Typology of teaching styles in primary schools. *British Journal of Educational Psychology*, 1975, *45*, 20–28.

Blank, M. Language, the child, and the teacher: A proposed assessment model. In H. L. Hom, Jr., & P. A. Robinson (Eds.), *Psychological processes in early education*. New York: Academic Press, 1977.

Bruner, J. S., Oliver, R. R., Greenfield, P. M., & Associates. *Studies in cognitive growth*. New York: Wiley, 1966.

Coombs, A. Educational accountability from a humanistic perspective. In M. Silberman, J. Allender, & J. Yanoff (Eds.), *Real learning: A sourcebook for teachers*. Boston: Little, Brown, 1976.

Cuffaro, H. K. The developmental-interaction approach. In Bank Street College, *Education before five*. New York: Bank Street College of Education, 1977.

De Cecco, J. P. *The psychology of learning and instruction: Educational psychology*. Englewood Cliffs, N.J.: Prentice-Hall, 1968.

Dworkin, N. E., & Dworkin, Y. S. Use of problem-solving strengths in dealing with disabled readers. *Reading Improvement*, 1977, *14*, 82–85.

Gagné, R. M. Educational objectives and human performance. In J. D. Krumboltz (Ed.), *Learning and the educational process*. Chicago: Rand McNally, 1965.

Hughes, M. M. *The earliest years*. Listener In-Service Cassette Library. Hollywood, Calif.: Listener Corp., 1973.

Johnson, D., & Johnson, R. *Learning together and alone*. Englewood Cliffs, N.J.: Prentice-Hall, 1975.

Kagan, J., Moss, H. A., & Sigel, I. Psychological significance of styles of conceptualization. *Monograph of the Society for Research in Child Development*, 1963, *28* (86), 73–112.

Klein, J. Making or breaking it: The teacher's role in model (curriculum) implementation. *Young Children*, 1973, *28* 359–366.

Klein, G. A., & Weitzenfeld, J. Improvement of skills for solving ill-defined problems. *Educational Psychologist*, 1978, *13*, 31–41.

Lundsteen, S. W. Measurement for creative problem solving in kindergarten children. Paper presented at the annual meeting of the American Educational Research Association, Boston, April 1980.

Lundsteen, S. W. A model of the teaching-learning process for assisting development of children's thinking during communication. *Journal of Communication*, 1968, *18*, 412–435.

Mager, R. F. *Preparing objectives for programmed instruction.* San Francisco: Fearon, 1962.

McClure, L. F., Chinsky, J. M., Larcen, S. W. Enhancing social problem solving performance in an elementary school setting. *Journal of Educational Psychology*, 1978, *70*, 504–513.

Millar, S. *The psychology of play.* Baltimore: Penguin Books, 1968.

Pulaski, M. A. Toys and imaginative play. In J. L. Singer (Ed.), *The child's world of make-believe.* New York: Academic Press, 1973.

Rosenberg, M. B. *Diagnostic teaching.* Seattle: Special Child Publications, 1968.

Shane, J. G., & Shane, H. G. Ralph Tyler discusses behavioral objectives. *Today's Education*, September–October 1973, pp. 41–46.

Smilansky, S. *The effects of sociodramatic play on disadvantaged preschool children.* New York: Wiley, 1968.

Spivak, G., & Shure, M. G. *Social adjustment of young children: A cognitive approach to solving real-life problems.* San Francisco: Jossey-Bass, 1974.

Spodek, B. *Teaching in the early years* (2d ed.). Englewood Cliffs, N.J.: Prentice-Hall, 1978.

White, B. L. *The first three years of life.* Englewood Cliffs, N.J.: Prentice-Hall, 1975.

Witkin, H. A., Dyk, R. B., Faterson, H. F., Goodenough, D. R., & Karp, S. A. *Psychological differentiation.* New York: Wiley, 1962.

CHAPTER 13

CHAPTER 13

Overheard in a teacher's lounge:
"There are so many rules and regulations
about what can and cannot be done in the
classroom for special children. I'll never
understand the laws, much less be able to
follow them to the letter."

CHILDREN WITH SPECIAL NEEDS

Norma C. McGeoch and Ellen Steadman

Federal and state laws, and community demands, now make it necessary for the schools to provide appropriate educational opportunities for all children—including those with special needs. The purpose of this chapter is to help teachers who are concerned about children with special needs.

Who are these children? They are children who differ from the norm, whatever the norm is, in a variety of ways and who need our sensitive concern and help. The ways in which they differ may be related to their culture, language, intelligence, creativity, emotional stability, learning ability, and physical ability. Obviously, a teacher may never have all kinds of special children; and certainly no teacher will have all at one time. But in the context of the present attitudes prevalent in this country and under current legislative mandates, it is becoming more and more typical that teachers will need to make provisions for some of these special children.

This chapter speaks to the following questions:

- What are the effects on the classroom of current community demands and legislative action regarding the economically disadvantaged and culturally and linguistically different child?
- What are the differences among various approaches to learning a second language, e.g., "immersion," "ESL," and "bilingual"?

- How do we meet the needs of gifted and creative children?
- What is Public Law 94-142 and what are the implications of main-streaming handicapped children?
- What can a classroom teacher do to help handicapped children learn?
- What attitudes are important in dealing with children who have special needs?

We shall first look at children who come from environments that create special needs. Among such children are those who are economically disadvantaged or culturally or linguistically different. Next we turn to the educationally different, including the gifted and the creative, the learning-disabled, the mentally retarded, and the emotionally disturbed. Then, we deal with the physically different, those handicapped in areas such as speech, vision, and hearing, and those having orthopedic and other medical problems. Last, we consider programs for early diagnosis and treatment of developmentally delayed infants. In each instance we examine legislation, attitudes, and appropriate teaching methods.

The Environmentally Different

During the late 1950s and early 1960s, writers, researchers, and President Johnson's "war on poverty" awakened America to the problems associated with the culturally different and economically disadvantaged. Infusion of massive financial support from the federal government precipitated programs dealing with the needs of children in this category.

ECONOMICALLY DISADVANTAGED CHILDREN Who are the *economically* disadvantaged children? They are generally identified as those in families where the income falls below a federally designated level. They may live in urban or rural areas. They may be any race or color. They may or may not be native English-speakers. Economic disadvantage exists in conjunction with, but also apart from, cultural or linguistic difference.

What can the teacher do to help the economically disadvantaged child? Once the teacher has determined which children in the class are economically disadvantaged, one step is to become thoroughly acquainted with the local, state, and national services available to the poor. Who, in the community, provides free immunizations, dental care, eyeglasses, counseling, help in finding jobs or financial assistance, parent education, and so on? Is there a local and state directory of such services?

Remembering that a quality educational program for *all* children is also a quality educational program for disadvantaged children, start with the strengths in the child's past experiences. Then move to provide additional experiences that develop concepts needed in school that an impoverished child may lack, e.g., a tradition of valuing literacy, books, and writing (see Weber, 1969).

The classroom teacher needs to observe an economically disadvantaged child carefully to determine the child's abilities and level of educational functioning. The teacher is then able to provide experiences appropriate to the child's stage of development. The teacher may need to create or adapt material to make the learning experiences understandable from the child's point of view and background.

Another important function of the teacher is to try to get the *parents* into the school, and the school into the home. Involvement is for economically disadvantaged parents as well as for other parents, and economically disadvantaged parents may need special encouragement to enter the "world of the school." (Education and involvement of parents are discussed in Chapter 15.)

CULTURALLY DIFFERENT CHILDREN

"I wish I knew how to get Tom to be more excited about things. He rarely indicates what he wants; he just accepts whatever I suggest."

The teacher making this remark interprets the child's behavior as extremely passive. The teacher knows that Tom understands, as his main language is English, but is not fully sensitive to one of the values of his American Indian culture—preserving an appearance of outward calm and deference to adult authority.

Who are the *culturally different* children? They come from various racial and ethnic groups that have their own values, life-styles, and customs, and sometimes a different language.

What can the teacher do to meet the needs of the culturally different? Teachers can make sure that the children see their membership in different cultures as a positive force. Thus the teacher can help to build rather than damage the children's self-concepts. Teachers need to understand that a second culture is a bonus to be capitalized upon in the classroom.

Not only do we want the children to know that we value their cultures; we also want the parents to sense our valuing. The teacher can invite parents to share traditional customs, foods, festivities, arts and crafts, music, and literature (oral or written) with the class. The teacher can enlist the parents as volunteers who not only provide assistance but also serve as role models for the children. Teachers need to encourage the exchange visits between home and school, particularly since these parents have not always been made to feel welcome.

LINGUISTICALLY DIFFERENT CHILDREN

Some children have not only interesting cultural differences, but also language differences. For example, one school in Arlington, Virginia, identified twenty-three different language groups among its student population (Clayton, 1978). This case is not at all unusual. This diversity is even more pronounced in cities such as New York, San Francisco, and Chicago. The needs of non-English-speaking (NES) or limited-English-speaking (LES) children have become an area of concern and controversy.

Since 1974 (when the Bilingual Education Act was passed) we have been a nation trying to respond to a court decision supporting bilingual programs. Ways of responding are various, and there has been little or no consistent precedent or research upon which to base decisions. Until the situation becomes clearer, you may have several options. Let's try to define them.

How do we teach the linguistically different?

Currently and historically there appear to be three ways to teach a language: (1) "immersion," or "total immersion," in which all instruction and communication are in the language to be learned; (2) "second-language instruction," in which the language to be taught is presented during a special subject period of the day (e.g., "English as a second language" or ESL); (3) "bilingual instruction," in which the language to be learned and the student's dominant language are intertwined during the whole day. As a variation of bilingual instruction, one sometimes finds an added language-instruction period tucked into the day. (In the United States this added period would be English as a second language, ESL.) Another variation is "bilingual-bicultural" instruction.

Immersion   Let's consider a Canadian example of the immersion type of program, the St. Lambert experiment in Quebec. In this program, English-speaking children were taught entirely in French for their first two years of schooling. Children could use English for spontaneous speech, but the teacher encouraged them to speak in French. The teacher always spoke in French. Thus the children learned to speak, read, and write in their second language. By the end of grade 1, the children were as fluent in the second language (French) as they were in their mother tongue (English) (Lambert, 1974; Lambert & Tucker, 1972; Swain, 1974). The total immersion program is also used by the armed forces and the diplomatic corps for personnel who need to acquire a new language very quickly. This method appears to be used successfully in countries with large immigrant populations with many different language backgrounds and strong motivation to learn the language in which most communication takes place (e.g., Israel and its Ulpan method).

Second-language instruction   In this case a language is taught as a secondary language during a special subject period of the day. Generally, a teacher trained in the skills of second-language teaching works with children individually or in small groups. The teacher starts where the child is and builds oral language skills and a vocabulary before embarking on a sequential program of reading and writing instruction.

Let's visit a third-grade classroom. A teacher comes in and takes Gustavo out. He has just come from Mexico and cannot speak any English. In a separate room the teacher uses a card file, lectures, newspapers, and other aids in order to elicit English vocabulary. This lesson is stressing shapes, colors, body parts, and family members. The teacher, using oral language (English) with the boy, is helping to develop his listening and speaking ability. Only later will reading and writing be introduced. This is an example of instruction called "English as a second language."

Bilingual and bilingual-bicultural instruction   Bilingual education uses the child's native language as the primary medium for the mastery of and instruction in the basic skills. In this country, English and the child's dominant language are used as mediums of instruction for all other areas of the curriculum. The "bi" in "bilingual" means "two," so that "bilingual" means "having two languages." One is the language of the school—English—and the second is the dominant language of the child (which may or may not be the dominant language of the home).

What is the dominant language of a child? Ideally it is the language that serves best for learning, *the language in which the child can do the highest-level, most abstract thinking.* Sometimes educators have assumed from querying parent or child, or from English tests, that the child's dominant language must be, say, Spanish. Then, upon further careful observation and testing—e.g., with repeating groups of numbers and phrases in reverse—it became clear that the child's command of Spanish was actually worse than the child's command of English. A whole new field of measurement has grown up around attempts to determine the child's dominant language. The dominant language could be, for example, any one of the 23 identified in the school in Arlington, Virginia, mentioned earlier, or any one of the eighty-two identified in the Los Angeles Unified School District.

Next, let's consider the term "bicultural." In a bicultural classroom the teacher will make use of many opportunities to include information and activities stressing the life-style, customs, vocabulary, music, art, and literature of the children's varying cultures. In most instances the term "bicultural" is rather misleading, since most children represent a multitude of cultural backgrounds. Before the year is out the children may have tried eating with chopsticks, breaking a piñata, writing to Kris Kringle, making Hopi pottery, and square dancing.

Issues and attitudes about programs for the linguistically different

Following our policy in this chapter of keeping our ears open to what teachers are saying, we stop by a faculty lounge and listen to part of a discussion dealing with bilingual education. The teachers represent various ethnic backgrounds—Anglo, Hispanic, black, second-generation European, and Oriental.

MS. JONES   I've just been reading that we have over 33 million individuals who live in homes where English is not the first language.

MRS. SMITH   This problem of educating minority groups with different cultures is new to me this year. Is this something new for educators?

MRS. BROWN   New? Not at all! In the 1800s schools enrolling immigrant children encountered problems very similar to the ones we have now. Poor ability in English language skills was said to be responsible for low school achievement, poor self-concept, truancy, and high drop-out rates (Hartmann, 1948; Ide, 1920). Sound familiar?

MR. JONES   Certainly does. Moreover, bilingual education existed for over 1 million children in the 1800s, for example, German-English in Pennsylvania, French-English in Louisiana, Spanish-English in New Mexico (Zirkel, 1977).

MS. BROWN   Why did the bilingual programs stop?

MR. JONES   A wave of nationalism in the 1890s put an end to the acceptance of "cultural diversity," and many states mandated the exclusive use of English. Indeed, in some states it was a "criminal act" to use any language other than English in the classroom.

MS. NOVAK   Quite right! I don't mean to sound un-American, but if people want to live in the United States, they should learn to speak English. My parents came from Europe, and they had to learn English. It didn't hurt them. They were happy to be here and proud to learn English.

MS. GARCIA   We don't want to lose our culture, as you did! Do you know what used to happen to Spanish-speaking children in schools? If they caught you talking Spanish, they would send you to the office, warn you, give you a lecture about not being a good American, say that your language was bad (U.S. Commission, 1973). They destroyed our children!

MS. ARMSTRONG   A *lot* of children out there need help. We need to be looking for *multi*cultural education. My black kids are in these schools. They know a lot about tacos and piñatas, but never get a chance to share our culture. We have a culture, too, you know!

MS. NOVAK   I agree. It's important for our children not to lose their own cultural identity. But they get bored and inattentive hearing everything first in English and then in Spanish. Why can't we have *multicultural* programs that give children a sense of pride, use a few words of the many languages represented, but teach English to mastery?

MR. THOMPSON   Well, you know a lot of my parents are saying that they bring their children to school to learn English, to succeed in an English-speaking society, and that that's my job!

MS. GARCIA Why don't you wake up and look at some facts? A large number of "limited-English" students have erroneously ended up in classes for the educable mentally retarded (Carter, 1970). Ideas that their language and culture are bad are reinforced by teachers' negative stereotypes (Wylie, 1976). Teachers give significantly less praise and encouragement to Mexican students than to Anglo-Saxon students (U.S. Commission on Civil Rights, 1973).

MR. JONES But try to think a moment of the greatest good for the greatest number. I met a teacher from a school where a bilingual-bicultural program in Spanish was required, since there were twelve Spanish-speaking kids and the school had hit the magic number. But he also had four Vietnamese children, four Taiwanese children and five Philippine children in his room. What was being done for them? Nothing!

MR. THOMPSON The cost bothers me—$500 million committed to bilingual education over the past ten years, and only ½ of 1 percent of that money went toward research to examine how effective the programs are for children (Troike, 1978).

MRS. TAYLOR I've been listening to all of you without saying a thing. To me, the final word is what I can see and feel in my own classroom. My children's words about how they like speaking their own language at the same time they learn English tell me my bilingual program is worth every cent. I feel deeply committed to the ideals of such a program and find that good things are happening to all my children.

From this discussion, you can see that bilingual education is received with mixed emotions. In the meantime, what can you do?

Tips for teachers

Some ideas follow that seem valuable no matter what approach your school is using. We divide them into three categories: language, classroom environment, and social enhancement.

Language
- Try to say at least a few words of the child's native language. In fact, go on and learn another language!
- If you do know the second language well, be prepared to switch back and forth from the child's language to English.
- Provide opportunities for English-speaking children to learn some words of the different languages of their classmates.
- Give direction or instruction in English and in other languages almost simultaneously.
- Label objects in the classroom in both languages.
- Have books available in both languages.

- Know and understand the particular linguistic difficulties your children are encountering. For example, did you know that there are only ten possible ways for a word to end in Spanish? Contrast that with forty possible endings in English. That makes thirty new sounds for Spanish-speaking children to hear and produce.
- Lotto-type games introduce new vocabulary painlessly.
- Use concrete objects and materials, letting the children handle and name them. With your bilingual aide (if you have one), give labels in English and then in the dominant language.
- As soon as it is feasible, have plenty of aides, volunteers, and parents available for children to dictate stories to and plenty of experiences to prompt dictation (in the dominant language, in English, or in a combination of the two). The language-experience approach is a natural, meaningful method for reading readiness and beginning reading. (See also the "key words" approach in Chapter 10.)
- Have parents come in and read to children. Bring in books from home to share. This practice may be your answer to those difficult-to-find materials. Read to them in both languages.

Classroom Environment
- Do use music. Encourage children to make up their own songs to preserve and read—in both languages.
- Interest centers are excellent places to encourage spontaneous, tension-free speech. Children can interact at the housekeeping corner, sand box, carpentry bench, story or puppet corner, and block area, to name a few. Interaction among children is an excellent means of learning.
- Capitalize on toys and games. These are remarkably similar throughout the world. Consider tag, marbles, and jumping rope.

Social Enhancement
- Build self-concepts. As teachers we need to build the positive self-concepts of *all* children. Social and emotional needs of youngsters affect their intellectual functioning.
- Be accepting of and interested in all children's cultures (positive attitude). Multicultural understanding is necessary for life in a global, pluralistic society. How lucky we are to have such a wealth of cultural diversity! What an exciting and challenging opportunity for growth and discovery! We can stress multicultural exchanges regardless of the language-learning approach.
- Invite parents and community representatives to explain and share national events, art, literature, architecture, and crafts. They can also serve as volunteers or aides in the classroom. Children usually relate to these people easily, see them as role models, and gain from the extra adult help.

Finally, children from diverse backgrounds usually exhibit more similarities than differences. Language development experiences which are enjoyable and productive for children in general are also optimal for them. (See Chapter 10.)

The Educationally Different

The foregoing section dealt with the child who is different environmentally: economically, culturally, or linguistically. In this section we move to the educationally different child, considering both the gifted and the handicapped.

Who are the educationally different and what do we do about them? Our stocks of information, the goals of research, the actions of courts and legislatures, even our attitudes are continuously evolving to meet the needs of the educationally different. Agreement on the accuracy of "current thoughts" presented here is not necessarily unanimous, even among experts in special education.

Children who differ from the norm in learning ability range from one end of various continuums to another. At one time intelligence—defined as IQ—was the main variable considered. In some cases IQ seems like a thermometer: IQs are described as "above normal" (130 to 140 or more), "normal" (about 100), and "below normal" (below 80). But learning ability may be affected by many factors other than IQ—e.g., adaptive behavior and social, emotional, and motor behavior. We need to be cautious about stereotyping and overgeneralizing about special children.

This section, dealing with educationally different children, includes discussions of gifted and creative children as well as those handicapped by learning disabilities, mental retardation, emotional disturbances, and other difficulties. We discuss a major piece of legislation (Public Law 94-142) dealing with the rights of these children as it affects schools and teachers. Teachers do feel affected, and we start each topic with a typical comment and related remarks.

GIFTED AND CREATIVE CHILDREN

"Sharon is such a bright child, functioning far above grade level. I'd like to see her in the program for gifted children."

"Sounds as though she really belongs there. Her sister is in my class and is really creative—but not all that bright. I don't think she'd qualify."

What is the distinction being made by these two teachers? Can a child be "gifted" and yet not "creative" or vice versa? Sometimes teachers tend to use such terms rather loosely and interchangeably.

The *gifted* child tends to have an unusually high IQ. In some states that have special funding for programs for gifted children, the qualifying IQ level is clearly stated. Children are "labeled" as gifted if they test above this score on an individually administered IQ test. They are usually recommended for this testing on the basis of scores on a group IQ test, the recommendations of their classroom teachers, or both.

Parents of gifted children have formed special interest groups to demand programs to meet their children's needs. Among these are enrichment programs—specially designed, adapted from existing materials, or made by teachers—to enhance the gifted child's learning. These programs expand the existing curriculum and provide additional high-interest materials at the child's level to be done at a pace set by the child.

Some schools provide special classes or interest groups to meet the special educational interests of gifted children. Some schools use grade advancement (skipping) or combination classes (grouping several grades together).

In some states and local communities, funds have been set aside for the development of programs to serve children identified as gifted (e.g., California's Mentally Gifted Minors—MGM—program). Districts anxious to obtain this additional source of funding are quick to identify their gifted children and to plan special programs for them. (See, e.g., Gallagher, 1975; Johnson, 1977; Wightman, 1977.)

What can the individual teacher in the classroom do to meet the needs and interests of gifted children?

- Encourage their curiosity, exploration, and questioning.
- Be willing to explore and to accept their alternative solutions to problems.
- Involve them in special projects that benefit them and can be of value to the class or school.
- Don't feel threatened if you don't know the answers to some of their questions. *Do* be willing to help them search for the answers.
- Encourage them to use a variety of resources—people, books, multimedia.
- Encourage higher levels of thinking. Questions and assignments should draw upon their abilities to analyze, synthesize, generalize, and solve problems creatively.
- Help them early to learn specialized reference skills that will help them throughout a lifetime of learning.
- Keep them motivated and constructively creating, as their high energy level can often be diverted into negative behavior.
- *Don't* fill their time *only* with errands, clerical jobs, or helping others in the class.

- Do, however, encourage them to accept their special gift as a responsibility, not just a privilege. They need to learn to value the contribution of all people and perhaps to tutor or guide other children.
- Remember, intellectual giftedness does not necessarily mean a totally integrated child. Often gifted children need help in developing balanced self-concepts and healthy social relationships.

The *creative* child may not necessarily have an exceptionally high IQ or unusually high achievement. Often, however, creative children do these kinds of things:

- Behave in ways that conflict with the teacher's expectations
- Question and challenge authority
- Become intensely absorbed in what they are doing
- Become extremely animated and physically involved
- Appear overly eager to share their discoveries with others
- Note relationships among apparently unrelated ideas
- Manifest curiosity, digging for information
- Take independent action
- Show willingness to consider strange ideas
- Display a tendency to seek alternatives and to explore new possibilities
- Demonstrate a particular talent (Adapted from Torrance, 1969)

What can the teacher do to encourage the child's creativity? The following are six suggestions:

1 Allow time for creative explorations of ideas (e.g., brainstorming) and materials.
2 Try out some of the ideas that come from the children.
3 Encourage children to make decisions.
4 Allow time for children to let their minds wander through daydreams and reflections.
5 Encourage children to express their thoughts and feelings in music, poetry, art, storytelling, movement, and writing.
6 Try not to squelch "wild" ideas and schemes. They may be the products of future Einsteins.

Although attitudes are certainly important when dealing with talented and gifted children, even more careful scrutiny and change in attitudes may be needed when it comes to dealing with mainstreaming. In the next section we examine, among other things, the legislative trends that have lifted our awareness concerning the handicapped.

EDUCATIONALLY
HANDICAPPED
CHILDREN

Legislative trends (Public Law 94-142)

Overheard in a faculty lounge: "What's all the excitement about mainstreaming? All we're doing is putting problem children back into the classroom again!"

Teachers' concerns, like the one just quoted, are common. Even without mainstreaming, many classes are already overcrowded, and if the paperwork alone is not handled well (using simplified checklists, for example), it can be somewhat overwhelming. But it must be pointed out that children who found it difficult to cope with the usual classroom environment were often tragically misplaced in the past. A child who did not speak English, for example, might be placed in a class for the mentally retarded. It became apparent that some reforms were needed in placing and evaluating children who need special education.

The rights of *all* individuals are important. The legislation of 1975 providing for the education for all handicapped children (Public Law 94-142) establishes a legal base for free and appropriate public education. This piece of legislation guarantees:

- Access to free and appropriate public education for individuals from ages three to twenty-one.
- Financial assistance to state and local agencies for the education of the handicapped.
- Due process of law for parents and children to ensure appropriate identification, evaluation, and placement. (Hearings can be initiated by parents.)
- A written yearly "individual education plan" (IEP) for each child. (This individualized plan involves parents, administrators, persons trained in diagnosis, teachers, and the *child*). It is not just a traditional prearranged program. (See Safford, 1978, for sample IEPs.)
- Education in the least restrictive environment.

The phrase "education in the least restrictive environment" implies that children are to be placed where they will learn best and where they can manage in the most normal manner. Thus, if special children are able to manage in the regular classroom (with architectural assistance and other aids), they are encouraged to do so. If not, one tries to have them in the regular classroom as much as possible, but with the help of some special classes. And so the situation continues, as shown in Figure 13-1. This figure gives a description of the different levels one encounters in trying to find the least restrictive environment for a child. (The idea is somewhat analogous to giving the least medicine that will cure a disease.) The tapered shape of the diagram shows the difference in numbers involved at the different levels of restriction. Note that the most

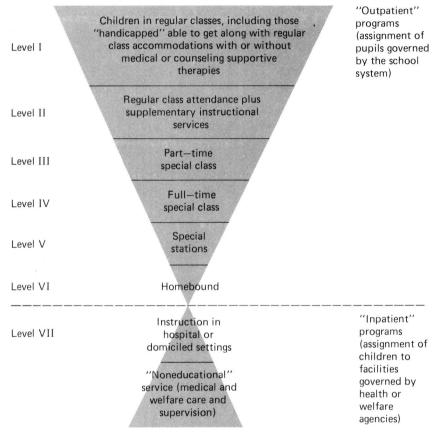

Level I — Children in regular classes, including those "handicapped" able to get along with regular class accommodations with or without medical or counseling supportive therapies

Level II — Regular class attendance plus supplementary instructional services

Level III — Part—time special class

Level IV — Full—time special class

Level V — Special stations

Level VI — Homebound

"Outpatient" programs (assignment of pupils governed by the school system)

Level VII — Instruction in hospital or domiciled settings

"Noneducational" service (medical and welfare care and supervision)

"Inpatient" programs (assignment of children to facilities governed by health or welfare agencies)

Figure 13-1
Finding the least restrictive environment. (Source: Deno, 1974, p. 66.)

specialized facilities are needed by the fewest children on a long-term basis (Deno, 1974).

The idea is to move children down the diagram toward the bottom levels only as far as absolutely necessary and to return the students to regular classrooms as soon as possible. The trend is toward fewer specialized places and more diverse "regular" places with support services—that is, toward moving specialized instructional systems into the mainstream wherever feasible. Along with this trend go removal of architectural barriers; braille and mobility instruction for the blind; a more cooperative classroom social structure; broad team approaches to planning; and recurring, specialized diagnostic appraisal. It is felt that the rich offerings of regular schools and classes need to be opened as widely as possible to all children. If Public Law 94-142 is to succeed in its objectives, classroom teachers need adequate support services: assessment systems, sequences, objectives, resource teachers, aides, methods and materials, smaller classes, and released time for special in-service training (Kavanagh, 1977).

Who are the handicapped?

Under Public Law 94-142, the handicapped include those with any physical or mental impairment substantially limiting one or more major activities:

- Mental retardation
- Impaired hearing
- Impaired speech
- Impaired vision
- Emotional disturbances
- Learning disabilities
- Orthopedic problems or other forms of impaired health

Even though children rarely fall into clear-cut categories (derived from medical or psychological classification systems) and even though these labels should not be rigidly accepted when educational plans are being developed, terms like those listed above are needed for communication. Some children, of course, are multiply handicapped. Exceptions are to be viewed against the background of a continuum of general individual differences, strengths and weaknesses, and learning styles. Actually, teachers will find that the range of abilities to be dealt with has been extended relatively little.

Mainstreaming

The Bureau of Education for the Handicapped estimates that over 1 million handicapped individuals have been totally excluded from school. It seems high time to provide the most appropriate education for each child in the least restrictive setting.

The integration of handicapped children with the regular school population has been called "mainstreaming." The concept is certainly not a new one for many preschool programs. Children with special needs have often been accepted into preschool programs (Northcott, 1970). Placement of such children, usually involving consultation with parents and perhaps pediatricians, was considered a "normalizing" experience for them. In addition, teachers and children became sensitized to the world of the special child.

Head Start, in 1972, stipulated that 10 percent of its enrollment had to be available to handicapped youngsters. Head Start, therefore, has been mainstreaming handicapped children for quite a few years now (Klein, 1975).

Let's turn now to look at some of the types of handicaps that will be mainstreamed into the regular classroom, considering first the learning-disabled, then the mentally retarded, and last the emotionally disturbed. In each section, we give diagnostic clues and tips for teaching.

Learning-disabled children

> "Doug never finishes anything. Either he can't remember what to do or he loses interest or he is daydreaming. I don't know what the problem is—he seems smart enough."

Doug, a school-age child, has a learning disorder that manifests itself as a problem in writing; and there is a discrepancy between his potential intellectual ability and his achievement. Although a recent intelligence test indicates that Doug has an IQ of around 110, he fluctuates in his performance and he cannot succeed on his expected level.

A child who is linguistically disabled, learning-disabled, or both is one who, according to a multidisciplinary team, is not making achievements commensurate with his or her age and ability levels in one or more of the following areas: oral expression, listening comprehension, written expression (including spelling), basic reading skill, reading comprehension, mathematical calculation, or mathematical reasoning. (The terms "linguistically disabled" and "learning-disabled" are not used to refer to those children who exhibit discrepancy between ability and achievement which is primarily the result of visual, hearing, or orthopedic handicap; mental retardation; emotional disturbance; or environmental, cultural, or economic disadvantage.) "Learning-disabled," a term of the 1970s, encompasses earlier labels such as "minimal brain dysfunction or injury," "specific learning disabilities," "perceptually disabled," and "neurologically impaired."

One possible characteristic of the learning-disabled child is called "hyperactivity" (it should be stressed that not all learning-disabled children are hyperactive). "Hyperactivity" is defined as "a consistently high level of activity that is manifested in situations where it is clearly inappropriate [*for the age of the child*] and is coupled with an inability to inhibit activity on command" (Ross & Ross, 1976, p. 288). (What is normal for a three-year-old may be "hyper" for a first- or third-grader.)

The terms "hyperactive" and "hyperkinetic" have, however, been abused. Some educators have fallen into the trap of attaching these labels to youngsters who are simply active, energetic, and curious. Much controversy has been generated in the last decade over the treatment of such children with methylphenidate drugs such as Ritalin. (We really are not yet aware of the full effects of drugs of this nature.) Another controversial program stresses dietary control of such substances as artificial coloring and food additives (Feingold, 1975).

Clues to learning disabilities   Teachers, who work with children on a daily basis, are in a position to spot clues to a learning problem. One task force generated ninety-five such clues (or descriptors). Each child will exhibit a different selection of these. A few of the signals are these:

- The child has a short attention span for his or her age.

- The child is overly distractable for his or her age (has figure-ground problems), or has impaired concentration.
- The child throws tantrums frequently when crossed, and has difficult relations with peers.
- Once started, the child is unable to stop laughing (an example of verbal or motor perseveration).
- The child is generally awkward.
- The child confuses similar words and letters (and has other academic difficulties).
- The child has difficulty remembering.
- The child talks well but can't put a puzzle together (i.e., shows a discrepancy among abilities). (See also a reference such as Wallace & McLoughlin, 1975.)

Tips for teachers What are some of the things the teacher can do to meet the special needs of the learning-disabled child?

- Place the child close at hand so that extra help can be given easily.
- Minimize distractions—the learning-disabled child has a tendency to pay too much attention to everything.
- Simplify the child's environment, and decrease the number of choices he or she is faced with.
- Use concrete materials and multiple sensory experiences—the older learning-disabled child may still have difficulty understanding abstract ideas in some areas. (Again, there will be a discrepancy among abilities.)
- Avoid unnecessary frustrations; for instance, don't assign tasks that the child cannot do.
- Have reasonable expectations—it takes longer for a learning-disabled child to complete an assignment.
- Break work into small segments. A large task overwhelms the learning-disabled child.

Basic principles of appropriate teaching—working from the child's strengths, individualizing, and giving concise directions—are just as useful for the learning-disabled child as for any child. Also, the idea of "nothing in excess" is worth remembering. For example, while some learning-disabled children may profit from a simplification of their environment, don't make their space bleak and barren.

Among the general principles that are useful in helping the educationally handicapped are: (1) Look for signs of *tension* in children, and try to pinpoint causes of tension. You might perhaps make the environment more soothing. (2) Help children to keep at it, to *persevere*. (3) Use *multisensory* approaches to learning. (4) Help children to get blocked responses flowing by using the technique of *initial cueing* (Cheek, 1978). Let's examine each of these principles in turn.

1   The teacher needs to find ways to relieve children who show signs of *tension* or "up-tightness" (characteristic of some learning-disabled children). Such signs are sweaty palms, upset stomach, and flushes behind the ears; in human beings, such reactions indicate readiness to flee or fight for survival, and in such a state abstract thinking and learning come virtually to a standstill. Perhaps some soft music, breathing and relaxation games, or just a reassuring hug and assurance that the child is on the right track might help.

2   Helping the child to *perserve* also requires much more attention from the teacher than would be the case for the "normal" child. Feeding the child a task in very small, nonthreatening, easily digested portions—one problem at a time, one task to a page, one direction at a time—may be the answer. Careful thought about inherent rewards helps, too.

3   Learning can take place through all five senses; and learning can be stored by means of all the senses. Educationally handicapped children have a better chance to learn through a *multisensory* approach; therefore, the teacher needs to be willing to invest as much time and energy as necessary to involve all the senses in building deep and lasting concepts. Let the children *clap* their numbers, *see* their numbers, *feel* their numbers—even *eat* number-shaped cookies that they have made. Relationships needed for lasting learning are built layer upon layer of varied, multisensory experiences.

4   It is important to be patient and willing to assist these children with strategies for getting started. Sometimes educationally handicapped children appear to block in responding to tasks or starting work. This does not necessarily mean that they cannot come up with the answer or do the work. Often they just need help in getting started. Saying the first words or doing the first part of the task in unison with the teacher may help. For example, the teacher may say: "2 + 2 is . . .", instead of "What is 2 + 2?" Aids like this are called "initial cuing."

Remember, these children *can* produce. They do not want sympathy and leniency that permits them to avoid what the others in the class are doing. What they do want is the respect that comes from accomplishing a task set for them, reasonable limits and standards (consistently adhered to) that they can meet, and the encouragement and assistance needed to do what *you* and *they* know they *can* do.

Many of these teaching tips also apply to the mentally retarded child—the topic of the next section.

Mentally retarded children

> "Melinda is so slow, and she can't play many games with other children. She doesn't remember from one day to the next how to play most games."

A mentally retarded child is one who is below average in overall intellectual functioning and has disorders associated with adaptive behavior (maturation, learning, or social skills). A student who is mentally retarded is one whom a licensed or certified psychologist (or some other qualified person) has determined to be functioning more than two standard deviations below the mean on individually administered scales of verbal ability, nonverbal ability, and adaptative behavior. For educational purposes, IQ alone does not determine whether or not a person is mentally retarded. Mentally retarded children are usually classified as follows:

Educable mentally retarded (EMR) or moderately intellectually limited. The "educable mentally retarded" have IQs, in the 50–80 range. They are unable to profit from regular methods of instruction; but they do have potential in academic subjects at a minimal level, social adjustment sufficient to get along in a classroom, and the possibility of developing occupational abilities that will allow for at least partial self-support as adults.

Trainable mentally retarded (TMR) or severely intellectually limited. These children have IQs in the 25–50 range. They have the potential for learning self-help skills, social adjustment, and some simple tasks.

Down's syndrome. Down's syndrome, or mongolism, is a specific form of mental retardation arising from chromosomal abnormality. Children with Down's syndrome characteristically have broad faces, flat noses, and slanted eyes. They are generally pictured as cooperative and affectionate, though of course there are individual differences in temperament. Retardation is moderate, so that these children can profit from structured language-development programs under the guidance of a caring teacher.

Mental retardation is also classified by cause. We currently know of about seventy causes; some causes we still don't understand. Known causes include diseases contracted by the mother during pregnancy, trauma at birth, diseases of the newborn, and lack of stimulation in infancy (Bradley, 1970; and see our Chapter 4).

Clues to mental retardation A combination of some of the following characteristics may signal mental retardation:

- Delayed coordination of motor skills, e.g., walking
- Delayed language skills
- Lack of inquisitiveness and desire to learn
- Persistence of infantile habits beyond the age when they are usually dropped; immaturity in comparison with peers
- Slow academic progress not explained by other factors
- Inability to follow directions and to comprehend conversations

- Consistent preference for playing with younger children
- Inadequate social adjustment
- Inability to comprehend the "why" of things; delayed ability to conceptualize; poor memory

Tips for teachers What are some things that the teacher can do to meet the special needs of mentally retarded children? These children can be taught in regular classrooms, given special provisions. Teachers can help them with social skills, self-help, and language skills through orderly programs.

- Be sensitive to the child's needs; praise the child for the completion of tasks no matter how small.
- Demonstrate that you care about the child, but be firm and consistent.
- Be aware of the child's capacity and do not force the child to attempt achievement beyond his or her capacities. Adjust your speed, pace, and tempo to the child, accepting the child as he or she is at that moment.
- Teach by gestures and concrete examples as much as possible.
- Help to give the child as much proficiency as possible in certain skills; e.g., jumping rope and dancing.
- Use a multisensory approach to learning. For example, Melinda is working with the number 4. She can:
  - Clap four times
  - Throw four Nerf balls (soft and spongy)
  - Wash four apples
  - Choose four people
  - Write four 4s on a page
  - Listen to four bells
- Have a talk with the child's parents and physician to help yourself understand the child better.
- Help the child develop acceptable attitudes toward family, school, and self.
- Give the child plenty of chances to learn and to overlearn in order to build a sturdy foundation for future expansions of his or her skills.
- Keep in mind the goal of helping the child become socially, personally, and, eventually, economically self-sufficient.

Remember that a mentally retarded child has the same emotional and social needs as an intellectually normal child. That is, he or she needs friends, acceptance, and love. Learning, language and problem-solving skills are less adequate than the skills of other children at the same chronological age but similar to those of children at the same mental age (see Jordan & Dailey, 1973).

Emotionally Disturbed Children

"Gigi blows up over the smallest matters. She loses control and sometimes hurts the other children. I've tried everything I know, and still this behavior continues. I don't know what to do."

An emotionally disturbed child is one who has the following traits (as evaluated by qualified professionals):

- An apparent inability to learn for which there is no medical, sensory, or intellectual basis (i.e., which is not due to a handicap)
- An inability to form or maintain relationships with other children or adults
- Inappropriate types of behavior or reactions under normal conditions
- A general, pervasive unhappiness or depression under normal circumstances
- A tendency to develop aches, pains, or fears when confronted with school or social problems (Department of Health, Education, and Welfare, 1977)

The presence of any one of these characteristics affects the child's learning.

Clues to emotional disturbance Some signals (besides those just mentioned) that may indicate an emotional disturbance are:

- Misbehavior for no apparent reason
- Emotional behavior not typical for the child's age
- Explosive reactions to minor incidents
- Frequent unhappiness in normal circumstances
- Withdrawal

Sadly, we still know very little about emotional disturbances in children. Emotionally disturbed children will have their own individual kind of learning problems.

Tips for teachers A few general things that the teacher can do to meet the special needs of the emotionally disturbed child are:

- Accept the child as he or she is, and try to build the child's trust.
- Eliminate or reduce opportunities for failure.
- Individualize instruction.
- Try to determine and reduce anxiety-causing situations.
- Show understanding of the child's feelings, but set firm limits on behavior.

- Be firm, fair, and consistent (provide stability and avoid being manipulated).
- Help the peer group to accept and encourage such children while influencing their behavior.
- Provide opportunities for autonomy and decision making—for more mature behavior.
- You are probably going to need help—get it (e.g., contact the school counselor or psychologist).

By easing the burden of high-pressure situations, the teacher can provide a comfortable and less restricted learning environment, one that may ease the child's disturbances. (See Chapter 14 for ideas on discipline.)

Some final thoughts on teaching the educationally different

In this section we have considered the needs of educationally different children, some clues to help in detecting such children (diagnosis comes before teaching), and some tips on teaching them. In the case of the gifted or creative child, what appears to be much more important than any specific type of program or materials is (as usual) the teacher's attitude. If the attitude is one that encourages questioning, curiosity, exploration, and elaboration, allows for alternative solutions, and is willing to confess "That's something I never thought of" or "I really don't know the answer to that. But where could we go to find out?" then these children can begin to achieve their fullest potential.

Next, we talked about children who are educationally handicapped by learning disabilities, mental retardation, or emotional disturbances. Here too, the teacher's attitude and developmental knowledge are highly important. The attitude of the more "normal" peers is important, and teachers can prepare for the possibility of some initial cruelty in the form of ridicule and aversion. Preparation involves talking with classmates, parents, and other school personnel.

Next, we look at another group of children. These children are physically different.

The Physically Different

Under the terms of Public Law 94-142, children who are physically different (including those with speech, vision, and hearing disabilities as well as orthopedic handicaps and chronic physical problems) are to be educated in the least restrictive environment in which they can successfully function. Many of them may be placed in the regular classroom. This section attempts to provide an introduction to the problems of the physically different, some clues that might help the teacher spot undiagnosed problems, and some tips for dealing with these children in the regular classroom. No one expects the classroom teacher to be a medical expert. Each of us who works with these special children has to be willing to turn to professionals for guidance and to plan and implement a program to meet the needs of *all* children. You can enhance your knowledge of effective teaching strategies through reading, course work, and exchanging ideas with other teachers. We also consider programs for developmentally delayed or "at-risk" infants, out of our firm conviction that early attention to some of these problems may greatly alleviate or even eliminate some of them.

SPEECH-HANDICAPPED CHILDREN

"Kathy is so hard to understand. Sometimes I don't talk to her just because I know I won't know what she is saying."

Slight defects can seem severe to a child because of the importance of speech and the pressure to be understood by others. A speech handicap is present when speech patterns draw attention to the manner of speaking rather than the content of speech.

The ability to articulate (including pronunciation and language usage) is a developed skill, just as intellectual skills are. As a child grows, speech and language usage normally improves. When analyzing the speech of a student, the teacher needs to consider if the mistakes are unique to this child or if other children of the same age make similar errors. If the mispronunciations or words used are typical of children that age, then the mistakes are generally developmental in nature and will be corrected in time and with exposure to appropriate role models.

Some errors are not developmental. Some have a medical basis and others are due to faulty signals from the brain. Children who characteristically make such errors will need special help from an individual trained in speech pathology. A surprising number of children do not hear well (Hendrick, 1975), and inadequate hearing is at the root of their speech problems.

Defects in *voice quality* are not developmental. Poor voice quality is manifested in persistent hoarseness, harshness, breathiness, stridency, or nasality. Those disorders can be due to improper use of the voice or illness. Children whose voice quality is poor need to be seen by a doctor to determine the cause of the problem and possibly for medical treatment for correction. When the defect in vocal quality is due to misuse, the child can usually benefit from speech therapy.

Clues to speech handicaps

Some signals that might indicate a speech handicap include:

- Consistent mispronunciation, not appropriate to the child's age (e.g., /l/ for /r/, /f/ for /th/; sounds omitted or distorted)
- Substitution (e.g., wed/red; widdle/little)
- Omission (e.g., cool/school; top/stop)
- Distortion (e.g., shtop/stop)
- Shyness; absence or near-absence of speech
- Stuttering
- Cleft palate, harelip, or both
- Poor speech quality (harsh, hoarse, high, husky, nasal, breathy, and so on)

Tips for teachers

Stuttering In working with stutterers, remember that very severe stuttering requires referral to a speech therapist. Here is some advice for the teacher.

- Don't refer to the stuttering problem.
- Help the child to relax.
- Be aware of situations which increase the problem.
- Encourage active participation when the child feels comfortable about it.
- Reduce the demand for speech when stress occurs.

The sand table and water table, puppets, dramatic play, and movement are all useful in eliciting spontaneous speech. Singing and choral reading are beneficial; some stutterers lose their stutters when engaged in these activities (Gearheart & Weishahn, 1976).

Articulation problems Because of developmental constraints, schools do not typically make referrals for working with articulation problems before the end of the first grade.

The following four specific approaches are those usually recommended:

- Help the child to *hear* the error. Use a tape recorder and present the child with correct and incorrect examples. Have the child speak into the recorder.
- Provide a *model* for correct usage. Encourage the parents to model correct usage also.
- Help the child *produce* the correct sound. Make rhyming lists; use puzzles and games.
- *Use* the word correctly in familiar stories.

HEARING-IMPAIRED CHILDREN

"You know that new boy, Tom, in my class just doesn't seem to respond to directions. I wonder if he could be hard of hearing."

Warning sirens, approaching trucks, words of affection, falling rain: most of us are aware of the sounds around us. But about 16 million Americans have impaired hearing; about half a million are profoundly deaf. A child with some hearing can use it in learning, but children utterly unable to hear have to learn entirely through their other senses. This restriction can, of course, have a profound effect. Other factors affecting learning abilities of a hearing-impaired child are age at which the loss occurred, type of loss, and amount of correction possible. Disorders of the middle or outer ear often can be corrected through surgery or hearing aids. Disorders of the inner ear and disorders related to brain damage are best treated through therapy to teach compensatory skills. The teacher needs to be aware of the corrective program being used for each hard-of-hearing child in the classroom and to make appropriate adaptations.

Clues to hearing impairments

Signals that might indicate a hearing impairment include these:

- Speech is delayed or hard to understand.
- Vocabulary is extremely limited.
- The child stares blankly when spoken to.
- The child holds the head to one side in an attempt to hear better.
- The child is inattentive.
- The child is unwilling to join in activities.
- The child is unable to follow directions (and may respond physically to sound without understanding).
- The child is easily distracted.
- Certain sounds are perceived while others (e.g., higher-frequency sounds: "s" "t" "th" "sh") are not. (The child may hear some speech as a jumbled mass of noise.)

Tips for teachers

In the classroom, the teacher can take some relatively simple steps to meet the needs of the hearing-impaired child.

- Seat the child in the middle of the class, close to the front.
- Keep the source of light behind the child to facilitate speech reading.
- Get the child's attention before speaking to him or her. Speak clearly and without exaggeration.
- Provide visual materials and instructions.
- Monitor hearing aids to make sure they are turned on and working.
- Use a "buddy" at times to help the child do such things as find the right page, follow oral directions, and go over assignments.
- Do not attempt to force a shy child to join in. A tension-free environment with rich interest centers will encourage exploration.

VISUALLY IMPAIRED CHILDREN

"Jane's eyes are so swollen and red-rimmed. She is forever rubbing them. I wonder if she is getting enough sleep."

No, Jane doesn't need more sleep! Jane needs to see an ophthalmologist who can diagnose and treat problems and diseases of the eye. Jane may have a visual handicap.

Visually handicapped children are those who are unable to learn through materials that are presented to, and understood by, sight. A child with impaired vision has to learn through his or her other senses or through special materials prepared for the partially sighted.

Adjustments have to be made in the classroom for students who have some residual vision. (At one time blind children were taught in special classes; now some are successfully mainstreamed.) If and when it is found that Jane has a severe visual impairment, she may work in the regular classroom and be seen by an *itinerant resource teacher*. This teacher travels from school to school and sees children on a regular basis.

Depending on the scope of the problem, the itinerant teacher might help Jane with magnification devices, books with large print, or—if the condition is severe—braille and taped materials. Jane will have training in typewriting, perhaps in mobility orientation, and probably in listening skills. Aside from these sorts of training, she will follow the regular curriculum.

Clues to visual impairment

Some signals noted by the National Association for the Blind include these:

- The child favors one eye by shutting or covering the other ("lazy eye").
- The child blinks more than usual.
- The child squints.
- The child holds objects unusually close or unusually far away.
- The child complains of headaches or dizziness.
- The child has problems with reading and with written assignments.
- The child's eyes move excessively.
- The child's eyes are watery.
- The child (who has learned to read) reads for short periods, reads slowly, and hesitates over words.

Tips for teachers

Teachers can help children with impaired vision in various ways:

- Seat these children so that they can best see the board, at desks that can be adjusted so that materials are easily visible.

- Provide lighting that does not cause glare or cast shadows.
- Use books with large print, magnifying equipment, and large-print typewriters.
- Use materials which encourage tactile, auditory, and kinesthetic exploration.
- Provide games and puzzles with raised surfaces.
- Provide unglazed paper, soft black pencils, and black felt-tip pens.
- Provide a helper (or a rotation of helpers) who can tape assignments and help with directions by reading them aloud.
- Keep the noise level low, if auditory clues are necessary for orientation.
- Use materials that appeal to various senses. (Children learn by doing, and exceptional children need to touch, smell, taste, hear, see, and manipulate in order to make sense out of their world.)
- Use touch and auditory contact. (Remember that a child who can't see you well will miss out on eye contact. Call the child's name; and touch the child to acknowledge, say, a job well done.)

ORTHOPEDICALLY HANDICAPPED CHILDREN

"Butch has artificial legs. I wonder if I'll have to spend a lot of time attending to his physical needs."

Children who wear prosthetic devices are usually pretty adept at handling themselves and their own needs. But some special provisions and additions may have to be made in the school building: equipment such as wheelchair ramps, wide doorways, handrails, adjustable desks, typewriters, and page turners is needed for unrestricted access to an education. Public Law 94-142 provides funding for architectural changes.

Problems arise when, because of attitudes founded on misinformation, students and teachers do not accept a physically handicapped child. In order to know what to expect of physically handicapped children, teachers and classmates must be aware of these children's actual capabilities.

Orthopedically handicapped children can be the least difficult to integrate into the classroom because most often they have no intellectual disorders and can fit into the mainstream fairly well. They have the same social and emotional needs as other children. Their disability may be frustrating at times, and they have to deal with limitations of their particular handicap. Role playing, dramatic play, and puppets are good avenues for growth and expression.

CHILDREN WITH OTHER PHYSICAL HANDICAPS

Mainstreaming children with special needs can bring children with other physical handicaps into the regular classroom, as educators attempt to find the "least restrictive environment" in which children can successfully function. Such physical handicaps include those associated with cerebral palsy, epilepsy, and other chronic problems such as cardiac and respiratory disorders, diabetes, and malnutrition. Teachers need to be prepared to learn about these various disabilities and to explore the best ways to meet the needs of children who have them.

DEVELOPMENTALLY DELAYED OR HANDICAPPED INFANTS

Regional centers serve children too young (below age three) to come under the provisions of Public Law 94-142. These centers serve as central points for identification, assessment, and referral of individuals with developmental disabilities such as mental retardation, cerebral palsy, epilepsy, and autism. Services such as those offered by the regional centers are becoming more numerous.

Attention has been directed to *early* identification of children with developmental handicaps and to the development of programs and materials for working with such children. Such efforts have been most encouraging. The earlier these children are identified and the earlier such programs are begun, the more effective they appear to be.

An example of such a program is the San Juan Handicapped Infant Project (Richardson, Ogle, Tudor, Fey, McGagin, & Chang, 1975), in which parents participate in the activities with the infants. Some examples of activities are stroking different parts of the body while naming the parts, dangling bright objects in front of the children's faces in an attempt to have the children lift up their heads, and playing peekaboo. Each child has an "individual education plan" (IEP), which has been formulated by a team of trained individuals. The team includes a nurse, psychologist, speech therapist, physical therapist, educational coordinator, and pediatric therapist. A technician works with the parent in the home, helping the parent to implement the program on a daily basis. Every six months the child is reassessed and new (and ongoing) goals are discussed with the parent. "Intervention cards" designed for the San Juan Handicapped Infant Project describe activities to stimulate development:

- Sensory stimulation—including visual, auditory, olfactory, tactile, and vestibular experiences
- Gross motor coordination—including body posture, head and trunk control, equilibrium, mobility, and ambulation
- Fine motor coordination—including prehension, auditory-visual skills, and object concepts
- Language—including expressive and receptive language
- Social behavior
- Self-help—including feeding, dressing, grooming, and toilet routines

Education programs for toddlers and parents are other components of the total program found to be effective with developmentally delayed or high-risk infants.

Summary

All children are special. Some children, however, have needs that require unusual attention from the teacher and the school. We need to provide all children with the best educational experiences we can, although some decry the approaches or the costs of recently enacted legislation. Children represent our nation's greatest wealth and most important investment; we need to treat them accordingly. When we look at the real priorities, we see that we need to put our children first and provide each special child with the best, most effective, and least restrictive educational setting and guidance.

A key theme for each section of this chapter was *attitude.* Can you accept children who are environmentally different, educationally different, or physically different and assist with the individualized planning necessary to meet the needs of these children? Are you willing to try? It won't hurt you, and it could further both your own personal and professional growth and the social growth and responsibility of your "normal" children. Everyone can profit from this additional diversity. So much depends on a teacher's willingness to reach out, to be humanistic and enthusiastic, and to make every effort to be prepared. What a rewarding feeling it would be to know that through your willingness, care, and guidance you prevented the destruction of a child's self-concept!

This chapter has considered the needs of environmentally different children, dealing first with economically disadvantaged and culturally different children. Some specific ideas were to start with the child's strengths and provide additional experiences, to act as a resource for referring child and parent to agencies that can be of help to them, to value and feature all cultures in the classroom, and to build a bridge between home and school (*multicultural* emphases).

We considered the effect of recent interpretations of legislation on the linguistically different child and various teaching methods (total immersion, second-language teaching, and bilingual-bicultural instruction) that have evolved. A wide spectrum of opinions on this subject was heard. Whatever language-teaching approach is used, emphasis on the child's culture is paramount. Suggestions for teachers include gaining an understanding of the languages spoken by the children, learning another language, encouraging parents and community representatives to share ideas with the children, and using a language experience approach for building oral language skills and a readiness for reading. We should remember also that in our eagerness to promote certain separate cultures, we need to keep a balance, modeling a universal (not a tribal) morality and valuing all cultures.

Our consideration of the needs of the *educationally different* took us to both ends of the spectrum—from the gifted and creative to the mentally retarded. Differences in strengths of the creative and gifted child were clarified—in the hope of making teachers' expectations more realistic. As we moved into a consideration of the needs of handicapped and educationally different students, extensive consideration was given to the ramifications of Public Law 94-142, mandating the mainstreaming of children with special needs. The rest of the chapter was devoted to consideration of both educational handicaps and physical handicaps that teachers can expect to have to deal with the regular classroom. In the discussion of the educationally different, clues for identifying children and tips for teachers were presented with regard to the learning-disabled (including hyperkinetic children), the mentally retarded (including children with Down's syndrome), and the emotionally disturbed. In the discussion of the physically different, we dealt with impairments of speech, hearing, and vision, with orthopedic handicaps, and with chronic physical problems. We stressed the importance of guarding against overgeneralizing, of watching out for stereotypes concerning these children, and of having well-grounded developmental knowledge so that we realize which expectations are appropriate in relation to the child's age and which expectations are not.

Not all the answers are in this chapter; it has provided a base from which concerned teachers can grow in their relationships with "special children." Approach your children with a sense of confidence and caring. Remember that all children are special—and so are the teachers who care.

A final comment, from a teacher: "I think I *can* survive—as long as I know I can continue to learn!"

References

Bradley, R. C. *The education of exceptional children.* Wolfe City, Tex.: University Press, 1970.

Carter, T. P. *Mexican-Americans in school: A history of educational neglect.* New York: College Entrance Examination Board, 1970.

Cheek, W. Chairman of Special Education Department, North Texas State University. Conversation, November 20, 1978.

Clayton, M. S. Meet Nina O'Keefe. *Today's Education,* 1978, *67*(3), 74–75, 77–78.

Deno, E. Special education as developmental capital. In G. J. Warfield (Ed.), *Mainstream currents.* Reston, Va.: Council for Exceptional Children, 1974.

Department of Health, Education, and Welfare. Education of handicapped children, P.L. 94-142. *Federal Register,* August 23, 1977. (Pt 2).

Feingold, F. Hyperkinesis and learning disabilities linked to artificial food flavors and colors. *American Journal of Nursing,* 1975, *75,* 797–803.

Gallagher, J. J. *Teaching the gifted child* (2d ed.). Boston: Allyn & Bacon, 1975.

Gearheart, B. R., & Weishahn, M. W. *The handicapped child in the regular classroom.* St. Louis, Mo.: Mosby, 1976.

Hartmann, E. G. *The movement to Americanize the immigrant.* New York: Columbia University Press, 1948.

Hearing Before U.S. Commission of Civil Rights. San Antonio, Tex.; December 9–14, 1968.

Hendrick, J. *The whole child: New trends in early childhood.* St. Louis, Mo.: Mosby, 1975.

Ide, G. G. Spoken language as an essential tool. *Psychological Clinic*, 1920, *13*, 216–221.

Johnson, B. "What can you do for the gifted on Monday morning?" *Educational Leadership*, 1977, *35*(1), 35–41.

Jordan, J. B., & Dailey, R. F. (Eds.) *Not all little red wagons are red: The exceptional child's early years.* Arlington, Va.: Council of Exceptional Children, 1973.

Kavanagh, E. A classroom teacher looks at mainstreaming. *Elementary School Journal*, 1977, *77*(4), 318–322.

Klein, J. W. Mainstream the preschooler. *Young Children*, 1975, *30*, 317–26.

Lambert, W. E. A Canadian experiment in the development of bilingual competence. *Canadian Modern Language Review*, 1974, *31*, 108–116.

Lambert, W. E., & Tucker, G. R. *Bilingual education of children: The St. Lambert experiment.* Rowley, Mass.: Newbury House, 1972.

Northcott, W. H. Candidate for integration: A hearing impaired child in a regular nursery school. *Young Children*, 1970, *25*, 367–380.

Richardson, R., Ogle, R., Tudor, M., Fey, K., McGagin, C., & Chang, V. M. H. *San Juan Handicapped Infant Project: Handbook.* Carmichael, Calif.: San Juan Unified School District, 1975.

Ross, D. M., & Ross, S. A. *Hyperactivity: Research, theory, action.* New York: Wiley, 1976.

Safford, P. L. *Teaching young children with special needs.* St. Louis: Mosby, 1978.

Swain, M. French immersion programs across Canada: Research findings. *Canadian Modern Language Review*, 1974, *31*, 116–129.

Torrance, P. E. *Creativity.* Belmont, Calif.: Fearon, 1969.

Troike, R. C. *Research evidence for the effectiveness of bilingual education.* Rosslyn, Va.: National Clearinghouse for Bilingual Education, 1978.

U.S. Commission on Civil Rights. *Teachers and students, Report V. Mexican American education study: Differences in teacher interaction with Mexican American and Anglo students.* Washington, D.C.: U.S. Government Printing Office, 1973.

Wallace, G., & McLoughlin, J. A. *Learning disabilities: Concepts and characteristics.* Columbus, Ohio: Merrill, 1975.

Weber, E. *The kindergarten: Its encounter with educational thought in America.* New York: Teachers College Press, 1969.

Wightman, M. The gifted, talented child. *Education Digest*, 1977, *43*(1), 51–53.

Wylie, R. E. Research. *Childhood Education*, 1976, *53*(2), 111–115.

Zirkel, P. The legal vicissitudes of bilingual education. *Phi Delta Kappan*, 1977, *58*, 409–411.

CHAPTER 14

*It is what we are usually like at our best
(not what we are occasionally like at our
worst) that counts.*

—Mary B. Hoover

SETTING THE TONE

Rose Spicola

In Chapter 1 you met three students—Chris, Pat, and Lee—who were considering careers in early childhood education. In this chapter you meet them again briefly (in the same faculty advisor's office), voicing some of the concerns that you probably have. The three students have just completed their credential requirements. Lee will start work (as you might guess from Chapter 1) in an infant-toddler center, Pat as a preschool teacher, and Chris in a kindergarten–grade 1 combination. (Early experiences do leave long-lasting impressions—even on young adults.) Let's listen to them.

"You know you helped us to decide on early childhood education as a career, and we've learned a lot this year. But we're worried about how to get ready for September and what to do the first day. We still have lots of specific questions, such as these:"

- How and when do I start planning, and what kind of planning should I do?
- What are effective ways I can organize my room?
- What do I do during the first days?
- How do I handle discipline?
- How can I make a really "special place" for children to learn and grow?

This chapter attempts to answer these questions. It is essentially a "how-to-do-it" chapter. Before we continue, we think it is important to establish a major principle: *no one but you* can "set the tone" of your classroom, either physically or as a matter of attitudes. Your classroom can be chaotic; or it can be a pleasant, orderly, clean, esthetic, and interesting environment. It can be a dictatorship; or it can be a place where children function within clearly drawn limits yet have the freedom to express their ideas and to develop according to their own needs.

The primary influence in any classroom is the teacher. Everything you do, including all the nonverbal behavior (eye contact, voice qualities, facial expressions, gestures), conveys powerful attitudes to your children. A teacher can "invite" (encourage, support) or "disinvite" (discourage, antagonize) children in a multitude of ways (Ginott, 1972; Purkey, 1978).

> I have come to a frightening conclusion. I am the decisive element in the classroom. It is my personal approach that creates the climate. . . . As a teacher I possess tremendous power to make a child's life miserable or joyous. (Ginott, 1972, p. 15)

Setting the tone of your classroom begins long before the first day of school, with careful planning and attention to detail. It doesn't happen instantaneously but is accomplished slowly, like the painting of a picture. The process of setting the tone cannot be rushed. Don't get discouraged. Your patience and your belief in what you are trying to accomplish, plus your faith in your children, will get you through this sometimes difficult first encounter with the world of young children.

How and When Do I Start Planning, and What Kind of Planning Should I Do?

Your planning starts long before the children arrive on the scene. You need to identify major goals and objectives, do some long-range planning of activities, and then organize your space and materials in a way that will enable you to carry out those plans. School policies need to be studied, resources need to be identified, and safety provisions need to be considered.

LONG-RANGE PLANNING   How does one plan for the year? That depends to some extent on the age of the children and the type of setting in which you will be working, but certain general principles are the same. There are written guides that suggest objectives and activities for the accomplishment of various goals. Different guides are appropriate for different groups of children—infants, toddlers, preschoolers, kindergartners, and primary-grade children. In most instances, your principal, head teacher, or director will provide you with the material adopted by your district or center. (For additional ideas, you can turn to your local college library.)

It is important to think through the whole year. Units of work may be planned around themes; e.g., "use of our senses," "living things," "use and conservation of energy." You will want to collect materials dealing with these (e.g., films, filmstrips, records, books, ideas for artwork). One plea: Don't allow your entire year's curriculum to revolve around holidays. There are so many more enriching themes.

As a beginning teacher, you will probably want to plan your themes in a more structured manner than will be necessary after you've gained some experience. Still, bear in mind that the interests which the children demonstrate can also give you ideas for themes as the year progresses. Sometimes it might even be advisable to drop one of your planned themes if there is not enough interest. After all, *process* is at least as important as content. It's important for children to inquire, classify, and solve problems, for example, whatever the content.

Your long-range plans need to be organized so that you can arrange appropriate materials, resource persons, and field trips. In planning field trips, you will need time to check safety regulations and travel costs, get permission slips, and visit some of the sites personally. Letters have to be written, and telephone calls have to be made, sometimes months in advance. In addition, films and other audiovisual materials have to be ordered very early if you wish to have them for certain topics and units.

By planning the whole year, you will avoid (to some extent) that last-minute rush to cover subjects and topics. And by developing themes or units, you can integrate much of the work in your learning centers.

Long-range planning is not to be so tightly sequenced, however, that you always know exactly what you will be doing on a given day. Instead, it helps to be flexible and creative in using unforeseen events and happenings. It's when you don't have a long view of the year that you tend to structure too tightly and to lose spontaneity.

Some of your planning must relate to the staff. Since teachers may be expected to coordinate the work of several adults who interact with their children, this coordination needs to be part of your long-range planning. These adults may include other faculty members who team up, special staff members (e.g., music, movement, and speech teachers), paraprofessional aides, and volunteers. In sum, your planning is highly likely to include managing human resources; the days of the single teacher reigning supreme over a class behind a closed door are generally past. (Chapter 15 presents ideas for effectively working with volunteer parents, aides, and others.)

SHORT-RANGE PLANNING

Once you have the year tentatively blocked out, you can plan special events or activities for each week as it approaches.

These activities are best not planned just in your head. It's important to get the plans down on paper in some kind of consistent and readable form. Why? There are several reasons. Often the head teacher or principal chooses to observe your teaching and can be more constructive in offering you suggestions and guidance if your plans are available. Written plans can be shared more readily with your fellow teachers and so offer the opportunity of expanding one another's ideas. Since it is unlikely that only one adult will be working with a group of young children, your weekly plans are an effective tool for making decisions jointly, generating ideas, solving problems about individual children or the group, and ensuring consistency and continuity. Finally, a weekly session devoted to making a written plan provides the structure that forces you to organize your own thinking and resources.

For example, when you "suddenly" say, "Let's take a walk and see how many leaves we can find," you will have done some careful planning. You will know, for example, the street on which the class is likely to find the most leaves; you will have notified the head teacher of where you and your children will be (in order to comply with the rules of your school or center); you will have consulted with the librarian and brought back a selection of books about leaves to share with the children; and you will have prepared waxed paper, an iron, and other supplies so that the children can make waxed leaf impressions.

One reminder—planning needs to be done in terms of the *whole group, small groups,* and *individual children.* For instance, the whole group may take a walk to find the leaves. Small groups of children may be involved in various activities when you return from the walk. One group may choose to make the wax impressions of the leaves, another may choose to look at the library books, and a third may listen to a record about falling leaves. A fourth group may be creating a collage, and a fifth may be dictating a story about the walk. Why the small groups? Small groups allow for more interaction among children, greater participation by each child, and more attention by adults to individual children. Small groups require considerable organization, and your weekly plans will reflect this.

We also need plans for the needs of individual children. For example, your plan book might contain the note, "Vicky needs more opportunity to verbalize. Involve her in the dictation group. Richard is still unwilling to do anything messy. Try getting him to use paste for a leaf collage."

In short, the idea is to let your weekly lesson plans make it clear how you wish to accomplish your long-range goals through your short-term objectives and activities. Keep in mind, of course, that you will want to leave yourself room for flexibility, for modification or postponement of activities. Your plan book, a working document with deletions, additions, and evaluations, is one of your prime tools for promoting children's growth.

RECORD KEEPING   Record keeping is essential to an evaluation of children's growth. Professionals such as doctors and dentists keep careful records on each patient, and you too will be more secure with detailed records. Professional early childhood educators should keep a *personal folder* on each child. Such a folder might contain:

Samples of the child's work in different areas (don't send it all home).
Anecdotal observations made as the child is seen in various centers. (Is this child always alone? Is Joe able to complete the puzzle? What kinds of sentences can Mary use? How does Tom spend his time outdoors?)
Records of conferences with children and parents (with short accounts of discussions).
Records of any tests given to the child (see Chapter 7).

Records should be so complete that you can sit down with a parent, supervisor, or administrator and explain a child's growth in the various areas as precisely as possible. This does not mean that you may not have questions about the child. (Many times behavior and growth are not consistent, and this puzzles us all.) But the folder is the basis upon which you make plans for working with each child to meet his or her needs.

Keep a notebook handy, take notes every day on several children, and your folders will grow. Make a practice of keeping some work each week and then keeping records won't be such a chore. (See Chapter 7 for samples of record keeping.)

What Are Some Effective Ways of Organizing My Room?

We have just discussed one dimension of setting the tone: planning. Another dimension is organization. Organization is a tool for implementing plans. It includes not only the organization of space and materials, but also the organization of time.

ORGANIZATION OF SPACE Space influences human behavior (Almy, 1975). Both indoor and outdoor space must be organized well in order to create an esthetic environment. Quiet areas need to be separated from noisy ones; quiet nooks need to be provided so that children can get away from the group. Not long after the ink is dry on your teaching contract, you need to visit your classroom and begin the process of arranging the physical environment. Try to visualize what arrangement you want to have ready to greet your children (and their parents) on the first day of class. The age of your children will help you decide what is most appropriate for each group.

Areas

Infant-toddler settings In selecting and arranging elements in an infant-toddler setting, those responsible might consider the following: quiet areas for undisturbed naps and eating; a comfortable place for changing diapers; a large rug area where children can creep, crawl, and explore; and perhaps an isolation area for babies or children who become ill. Figure 14-1 is an example. (Recall also the description in Chapter 1 of the Maddox Corporation's day care center.)

Preschools and kindergartens Preschools (Figure 14-2) and kindergartens (Figure 14-3) warrant a good deal of thought about where children will place their outer clothing, where they will go when they enter the room, how tables are grouped, how individual areas are to be created within the room, and how traffic lanes can be kept clear so that children can walk without bumping into furniture or each other, or treading on each other's work. Try to keep the room uncluttered and open. An art center—where shirts or smocks are used for the protection of children's clothing, and other items, such as scissors and scraps of

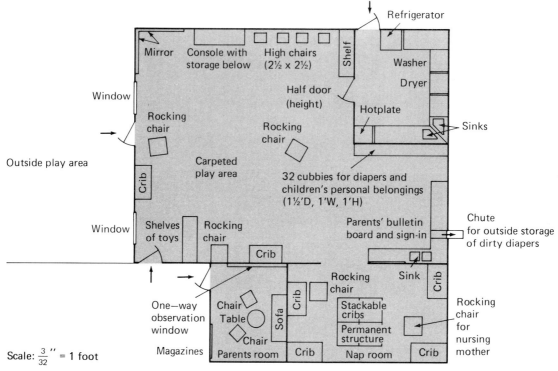

Figure 14-1 *Plan of an infant center. All rocking chairs 2½ by 2 feet; all cribs 2½ by 4 feet. (Source: By Naomi Goldsmith.)*

material, are in use—will need adjoining storage places. Drippy paintings can often be accommodated on a clothesline or high racks indoors. For preschoolers and kindergartners, you'll also need to plan for other areas—blocks and housekeeping, for instance.

Primary schools For primary students, consider arrangements of desks, placement of the teacher's desk, a dramatic-play area (instead of a housekeeping area) or a puppet theater, and a language center for writing and reading. You may also have a rug area, various learning centers, and centers for special activities.

You'll want to balance quiet areas and noisy ones. The library area will need to be away from records or blocks. Create clear, physical spaces by the way in which you arrange tables, bookshelves, rugs, pillows, and other furniture and equipment. You don't want children dripping paint over library books or puzzles being assembled in the line of traffic.

Remember—children love to be snug in corners or other partly enclosed spaces.

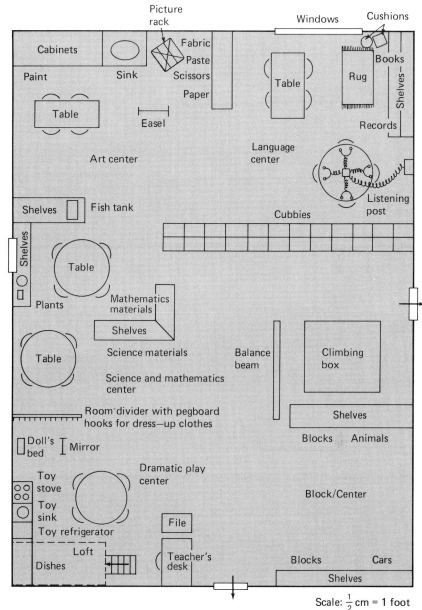

Figure 14-2
Arrangement of space in a preschool room (3- to 5-year-olds). (Source: Schickendanz, York, Stewart, & White, 1977, p. 21.)

Figure 14-3 *Arrangement of space in a kindergarten-primary room.*
(Source: Adapted from S. N. Kaplan, J. A. B. Kaplan, Madsen, & Taylor, 1973.)

Storage

Where will the children's possessions be stored? You may want to purchase some plastic or cardboard storage bins, or make them from divided corrugated cartons or commercial ice cream containers. Children will be encouraged to bring toys, games, and books from home (to donate or share) if they are assured of a safe place to put them.

Those working with infants and toddlers need to take care to keep clothing, food, and other essentials separate and accessible to caretakers and parents.

A note on adaptability

Of course, even with all the planning you can do, you may still find that your physical arrangements are not working out. This is common. Rearrange, with the help of the children. You will be surprised at how they can sometimes solve your problem or come up with fine ideas. (The same is true for any activities you may have planned.)

ORGANIZATION OF MATERIALS

You will want to consider carefully what materials, equipment, and supplies you will need. What you decide upon will be based on what you know about the individual children in your care, the goals of your program, meaningful objectives, and other matters such as costs, durability, flexibility, and safety.

Indoor materials

Collecting materials In general, you can begin collecting inexpensive materials (which will fit into any sound developmental program), such as puzzles, records, pictures, materials to be manipulated, rock collections, newspapers, pieces of wood (from a lumber yard, construction site, or cabinetmaker), old radios, tools, pieces of fabric, old clothes. Even old containers can be used for mixing paints and storing scissors. Try to find a typewriter, clocks, old Halloween masks, party decorations, boats, hats, toys, and shoes. You will find lots of uses for these items in different learning centers. Even a discarded mailbox is useful for teaching children how to address and mail letters to each other. If you're going to have a dramatic-play center, you'll need to start collecting, e.g., shoes, wigs, hats, pieces of fabric. If you want a puppet theater, it may have to be constructed. (Place it in an area where children can at times perform for other children.) What puppets do you want? Will you make them? Will they be animals or people?

Table 14-1 gives an idea of the wide variety of equipment typically found in preschools.

Begin thinking tentatively about the things you want to collect for the first day of class. Supplies should be handy, so that children can begin learning how to get them and use them without your having to do it all or having to get into long explanations. If you want art activities the first day, will you have water in the room or will it have to be brought in? If you can't, or don't want to, have water in the classroom, you may want the art area close to the door (or perhaps outside the room) so that children won't have to carry pails of water through the room. These are some of the details you will need to visualize and some of the items you'll need to collect.

Table 14-1 SUGGESTED MATERIALS TO EQUIP A PRESCHOOL

SUPPLIES AND EQUIPMENT

Art materials and supplies. Brushes varying in size and length of handle, easels, clay, crayons, powder paint, finger paint; muslin, oilcloth, paper for finger painting and crayons, newsprint, tagboard; paste and brush, blunt scissors; yarn, sewing basket with varying sizes of thread, and large-eyed needles.

Woodworking. Claw hammers, nails of assorted sizes, files and cards for cleaning files, scraps of soft wood and beaver board, saws, screwdrivers and screws of assorted size, workbench with clamps, yardstick and rulers, hand-drill, monkey wrench, planes, sandpaper, dowel rods, screw eyes, pliers, paint, varnish, shellac, brushes, linseed oil, and paint remover.

Science. Aquarium and herbarium with cover (material for making), barometer, thermometer, compass, cage for pets, magnifying glass and access to microscope, horseshoes, glass jars with lids, preserving fluid for specimens, tuning fork, prisms, collection of various types of magnets, iron filings, blotters, seeds, gardening tools, watering cans, weathervane and weather glass, measuring vessels, and spoons.

Musical instruments. Autoharp, drum, rhythm sticks, songbells, tuned time bells, tomtom, triangle, tone blocks, xylophone, piano and bench, phonograph and recordings; also radio and television available for special purposes and for special occasions.

Water play. A wading pool, hoses, a tube, a table with metal or plastic pans, and a place to wash doll clothes.

Toys. Playhouse toys, water play equipment, puzzles of varying types and difficulty, games, transportation toys of all types, building blocks, and other manipulative construction toys.

Wheel toys. Wagons, tricycles, "kiddie-kar," wheelbarrow, trucks, tractors, boards equipped with large casters.

Stationary play equipment. Jungle gym, climbers of different varieties, slides, swings, bridges, ladders, boards, mazes, gangplanks, pools, sandbox, platforms.

Sandbox. Buckets, spades, spoons, sieves.

Numbers. Dominoes, calendar, measuring cups, containers, measuring spoons, play money, scales, rulers, yardstick, tape measure, peg boards, games, abacus, collection of articles for counting such as beads, buttons, sticks.

Audiovisual facilities. Films and filmstrips; record player and recordings; globe, maps, pictures, picture books, costumes, magazines and catalogs, and access to projectors, screen, and tape recorder.

Animals. (See "Animals" in this chapter.)

Housekeeping equipment and supplies. Suitable and in sufficient quantity—stove and refrigerator may be on casters. If stove not available, a hot plate can be substituted. Equipment for cleaning up "spills" and for child care of room; tissues, paper towels, and roll of brown paper.

Storage. Ample cabinet spaces and shelves, filing cabinet.

First aid and safety. Large Red Cross first aid kit for emergency, and smaller kit for daily use. Fire extinguisher easily accessible and in good condition at all times.

Miscellaneous supplies. The teacher will need forms for admitting child, for recording progress and personal data, and for transmitting child's record. She will also need a pencil for china marking, twine, pencils, paste, and pastebrushes, boxes for storing, beads and beadlaces, chart rack, large scissors, colored and white tissue, colored construction paper, cleaning tissue, paper towels; roll of 36-inch brown paper, materials for making finger paint and other art media; adhesive and mending tape, scotch tape, masking tape, chalk, erasers, stationery and envelopes, stamps, a marking pad and pencil, erasers, paper clips, large crayons of black and primary colors, pencil sharpener, pen holder and assorted sizes of lettering pens, India ink, felt marking pen, pins (straight and safety), stapler and staples, eyelet punch and eyelets, reinforcements, and rubber bands. The teacher will need access to a primary sized typewriter, typewriter ribbons, paper and carbons, and to a duplicator, carbon and paper for duplicating.

Table 14-1 (CONTINUED)

FURNITURE

Tables. These should be varied as to height, ranging from 15 to 22 inches high to fit the sizes of the children. Differing shapes provide for a variety of uses.

Chairs. They should be stackable, light enough for children to handle, movable without undue noise. Chairs should be in varied sizes, from 14 to 20 inches high, depending on ages and sizes of children. Check by placing hand, palm down, between front of chair seat and upper part of child's leg; space will not be adequate for adult hand if height is correct. Larger chairs for teacher and other adults are needed.

Display racks and bookshelves. Preferably movable on casters—shelves easily accessible to child.

Clock. Large face with arabic numerals, preferably black hands on white face.

Easels. Easily adjustable to child's size (so that elbows are even with bottom of paper); portable with washable surface includes trays to hold cans of paint and provide clips to hold paper.

Source: Adapted from Leeper, Dales, Skipper, & Witherspoon, 1974, pp. 443–444.

Storing materials You may ask, "Where in the world will I put all this?" Part of the answer is, of course, that it won't all be in use at the same time. You will put out different materials as you work in different curriculum areas. If you put out too much, the children will be confused and not really able to explore thoroughly. The other part of the answer is that you will have to set up some system for storing materials so that they will be secure and out of the way, but easy to get.

Using commercial materials You will probably have in your classroom some commercial materials. For a kindergarten–first grade, for instance, you will have readers, packaged materials, and some workbooks (perhaps cut apart and filed by skills) for use by those who really need them. Here again, only you can decide how to use these materials. Just because they are available does not mean they will meet the needs of your children. Check all materials carefully. Learn the goals and objectives of each commercial program; study and try out the activities. Then you'll be better prepared to match the materials to your children's needs.

It's probably safe to say that commercial programs should only be a small part of the materials you use with your children and that some of these prepackaged activities are not appropriate for the children in your care.

Outdoor equipment

Until very recently, equipping the outdoor area in a preschool, kindergarten, or primary school meant sinking metal swings, slides, teeter-totters, and an occasional piece of climbing apparatus into solid concrete.

The trend today, however, is toward designing novel, relatively less expensive, and more attractive equipment. Often the new equipment is movable; it is usually multipurpose and created from natural materials like wood, rope, and rubber. The British have experimented with "adventure playgrounds" using very little hard surface area and capitalizing on trees, rocks, and hills.

Boards, sawhorses, barrels, rubber tires, and hollow tubes and blocks are all ideal for use with a variety of balls and wheeled toys. The use of "junk" materials and the labor of the school maintenance crew or parents make a little money go a long way toward equipping a center with outdoor equipment. A covered area, protected from sun and rain, is also highly desirable, as are areas set aside for digging (a sand pit), for water play, and for gardening. A storage area for large equipment makes the material readily available to the children but protects it from vandalism.

A note on safety

When equipment is purchased or collected, consideration must be given to safety. Items with small parts that are easily removed are extremely dangerous for infants, who tend to submit everything to the "taste test." Items that can be stood on or climbed on have to be sturdy enough to hold the weight of many children hour after hour. Paint used on any equipment must be nontoxic. Poisonous materials must of course be stored far beyond children's reach. Teachers need to exercise good judgment about what limits to set for children, what risks children tend to take, and what situations the children are likely to find themselves in.

ORGANIZATION OF ACTIVITIES: A BALANCED CURRICULUM

There are many ways to organize classroom activities; you will have to decide for yourself which way is best for you and your children. You will want to organize your half- or whole-day schedule in such a manner that you balance the curriculum and your teaching-learning strategies. There needs to be a balance between working alone and with others in a group (between independent and cooperative goal structures) and among a great variety of subject areas: art, music, mathematics, science, language arts, health, physical education, and creative dramatics. There should also be a balance between active and quiet activities.

Below, we discuss an important aspect of organizing activities: learning centers. We also discuss (briefly) one specialized type of learning center: the animal center.

Learning centers

Many teachers of young children have found that preparing learning centers or activity areas is an effective way of organizing classroom activities. Centers encourage independent growth and give a teacher time to work with small groups. The age of the children, the space and materials available, and the goals of your curriculum will suggest what centers you will need and how often you change them.

Types of centers for young children vary. For very young children, you'll want a playhouse or a housekeeping area, a block corner, a painting area, other art areas (say, for clay, pasting, and cutting), a book area, a woodworking area, a sand and water play area, and science and mathematics areas. For kindergarten and primary grades, some of these same centers will be included, but the level of activity will be quite different. Your mathematics and science center will have much more complex materials for five- to eight-year-olds than for preschoolers. In addition, you'll need a language arts center which includes reading, writing, spelling, and other language activities. Your playhouse might be replaced by a puppet theater or grocery store for older students.

Temporary centers may be set up while you are studying some special area. For example, you may want a dental office for two weeks while you're studying dental care: a rocking chair can serve as a dentist's chair, and pieces of string with stirrers or spoons attached can be the dentist's equipment. Some centers can have multiple uses. A grocery store will illustrate how one shops for food and other items, how to make change, how to have a balanced diet, how to budget. When an area seems to lose popularity for a while, then you might withdraw it and perhaps reintroduce it later.

Ideas for learning centers are many. The only limit on the variety of learning centers in a classroom is the imagination of the teachers, aides, and parents who create them. Broman (1978) provides an exhaustive listing, from which examples are given in Table 14-2.

How do you get started? Teachers have experimented with various ways of easing into a learning-center approach. Generally it is best to start with two or three centers at most, teach the children how to use them, and operate them for a while before adding more. The construction of each center is time-consuming, and the preparation of more than two or three can be quite an undertaking. Children also need time to develop the self-management skills needed to function in a learning-center environment. Starting with too many centers can confuse children; although choices are desirable, too many choices tend to overwhelm young children.

Some teachers like to introduce the center approach in just one curriculum area, offering, for example, a choice of three or four different science centers. Other teachers have indicated that they like to use centers for a limited part of the day (e.g., from 10 to 11 A.M. daily) or for a specific day (e.g., Friday is "center day" in many schools).

Before increasing either the number of centers or the time allotted to activities involving them, teachers and staff need to be comfortable

Table 14-2 SOME SUGGESTED LEARNING CENTERS

Reading center Made up of books and space to sit or lie to "read." Magazines and newspapers are also appropriate. Include a rug, pillows, shelves, display racks, bulletin boards, and a rocking chair. Space should have minimum traffic and noise.

Creative writing center Made up of tables, chairs, writing materials. Might include paper, pencils, typewriter (if available), crayons (for illustrating and writing), display space for finished projects. Children can make up their own writing technique or can dictate to the aide or teacher.

Listening center Made up of audio equipment, headphones and jacks, recordings, blank tape cassettes, storage shelves (for phonographs, tape players, recordings). Recordings may include music for appreciation, story records, teacher-recorded books on tape, or teacher-recorded individual activities. Commercially prepared audio materials are also appropriate. Include blank tapes for children to record on. This is one way a story can be shared with other children.

Viewing centers Made up of a television set, 8 mm and/or 16 mm projectors, 35 mm filmstrip viewers, several headsets and jacks, and a small screen recessed from light as much as possible. Storage space for films, strips, and equipment is needed.

Creative dramatics center Made up of props useful for acting and storage space for them. Clothes could include old hats, coats, dresses, shoes, canes, gloves, scarfs, aprons, and such. Children should be encouraged to dramatize stories and poems, role play their problems, and engage in exploratory movement.

Mathematics center Made up of mathematical activities, math games, math puzzles, geometric tools and materials, or books with math activities and puzzles in them.

Painting center Made up of easels, paints, brushes, smocks, and bulletin board for display. Paints may include (according to age) tempera, finger, chalk, water color, polymer, or oils. Children should be encouraged to illustrate creative stories and real events, to prepare posters and murals, and to produce individual creative expressions.

Sand table center Made up of a 3- × 5-foot (or larger) table with 4- to 6-inch sides, lined with galvanized tin, and half filled with fine sand. Children should be encouraged to portray visually ideas and problems. Projects can include a map of the community, a model of a conservation project, or creative expressions.

with the learning-center approach; techniques of recording children's work and monitoring their progress need to be refined, and management skills need to be effectively exercised.

Remember that for the children these procedures need careful explanation. Take all the time you need to demonstrate how one uses a center. One technique is to guide the children through role-playing situations. For example, have the children enact a situation where one child goes to the painting center and finds two children already there. What does the child do? This attention to clarifying the routines will eventually pay off by establishing the management tone you need.

There is much that you can learn by observing the activities in each center. Some of the best teaching can be done in this way. Some materials

Table 14-2 (CONTINUED)

Garden center Made up of sunny ground where children can plant and tend flowers and vegetables—where they can learn biology and responsibility—and where some can find their own expression. Try scheduling a parent or two to help here two or three times each week in season.

Games and puzzles center Made up of space to spread out a variety of games—and storage space. A wide variety of games and puzzles suitable for the range of abilities and interests of the children.

Biological science center May include an aquarium, a terrarium, a cage of gerbils or mice, seedlings and plants, specimen collections of any sort of biological phenomena, a microscope and slides, materials for conducting biological examinations and experiments, a bulletin board, field manuals.

Clay center Made up of a sturdy table, a crock of ready-to-use clay, a drying rack, a wire for cutting clay, and a few simple tools for shaping. A kiln would be helpful but not essential. Children should be encouraged to express themselves in three-dimensional form as well as two. Illustrations of stories, books, models, and artifacts as well as creative expressions encouraged.

Construction center Made up of a work bench (with vise) tools (hammers, saws), expendable materials (nails, glue, sandpaper, paint, wood, plastic, wire, metal). Children should be encouraged to make specific things the class needs (a birdhouse, an easel), and also to be creative in making decorative items (a wood, wire, or metal sculpture, a mobile). Cabinet makers and lumber companies will usually donate wood scraps to teachers. Fathers or mothers may be willing to help here two or three times a week.

Block center Made up of appropriate size blocks for the age group in sufficient quantity; bins for storage; and flat, clear space for building. Blocks are a creative learning device for all ages.

Cooking center Made up of a one- or two-burner hot plate, pans, utensils, paper towels, paper plates, and so on. Cooking center activities can be extended by use of ovens and sinks in cafeteria. Materials and ingredients needed in specific activities can be brought the day needed to avoid spoilage.

Source: Broman, 1978, pp. 440–447.

children manipulate let the children direct themselves and correct themselves. You can ask questions: "Does this block match this one?" "Where do the knife and spoon go when you set the table?" You can model appropriate behavior: "This is a way to see if the number of buttons is the same." "Here is the way to write 'Santa Claus.'" "I can measure how long this is with the ruler."

Once you have opened a center, you will, of course, want to use many open-ended questions to stimulate divergent thought. Examples follow:

"What else could you do with these blocks?" (multiple alternatives)
"What do you want to try next time?" (alternative hypotheses)

"What do you think will happen if you push on that?" (predicting consequences)

"Does it make any difference if you do it Susan's way? . . . Why?" (testing hypotheses)

"I wonder why that picture fell off the wall." (cause-effect thinking)

"What do you think we could do about it?" (problem solving)

Once the routines are established for each center, you will begin to find the time you need to work informally in some centers with children who need help or formally with small groups in some type of direct instruction. You can also begin helping children who need individual help.

The values of learning centers are readily apparent. Your centers or activity areas give children a chance to work on their own, freely and independently. A child finishing one activity can check to see if another area is available; if not, then he or she can go elsewhere. With older students, you might set up a system where each child is expected to work in three areas during the day (you may select the language center, the library, and the mathematics center, for instance) but is otherwise free to choose other centers. Some teachers prefer the sign-up method for management of the centers. Some teachers are committed to a "trust-the-child" approach and find that it works well.

Animals

If you want animals in your classroom, there are matters of safety and health to consider. First, be sure your school or center allows animals. Find out exactly what care will be needed. Perhaps you will want to wait until you have had an opportunity to work with your children before you decide on a particular animal. It may be that you will want an animal only for certain curriculum units. Consider all problems of care when your center or school is not in session.

ORGANIZATION
OF TIME

Pace and regularity

Will your classroom move to a fast beat or a slow one? Too much hurry or too strict adherence to a rigid schedule will defeat most children. Children are most comfortable with a consistent and familiar structure. Lay and Dopyera (1971) suggest, however, that under some conditions regularity can be stultifying. Introducing new materials gradually as the program progresses enlivens the classroom. The pace should be unhurried. Give children extra time to work if they are engrossed in a project.

Scheduling

Scheduling is one of those areas of life where one can get too much of a good thing. It is important to set aside time for each day's activities. There is also a certain degree of comfort for young children in being able to anticipate "what comes next." It is only when flexibility and creativity are sacrificed to following an exact pattern that we have too much of a good thing.

When time is blocked into small segments on the basis of activities or subject-matter areas, we tend to find all children in a room engaged in the same activity at the same time, with the clock signalling an end to the activity for all the children simultaneously.

An alternative to scheduling time into periods is to use some variation of the "integrated day." If teachers are concerned with individualizing instruction and developing autonomy in children, they can make plans that allow many program strands to operate at the same time. Then children can move from one curriculum area to another at their own pace (Spodek, 1978). In the integrated day there are usually no set time slots, and the activities are—as the term implies—integrated. For instance, while one group of children is observing hamsters, another group may be reading about them, another writing about them, another rendering them artistically, and another calculating their weight.

It is important that you and the children develop the schedule together. You need to have a schedule set up for the first week, but be ready to modify it as soon as the children indicate that they're ready for more responsibility. Try to keep your schedule as open as possible so that the children can work longer or shorter periods according to their interests.

Infants and toddlers tend to establish their own schedules. We want as few constraints as possible in developing schedules for infants, toddlers, preschoolers, and kindergartners; but we do have to operate within set times for arrival and dismissal in preschool and kindergarten. It is generally helpful to schedule a planning period with the children, followed by time to carry out the plans (the general work or activity time). Cleanup is a necessary corollary to work time and ideally is followed by some informal evaluation of the activities. Other blocks of time will be needed for naps and for eating (either snacks or lunches).

Primary teachers are bound by more constraints. They must build their schedules around arrival and dismissal; the programs of special teachers in art, music, movement, and science; the hours during which they have aides or volunteers in the room; their own scheduled lunch hour; their own free periods; and the shared use of special equipment or facilities. There may be also district or state requirements setting minimum hours per week for certain subjects.

What Do I Do Those First Days?

We have discussed long-range planning and short-range planning. We now turn to the special planning for the first few days. Because we will say a few things we've said before, this section will serve as a handy collection of reminders.

Many of the ideas to follow apply across a large range of ages, but we are primarily concerned here with young children, for whom this is the first experience of school. We are speaking to first-time teachers, too. Of course you'll be a little nervous the first day; that is normal. Even experienced teachers are somewhat nervous on the first day of a new school year. You can plan well and thereby take away some of the tension—but not all of it.

MEETING CONCERNS OF PARENTS Some parents will be reluctant to leave their children. If the child seems calm and adjusted, tell the parent that you will make time for him or her to visit and talk another day. A smile will do wonders to reassure them. Most of the children and parents will accept the situation, and you will probably have only one or two cases that you must really work with. If some children seem upset, let their parents stay with them a little while. When these children become involved in an activity and forget their fear, the parents can see that they are content and learning. Most of the children who cry will stop fairly soon. If there is overt fearfulness or anxiety, the parent may have to stay longer. Some young children have been known to run away, and so it is better to keep the parent around. This may have to be done for several days, until each child can stay without the presence of a parent.

Even from the first day, you can help meet many of the general concerns of parents by keeping them *informed* about your program. Near the beginning of school you might send home a newsletter or a simple note describing the activities that are going on in the classroom and what purposes they serve. For example: "This week we are baking cookies. Children will learn to count, measure, mix, handle ingredients, follow directions; they will learn that there are substitutes for sugar in cookie recipes." Since parents are your most important allies, get them involved early on by inviting them to observe your class. Show that you care for their children. (See Chapter 15, on involving parents.)

GETTING TO KNOW THE CHILDREN Perhaps the best way of dealing with edgy children—and edgy parents—on the first day is getting each child involved in some interesting or well-loved activity such as working on a puzzle with someone, playing with blocks and toys, or working on an art project. It may take a warm reassuring hug on your part, or an invitation to sit with another child, but you will be surprised at how well you will be able to "feel" your way out of the problem.

You will want to introduce the children to each other and to everyone who works in the classroom. Name tags worn during the first week will help you to learn the children's names quickly. It is important to use a child's name rather than a cold "you." Introduce yourself and anyone else who works in the room. Make sure each child tells what he or she likes to be called. Use games and songs to help the children learn each others' names. Incidentally, it will make life far easier for you if you can arrange for preregistration visits or staggered entrances on the first day of school.

ARRANGING FOR THE FIRST ACTIVITIES

Individual activities

You will want to make some quiet activities available. As was just suggested, have some puzzles, play dough (highly recommended), paper, toys, and books out and explain how to work with them. It is equally important for the children to start learning how to put these materials away safely and clean up. From the first day, stress each child's responsibility for putting things away.

Group activities

On the first day, consider a rhythm or music activity. It would be great if you could teach your children a simple song or have them sing a song they already know. One of the children might teach a song to the others. (What is appropriate here depends on age, of course. See the section on music in Chapter 11 for more detail.)

You might prefer to have a rhythm or movement activity. An enjoyable action song such as "Skip to My Lou," a marching song, or a clapping or performance song can combine music and movement. Don't forget that *you* participate in all exercises, too—which means you jump, you skip, you clap hands.

Story time

Consider having a short period reserved as story time, or slip it in (like spices in a good meal) when you gather two or three children around you. From the beginning, you want to cultivate the sharing of good literature with your children, no matter what their age. Read the story with animation; show children the pictures; perhaps act out little bits; involve the children, talk about the story while you're reading it or afterward. "Now I wonder what Cinderella is going to do." "What would you have done if you were the wolf?" "What part of the story did you like?" "How would you have ended the story?" Sometimes substitute your children's names for the characters' names to catch egocentric interest. (See Lundsteen, 1976, chap. 5, for many ideas for primary grades; and the section on literature in our Chapter 10.)

INTRODUCING ROUTINES

Routines seem to center on the processes of arriving, departing, eating, using the toilet, resting, and working. We discuss each of these below and then make some comments on transitions between activities.

Arriving

Arrival practices differ for different ages and different settings. Most infant and toddler centers require the parent or guardian to come in with the child and then turn the child over to one of the staff members with any information that might be important (e.g., an eating or sleeping problem; irritability). Often the baby's belongings and food are put in a special place, and the parent signs in, noting any significant information. Preschoolers are usually delivered to the gate of the play yard or to the door of the school. Some centers do not allow the children to enter until a certain time, when they line up and enter together. Others prefer to let each child enter when he or she arrives, so that the children are given the opportunity to greet the teacher and interact on a one-to-one basis. In this more developmental approach, the children may start work immediately in an area of interest. But in some centers the children wait until all have arrived; then there is some kind of formal opening exercise or group meeting; and then the children disperse to activities. Whatever the approach (open and developmental, or more traditional), it needs to be made clear to the children from the first day.

Departing

On the first day, dismissal time may seem to come very slowly for some children. Try to keep such children busy. If asked when they are to leave, point to a clock and say, "At 11:00" (or whatever time) "we will go home." Be sure to plan dismissal time, or there will be chaos. Cleaning up, collecting work, getting any clothing that was brought—all this is best done in a certain order. You decide, and show the children how to do it. When the children are ready to leave, take a minute or two to encourage them. Go over with the children all the work that was done and give them a preview of what they will be doing the next day. Remember to *provide more time for every step of your day at first;* later on, as the children become more familiar with the routine, things will go faster.

   If parents are waiting, you may let them in; if the children take buses, walk them out and wait until the bus arrives (unless someone else has that duty). If a parent is late, stay with the child. You may also have to call a parent or relative if a child seems to have been forgotten. Be responsible.

Eating

At some time during the day, whether you are on a full- or half-day schedule, you'll want time for some refreshments. Again, what you have and when depends upon the age of the children. With older children, you'll want to establish the routine on the first day; with younger children you may have to do the serving for a while until you can train some young assistants. Show children how to wait to be served, how to use a napkin, where to put empty cups or cartons. Take time to establish a quiet, calm atmosphere for snack time. Manners can certainly be taught or improved during this activity.

Some developmentally oriented teachers prefer to set out snacks and allow children to help themselves when *they* choose to have their own snack time, alone or with a friend. The process and any limitations need to be made clear not just on the first day, but for several days thereafter.

Using the toilet

An important item of business is toilet routines. If you have toilet facilities in your classroom, many problems are solved; but if they are in another location or on the other side of the building, things get a little more complicated. (By the way, it may be smart to have some extra clothes on hand in case of "accidents.")

Show the children the facilities, demonstrate how to flush, how to wash the hands after using the toilet, and how to use *one* paper towel. (And don't be surprised if you have many requests to use the toilet after this demonstration.)

Some children will be hesitant and need to have their fears allayed. They need to have a clear understanding of what procedures they are to follow. Do they have to ask permission? May they use the facilities at any time? Be sensitive to individual differences in a sensitive area that can cause embarrassment.

Resting

Children in full-day centers will generally nap each afternoon. The need for sleep varies, and teachers need to take this variation into account. If a child cannot sleep, encourage him or her to rest, perhaps with a favorite toy or picture book. The room needs to be darkened, activity avoided, and perhaps some soft music played. It is important, with routines, to keep the daily expectations and order of events the same.

Working

Introduce just a few activities and demonstrate how the equipment is to be used. After the children have worked, show them the routines for cleaning up. For example, show them how to put away puzzles, drawings, paintings, and toys in their proper places. It is best to demonstrate and not to assume that children can do this. Be prepared to repeat your instructions and demonstration several times in the first days or weeks. If you have children who speak little English and you don't have a bilingual aide, you will have to proceed slowly and demonstrate even more carefully (see Chapter 13).

Transitions

Many beginning teachers find that classroom activities go along very well until there has to be a change from one activity to another, and then everything seems to go wrong. Think through all the transitions that have to be made during the day and visualize how they can be simplified or smoothed.

First, establish a consistent way of getting the children's attention. Your method may be a note on the piano, a rhyme, or a simple song; you decide what's best according to the age of your children. With older students, a simple call—e.g., "Boys and girls"—may do.

Try to ease a changeover in activities by giving advance notice. For example, say, "In a few minutes we'll start our cleanup." Then, gently, start assisting the children who are ready and need help. If a child is in the middle of something really important or is about to complete a project, allow a few more minutes or promise an opportunity to get right back to it after completion of another short task. The idea is not to get bogged down in these transitions and not to expect all children to finish exactly at once.

Remember that switching time frames is hard on young children; have as few switches as possible.

HANDLING THE INITIAL ADJUSTMENT PERIOD

The most important tasks ahead of you during the first few weeks are learning as much as you can about each child and helping each child through the initial adjustment period. Some of your children will have had much relevant experience in a school setting or at home, which will mean that they can move much more quickly than the other children into learning activities of all kinds. Other children will lack experience or may have had little parental help; they will need much patience and guidance on your part.

During the initial adjustment period, you may feel as though you are in a frozen time frame, making no progress. Don't try to hurry this period. Keep working toward smoothing out routines, getting the children to gradually become more independent, and eliminating confusion.

Encourage the children by praising the things they do well. Be positive. (You may want to tape-record yourself the first few days to be sure you're not reinforcing poor behavior.) Spend the time you need early; this careful attention to detail will pay off later.

If there are recurring problems at certain times, or in certain learning centers, talk the matter over with the children. Try to let them help you resolve the situation. Try to identify each problem clearly: is it organizational, environmental, interpersonal, or personal? After watching and listening, select from among appropriate problem-solving strategies, such as changing the environment, giving information, expressing your reaction directly, and negotiating (see Chapter 12).

What Are Effective Ways of Guiding Children's Behavior? —Some Thoughts on Discipline

This section explores modern principles and strategies useful in long-range planning for effectively guiding children's behavior. The management of the behavior of a group of children—traditionally referred to as "good discipline"—occupies a large part of teachers' thoughts, especially preservice teachers.

When you are approaching any major educational area, considering its major goals helps to give perspective. The overriding goal in the use of discipline is ultimately the development of children's *self-discipline*. Throughout this book there has been an emphasis on encouraging self-discipline. In this section, you will find ideas stressing positive, interactive, productive communication. You will find suggestions to make life less painful and more conducive to growth, for both teacher and child.

DISCIPLINE AND DEVELOPMENTAL STAGES

For children in the *sensorimotor stage*, discipline tends to be nonverbal and is often simply an assertion of power by the caretaker: e.g., removing something dangerous or valuable from a child's grasp. Still, the caretaker should act as gently and respectfully as possible.

For children in the *preoperational stage*, adults may be able to set limits—a method advocated by Ginott (1961)—using some verbal explanations, which increase as the child's language increases.

For children in the *concrete-operational stage*, expanded explanations can be used. Once the child has language and can reason at appropriate levels, strategy can focus on reasons for, interpretations of, and logical consequences of misbehavior (Dreikurs & Cassell, 1972; Gordon, 1970).

But there are not as many developmental restraints as you might think. Children cannot reach higher levels unless adults continually give them opportunities to do so—that is, unless adults go beyond assertion of power (e.g., "You just do it because I said so!").

STRATEGIES
FOR DISCIPLINE

Setting limits

We now examine five steps in setting limits (Ginott, 1961), using as an example a child who is about to hit you or another child.

*Steps in Setting Limits**

1 *Recognize the feeling by expressing it.* "You are feeling angry with her." "You want to hit me." Often simply expressing feelings is enough to stop the unacceptable behavior.
2 *Set the limit.* Be clear and concise in saying what is unacceptable conduct: "I'm not for hitting." (Note the wording here; the reasoning is that this form arouses less resistance than the imperative: "Stop hitting.") If possible, set the limit *before* the child acts but when his or her *intention* is apparent.
3 *Provide at least one acceptable alternative.* "You may pound the wood with the hammer or hit the doll." Usually, these three steps are enough, although you may need to go through them several times. If the unacceptable conduct has already occurred, do steps 1, 2, and 3 together. If the child persists in the unacceptable behavior, go on to 4 and 5.
4 *Provide a choice that represents a natural consequence of the unacceptable behavior.* "Either stop hitting or leave the area." "If you go on jumping on the couch, you are choosing to leave the room." Give this "choice statement" *only once.* If the child still persists, go to step 5.
5 *Act.* Do not delay. Impose the consequence you have specified. You may again reflect feelings. "I can see you're angry, but you chose to leave the room."

No society can survive without placing some limits on the behavior of its members. Be clear about your limits. Let the children understand what is appropriate behavior and what is not.

In addition to ideas on setting limits, Ginott (1961) also has some

* Adapted from Dr. Garry Landreth, Texas State University, who based this structure on ideas of Bixler (1949) and Ginott (1961).

worthwhile ideas for communicating with children. Remember to speak in ways that preserve the child's self-respect as well as your own. Statements of understanding or recognition of feelings should *precede* statements of advice or instruction. One of the reasons for this approach is to lessen conflict. When you praise, Ginott recommends mentioning only the child's efforts and accomplishments, not character and personality; it is difficult to live up to "You're such a good boy (or girl)"— instead, say, "You tried hard to get those brushes really clean." As for feelings, Ginott thinks adults need to let children know how they feel, too, as long as they express their feelings appropriately. Avoid threats, bribes, promises, sarcasm, sermons, and rudeness. Finally, give children opportunities to be responsible—directly and indirectly—by having some voice in decision making.

Understanding goals of misbehavior

Another strategy for discipline is described by Dreikurs and Cassel (1972), with reference to children under the age of ten. They suggest that we can deal with children's misbehavior by understanding the goals that prompt it:

1 To gain attention
2 To display power
3 To gain revenge
4 To express inadequacy and passivity; to give up

Let's examine each of these.

Attention "Only when people pay attention to me do I belong." A child who wants attention may show off or make demands. Typically, the teacher's reaction is annoyance: "This child takes too much of my time!" But attempts to correct this behavior without understanding the goal that prompts it may stop it only temporarily.

Dreikurs and Cassel suggest, first, that "diagnostic" questions be asked: "Could it be that you want me to notice you?" "Could it be that you want me to do something special for you?" The phrasing should be tentative, since the child may not be aware of his or her own motivation.

Corrective procedures follow diagnosis. Dreikus and Cassel insist upon *not* giving attention when the child demands it. Ignore the child; and do not show annoyance. Be firm and consistent. *Do* give the child attention when he or she is not making a bid for it.

Power "I count only when you do what I want, when I am the boss, or when I am proving that no one can boss me." Or: "If you don't let me do what I want, you don't love me." A child whose goal is power may argue, have temper tantrums, lie, and disobey. Typically, the teacher's reaction is anger: "Who is running this class?" In response to inappropriate correction (e.g., "You'll do it or else!"), the child may intensify the misbehavior or may submit only with defiance.

To diagnose this goal, which may be conscious or unconscious, first ask the same question suggested above: "Could it be that you want me to notice you?" Then ask: "Could it be that you want to be boss?" Or: "Could it be that you want to show me that you can do what you want to do? And that no one can stop you?"

The corrective procedure Dreikurs and Cassel suggest is, first of all, to avoid either fighting back or giving in. Fighting back or giving in only increases the child's desire for power. Instead, withdraw from conflict. Next, help the child to see how to use power constructively by helping and cooperating. Respect the child's constructive efforts, and enlist the child's help in constructive agreements.

Revenge "I try to hurt as I feel I have been hurt by others." "I cannot be loved; my only hope is to get even." The child may whose goal is revenge may kick, bite, and scratch, viciously hurting animals, other children, and adults. Unfortunately, the teacher's reaction is typically outrage, personal dislike of the child (which may lead the teacher to retaliate), or a feeling of deep injury: "How mean!"

To diagnose, ask, "Could it be that you want me to notice you?" and "Could it be that you want to show me that no one can stop you?" Then ask, "Could it be that you want to get even?" Or: "Could it be that you want to hurt me and the children in the class?"

Dreikurs and Cassel suggest these corrective procedures: Do not say that you are hurt, and do not behave as though you are. Apply natural consequences: "Someone else will have to feed the animals; they are not for hurting." "You will need to play quietly with the clay or finger paint until you feel you can come back to the group." "I will need to hold you still for a few moments until you can control yourself, so others won't get hurt."

Physical punishment makes the situation worse. Instead, show love and build a trusting relationship. Enlist the help of the group or of individual children to give encouragement. This kind of situation is urgent and needs immediate attention.

Passivity "You can't do anything with me." "I am helpless." The child who wants to express inadequacy may respond only passively or fail to respond at all. The teacher may react by finally throwing up the hands and tending to agree with the child that nothing can be done.

To diagnose, ask, "Could it be that you want to be left alone?" Or:

"Could it be that you feel you are no good and don't want people to know?"

The corrective measures Dreikurs and Cassel suggest are: Stop criticism. Say, "I'm not giving up with you." Don't be discouraged. Encourage *any* positive attempt, no matter how small. Get other children to help make this child feel worthwhile. Above all, do not be lured into pitying the child. Seek outside help if necessary.

The "no lose" method

Gordon (1970) does not suggest a "best" solution to any problem; rather, he proposes a "no lose" approach to problem solving. For the adult, this entails *active listening* as a method of influencing children to find their own solutions to their own problems.

Gordon distinguishes "no lose" situations from "win-lose" situations. There are two kinds of "win-lose" situations. In the first, adults win because they use their authority, power, and superior knowledge and experience. When the adult always wins and the child always loses, children feel resentful, unimportant, and unworthy; and communication between adult and child breaks down. In the second type of "win-lose" situation, children win because the adults do not want to lose their love, have mistaken beliefs about permissiveness, or are too tired or uninterested to negotiate.

In a "no lose" situation, adults and children solve conflicts by finding solutions acceptable to both—i.e., by negotiating. The "no lose" method consists of these steps:

1 Identify and define the conflict. (Example: Both child and adult agree that the child does not want to put on a smock to paint.)
2 Generate possible alternative solutions. (Example: The child can wear an old shirt or take off his or her own shirt.)
3 Evalute the alternative solutions.
4 Decide on the best acceptable solution.
5 Follow up to evaluate how it worked.

This method is for not teachers—or parents—who are always in a hurry or always busy. But it is important and worthwhile because it can help children develop as fully functioning, self-respecting, responsible individuals and it makes for mutual respect between adults and children.

Behavior modification

"Behavior modification" can be defined as manipulating the behavior of organisms through reward. If you know what constitutes a reward, you can control behavior.

Behavior modification consists of these steps: (1) Pinpoint the problem behavior. (2) Records its frequency. (3) Apply reinforcers and consequences tied directly to a corresponding desired behavior. (4) Evaluate progress. This cycle is repeated until the problem behavior disappears.

The concept of rewards is basic to this method. You decide what is rewarding for the child and give the reward when the child behaves appropriately. Sometimes the reward is given immediately; but sometimes tokens are given which may be exchanged for rewards later.

Rewards—or "reinforcers"—are supposed to be gradually eliminated, so that children behave appropriately without them. This elimination is accomplished by moving from concrete rewards (e.g., candy) to less concrete rewards (e.g., being allowed to choose an activity) to social rewards (e.g., a smile), to internal rewards (feeling good about one's own behavior).

Many people have reservations about this method. It can be argued that behavior modification focuses on symptoms rather than underlying causes; that it places the control of behavior outside of the child; that it limits children's autonomy; and that it does not really lead to understanding what responsible behavior is. Some people also feel that it smacks of bribery and develops children who consider rewards to be their right and perform only when rewarded. It may also be necessary, some believe, to keep increasing rewards: a six-year-old may settle for candy, but an adolescent may demand a car. (For detailed descriptions of behavior modification, see, e.g., Madsen & Madsen, 1970.)

DEALING WITH SPECIFIC PROBLEMS

We now apply some of these ideas on discipline to a few specific problems—those most frequently mentioned by teachers.

What do you do when children run around the room, knocking into people and things? As you settle them down, try to understand. Are they hungry? Scared? Frustrated? Excited? Was the story too long? Was a transition too abrupt? What time of day is it? Who is involved?

Avoid anger, particularly a loud, angry voice; retaliation usually makes the situation worse.

If the problem persists, help the children develop self-control: (1) Warn them. (2) Remove problem children from the group and keep them with you. (3) Wait for these children to decide to return to the group. (4) Help these children to return and be more successful (Hendrick, 1975). You might say, "No more running for now; people and things are not for knocking into. Play here with me for a while and let me know when you feel you can return quietly to the block area. I'll go with you to help." Allowing time out to go to the toilet may also cool events down appreciably.

What do you do when children just stand around? First, try to find out why. Do they feel helpless? Or are they tired or ill? Then, let them know that if they want help, you will not neglect them or pressure them. You might say, "If you want to watch for a while, that's OK. And when you want help or want to talk, let me know."

What do you do when there's a fight? First, stop the fight. Reasoning may not be enough; use the "football carry" if necessary (hoist the child onto your hip with head forward and feet stuck out behind). When you have brought the battle to a halt, you talk—*briefly*. You might say, "I know you feel mad" (reflection of feelings), "but that's enough. We'll talk later." Steer the fighters into an engrossing activity. Still later, you help them talk it out—when they are calm enough to listen to each other. Your aim is not to take sides or to get the facts but to help them express their feelings, negotiate, and solve their own problem.

What do you do when a child bites? Be alert and react quickly and consistently. Get right down to the child's eye level, saying, for example, "People are not for biting. We want everyone to be safe." You may have to hold the child in a nonpunitive way. Don't demand apologies; if you get any, they will be only empty gestures. Spitting (in a clearly designated place) may help a child who is too angry to talk. A child who bites frequently is tense and very troubled; get help.

IN CONCLUSION: DISCIPLINE

We conclude this section by listing some ideas worth remembering.

1   Be developmentally oriented. You may need to adjust your methods to the child's cognitive and language abilities. But remember that children need respect at every stage of development.

2   Keep in mind the primary goal: self-control. Strive for long-term autonomy rather than external control. We have not thus far used the word "conscience," but that is really a synonym for "antonomy" in this context. Research suggests that development of conscience goes along with warm, nurturing parent-child and teacher-child relationships, and with the ability to reason and to grasp consequences (Sutton-Smith, 1973).

3   Consider carefully what rules and limits you really need and what is really appropriate for children at different ages. Be realistic.

4   Try to let children understand the *reason* for every rule. Explaining why, for example, there can be no running and knocking into things and people in the classroom is a lesson in language and rational thinking. Give children opportunities to understand the natural consequences of their behavior.

5   Be understanding and flexible. Flexibility is especially necessary with younger children. Part of being flexible is to fit a method of discipline to a given child in a given situation.

6   Be consistent in enforcing important rules—especially safety rules.

You cannot let the children throw pebbles one day but not the next. Help the children understand that flexibility is not inconsistency: "John doesn't feel well today; it's all right for him to rest instead of work."

7   Never confront, nag, yell, threaten, or ridicule.

8   "Accentuate the positive," as the saying goes. Let children know what is appropriate behavior, and reinforce it when it occurs.

9   Act quickly and firmly to prevent injury or destruction. Make sure your classroom is safe (physically and emotionally) for each of your children.

10   Help children maintain their dignity. If you have to step in to help manage a child who cannot seem to control his or her behavior, do as little as is necessary. Simply moving toward a child or distracting a child may prevent misbehavior, but you may sometimes have to sit apart with the child and talk quietly. When things have cooled down, then you can try to help children to solve their own problems.

11   Even if you see a child do something wrong, don't force the child to admit guilt. Elkind explains that the "assumptive reality" of a situation may cause a child to genuinely believe that he or she is innocent. It's far better to simply and clearly state, "You took the pencil; let's return it" (Elkind, 1974, p. 86). But you should guide children to take responsibility for their actions. You can sometimes do this by persistently asking, "What did you do?" (see Glasser, 1969).

12   Remember that an interesting, colorful, appropriate environment with appealing activities for all is the best means of preventing problems. Within this environment, observe the children carefully, so that you can spot the signals if something is going wrong.

How Do I Create a Special Place for Children to Learn and Grow?

You undoubtedly are anxious to create, in your room, the optimal environment for young children. What does that entail?

AN ESTHETIC ENVIRONMENT   Your room arrangement need not be drab, colorless, or regimented. Displays of children's work (as well as yours), mounted carefully, a pleasant atmosphere, an interesting stock of children's books, groupings of furnishings, some wall decoration, hanging plants, a rocking chair or an armchair in bright colors, pillows or a rug on the floor, posters, curtains, pictures, a giant stuffed animal or a beanbag seat or two—all these have appeal for both boys and girls. Plants on shelves and most things hung at children's eye level will contribute to an eye-catching environment for you and the children.

Bulletin boards can also be attractive. Swatches of material, children's work, and eye-catching posters or pictures can be displayed on these bulletin boards. You may want to change the theme at various times, centering on some unit of work you are doing. Bulletin boards are instructional tools. They can be integral parts of learning centers. They may also hold important notices for children and staff members. Don't spend time and energy turning bulletin boards into professional "window dressing," or backdrops for thirty identical pumpkins; see them as colorful and significant teaching-learning aids.

HARMONIOUS RELATIONSHIPS Throughout this chapter we have stressed the *tone* of your relationship with the children and the staff and the tone of the relationship you encourage among them. Here are ten important ideas for you to remember:

1 Show respect for the children's interests and be involved in what they are doing.
2 Speak in a normal and pleasant tone.
3 Serve as a role model—treat the children courteously.
4 Help the children aspire to improve.
5 Expect children to treat each other courteously.
6 Listen carefully to what children are saying.
7 Make each child feel a part of the class.
8 Use discipline quietly.
9 Provide plenty of one-to-one contacts.
10 Help each child maintain his or her dignity.

You're planning a special world for your children, specifically designed for them. Through your organization of long- and short-range goals, you can create a place so well-suited to your children that they don't want to leave when it's time to go home.

Summary

Our three students in early childhood education, Chris, Pat, and Lee, learned that the primary influence in setting the tone of any classroom is the teacher.

One of the fundamentals of setting that tone is careful planning long before the children arrive. Major goals and objectives need to be identified, long-range plans set in motion, and space and materials organized. Short-range planning (weekly and daily) needs to take into account plans for the whole class, for small groups, and for individual children. Record keeping is important in keeping track of each child's progress and will help you in discussing that progress with parents and others who work with the child.

After discussing planning, we addressed several topics having to do with organization as a means of setting the tone: organizing (1) space, (2) materials, (3) activities, and (4) time. Organization of *space* needs to take into account the areas appropriate for children at particular ages, storage, and flexibility or adaptability. The old adage "A place for everything and everything in its place" applies here. Organization of *materials* includes indoor and outdoor settings. Outdoor equipment particularly needs to be selected with attention to cost, safety, and multiple uses. *Activities* may be organized in a variety of learning centers, and consideration was given to ways of getting centers started We also took a brief look at animals. *Time* can be organized in terms of pace and blocks of time. An "integrated day" allows individualized instruction and helps develop autonomy in children. In organizing time, the teacher needs to be able to work cooperatively with aides, other faculty members, parents, staff—and, of course, children.

The next section of the chapter provided specific suggestions about what to do during the first days of school. It dealt with meeting concerns of the parents, getting to know the children, and orienting children to their new setting by means of activities and routines.

We presented various practical ideas in the area of discipline and management. These included setting limits, understanding children's motivations for misbehaving, negotiating in "no lose" situations, and behavior modification. We stressed that the central purpose of discipline is to help the child achieve self-discipline. Effective communication, firmness, kindness, and respect are at the heart of dealing with negative behavior in children.

Finally, we discussed the creation of an esthetic and harmonious environment—a special place where both children and learning flourish.

References

Almy, M. *The early childhood educator at work*. New York: McGraw-Hill, 1975.

Bixler, R. Limits are therapy. *Journal of Consulting Psychology*, 1949, *13*, 1–11.

Broman, B. *The early years in childhood education*. Chicago: Rand McNally, 1978.

Dreikurs, R., & Cassel, P. *Discipline without tears* (2d ed.). New York: Hawthorn Books, 1972.

Elkind, D. *Children and adolescents*. New York: Oxford University Press, 1974.

Ginott, H. G. *Group psychotherapy with children*. New York: McGraw-Hill, 1961.

Ginott, H. C. *Teacher and child*. New York: Macmillian, 1972.

Glasser, W. *Schools without failure*. New York: Harper & Row, 1969.

Gordon, T. *Parent effectiveness training*. New York: Wyden, 1970.

Hendrick, J. *The whole child: New trends in early childhood.* St. Louis, Mo.: Mosby, 1975.

Hoover, M. B. *The responsive parent.* New York: Parents Magazine Press, 1972.

Kaplan, S. N., Kaplan, J. A. B., Madsen, S. K., & Taylor, B. K. *Change for children.* Pacific Palisades, Calif.: Goodyear, 1973.

Lay, M., & Dopyera, J. *Analysis of early childhood programs.* Urbana, Ill.: ERIC Clearinghouse on Early Childhood Education, 1971.

Leeper, S., Dales, R., Skipper, F., & Witherspoon, R. *Good schools for Young children* (3d ed.). New York: Macmillan, 1974.

Lundsteen, S. W. *Children learn to communicate.* Englewood Cliffs, N.J.: Prentice-Hall, 1976.

Madsen, C. H., & Madsen, C. K. *Teaching/Discipline: Behavioral principles towards a positive approach.* Boston: Allyn & Bacon, 1970.

Purkey, W. W. *Inviting school success.* Belmont, Calif.: Wadsworth, 1978.

Schickedanz, J., York, M., Stewart, I., & White, D. *Strategies for teaching young children.* Englewood Cliffs, N.J.: Prentice-Hall, 1977.

Spodek, B. *Teaching in the early years* (2d ed.). Englewood Cliffs, N.J.: Prentice-Hall, 1978.

Sutton-Smith, B. *Child psychology.* Englewood Cliffs, N.J.: Prentice-Hall, 1973.

CHAPTER 15

Parents are, indeed, the child's first teachers,
and the home is actually the first classroom.

—T.H. Bell (former United States
Commissioner of Education)

BEYOND THE SCHOOL: INVOLVING PARENTS AND THE COMMUNITY

Paulette Fuller and Gloria Tansits

The last quarter of the twentieth century will probably be recognized as the era when parents, professionals, and society as a whole have come to realize that education starts long before and continues long after the hours a child spends in school. The school setting extends far beyond the four walls of the school, into the home and the larger community.

Programs that have evolved in response to this recognition include involvement of parents, primarily as volunteers or members of advisory councils; parent education for parents of young children or as preparation for future parenthood; efforts to combine parent education with direct involvement; and efforts to utilize effectively the resources of the community. This tapping of resources is cutting across cultural and socioeconomic backgrounds, and bringing a cross section of American society into our schools. We consider involvement of parents and community in the course of answering the following questions:

- What is "parent education," and why is it important?
- Why and how can parents be involved in the school?
- How can parent volunteers be effectively recruited and trained?

- How can parent-involvement programs benefit children with special needs?
- What community resources can serve the needs of young children?

In the past, any orientation or "education" for parents was provided informally on a "catch-as-catch-can" basis. Occasional contacts with parents provided the "education" component while parent volunteers, when present, provided an extra pair of hands. Our philosophy of teaching-learning, with its commitment to openness in educational practices, individualization, and partnership between home and school in the education of children, makes that kind of help essential. It also means greater attention to the background parents bring to their work in the classroom and to their role as parents.

Much of the information in this chapter dealing with parents is also applicable to other adults in the classroom and to the whole range of early childhood education, from day care for the very young through the primary grades. In many instances the functions assigned to a parent volunteer or to an "aide" differ only in that the aide is being paid. In many instances the aides are drawn from the ranks of parent volunteers who decided to move onto a career ladder (that perhaps culminates in a teaching position at a later time). (Recall Chapter 1.) You, the future teacher, will find this information helpful—not later when you begin work with parents and aides in your own classroom—but right now as you serve as an aide or engage in observation and participational field-work in preparation for your career.

Parent Education

Parents are the earliest and most influential teachers of their children. Their effectiveness, however, depends upon their knowledge, their experience, and their interest in helping their children lead fulfilling lives. This is where parent education can make a difference. What is parent education? Why is it important? For whom is it intended? How can it be implemented to meet the needs of the parents it serves? The following sections will provide some answers to these questions.

PREPARATION FOR PARENTHOOD Programs in preparation for parenthood are directed at school-age and adult expectant parents as well as adolescents who are interested in acquiring the skills of parenthood for the future. Such programs emphasize prenatal experiences: procreation, pregnancy, and childbirth. Classes on methods of childbirth (such as natural, or prepared, childbirth) are very popular—especially those on the Lamaze method and the LeBoyer method (Caplan, 1977; Morrison, 1978).

Most of these programs do not take up the skills of parenthood other than the physical necessities of infant care. But one program—"Education for Parenthood"—does provide information and practice designed to enable its members to become effective parents. "Education for Parenthood" was launched as a joint program by the U.S. Office of Education and the Office of Child Development in 1972. The curriculum for the program is called "Exploring Childhood." It is a one-year elective course for boys and girls in grades 7 to 12 which includes classroom study (films, filmstrips, audiocassettes, discussion of field experiences), independent research projects, and fieldwork in day care centers and nursery schools. It is too early to say how effective this program will be or whether others will follow; but the students have been generally enthusiastic (Bell, 1976; Kruger, 1972; Ogg, 1975).

A number of school districts have come to terms with the fact that many young women are becoming mothers while still in high school. Programs have been developed which provide prenatal counseling, services, information and continuing guidance and education after the birth of the baby. Usually the young mother continues with her high school classes while the child is cared for in an infant center. Part of the curriculum for the mother deals with child development and child care and education. A major portion of the program involves applying skills and information to the care of the child under supervision in the center. Some of these programs are using materials from the "Exploring Childhood" program.

CHILD REARING Modern parents shopping for information on children will find it in a variety of places and forms:

- Adult education classes in high schools and community colleges
- Discussion groups
- Programs in school settings, home settings, and combined settings

Adult education

Courses in parenthood are generally offered to adults in high schools and community colleges, though some do involve both parent and child. At the Whitney Community Learning Center in Cerritos, California, for example, it is the parent who is enrolled as the student, but parents bring their children to the center's preschool in order to interact with the children while learning the skills of parenthood. Learning such skills is the main objective of the program; but the child's early education is a secondary objective (Ohnersorgen, 1978).

Discussion groups

Discussion groups usually involve adults only.

One of the most popular programs, "Parent Effectiveness Training" (PET), tries to build parents' confidence and teach communication skills to improve the parent-child relationship. It emphasizes treating children as people and advocates a "no lose" method of dealing with conflicts between adults and children (Gordon, 1970; we discuss this method in Chapter 14). PET appears to be an effective type of parent education in that it changes parents' attitudes in a psychologically healthy direction (Duffy, 1974). Since its inception in 1970, PET has led to related programs, books, and activities. Similar programs include "Child Management: A Program for Parents" (Smith, 1966); "Parenting Skills" (Abidin, 1976); and "Systematic Training for Effective Parenting" (STEP) (Dinkmeyer & McKay, 1976).

A totally different approach, based on a behaviorism, is provided by Becker (1971). His system trains parents to use behavior modification to shape children's behavior, on the basis of principles of reinforcement and extrinsic rewards. (See Chapter 14.)

Parent-child programs

A third type of parent education focuses on the cognitive development of the child. Parent education is closely related to parents' involvement in the child's school—each reinforces and adds depth to the other. Some of these programs teach parents how to conduct practical activities in the home which are designed to enhance the child's cognitive development. (See Chapter 5.) Parent-child cognitive education takes various forms, including parent-child centers, parent cooperatives, workshops, small groups, and home-visit programs:

- *Parent-child centers.* Parent-child centers attempt to provide an integrated program of education for both parent and child. Parents bring their children to the center to interact with other children in the center's preschool. Some programs operate daily, others less frequently. Some programs are geared toward toddlers, others toward three- to five-year-olds. As the children learn through play, parents have the opportunity to practice skills learned in their own sessions, which are often conducted in a series of eight to twelve two-hour weekly programs. During a session, there is a discussion about some topic related to child development. Parents also watch films, slides, and demonstrations and participate in role-playing situations. New toys may be introduced, with explanations of their educational potential and how they can be used with children. These centers represent a wide range of philosophies: some provide a very open structure, allowing for exploration; others have highly structured "intervention" programs aimed at specific physical-motor or cognitive skills. Some centers have a wide range of ongoing activities (e.g., sewing, cooking) designed to help parents in their everyday lives. A center may contain a library of books, toys, pamphlets, and educational materials which parents can borrow. Some centers may even offer transportation to parents when necessary.

- *Parent cooperatives.* Parent cooperatives have actually pioneered parent-child centers. These cooperatives are geared primarily to the needs of middle-class families. They provide preschool experience for children, generally in a center under the supervision of a trained professional, and their primary purpose is the education of the child rather than the parent. Parents take turns assisting the teacher each day, thus lowering costs and learning to work with children. In these programs, parents generally work with groups of children so as to improve the adult-child ratio. Since the purpose is generally *not* to teach parents or parent-child pairs, parents are not expected to work individually with their own children. However, many ideas and skills are naturally transmitted to the parents.

- *Workshops.* Workshops are usually open to large groups and therefore are likely to be conducted in public spaces. Both parents and school staff members can benefit from workshops in teaching-learning activities and devices. Workshops may also deal with learning children's games, songs, and dances, and may include lectures, films, and panel discussions.

- *Small groups.* Small-group meetings in homes or other neighborhood settings can sometimes reach out more effectively than large groups. Talking around a neighbor's kitchen table is nonthreatening and informal; parents can express feelings and attitudes freely in a comfortable atmosphere. This type of setting lends itself to discussion of "delicate" topics such as toilet training, masturbation, and sex education.

- *Home-visit programs.* Home-visit programs use professional educators or paraprofessionals, preferably from neighborhood cultural groups, who can readily identify with the families they serve. Gordon (1970) suggests that the best teacher of parents is someone from a similar culture. Home visitors bring a curriculum to parent and child at home. During their weekly visits, they interact with the children in the family, teach parents specific tasks to do with the children, demonstrate the tasks with the children, and observe parents working with their own children. They also counsel parents on program services and act as a referral service to outside agencies. This one-to-one format can work excellently. Some programs combine home visits with a center-based program for preschoolers. Home-visit programs can also include television broadcasts, parent education classes, group discussions, toy lending libraries, and supplements such as dental, medical, nutritional, and social services.

MASS MEDIA When no formal parent education programs is available, an alternative means of parent education is the mass media. There are many useful television programs, "how-to" books, and journal articles.

Involving Parents as Volunteers

For decades, individuals have volunteered their services in hospitals, libraries, and other charitable organizations. Such services were usually limited to those institutions and were often viewed as a casual activity for leisure time. Volunteer services today, however, are based on an acceptance of the facts that community services are everyone's concern, that the school is an appropriate agency to utilize volunteer services, and that parents are an ideal population to provide such services (Taylor, 1972).

WHY INVOLVE PARENTS? The 1960s and 1970s have witnessed increased concern and involvement in public education and a great increase in volunteer programs, resulting from a variety of factors. Seven reasons why increased involvement is important and useful follow.

1 *Parents should have a voice in decision making.* Many people feel that if they or their children are going to be affected by decisions made by educators, they have the right to have a voice in making those decisions. Lasting and constructive change and improvement are most likely to happen if those affected are involved in the planning (Wohlforth, 1977).

2 *Federal and state guidelines often require participation by parents.* Federal and state guidelines for many specially funded programs have made parent participation mandatory. Examples are Head Start (Chapter 3) and Public Law 91-142 (Chapter 13).

3 *Parents are a valuable resource.* Parents offer potential assistance in most areas in which human beings possess talents. The resources they provide can help to improve instruction, enrich the curriculum, and increase relations between the school and the community.

4 *There are benefits to teachers.* Volunteers can relieve teachers of many chores which take up time that could be used for more important educational purposes, such as small-group and individualized instruction.

5 *There are benefits to parents.* Parents working in the classroom learn firsthand how different children are from each other and how one

can respond to their differences. One mother related to a school principal that she had much more patience with her own child after working with other children and their varying learning styles.

Volunteers are also able to gain knowledge and understanding of curriculum materials and what the school is teaching and why. The parent does not have to depend solely on the child to unravel the mystery of school. ("What did you do in school today?" "Oh, nothing!") Consequently, conferences with parents become more meaningful and parents are better able to help their children at home.

Volunteering often leads to paid positions for many parents. As the volunteers are trained and learn new skills, they are hired as paid aides because they have the necessary knowledge and experience for the job. Many principals have happily complained that they have lost some of their best volunteers by indirectly training them for paid positions. Parents who feel that they are unskilled often gain the self-confidence needed to seek paying jobs after they have had successful "careers" as volunteers.

What about the benefits to parents whose very young children are receiving day care? When parents attend sessions at the child's day care center, they get an idea of the impact the facility is making on the child. Head Start, for example, spreads its impact throughout the family. When parents visit, bringing even younger children with them, the day care teachers can not only establish rapport with the parents but also get to know the younger children in the family. Many possibilities for involving parents are presented to Head Start clients: meetings with parents, mini-courses on discipline or child development, multicultural and bilingual programs, health and nutrition guides, government bulletins, and educational information. Furthermore, Head Start day care centers are in contact with local schools to help smooth the transition up the educational ladder. It is hoped that parents will establish habits of close contact with the day care center and continue this kind of involvement as their children grow older and progress in school.

6   *There are benefits to children.* Adult tutors can work on a one-to-one basis or with small groups, not only giving students a chance to meet and interact with other adults besides the teacher but providing them with increased individual attention. Parents can set up and supervise learning centers in science, cooking, art, and other areas. Parents also contribute indirectly to the child's self-concept by participating in the classroom program. One third-grade teacher reported how a student in her class sat proudly and displayed a huge smile the entire time his mother shared family pictures and souvenirs of a trip to Australia.

7   *Parents can help form a bridge between cultures.* An effective volunteer program promotes a closer relationship between the community

and the school. For many parents, especially those living in poverty or in areas where little or no English is spoken, there is a sharp line between their world and the world of the larger society. The school has, traditionally, been seen as the representative of middle-class values, and as such has almost been a "forbidden world" to many parents. We see the school as serving the function of a bridge between cultures—a place where parents will feel welcome, comfortable, and valued. We see the school as a place where parents of other cultures gain and use skills that will assist them and their children in joining the society they live in while retaining the values and traditions of their own culture.

PREPARATION FOR A PARENT-INVOLVEMENT PROGRAM

Suppose that your school has decided on a parent-involvement program. What do you need to know and do? Such programs are subject to the "bandwagon" phenomenon. By this we mean that often schools or districts jump on the bandwagon of a popular concept without adequate preparation to ensure its success. Preparation is essential; without it, you can be sure that the program will fail.

First, there must be a *decision* to institute a parent-involvement program. This decision must be made by all those who will be concerned.

Second, the decision should be followed by *assessment of needs*, to determine the major needs of the school and the parents.

Third, *studying information about existing programs*, visiting some exemplary programs, or inviting personnel from such programs to talk to parents and staff members are all helpful in establishing objectives.

Fourth, some means of determining whether or not objectives are being met (*evaluation*) should be established.

Fifth, since leadership is very important in getting a program under way, *a leader or coordinator must be selected*.

Finally, *teachers and staff must be informed* about all the possibilities of the program.

To summarize, the preparation phase should include:

- Decision to implement a parent-involvement program
- Assessment of needs
- Study of existing programs and establishment of objectives
- Determination of means of evaluation
- Selection of leaders
- Orientation and preparation for staff members

HOW MIGHT PARENTS BE INVOLVED?

There are innumerable ways that volunteers can assist in the instructional process. While some parents will want to assist the teacher, others will prefer to do clerical work or artwork or correct papers. Duties will vary from classroom to classroom and from volunteer to volunteer.

Tasks parents can perform in the classroom

The variety of jobs that volunteers can perform is extensive. Some of the most valuable ways that parents and community members can assist the educational process are discussed below.

Tutoring Tutoring individuals or small groups can help children develop at their own pace in a particular subject area. While children receive extra attention and reinforcement from other adults, the teacher is free to spend more time giving special help to individuals who need additional instruction. Volunteers can:

- Listen to an individual child
- Give one-to-one help in reading, mathematics, etc., as a follow-up to concepts already taught by the teacher.
- Give individual help with writing and spelling
- Assist children who have missed instruction because of absences
- Assist children with correct formation of letters and numerals
- Assist those few children who need practice with word, phrase, or number flash cards

Subteaching tasks Certain assessment tasks and instructional procedures benefit from a division of responsibility. In these areas, help from volunteers can greatly increase a teacher's efficiency. The teacher must judge how much responsibility the volunteer can comfortably assume. Volunteers can:

- Read stories to children
- Read spelling or vocabulary lists
- Listen to children practice oral reading
- Assist children with compositions
- Assist with assessment procedures
- Work with children in creative dramatics
- Supervise small-group games
- Assist with playground supervision
- Assist with art and music activities
- Assist pupils with independent work
- Help pupils find reference materials
- Translate for children whose dominant language is not English

Enrichment of the curriculum Within the ranks of the school's volunteers, there may be individuals who excel musically or who are artistically or mechanically skilled. Often parents are willing to share their expertise in cooking, sewing, carpentry, and other areas. Multicultural education can be integrated into the educational program by parents who can share materials and traditions of their culture. Parents' jobs, hobbies, crafts, and talents offer a resource that can enrich the curriculum as well as guide children in career aspirations and effective use of leisure.

Clerical and housekeeping tasks   There are many necessary "non-teaching" tasks that volunteers can perform. Collecting lunch money, grading papers, getting supplies, and setting up displays are just a few examples. However, the role of the volunteer should not be reduced to just clerical and housekeeping chores. Though they can be involved in some of these duties, parents need tasks that will make them feel helpful, useful, and involved (Maerowitz, 1973). Volunteers can:

- Type children's stories
- File materials
- Take roll
- Grade papers and workbooks
- Put lessons on the chalkboard
- Assist in typing children's compositions for "publication," correcting invented spellings, and binding stories into books
- Secure children's literature collections from the library and return them
- Arrange instructional bulletin boards or assist children in arranging their own
- Keep track of children's work and progress
- Develop resource files (pictures, poems, finger plays)
- Prepare tapes for lessons at listening centers
- Type and duplicate instructional materials
- Gather and distribute materials, supplies, and equipment

Housekeeping tasks that volunteers can perform (thereby releasing the teacher for work with children) include:

- Washing paint jars and brushes
- Setting out art materials
- Sorting and storing games and activities
- Assisting with general classroom maintenance beyond what children can do

Preparation of instructional materials   Volunteers often assist the teacher by preparing instructional materials, either in their own homes or in school. Many schools have set up resource centers where parents can make games and other materials. These centers sometimes also serve the purpose of providing an opportunity for parents to interact with each other and share common concerns.

Other ways volunteers can be used include participation on field trips, help as "room mothers," and assistance with initial screening and assessments. Effective use of volunteers depends on the needs of the classroom and the abilities of the teacher and the particular volunteer.

It is important that the teacher help the volunteer grow in skills that will fit the needs of the classroom. The volunteers may be assigned to a variety of tasks so that they become proficient in many areas, thus increasing their value as "experienced" volunteers. The objective is not to make each volunteer a narrow specialist or a jack-of-all-trades but to utilize all the volunteer's capabilities and to keep the job interesting and productive. Bear in mind that it is as volunteers that many parents first become interested in working with children and aware of their own abilities in the field.

Advisory committees

Involvement in the classroom is only one aspect of volunteering. Another way that parents act as a resource to the school is through their participation on school advisory committees. These committees are usually composed of parents, teachers, aides, the school administrator, and representatives from the community at large.

Advisory committees generally meet on a regular basis and give parents an opportunity to provide input on issues involving the school program. Serving on these committees also enables the school staff to keep a finger on the pulse of the community (Morrison, 1978).

The functions of advisory committees usually include involvement in assessment of educational needs, planning of educational programs, budgeting resources, defining the goals of the school, and evaluating the school and its academic effectiveness.

Most parents do not come to the advisory committee with the skills necessary for involvement in the decisions that have traditionally been made only by educators. However, when given the background information, explanations, and some training, parents become informed and valuable members of the team.

Opportunities for meaningful contributions in terms of committee action are often limited because, by definition, the parents' advisory committee serves only an advisory role. Part of the problem has been the reluctance of administrators and other school staff members to include parents in decisions that might affect policy. Some educators fear that they will lose their professional standing or jeopardize their professional role through such advisory groups. However, through this involvement process, parents come to understand more fully the complexity of the school program. Parents become partners in the instructional process, but the professional educator has the responsibility for setting the direction.

Once you understand the importance of involving parents and the tasks they might perform, the next job is recruitment. If you are, or become, a teacher attempting to recruit volunteers, here are five helpful hints.

1 *Be patient.* For many years parents were told, "Don't call us, we'll call you if we think there's something you ought to know at school." Consequently, many parents aren't quite sure how to react to the sudden "Come join us" invitations issued by teachers, parent volunteer coordinators, and the principal. It may take time to change some feelings and attitudes.

2 *Go after the volunteers.* A successful recruitment program will go after the volunteers, not wait for them to come to the school. Personal contact really helps convince parents that they are needed and wanted. "Back to school" nights, parent conferences, kindergarten orientation, and PTA meetings are a few places to start. However, they are only the beginning. It is important to be creative and use every available resource.

3 *Be warm and friendly.* No plan for recruitment, however well developed, will succeed if people don't feel friendliness and sincerity. Condition of clothes, color of skin, language spoken, and amount of education do not determine a productive volunteer. Be sensitive to individual differences.

4 *Put out the welcome mat.* Invitations to the school will be more "believable" if parents really feel they are welcome when they arrive at the school. Provide a "parent-staff room" with comfortable chairs, refreshments, and opportunity to interact informally.

5 *Make it easy to serve.* Keep rules, regulations, and even training sessions to a minimum. It is important to get people working with people.

Who does the recruiting?

Recruitment can be basically the responsibility of one person, or it can involve the entire school staff. This depends on the program and the need of each school. In many cases, each teacher recruits volunteers for his or her classroom. This is often the most effective way, because parents feel special when approached personally by their child's teacher. Even schools that have designated specific staff members to organize the volunteer program find that the classroom teacher is still one of the best recruiters.

A "parent volunteer coordinator" can be either a teacher, a paid aide, or another volunteer. The main duties of the coordinator are to recruit, train, and generally coordinate the volunteer program. This person often acts as a liaison between the community and the school.

Who are potential volunteers?

The possibilities are almost endless. Do not overlook anyone in the community who enjoys working with others and has some extra time. Parents are probably the largest and most interested group of potential volunteers. Senior citizens, retirees, and grandparents represent a group of citizens that have not only skills and talents to share with children but the time to share them. Contact a local senior citizen organization and offer to talk at a meeting about the volunteer program at your school.

Neighboring schools and colleges may give credit to students who tutor on a volunteer basis. Home economics classes and teacher education courses often require field experiences involving children. Dance groups, drama classes, and singing groups from junior and senior high schools need audiences for their programs. While the older students are able to practice their performance, the younger children receive the enrichment that such productions offer.

Techniques for recruiting within the school community

There are many ways of contacting parents and explaining the volunteer program to them. The more information that goes out into the community, the more parents will come to the schools. Some of the techniques and opportunities for recruiting include:

- *Registration.* When parents come for day care and kindergarten preregistration, explain the program and ask them if they would like to participate.
- *Parent conferences, home visits, and phone calls.* When the opportunity is there, use it.
- *School meetings, teas, newsletters, and evening programs.* Have your sign-up sheets ready.
- *Questionnaires.* Fliers sent home can provide a resource file listing skills, talents, and interests of parents.
- *Children's requests.* It is amazing how successful this approach is with parents, how many respond to invitations written and designed by their own children.

Techniques for recruiting within the community at large

There are many people within the community, not necessarily parents of children in your school, who have much to contribute to the school program. It is important to use every available resource to contact and involve volunteers from the community at large. Remember that these potential volunteers usually don't attend school meetings or get the newsletters and fliers that go home with the children; they have to be reached in other ways.

Many volunteers are recruited by other volunteers who speak at meetings of service clubs and other organizations. Sometimes just asking everyone to bring a friend or neighbor to a meeting or tea at school gets enthusiastic response.

Use all available media for publicizing the volunteer program. Don't overlook the local newspaper. Editors are often willing to do an interview or at least a community service announcement.

Let the newspaper keep you informed. Watch for articles about people with special skills. Contact them and invite them to your school to share their special talent with your students. At one school in Hawaiian Gardens, California, the reading specialist contacted an author of children's books who had been written up in the newspaper. She came to the school and was delighted to do story hours for the primary-grade children.

Other schools use other techniques: at one, a committee of parents contacted local merchants and industries to arrange either for the children to tour the business or for the business to come to the school. (For example, children were able to watch sheep being sheared and a horse shoed right on the school grounds.) Another school uses spot announcements on the radio to reach potential volunteers.

Post "advertisements" in stores, banks, restaurants, and community colleges. Be sure to give the name and phone number of the person at school to be contacted.

Contact service clubs, churches, and existing volunteer organizations to inform them of your program and make it known that someone from the school is available to talk or show slides about the school volunteer program at their meetings.

ORIENTATION AND TRAINING OF PARENTS AND STAFF

Once you have parents lined up and ready to volunteer, it is important to prepare them so that their efforts will be successful and satisfying for themselves and the children. However, training is not just for the parents.

Staff preparation

Often schools are concerned with "training" the parents to be involved but do not consider the importance of developing *readiness* on the part of teachers and staff members to ensure that they will work effectively with the volunteers. Teachers need to develop positive attitudes toward the use of parents; they must sincerely want the assistance of volunteers in the classroom. Teachers need to be prepared for the fact that at first there may be additional work involved. But effective organization will guarantee that the value of the volunteers will soon more than repay this extra work.

Teachers need to understand the importance of open and ongoing communication, of allowing the volunteer ample (but not too much) time for observation. Such observation builds familiarity with the routines of the classroom, a relationship with the children, and the volunteer's self-confidence. The teacher's aide (if there is one) and the children need to be prepared for the volunteer. That is, children need to be oriented to the role that the volunteer will play.

Have the classroom set up so that the volunteer can enter the room, consult a plan board and begin work. Allow a place for the volunteer to record what work the children completed, observations about how the children worked and played, and suggestions.

General orientation session

Some administrators may plan a general orientation session for volunteers, possibly with, e.g., slides, videotapes, role playing, and small group discussions. If responsibility for this orientation is not assumed by someone else, then the teacher will need to cover the following points.

Philosophy   It is important that parents understand how the staff members feel about all children as well as how they feel, e.g., about individualization of instruction, the open classroom, and creativity.

Procedures   School procedures are easily overlooked because everyone familiar with the school knows them and takes them for granted. Some things you might want to consider doing during orientation are these:

- Tour the facilities.
- Introduce all the staff members.
- Call attention to procedures for signing in and out.
- Discuss whom to call when the volunteer can't come.
- Outline schedules: arrival, lunch, and dismissal; recess and coffee breaks.
- Discuss procedures during drills of various kinds (e.g., fire drills, weather alerts) and their purposes.

Child development   Explain what is reasonable to expect of children at various stages of development. (A mother of a precocious first-grade child may not realize that there are first-graders who cannot hold a pencil.) It is important to outline the expectations for the age group.

Offer suggestions of some ways volunteers can cope with children's aggression, independence, or dependence. (See Chapter 14.)

Responsibilities of volunteers   Explain the necessity for a chest x ray, consistent and regular attendance, and the avoidance of discussions about individual children.

Some of the information given in a general orientation session can be put into a volunteers' handbook that can be read at leisure as well as used for quick reference. Such a handbook can also be given to parents who start volunteering after the general orientation session has taken place.

Concerns and questions of aides and volunteers

What are some of the aspects of volunteering or being a paid aide that should be clarified? The following list gives some examples:

As a Teacher's Aide . . .

1   Will I work directly with children?
2   With which age group or groups will I be working?
3   What duties will I have?
4   What skills must I have now in order to do an efficient job?
5   Will I have the opportunity to learn how to operate school equipment such as duplicating machines and audiovisual equipment?
6   What is my role when a child requires disciplining? Should I speak to the child directly? Should I just refer the child to the teacher?
7   Will I be responsible for *teaching* children?
8   Will I be asked to plan activities or create materials or is my role to carry out plans made by the teacher and to construct materials as I am directed?
9   Will I find myself encountering parents? What should I say to them? Should I limit my conversations with them?
10   What should the children call me? Should they say "Mr. X," "Mrs. Y," "Ms. Z," or "Miss Q," or should they use my first name?
11   Should I expect to take work home with me for completion or correction?
12   Where is the school's central supply room? Am I allowed to obtain materials for my classroom teacher? What is the correct procedure? What are the limits to quantities obtained?
13   Are there special events which may require my attendance during times other than assigned work hours? When and how frequent are these events?
14   What facilities am I authorized to use (e.g., teachers' lounge, restroom)?

15   Will my performance as an aide by evaluated? Who will rate me? In which areas will I be rated?*

Specific training for helping in the classroom

It is what you do with parents and others once you have them in the classroom that will really determine whether they develop into reliable volunteers or fade out of the picture. However, since each volunteer and each teacher is different, there is no one way to train volunteers for specific classroom tasks. Consequently, some of the most intensive and meaningful training will be given by the teacher and will be individualized for each of the volunteers.

Teachers may have to spend some recesses or lunch periods planning and talking to parents, but the results are well worth the effort. Following are seven general guidelines to keep in mind when training parents for specific classroom work:

1   *Analyze each volunteer's strengths and weaknesses.* For example, ask the volunteer to read a story to a small group, play a game with several children, transcribe a story dictated by a child. You can then observe the volunteer actually working with children and determine how much additional training or guidance the volunteer will need. Nervousness, degree of confidence, ability to solve problems, and ability to change pace when necessary are the kinds of things a teacher can note and use in planning an effective training program.

2   *Make a plan.* A good training program does not have to be complicated. However, it should reflect the needs of the individual who will be involved. Some administrators have arranged released time for teachers so that they may plan together with their volunteers. The plan should include the kinds of things the volunteer will be doing along with some specific suggestions.

3   *Put each volunteer to work.* Assign a specific job to the volunteer, and provide a short explanation of its importance. Volunteers do not come to sit and observe the teacher. If they do not feel that they are needed, most will not return. Be sure to let your volunteers know that they are contributing and are an important part of your classroom program.

4   *Give specific directions.* It is also helpful to write the directions for the task you want a volunteer to do on a card instead of giving them orally. This enables the volunteer to reread the assignment if necessary without having to interrupt the teacher.

5   *Vary assignments as much as possible.* This ensures that volunteers will be trained in several areas.

* Compiled by Diane Asari (former aide, now teacher), Long Beach Unified School District, Long Beach, California.

6 *Explain general routines.* Volunteers can be trained to take over many of the nonteaching tasks so that more of the teacher's time will be spent teaching. Volunteers should understand classroom and general routines. These are often overlooked because they are taken for granted. However, every volunteer should know:

- Where to put coats, purses, etc.
- How to help children clean up and get ready for the next activity
- Where to look for plans or instructions for the day
- Where to put evaluations or anecdotes regarding children with whom they have worked
- How to record children's progress
- How to conduct opening routines (taking attendance, saluting flag, collecting milk money, etc.)
- Where materials are kept
- General classroom schedule and dismissal procedures
- Emergency procedures

7 *Use games effectively.* Volunteers need to be taught that games in a classroom are used for many reasons, including reinforcement of academic skills, development of social skills, extension of attention span, and building positive self-concepts. Be sure the volunteers know the purpose of the game as well as how to play it. Since volunteers often *make* many of the games used in the classroom, it is doubly rewarding when they are given an opportunity to see the children use the games they have made.

8 *Explain techniques for managing a center or teaching a small group.* Parents generally want to work with children and usually learn very quickly; a short demonstration and explanation will get them started. Talk over the experience whenever possible and stress such things as *letting the children discover as much as possible for themselves* and maintaining appropriate standards of behavior. When working in a learning center, volunteers should know such things as the purpose of the center, who can use it and when, and record-keeping procedures.

While most volunteers are not trained teachers, it is important to remember that they can do much more than just housekeeping chores. It is up to the classroom teacher to keep parents interested in children and education throughout the year. Listen to your volunteers and respect their opinions even if you don't always agree with them.

HOW TO KEEP THE VOLUNTEERS COMING BACK

The following are five ways to increase the probability that your volunteers will return.

1 *Use their talents.* In order to use volunteers effectively and keep them coming back to the school, it is important to make *maximum use*

of their talents. Volunteers who are inappropriately placed will not return even though they may have been enthusiastic when they started. Although it may sound simple, matching volunteers to the right activities will require patience and flexibility. You can refer to questionnaires to find out your volunteers' hobbies, interests, and occupations. By asking parents, you can find out the kinds of activities they *want* to do.

2   *Preserve their group identity.* Preserving the volunteers' sense of group identity can be accomplished by regular meetings at school or in private homes. If appropriate professional library materials can be collected, a further boost may be given to group identity during the sharing and discussion of materials kept, say, in a corner of the "staff lounge" (which is not called the "teachers' lounge").

3   *Show appreciation.* If you want your volunteers to return, make them feel welcome, needed, and appreciated. Simple, but often overlooked, ways of making parents feel part of the school team include giving specific compliments, stressing the positive aspects of a volunteer's help, giving constructive suggestions, receiving and giving immediate feedback, and smiling and saying thank you. Other ways to show appreciation to volunteers for their time and effort include:

- Special lunches, teas, or parties given by the school staff
- Recognition programs where certificates are given
- Thank-you letters written by the students or cards made by the children at holidays
- Bulletin boards displaying photographs of volunteers and descriptions of their contributions
- Press releases to neighborhood newspapers or district newsletters telling of unique or unusual volunteers and work they have done

4   *Provide creature comforts.* Be aware and show concern for your volunteers' comforts. Make arrangement for coffee breaks and arrange a comfortable place to take them.

5   *Appeal to ideals.* Teachers and administrators need to do everything they can to get across to volunteers the idea that by working at school they are helping children and improving the school and community.

SOME COMMON PROBLEMS

Working successfully with parents and volunteers takes skill and understanding. A volunteer program will generally present problems (or challenges). However, if you are aware of them, some of the problems can be anticipated and their effects minimized (Morrison, 1978). An elaboration of six common difficulties in working with volunteers follows.

1   *No-shows.* One of the major concerns of teachers working with volunteers is planning for their arrival and then finding that they do not show up. Often a new volunteer is late or absent because it is easier to

find an excuse to stay home than face a new situation in which the volunteer feels insecure and uncomfortable (Hendricks & Enk, 1976). It takes time for the volunteer to feel needed and successful and to develop a feeling of responsibility.

Until you have volunteers that are committed to your program, there are several things you can be prepared to do to cover for a no-show.

- Find a parent who would be willing to substitute at irregular times.
- Plan an additional activity that does not require close supervision.
- Close a learning center or postpone work that was planned. Children can be reassigned to other centers or volunteers or given additional independent assignments. Have some emergency learning activities.

When they return, let your volunteers know how much they were missed. If they do not call, get in touch with them so they will know that you still need them.

2 *Classroom discipline.* Another area in which problems sometimes surface is classroom discipline. While some teachers complain that parents don't exercise enough discipline, others say that parents discipline too much (Morrison, 1978). Volunteers need to be informed of standards of discipline in the classroom and the rules students are expected to follow. They should also be instructed in techniques for maintaining order without destroying a child's self-image. While the teacher is responsible for setting the tone and direction of the discipline process, the parent should know what to do when a child disrupts the class or displays inappropriate behavior. (See "Setting Limits" in Chapter 14.)

Children should be aware that volunteers are there to help them with their work and not to teach them how to behave. The volunteers' time is valuable, and students need to make the time count. Children's respect for the volunteers must be ensured.

3 *Overstepping bounds.* Occasionally there will be a volunteer who will go beyond offering suggestions and attempt to "take over" the classroom. It is up to the teacher to establish limits, welcoming suggestions but clearly retaining decision-making authority (Hendricks & Enk, 1976). The duties and responsibilities of the volunteer may have to be reviewed and emphasized in an individual or general meeting.

4 *Parents as teachers of their children.* A question that arises frequently in regard to involvement of parents is whether or not parents should be allowed to volunteer in their own children's classrooms. Many teachers worry that parents will give too much attention to their own children or that the children will become overly dependent on their parents. However, such cases are rare. Instead, by working in their own children's classrooms, parents are able to become familiar with the

learning materials and the way they are used in that particular classroom. Parents are then better prepared to help their children at home. They are also able to see that their time and talents result in more individual attention for their own children as the teacher is relieved to work with smaller groups of children.

It is not unusual for a teacher to feel uncomfortable and inhibited when a parent watches his or her own child being taught or disciplined (Morrison, 1978). However, it is important to remember that the volunteer is there to help children, not to observe the teacher. Keep parents involved with other children, doing absorbing and rewarding tasks, and there will be little time for observation of the teacher.

If a situation does occur where a parent-child relationship has negative effects, it is best to reassign the volunteer to another classroom or to the office.

5   *Volunteers who speak little or no English.* Volunteers who speak another language can be a genuine asset to your program, especially if you have children who speak little or no English. They can help tutor, work in bilingual learning centers, or even teach a second language to those who speak only English. They can also be assigned to areas, such as crafts, art, and housekeeping, where language is not involved.

6   *Rumors, gossip, and criticism.* The training program or volunteers' handbook is an appropriate place to stress that what happens at school is always confidential and that gossip about test scores or other personal matters may be harmful to a child if it is discussed outside of school. Volunteers need to learn what information is useful in dealing with a child and what information is self-defeating. At the same time, staff members need to set the tone for volunteers and should be careful not to gossip among themselves.

EVALUATION   Evaluation of the effectiveness of your parent-involvement program needs to be an ongoing process so that you can make changes when they are needed. Procedures for how you are going to evaluate the program need to be established from the start and need to include evaluation of attitudes as well as behaviors. Evaluation includes assessments by the volunteers, the staff, and the children. Information derived from the evaluation is used to modify the program and to plan for the future.

A FINAL THOUGHT   We have considered the varied benefits of involving parents in the educational program both as members of advisory councils and as volunteers. Methods of recruiting and training and retaining parent volunteers were discussed in detail. We have also considered some of the problems entailed in starting and carrying on such programs. You may now be wondering what's really in it for you, professionally.

Perhaps the best answer is this: With aides and volunteers, you have more "teaching power." By that we mean you have more time to be a thoughtful teacher, more time to allow young children to think for themselves and to encourage their creative problem solving. Without this "people help," you may find that you have so many routine duties—so much to do at the same time—that your highly sensitive decisions about each child's growth and development may have to be sacrificed to preserve the smooth, crisis-free, machinelike functioning of the "good" teacher's class. "People help" can release you to promote children's imaginations, their caring for one another, their varied language activities (rather than silence), and in general the fulfilling activity that you, as an educated professional, can offer children. Of course, it is possible to have a room full of help and still fail to make these sensitive decisions. But given your planning, practice, and the breaking-in period, if you keep the theme of this book (creative problem solving) in mind, you can use the relief provided by these volunteers to enrich the "life drama" of your classroom. And if they remain your helpers for a period of time, they, catching your spirit of creative problem solving, will enrich the lives of children wherever they go.

Parent-Teacher Conferences

Parent-teacher conferences were used, in the past, only to inform the parents of their child's behavior and academic progress in school. But the parent-teacher contact can be expanded into a relationship enabling the teacher to become an effective educator of parents. Annual, semiannual, or more frequent parent-teacher conferences can be a vital source from which parents can learn skills of parenthood uniquely designed for their own children. The one-to-one meeting of parent and teacher provides a golden opportunity for the ideal teaching-learning situation. These conferences also open up two-way communication between the home and school. Parents have a chance to ask questions, voice concerns, and—most important—give the teacher valuable information about what the child is like outside the school. The teacher can also get many clues about family interactions that affect the child. There are several important factors to keep in mind when conducting parent-teacher conferences:

- Communicate with parents on their level. Don't use a lot of educational jargon.
- Make the parent feel relaxed. Many parents have not been back to school since they were students, and returning often makes them feel uncomfortable.
- Conferences can be held in the child's home as well as at school. Some parents feel more comfortable on their own home ground.

- Avoid sitting behind the teacher's desk. Meet the parents on equal terms—perhaps around a table.
- If parents do not speak English, arrange for someone to help with translation.

Both the teacher and the parents need to give each other information and at the same time, learn more about the child. It is important to be aware of the kind of information that will be helpful to the parent, as well as to you, the teacher. Be prepared to discuss the following kinds of information, which will be helpful to the parent as well as to you, the teacher:

- The child's abilities, including specific skills he or she has mastered and the level of difficulty at which he or she is working
- How involved the child is in classroom activities
- The child's attitude toward school and other children
- The child's work and play habits, including starting and finishing projects on time, working independently, and following directions
- Successes and challenges—including areas in which the child has shown improvement and areas where more improvement is needed
- How the child has been placed in groups for purposes of instruction
- Samples of the child's oral and written compositions, tapes of language samples, test results, drawings, artistic expressions, and other records
- Anecdotes that demonstrate the child's problem-solving abilities; samples of work showing unique ways of solving problems (see Chapters 7 and 12) (adapted from Alum Rock School District, n.d.)

When the conference is over, parents should have a good idea of how their children are doing in school, and, if there are any problems, what they, as parents, can do to improve the situation.

Some kinds of information that you, the teacher, might want to gain from the parents include:

- Health problems the child might have
- Emotional problems or areas of strength
- Unusual experiences, such as a death in the family and serious illness
- How the child feels about school
- How the child cooperates at home—work habits, acceptance of responsibilities, getting along with other family members
- The child's after-school activities
- The child's special interests or hobbies
- What the parents feel are the child's strong points; areas where they see improvement—e.g., in academic and nonacademic areas and in the integrative processes (such as play and creative problem solving)
- Ways in which the parents feel the school can most help their children

Day care teachers of very young children may want to know which family members are closest to the child and what the child calls each of them. It would be helpful to know about the presence of pets, favorite toys, and the amount and type of television programming viewed. One day care worker asks, "Who talks to this child?" The principal vocabulary encoder plays a powerful role in the oral expression of children.

At the end of the conference, you should have a better idea of what the child's home life is like, be aware of his or her special interests, and, most important, have a better understanding of the child as an individual and a member of a family group as well as a member of the class.

Parents and Children with Special Needs

Parents of children with special needs are now becoming more involved in their children's education.

THE HANDICAPPED Are there any special techniques needed in dealing with parents of handicapped children? Connolly (1978) notes that many parents of handicapped children carry unrealistic burdens of guilt regarding the child. Often, they are frustrated in their aspirations for the child. They may focus this frustration on the school personnel who identify the child's learning problems. Some parents try to escape the problem by refusing to acknowledge that it exists. Connolly recommends certain techniques teachers can use when counseling parents:

- Understand your own biases and prejudices in dealing with the problem.
- Empathize with the parents; try to understand their perspective.
- Use effective communication skills—interpreting both verbal and nonverbal cues, sharing openly results of evaluations, and encouraging parents to respond.
- Make some concrete suggestions about what parents can do to help their child.
- Help the parents to see the positive, unique, and interesting qualities of their child.

Among the topics to discuss with parents:

- The child's management skills
- Social skills and self-sufficiency
- Strategies for coping, accepting, and understanding
- Language development

(Incidentally, most of these topics are equally relevant when dealing with parents of nonhandicapped children.)

THE GIFTED Teachers and parents of gifted children need to find ways to keep these children's interest alive. O'Neill (1978) found a method of doing this which not only benefitted the children, but involved the parents as well.

O'Neill provided assignments to be completed by the children with parental assistance. The assignments involved group projects, theme projects, and independent projects. Feedback by parents during conferences and at the end of the year was enthusiastic. She concluded that her program provided the extra challenge needed by gifted children and an opportunity for parent and child to work together, and enabled the child to feel that the parents were interested in his or her education. Organizations of parents of gifted children exist at the national and local level. They provide enrichment activities during and after school hours. Their meetings usually include an educational component—particularly geared to the problems of living with and educating a gifted child.

Classroom doors in the past were often closed to parents (except on "open school day"). The trend today is to involve the parents as much as possible in their child's education. Through parent-child centers, home visits, and parent conferences, educators are encouraging involvement of the parents in children's programs. They are reaching out for children in infancy through the school-age years—for children with special needs, the handicapped, the gifted.

Involving the Community—The Untapped Resource

In the past, "education" took place solely within the four walls of the school. Now there is increasing recognition that this is only one place where education begins. Efforts are being made to move beyond the school in order to tap the resources of the larger community.

Community involvement in the educational process can happen in many different ways. However, it has taken public education a long time to realize the potential support the local community can provide the school. Fortunately, educators are finally taking advantage of the almost unlimited resources the community can offer. From career education to public service agencies to additional volunteers, community involvement can provide a positive addition to any school program.

CAREER EDUCATION As mentioned earlier in this chapter, local businesses are often willing to share their craft or expertise with children. What better way for students to begin learning about careers than seeing firsthand the variety of jobs that are performed daily in their own neighborhood?

While many schools incorporate field trips or career education into the social studies curriculum, one has developed its entire reading program around the study of parents' occupations. The program uses a language experience approach to reading and provides each student with a firsthand look at the "world of work" by studying parents' occupations. The school is located across the street from a large fruit factory which employs many parents. When safety rules prohibited children from touring the plant, the company allowed parents time off work to come to the school to talk about their jobs.

PUBLIC SERVICE AGENCIES

Schools often identify problems that children are having and readily bring them to the parents' attention. However, parents are often left to act on their own when it comes to solving such problems (Morrison, 1978). When children have been identified as having physical or mental handicaps, referrals to outside agencies are sometimes the best direction schools can give to parents. Even if one agency cannot deal with a specific problem, it can usually provide information about where the parent can go to receive help.

Many Head Start programs give all parents a directory of services available to them in the community. The telephone numbers listed include emergency services such as police, rescue squads, neighborhood counseling and legal services, mental health agencies, and hospitals.

All the following can help provide information and services to children and their parents. It would be useful to have the local telephone numbers available to give to parents when needed:

- Local hospitals, including county, private, university, pediatric
- Public health clinic
- Mental Health and Retardation Association
- American Red Cross
- March of Dimes
- Social Security Administration
- Welfare office
- Day care and Head Start programs
- Family counseling services
- Dental emergency service
- Local service clubs that will purchase dental work, glasses, etc., for those who cannot afford them

VOLUNTEER SERVICES

As we noted earlier, parents are not the only sources of a volunteer program. Senior citizens and students can make valuable contributions. Children can gain the concept of growing old and remaining a useful member of society (in spite of our highly youth-oriented culture). When retirees share their talents, they are rewarded by the enthusiasm of the children. One location has a program called "DOVES" (Dedicated Older Volunteers in Educational Services). College and high school students specializing in drama, foreign language, and physical education provide other possibilities for enriching young children's curriculum. These resources include people who can help schools and provide special facilities or environments conducive to learning, e.g., museums, parks, colleges, and hospitals. All stretch the borders of the educational environment.

Summary

The presence of this chapter in a textbook on early childhood education indicates an awareness of the fact that education extends far beyond the time or space limitations of the school into the home and the community. This chapter has dealt with the areas of parent and community involvement. We have considered the value of involving parents in the educational program—value to teachers, children, and parents. We discussed not only methods of recruiting, training, and retaining parent volunteers, but also ways teachers can use the services of such volunteers most effectively. We discussed some of the problems involved in developing and carrying out volunteer programs. We stressed the importance of involving parents from different socioeconomic and cultural groups in an attempt to bridge the gap between home and school. This chapter also considered the value of involving parents on advisory committees and the importance of helping parents to develop the skills needed to succeed in this role.

We dealt with parent conferences as providing a special opportunity for teachers and parents to exchange information. And we found that the needs of special children are better met if parents and teachers work together as a special team.

Recognizing the need to extend the geographic borders of the educational environment beyond the limitations of the school, this chapter has considered various ways to tap the resources of the community to benefit young children and their families. Included among these resources are opportunities for career education (even for our youngest citizens), use of appropriate public service agencies, and use of people and facilities of the community.

Finally, this chapter has taken notice of the fact that the personnel and facilities of the school cannot possibly adequately meet the needs of children in our complex society. The personnel needs to be expanded to involve parents—the first and most important educators of children. Together, parents, teachers, and community, using the facilities of the community and the school, will better meet the needs of young children from a variety of cultural and socioeconomic backgrounds. This cooperative team can provide children with an education relevant to their needs and to the complexities of modern life.

A Look Ahead

The last portion, the Epilogue to this book, follows. It contains an affirmation of the theme of this book, some of the most important ideas, and a look to the future. You will have a final glimpse of our students, Pat, Chris, and Lee, as they enter professional life.

References

Abidin, R. R. *Parenting skills.* New York: Human Sciences Press, 1976.

Alum Rock School District. *The conference handbook: Getting the most from your parent-teacher conference,* undated.

Becker, W. C. *Parents are teachers: A child management program.* Champaign, Ill.: Research Press, 1971.

Bell, T. H. *An educator looks at parenting.* Urbana, Ill.: ERIC Clearinghouse on Early Childhood Education, 1976. (ED 127 547.)

Caplan, F. (Ed.). *The Parenting Advisor.* Garden City, N. Y.: Anchor Press/ Doubleday, 1977.

Connolly, C. Counseling parents of school-age children with special needs. *Journal of School Health,* 1978, *48*(2), 115–117.

Dinkmeyer, D., & McKay, G. D. *Systematic training for effective parenting, Leader's Manual.* Circle Pines, Minn.: American Guidance Service, 1976.

Duffy, V. R. *Changing parental attitudes through parent effectiveness training.* (Masters thesis.) Long Beach, California State University, 1974.

Gordon, I. J. Reaching the young child through parent education. *Childhood Education,* 1970, *46,* 247–249.

Hendricks, M., & Enk, J. *Lighten your load with volunteers.* Author, 1976.

Kruger, W. S. *Education for parenthood and the schools.* Urbana, Ill.: ERIC Clearinghouse on Early Childhood Education, 1972. (ED 184 022.)

Maerowitz, I. Parents! Bless them & keep them . . . in your classroom. *The Education Digest,* 1973, *38*(7), 38–40.

Morrison, G. S. *Parent involvement in the home, school, and community.* Columbus, Ohio: Charles E. Merrill, 1978.

Ogg, E. *Preparing tomorrow's parents.* New York: Public Affairs Committee, 1975.

Ohnersorgen, S. Speech presented at a meeting of the Phi Kappa Delta Honorary Education Fraternity. Cerritos, Calif.: Whitney Community Learning Center, 20 April, 1978.

O'Neill, K. K. Parent involvement: A key to the education of gifted children. *The Gifted Child Quarterly,* 1978 *22*(2), 235–242.

Smith, J. M. & Smith, D. E. P. *Child management: A program for parents.* Ann Arbor, Mich.: Ann Arbor Publishers, 1966.

Taylor, J. Make them welcome. *Instructor,* 1972, *82*(1), 54.

Wohlforth, R. Wanted: A Consumer-oriented superintendent. *Citizen Action in Education.* 1977, *4*(3), 1–15.

EPILOGUE:
THEMES, TRENDS,
AND ISSUES

TIME   Still the 1980s
SETTING   A faculty office, School of Education, Everyone's University
CAST   The professor; our students (Chris, Pat, and Lee)

This Epilogue finds our actors at the end to the first phase of their professional preparation. In their undergraduate work, they learned many theories, techniques, and skills. They found answers to many of their questions; they also learned that many trends present unanswered questions and unresolved issues.

The professor, having invited Chris, Pat, and Lee to help plan a workshop on "Trends and Issues for the 80s in ECE," pours each a cup of tea. "Glad all three of you could make it today. The trends and issues you've collected seem to fall into one of three areas:"

- Responsibility of family and society for quality child care.
- Theories of human development and learning.
- Teaching—an art or a science?

"I'd like to say something about the first one, *responsibility of family and society for quality child care*," said Lee. "What a controversial area! Some people seem to resent the government's involvement in child care programs because they say that such action is intruding into private matters and that raising children is the job of the family. Others claim that it is society's responsibility to help take care of those members of society, such as the educationally and economically disadvantaged, working mothers, and victims of child abuse, who need such care. Personally, I hope that more and more people will come to view all child care and ECE programs as helpful and educational in nature for all kinds of children. Child care centers are not just places to "dump" children while parents work. With trained personnel, they are places where the child's whole development may be fostered through prevention, stimulation, nurturance, and understanding."

"But," added Chris, "not everyone agrees *how* children develop. As a consequence, we are not always certain of the best ways to go about stimulating children's growth. What I'm talking about relates to trends and issues in the second area, *theories of human development and learning*. You'd be surprised how heated the arguments in this field can be! Some are convinced that children need to be molded by the environment and others firmly hold that children need to be left to develop on their own, without obstacles. After a lot of thinking I have decided I really agree most with the developmental-interactionist approach, because it takes into account both environment and the child's inherent qualities, development, and rate of growth. I think children have many abilities we don't give them credit for, and that they can develop if we let them. Sometimes we coddle and underestimate children. On the other hand, I, as a trained professional, can probably do many things to encourage and stimulate children. I think my knowledge of child development and my careful observation will help me decide what is appropriate. You look as though you have more to say about this, Pat."

"Yes—I'm thinking about the third area, *teaching—an art or a science?*" responded Pat. "Do we use teaching techniques with scientific objectivity or do we do things by impulse or intuition? I would say we use research findings to guide us to be scientific and objective, but a lot of what we do is flexible and creative, tailored to the individual needs of particular children at a given moment. I can't really say that one method is better than another. However, before I tried any method I would ask myself, 'In what ways can I increase this child's autonomy if I use this method? Are the integrative processes involved in play and creative problem solving being developed and used to the maximum?' For me, quality education shows respect for the child by encouraging these processes as well as serving all kinds of children. Therefore, I plan to choose my materials and methods carefully so that I can be deliberate in what I do. I don't want a hodgepodge of activities that doesn't make sense to me or the children!"

"Everything you have all said impresses me," said the professor. "Wish I had recorded it on tape to share with my classes! With such attitudes, I think you will agree with the new motto I'm putting up on my door:

IF YOU ARE EDUCATED TODAY AND QUIT LEARNING TOMORROW, YOU ARE UNEDUCATED THE DAY AFTER.

I have no doubts that each of you will continue learning for the rest of your lives about effective ways of guiding young children's learning."

Glossary

accomodation (Chapter 5; *see* assimilation)

The process by which the individual adjusts to reality. Accommodation involves combining new information with information already known and adjusting attitudes or behavior accordingly.

advisory committees (*see* school advisory committees)

affective domain (Chapter 3; *see* cognitive domain, psychomotor domain)

The area concerned with emotional, social, and creative development.

aide (Chapter 15; explained in Chapter 14)

A paid employee of the school district who assists the teacher in the classroom.

amniocentesis (Chapter 4)

The process of drawing fluid from the amniotic sac surrounding the developing fetus. Amniocentesis can be used to determine whether genetic irregularities (and possible handicaps) are present.

anecdotal record (Chapter 7)

The abbreviated factual description of a student's behavior observed in relation to a particular event oc-

curring in a school setting which, along with other descriptions compiled over a period of time, provides a continued and integrated picture of behavioral changes.

animism (Chapter 5)

A young child's belief that things in nature have life and purpose (e.g., the belief that the moon moves when you walk and keeps you company).

assessment (Chapter 7)

The process of gathering information, comparing it with a standard, and placing a value on that outcome based on its context.

assimilation (Chapter 5; *see* accommodation)

The process of taking in new information.

association (Chapter 12; *see* behaviorists)

The connection between stimulus and response.

auditory discrimination (Chapter 5)

The act of differentiating between sounds heard.

auditory memory (Chapter 5)

The mental capacity of retaining and recalling sounds heard.

authoritarian style (Chapter 6)

A style of relating to others (children) in which teachers or parents are controlling and aloof.

authoritative style (Chapter 6)

The style of relating to others (children) in which teachers or parents are firm, consistent, and clear in setting limits.

behavioral objectives (Chapters 12 and 3)

Aims established for a lesson or program that can be evaluated on the basis of observable behavior.

behaviorists (Chapter 5; *see* association, phenomenologist)

Followers of the belief that learning takes place by modifying behavior through conditioned responses to specific stimuli.

bibliotherapy (Chapter 6)

The use of books and stories for the improvement of behavior or attitudes.

body awareness (Chapter 8)

The perception of the relationship of the body to an object. Body awareness is learned through touch, vision, and kinesthetic sense.

body concept (Chapter 8)

The intellectual knowledge of the parts of the body.

body image (Chapter 8)

The feeling of one's body in relation to the world. The sum of all feelings concerning the body.

British infant school (Chapter 3)

A comprehensive educational program characterized by flexible, multiage grouping and active involvement of the children in learning at interest centers.

career ladder (Chapter 11)

The path by which one moves up in an occupation. For example, a person may volunteer in the classroom and after a certain amount of experience may become a paid aide. Continued experience in education and encouragement to attend related college courses may lead to employment in positions of greater responsibility.

cephalocaudal development (Chapter 4; *see also* proximodistal development)

Development that proceeds from top to bottom (from head to foot).

class inclusion (Chapter 5)

The relation that holds between one class and a second when every object that belongs to the first class also belongs in the second (Example: all red triangles are included in the class of triangles.)

classification (Chapter 5)

The operation of grouping objects and events into mutually exclusive categories on the basis of their common properties.

cognitive domain (Chapter 4; *see* affective domain, psychomotor domain)

The area concerned with the process of thinking.

compensatory education (Chapter 3; *see* intervention)

Instructional program designed to help overcome the gap between disadvantaged children and their peers.

concept (Chapter 5)

The meaning that results from the learner's integration of related perceptions.

concrete-operational stage (Chapter 5; *see* sensorimotor stage, preoperational stage, and formal operational stage)

The third stage of Piaget's four major developmental stages. Concrete-operational children are able to deal with concrete objects and objects easily imagined in a concrete way, using them to assist logical thinking processes.

connotative meaning (Chapter 5; *see* denotative meaning)

The colorations, imaginings, images, pictures, and feelings a word produces. The connotative aspects of a word are its shades of meaning beyond its literal meaning.

conservation (Chapters 5, 9, and 10)

The intellectual operation which includes a grasp of the fact that the way something looks from moment to moment need involve no change in the basic material.

construction (Chapter 9; *see* instruction)

The process of internally building up ideas based upon active involvement in experiences.

content emphasis (Chapters 5, 9; *see* process)

The emphasis on learning specific facts.

convergent thinking (Chapter 6; *see* divergent thinking)

The process of thinking involving the selection of *the* correct solution to a given situation.

creative problem solving (Chapters 1, 7, 10, 12, 15)

The process of reaching a solution to a problem through the use of divergent thinking.

criterion-referenced tests (Chapter 8; *see* norm-referenced tests)

Tests that compare a child's performance to mastery of the criterion or goal of instruction that the test is constructed to assess.

critical period (Chapter 3)

The period in which the greatest growth takes place in a particular area.

Cuisenaire rods (Chapter 4)

A set of oblong blocks, sequenced in size, used for developing number concepts.

culture-fair tests (Chapter 7)

Tests which include concepts within the realm of experience for children from any culture.

cumulative records (Chapter 8)

Files including confidential information gathered regarding a child's past behavior, performance on standardized measures, and accounts of past parent conferences. Cumulative records are usually passed from one year to the next.

day care (Chapter 2)

Any care a child receives in a program outside of the home for some part of a twenty-four hour day.

decoding approaches (Chapter 10)

Approaches to teaching reading based on relating the printed symbols to their oral counterparts ("sounding out" as opposed to "whole word" or "sight" methods). Decoding approaches typically emphasize phonics, linguistics, and artificial orthography.

denotative meaning (Chapter 5; *see* connotative meaning)

The literal aspects of the meaning of a word. (For example, the denotative meaning of "pig" involves the real animal, not messy persons.)

discipline (Chapter 14)

A system of rules designed to instill inner controls in the child leading to the gradual development of conscience and ego strength.

discovery learning (Chapter 12)

The inductive process of acquiring knowledge in an environment where the child is free to explore and investigate.

dishabituation (Chapter 4)

The ability of the infant to transfer attention from one stimulus to another.

divergent thinking (Chapter 6; *see* convergent thinking)

The operation of generating items of information where emphasis is on a variety of output and a search for logical alternatives (rather than one right answer.)

dramatic play (Chapter 10)
Spontaneous, make-believe activity, often involving props.

early childhood education (ECE)
any program designed for children from birth to age eight.

egocentric (Chapter 5)
Term applied to the characteristic of having or recognizing the self as the center of all things, being interested in one's personal needs and concerns.

EMR (Chapter 3; *see* TMR)
Educable mentally retarded. The phrase is applied to those having IQ's between 50 and 70. The educable mentally retarded can generally be accommodated in a school setting.

equilibrium (Chapter 5; *see* assimilation, accommodation)
The mental poise or the state of balance in which opposing forces exactly equal each other, and there are no challenges to existing understanding.

ESL (Chapter 13)
A program for teaching English as a second language.

evaluation (Chapter 7)
The process of assessing an individual or group and comparing performances with prior expectations.

expanded language (Chapter 10)
The method of developing oral language by enlarging on and interacting with the child's words, thereby extending vocabulary and concepts.

extrinsic (Chapter 3; *see* intrinsic)
Term describing an external reward system (in which rewards are, e.g., praise, food, prizes).

family grouping (Chapter 2)
The multiage grouping of children which provides opportunities for stimulation like those experienced within a family.

FES (Chapter 13; *see* LES, NES)
Fluent English-speaking.

figure-ground discrimination (Chapters 8 and 10)
The ability to perceive a specific figure in a complex setting.

flannelboard (Chapter 11)
A display board covered with flannel fabric, permitting cutouts to adhere to the surface. The flannelboard is a standard piece of preschool equipment.

formal operational stage (Chapter 5; *see* sensorimotor stage, preoperational stage, and concrete-operational stage)
The fourth stage of Piaget's child development levels. Formal operational children are characterized by an ability to reason without the presence of concrete materials, can use symbols and language as tools, and think about thinking.

formative evaluation (Chapter 7; *see* summation evaluation)
An evaluation which is ongoing during the implementation of a program and aids in the day-to-day planning for improvement of the program.

goal (Chapters 9, 10, 11, 12; *see* objective, learning activity)
A priority toward which specific objectives and related learning activities are directed for desired change in attitude or behavior.

goal structure (Chapter 12)
The individual, cooperative, and competitive ways in which children relate to each other and to the teacher in working toward the accomplishment of goals.

hearing acuity (Chapter 5)
The degree of sharpness of the ability to perceive sounds.

IEP (Chapter 13)

Individual educational program planned for children with special needs by teachers in cooperation with parents and children. IEPs are required by mainstreaming efforts of Public Law 94-142.

induction (Chapter 6; *see* deduction)

A process of reasoning from particular facts to a general rule.

inquiry learning (Chapter 12)

A process of acquiring knowledge whereby the child asks questions and the teacher responds with a yes or no.

instruction (Chapter 9; *see* construction)

The process of systematically imparting information.

intervention (Chapter 7; *see* compensatory education)

A specific attempt to modify the course of development, understandings, attitudes, or behavior.

intrinsic (Chapter 3; *see* extrinsic)

Term describing an internal reward system (in which rewards are based on individual satisfaction and are logically closely related to or part of the behavior or task).

intuitive thought (Chapter 5)

The mental process of immediate perception, arrived at without prior reflective thinking.

kibbutzim (Chapter 2)

Cooperative agricultural settlements where children generally live and learn with a peer group, spending part of each day with parents and siblings.

language experience approach (Chapters 10, 12)

An approach to teaching reading, primarily by a "sight word" method, using material dictated or written by the child.

laterality awareness (Chapter 8)

Awareness that two sides of the body exist separated by an imaginary line down the middle.

learning activity (Chapter 9 and introduction to Part Three; *see* goal, objective)

Specific experiences designed to achieve objectives leading to attainment of goals.

least restrictive environment (Chapter 13)

A setting in which to the maximum extent appropriate, handicapped children are educated with children who are not handicapped.

LES (Chapter 13; *see* NES, FES)

Limited English-speaking.

manipulative material (Chapter 5)

Objects a child can handle to reinforce a concept.

measurement (Chapter 7)

The process and outcome of gathering information about someone or some group and quantifying that information in some manner.

modeling (Chapter 6)

The technique whereby individuals (e.g., teachers) exemplify behavior which children imitate. Modeling allows children the opportunity to modify their behavior through perceptual learning.

myelinization (Chapter 4)

The formation of a protective sheath over the neurons enabling pathways to be established between the brain and the muscles. Myelinization is necessary for the coordination of movement.

needs assessment (Chapter 15)

The process by which data are gathered and used to evaluate specific knowledge, skills, or attitudes which are lacking but which may be obtained and satisfied through learning experience.

neonate (Chapter 4)

The infant during the first month of life.

NES (Chapter 13; *see* FES, LES)
Non-English-speaking.

nominal scales (Chapter 7)
Instruments that assess individuals and allow comparisons to other individuals.

norms (Chapter 5)
Standards derived from testing a large group of persons and used for comparison of an individual's score with the scores of others in a defined group.

norm-referenced tests (Chapter 7; *see* criterion-referenced tests)
Tests of achievement or ability, comparing an individual's performance to that of other similar individuals.

object constancy (Chapter 5)
A concept based on the principle that an object exists even when it cannot be seen.

objective (Chapters 10, 12); *see* goal, learning activity
A clear statement identifying ways of accomplishing goals through specific learning activities.

operant conditioning (Chapter 6)
The procedure of reinforcing responses as they occur in order to increase their frequency.

operations (Chapter 5, 6, 10, and 11)
Mental activities an individual performs in constructing and using information. Operations are activities having definite structure, usually in the special province of later childhood and adolescence, (e.g., adding, subtracting, measurement, classification).

ordinal scales (Chapter 7)
Instruments consisting of items selected and ordered in a sequence that has been identified through the observation of many individuals. Ordinal scales allow comparisons of present status to the previous performance.

percept (Chapter 7; *see* concept)
That which is grasped or taken in through the senses.

permissive style (Chapter 6)
A style of parenthood in which parents are warm but rank low in control in setting required standards for their children's behavior.

phenomenologist (Chapter 12)
One who is convinced that human learning requires development of an organized framework, an understanding of all the varied events and conditions in a situation. Phenomenologist (including cognitive developmentalists, developmental-interactionists, Gestalt-field theorists) concentrate on the ideal, essential elements of experiences.

phonics method (Chapter 10)
One of the decoding methods of teaching reading which concentrates on associating printed letters with their sounds.

planned variations (Chapter 3)
The concept of implementing varied and specific compensatory education programs in Head Start and Follow Through.

play group (Chapter 2)
A group consisting of one or two mothers (or a professional hired by the mothers) who meet with several children in a backyard or other available space to provide the children an opportunity to play and learn with their peers.

prelinguistic stage (Chapter 5; *see* protolinguistic stage)
A stage of language development corresponding roughly to Piaget's first major stage of intellectual development, sensorimotor. The prelinguistic stage is characterized by the child making reflexive sounds associated with physiological states and squealing and gurgling sounds called "cooing."

preoperational stage (Chapter 5; *see* sensorimotor stage, concrete-operational stage, formal operational stage)

Piaget's second major stage of intellectual development. The preoperational stage is characterized by symbolic knowledge that is still tied to the self and by illogical intuitions based on perception.

program evaluation (Chapter 7)

The assessment of the effectiveness of particular techniques or materials.

protolinguistic stage (Chapter 5) (*see* prelinguistic stage)

The stage of language development reached by children approximately twelve to twenty months of age. Children in the protolinguistic stage imitate sounds heard and show evidence of listening to simple commands.

process (Chapter 9; *see* content)

The "how" of learning, the action of an individual which involves the mind.

proximodistal development (Chapter 4; *see* cephalocaudal development)

The principle that development proceeds from the center to the outside.

psychomotor domain (Chapter 8; *see* affective domain, cognitive domain)

The area concerned with physical, motor, and perceptual development.

punishment (Chapter 14)

The infliction of a penalty on an individual (e.g., a child) because the person administering the penalty disapproves. The penalty may be a painful stimulus or denial or removal of a satisfaction (negative reinforcement).

reading readiness (Chapter 10)

The state or period in which the relationships, concepts, and skills deemed prerequisite to reading are built up.

reliability (Chapter 7; *see* validity)

The degree of accuracy of measurement of a test, its tendency to yield consistent and stable measures relatively free of error.

reversability (Chapter 5)

A concept based on the principle that a substance or event that is changed can revert to its original state. Reversability involves the possibility of performing an action in reverse. (e.g., heated, cooled; made fat, rolled thin) and the insight that for every action there exists another action that undoes it (e.g., addition, subtraction).

role playing (Chapter 6)

A method of instruction in which the children act out or imitate the role behavior of another person or the behavior not available in real life.

scheme (Chapter 5)

A system of connected thoughts which changes to take in and adjust to new information. Schemes are usually associated with sensorimotor intelligence, e.g., strategies for getting objects nearer to oneself).

school advisory committees (Chapter 15)

Committees composed of representative parents and taxpayers. School advisory committees meet on a regular basis to assist in planning the school program to meet local needs.

self-concept (Chapter 11)

A person's awareness of, identification with, and attitude toward his or her own being, physically, cognitively, and affectively.

seriation (Chapter 5)

The operation by which organized data or items are arranged in an order, each leading to the next according to some definite principle (concerning space, time, or logic).

sensorimotor stage (Chapter 7; *see* preoperational stage, concrete-operational stage, formal operational stage)

Piaget's first stage of intellectual development characterized by the child showing knowledge of objects tied to specific sensory awareness or to body actions. Children in the formal operational stage learn through physical exploration and sensory stimulation.

spatial awareness (Chapter 8)

The ability to perceive the position of objects in space.

stages (Chapters 5, 6, 11)

Levels of development involving more and more complex and integrated patterns of thought or other behavior. Stages are usually identified loosely with certain ages.

summative evaluation (Chapter 7; *see* formative evaluation)

Evaluation of the outcomes of programs after their completion

symbolization (Chapter 5)

A representation of something that stands for an idea or other abstraction. For example, a young child may use an acorn to represent a dish.

teacher-made tests (Chapter 7)

Tests constructed by whole school staffs, parents, and/or individual teachers.

temporal awareness (Chapter 8)

The ability to perceive the position of events in time.

TMR (Chapter 13; *see* EMR)

Trainable mentally retarded. The phrase is applied to those having IQs between 30 and 55. The trainable mentally retarded generally require special programs to develop skills in self-help.

validity (Chapter 7; *see* reliability)

The property of a test that reflects the extent to which it actually measures what it is intended to measure.

CREDITS

Chapter 1

Table 1-1, page 21. Adapted from: National School Boards Association. *Job descriptions in education.* Washington, D.C.: National School Boards Association, 1973. Copyright © 1973 by National School Boards Association. Reprinted by permission.

Chapter 2

Figures 2-1, 2-2, 2-3, 2-4, 2-5, 2-6, 2-7, 2-8, pages 40–41. From: *Nienhuis Montessori catalogue.* Reprinted courtesy of Nienhuis Montessori USA, Mountain View, California.

Chapter 3

Figure 3-1, page 62. From: Bernstein, N. An analysis of early childhood models along selected criteria. Long Beach, Calif.: California State University at Long Beach Foundation, 1972 (unpublished).

Figures 3-2, page 66; 3-3, page 67; 3-4, page 67; 3-5, page 71. Rayder, N. *Methodological and ethical problems of research in early childhood education.* San Francisco: Far West Regional Laboratories, 1976.

Chapter 4

Pages 83, 84. From: CRM. *Developmental psychology today* (2d ed.). New York: Random House, 1975. Copyright © 1975 by Random House, Inc. Reprinted by permission of CRM, a division of Random House, Inc.

Table 4-1, page 85. From: Dennis, W. A description and classification of the responses of the newborn infant. *Psychological Bulletin*, 1934, *31*, 5–22.

Page 87. From: Elkind, D., & Weiner, I. *Development of the child.* New York: John Wiley, 1978. Reprinted by permission of John Wiley & Sons, Inc.

Figure 4-2, page 90. From: Bayley, N. Comparisons of mental and motor test scores for ages 1 – 15 months by sex, birth order, race, geographical location and education of parents. *Child Development*, 1965, *36*, 379–411. © The Society For Research Development, Inc.

Table 4-2, page 93. From: Smart, M.S., & Smart, R. C. *Children: Development and relations.* New York: Macmillan, 1972. © 1972 by Macmillan Publishing Co., Inc. Reprinted with permission.

Chapter 5

Figure 5-4, page 116. Schulz, C. *Snowstorms are not caused by kicking a snowman!* © 1973 United Feature Syndicate, Inc. Reprinted by permission.

Figure 5-5, page 117. From: Wilson, J. A., Robeck, M. C., & Michael, W. *Psychological foundations of learning and teaching* (2d ed.). New York: McGraw-Hill, 1974. Reprinted by permission.

Figure 5-17, page 134. Johns, A. *Okay, Mom, I've done all the nooks. Now what's a cranny?* Cartoons by Johns. Reprinted by permission of the artist. First appeared in *Saturday Review*, June 1974.

Chapter 6

Page 156. Adapted from: McDavid, J. W., & Garwood, S. G. *Understanding children: Promoting human growth.* Lexington, Mass.: D.C. Heath, 1978. Reprinted by permission of the publisher.

Table 6-2, page 164. Adapted from: Hoffman, M. L. Moral development. In P. H. Mussen (Ed.), *Carmichael's manual of child psychology* (3d ed.). (2 vols.) New York: John Wiley, 1970. Reprinted by permission of John Wiley & Sons, Inc.

Chapter 7

Table 7-1, page 185. Adapted from: Wall, J., & Summerlin, L. Characteristics of standardized and teacher-made tests. *The Science Teacher*, 1972, *32*, 36. Reprinted by permission of *The Science Teacher* and the author.

Table 7-2, page 186. Compiled from information available in the following: (1) Buros, O. K. (Ed.) *Tests in print II.* University of Nebraska, Lincoln, Nebraska: Buros Institute of Mental Measurements/Gryphon Press, 1974. Also: Buros, O. K. (Ed.) *Eighth mental measurements yearbook*, 1978. (2) Lewis, M. (Ed.) *Origins of intelligence.* New York: Plenum Press, 1976.

(3) Spodek, B. *Teaching in the early years* (2d ed.). Englewood Cliffs, N.J.: Prentice-Hall, 1978.

Figures 7-1, 7-2, page 189. From: Cartwright, C., & Cartwright, G. *Developing observational skills.* New York: McGraw-Hill, 1974. Copyright © 1974 by McGraw-Hill Book Company.

Figure 7-3, page 192. From: Irvine Unified School District. *Mathematics profile K-3.* Irvine, California: Irvine Unified School District. Reprinted by permission.

Chapter 8

Page 214 and Figure 8-1. From: Capon, J. *Perceptual-motor lesson plans, Level 1* (5th ed.). Byron, Calif.: Front Row Experience. Reprinted by permission of the publisher: Front Row Experience, 540 Discovery Bay Blvd., Byron, Calif. 95414.

Page 215. From: Texas Education Agency. *Approaches to programs of motor development and activities for young children.* Austin, Texas: Texas Education Agency, 1977. Reprinted by permission of Texas Education Agency.

Page 216. Adapted from: Gerhardt, L. A. Movement. In C. Seefeldt (Ed.), *Curriculum for the preschool-primary child.* Columbus, Ohio: Charles E. Merrill, 1976. Reprinted by permission.

Figure 8-2, page 219. From: Cameron, W., & Pleasance, P. *Education in movement—Gymnastics.* Oxford, U.K.: Basil Blackwell, 1971. Reprinted by permission of Basil Blackwell Publisher.

Table 8-1, page 220. From: Stanley, S. *Physical education: A movement orientation.* Toronto: McGraw-Hill Ryerson, 1977. Copyright © by McGraw-Hill Ryerson Limited, 1977. Reprinted by permission.

Page 220. From: Fabricius, H. *Physical education for the classroom teacher.* (2d ed.). Dubuque, Iowa: Brown, 1971. Reprinted by permission of the author.

Table 8-2, page 222. From: Gilliom, B. *Basic movement education for children: Rationale and teaching units.* Reading, Mass.: Addison-Wesley, 1970. © 1970 Addison-Wesley Publishing Company, Inc. Reprinted with permission.

Chapter 9

Page 247. Adapted from: Engelmann, D., & Carnine, D. *Distar arithmetic I, An instructional system.* Chicago: Science Research Associates, 1969. © 1969 Science Research Associates, Inc. Adapted by permission of the publisher.

Figure 9-2, page 253. From: Nelson, L. W., & Lorbeer, G. C. *Science activities for elementary children* (6th ed.). Dubuque, Iowa: Brown, 1976. © 1967, 1972, 1976, Wm. C. Brown Company Publishers, Dubuque, Iowa. Reprinted by permission.

Chapter 10

Page 272. From: Lundsteen, S. Give your speaking voice a home improvement course. *Instructor*, 1979, *89* (1, August), 120–127. Copyright © 1979 by The Instructor Publications, Inc. Used by permission.

Page 282. From: Seuss, Dr. *The lorax.* New York: Random House, 1971. Copyright © 1971 by Dr. Seuss and A. S. Geisel. Reprinted by permission of Random House, Inc., and William Collins and Sons & Company Ltd.

Pages 298, 299. Adapted from: Allen, R. V. *Language experience in communication.* Boston: Houghton Mifflin, 1976. Copyright © 1976 by Houghton Mifflin Company. Used by permission.

Chapter 11

Page 327. From: Andres, P. Music and motion: The rhythmic language of children. *Young Children*, 1976, *32* (1, November), 32–36. Copyright © 1976, National Association for the Education of Young Children, 1834 Connecticut Avenue N.W., Washington, D.C. 20009. Reprinted by permission from *Young Children.*

Pages 330–331. Adapted from: Bayless, K., & Ramsey, M. *Music: A way of life for the young child..* St. Louis, Mo.: C. V. Mosby, 1978. Reprinted by permission.

Page 331. Adapted from: Nye, V. *Music for young children* (2d ed.). Dubuque, Iowa: Brown, 1975. © 1975, 1979 Wm. Brown Company Publishers, Dubuque, Iowa. Reprinted by permission.

Page 332. From: Margolin, E. *Sociocultural elements in early childhood education.* New York: Macmillan, 1974. Copyright © 1974 by Edythe Margolin. Reprinted by permission of Macmillan Publishing Co., Inc.

Chapter 12

Table 12-1, page 349. From: (1) Rosenberg, M. B. *Diagnostic teaching.* Seattle, Washington: Special Child Publications, 1968. Used by permission. (2) Adapted by E. J. Moore, Associate Professor of Education, University of Missouri—Columbia. (3) Table developed by Carol Mason Wolfe.

Table 12-4, page 377. Adapted from: Johnson, D. W., & Johnson, R. T. *Learning together and alone: Cooperation, competition, and individualization.* Englewood Cliffs, N.J.: Prentice-Hall, 1975. © 1975. Reprinted by permission of Prentice-Hall, Inc.

Chapter 13

Page 394. Adapted from: Torrance, P. E. *Creativity.* Sioux Falls, S.D.: Adapt Press, 1969. Reprinted by permission.

Figure 13-1, page 396. From: Deno, E. Special education as development capital. In G. J. Warfield (Ed.), *Mainstream currents*. Reston, Va.: Council for Exceptional Children. Copyright © 1974 by The Council for Exceptional Children. Reprinted by permission of The Council for Exceptional Children.

Chapter 14

Figure 14-2, page 423. From: Schickendanz, J., York, M., Stewart, I., & White, D. *Strategies for teaching young children*. Englewood Cliffs, N.J.: Prentice-Hall, 1977. © 1977. Reprinted by permission of Prentice-Hall, Inc.

Figure 14-3, page 424. Adapted from: Kaplan, S. N., Kaplan, J. A. B., Madsen, S. K., & Taylor, B. K. *Change for children*. Pacific Palisades, Calif.: Goodyear, 1973. Copyright © 1973 by Goodyear Publishing Co. Reprinted by permission.

Table 14-1, page 426. Adapted from: Leeper, S., Dales, R., Skipper, D., & Witherspoon, R. *Good schools for young children* (3d ed.). New York: Macmillan, 1974. Copyright © 1974 by Macmillan Publishing Co., Inc. Reprinted with permission.

Table 14-2, page 430. From: Broman, B. *The early years in childhood education*. Chicago: Rand McNally, 1978. Copyright © 1978 by Rand McNally College Publishing Company. Reprinted by permission.

Chapter 15

Page 474. Adapted from: Alum Rock School District. *The conference handbook: Getting the most from your parent-teacher conference*. Undated. Reprinted by permission.

Page 475. From: Connolly, C. Counseling parents of school-age children with special needs. *Journal of School Health*, 1978, *48* (2), 115–117. © by the Journal of School Health. Reprinted by permission.

INDEX

All page references in *italics* refer to material included in tables, figures, or the glossary.